ASBO NATION

The criminalisation of nuisance

Edited by P

First published in Great Britain in 2008 by

The Policy Press
University of Bristol
Fourth Floor
Beacon House
Queen's Road
Bristol BS8 1QU
UK

Tel +44 (0)117 331 4054
Fax +44 (0)117 331 4093
e-mail tpp-info@bristol.ac.uk
www.policypress.org.uk

© Peter Squires 2008

British Library Cataloguing in Publication Data
A catalogue record for this book is available from the British Library.

Library of Congress Cataloging-in-Publication Data
A catalog record for this book has been requested.

ISBN 978 1 84742 027 5 paperback
ISBN 978 1 84742 028 2 hardcover

Cover design by Robin Hawes
Front cover: Image kindly supplied by www.sxc.hu/
Printed and bound in Great Britain by Hobbs the Printers, Southampton

Contents

List of figures and tables

Figures

Tables

List of contributors

Daniel Briggs is a research fellow at the Crime Reduction and Community Safety Research Unit, London South Bank University.

Elizabeth Burney is Honorary Senior Research Fellow at the Institute of Criminology, University of Cambridge.

Rionach Casey is Research Associate at the Centre for Regional Economic and Social Research, Sheffield Hallam University.

Shami Chakrabarti is the Director of Liberty, the National Council for Civil Liberties.

Adam Edwards is Lecturer in Criminology at the School of Social Sciences, University of Cardiff.

John Flint is Professor of Housing and Urban Governance in the Centre for Regional Economic and Social Research, Sheffield Hallam University.

Carlie Goldsmith is a postgraduate researcher and part-time lecturer at the School of Applied Social Science, University of Brighton.

Mike Guilfoyle is a probation officer working in London.

Amanda Holt is a postgraduate researcher and part-time lecturer at the School of Applied Social Science, University of Brighton.

Mike Hough is Professor of Criminology and Director of the Institute for Criminal Policy Research at King's College, London.

Gordon Hughes is Professor of Criminology at the School of Social Sciences, University of Cardiff.

Jessica Jacobson is a Visiting Senior Research Fellow at the Institute for Criminal Policy Research, King's College, London.

Roger Matthews is Professor of Criminology at London South Bank University.

Gillian Mayfield is Public Safety Manager at Leeds City Council.

Brian McIntosh is a postgraduate researcher and part-time tutor in the School of Social Sciences, University of Cardiff.

Fiona Measham is Senior Lecturer in Criminology in the Department of Applied Social Science, Lancaster University.

Andrew Millie is Lecturer in Criminology and Social Policy in the Department of Social Sciences, Loughborough University.

Andy Mills is Head of Service, Community Safety at Leeds City Council.

Karenza Moore is a Lecturer in Criminology in the Department of Applied Social Science, Lancaster University.

Stephen Moore is a Reader in Social Policy at Anglia Ruskin University of Birmingham.

Judy Nixon is Principal Lecturer in Housing Policy at Sheffield Hallam University.

Paul Norris is a Senior Lecturer in Criminology and Politics at Southampton Solent University.

Sadie Parr is a Research Fellow at the Centre for Regional Economic and Social Research, Sheffield Hallam University.

Jo Phoenix is a Reader in Criminology in the School of Social Sciences, Durham University.

David Prior is a Senior Research Fellow in the Institute of Applied Social Studies, University of Birmingham.

Jago Russell is the Policy Officer for Liberty, the National Council for Civil Liberties.

Basia Spalek is Senior Lecturer in the Institute of Applied Social Studies, University of Birmingham.

Peter Squires is Professor of Criminology and Public Policy in the School of Applied Social Science at the University of Brighton.

Dawn E. Stephen is Principal Lecturer in Criminology in the School of Applied Social Science at the University of Brighton.

Stuart Waiton is a Sociology Lecturer at Dundee Abertay, a Director of the research group Generation Youth Issues, and a regular contributor in Scotland to the *Times Educational Supplement*.

Derek Williams is a Senior Lecturer in Criminology and Sociology at Southampton Solent University.

Introduction: why 'anti-social behaviour'? Debating ASBOs

Peter Squires

The original ambition for this collection of articles about the anti-social behaviour phenomenon in the UK had been to capture, in a single volume, a wide range of positions that one might take up in respect of the 'anti-social behaviour question'. The discussions were to address the first emergence of the issue, the differing interpretations of anti-social behaviour (ASB) and contrasting reactions to it. Further chapters were to explore the attempts to address it by both policy makers and professional practitioners. A selection of the emerging research evidence about ASB and the impact of research findings on policy making was also to be included. In this, then, the book aimed to embrace a broad debate about the contemporary significance of anti-social behaviour and what could, or should, be done about it. Accordingly, contributions were solicited from a wide variety of authors representing a range of agencies, interests and perspectives surrounding the ASB issue. Significant evidence of the rapid explosion of interest in the ASB issue might be derived from the rapidly growing literature emerging in all of the above areas even as this project itself was under way. Moreover, this field was not just growing in a quantitative fashion, new issues and perspectives were arising. Just as the government was developing and enhancing its array of ASB policies, interventions and legal powers, the debate about ASB – what it was possible to say about ASB – was also changing in a number of important ways.

At opposite ends of the spectrum of opinion on ASB were, on the one hand, those who might be considered ASBO 'enthusiasts' (Field, 2003), 'ambassadors' (as described in Squires, 2006) or other 'Blairite crusaders'. This group are generally convinced that anti-social behaviour is a major social problem and that the ASBO is a vital utilitarian response to be deployed, unapologetically, as and when necessary, to tackle trouble makers and to demonstrate to communities that their concerns were now being taken seriously. As a number of commentators have noted, perceptions are important in managing anti-social behaviour. On the other hand, at the other end of the spectrum, were those who, either reflecting a legal interest or training (Ashworth et al, 1998; Chakrabarti, 2006; Simester and von Hirsch, 2006; see also ASBOconcern.org.uk) or versed in the traditions of critical criminology (Squires and Stephen, 2005), tended to regard the ASBO as oppressive, potentially counterproductive and in breach of important principles of legal due process.

Unfortunately, despite initially favourable and promising reactions from those members of the 'enthusiast' camp originally contacted (be they members of central government policy units or representatives of those 'on-message' local authorities especially noted for their diligent pursuit of ASBO numbers), agreements to contribute to this volume could not be secured. Perhaps the demands of enforcement permit few opportunities for reflection, justification or evaluation, for certainly (as a number of contributors to this volume reiterate) a government in principle so committed to evidence-led policy making and 'what works' devoted relatively few resources to evaluating its ASB strategy, moving rapidly to multiply, develop and enhance its enforcement tools on the basis of little real evidence (see also House of Commons, 2005; Turner, 2006; Hodgkinson and Tilley, 2007). Such factors suggest that it is not unreasonable to regard the government's ASB strategy, in much the same way as its more general 'law and order' politics, as ideologically driven (Reiner, 2007). For this reason (among others) I have adopted a similarly 'ideological' classification of ASB commentators and commentaries in the discussion that follows (see Figure i.1 for summary). Admittedly, the 'fit' is not always perfect (few of us appreciate being too neatly pigeonholed) but it is notable how at least *some* of the contributions (see for example Chapter Two by Edwards and Hughes) explicitly embrace an ideological frame of reference in their analysis.

Although no 'ASBO enthusiasts' volunteered a contribution there are many shades of opinion reflected in the chapters that follow. At one point we considered compiling our own 'case for ASBOs', drawing upon the wide range of commentary, argument and justification emanating from the various levels of our burgeoning ASBO industry. In the end this strategy was rejected as somewhat artificial. In any event, whose 'voice' would articulate the pro-ASBO case? A tabloid journalist, with talk of 'neighbours from hell', family 'sin bins' (see Parr and Nixon, Chapter Nine in this volume), 'yobs', 'thugs' and 'scum', or would it be an ASB coordinator, working in a crime and disorder reduction partnership (CDRP), seeing vigorous enforcement as the key to protecting the vulnerable and the victimised? The plan to write an abstract 'case for ASBOs' also fell foul of an issue we have already referred to, the rapidly developing debate. The government's agenda had moved on, the wider Respect Agenda had been put in place, and new forms of professional practice were emerging that, while continuing to use ASBOs, saw them or employed them differently, as a last resort, as

---

Figure i.1: Classifying perspectives on anti-social behaviour and ASBOs

Positions taken: Not all being necessarily mutually exclusive!

Blairite Crusaders
> Authoritarians
> 'Hoodie Huggers'

Communitarianism(s)
> Accountability
> 'Social Capitalists'
> Preventionists

Social Democratic Welfarism
> Pro-Welfarist
> Support not Enforcement
> Last Resort
> Corporatists

Post-Foucauldians
> New 'Governance' Theorists
> Critical Practitioners
> Community Safety

Critical Legalism (*AsboConcern*)

Critical Criminologies

---

part of a graduated ('tiered' or 'stepped') response, as part of a package of measures or in conjunction with other, more supportive interventions (themes explored in many of the following chapters). Finally, of course, just as the book's manuscript was almost finalised, the Respect Agenda was quietly sidelined. In place of the Respect Task Force a much more broadly developmental Youth Taskforce was to replace it, this time located in the Department of Children, Schools and Families. Ed Balls, the Secretary of State responsible, had already signalled a new emphasis in the ASB debate with his suggestion that the awarding of an ASBO should be seen as a mark of failure: 'I want to live in the kind of society that puts ASBOs behind us' (*Guardian*, 27 July 2007).

In the end it was decided to draw the case for ASBOs more indirectly from the various pronouncements of one of their earliest and most enthusiastic advocates, the then Prime Minister himself, and to do so in a way that described the particular case for taking ASB seriously within a discussion of the wider social, cultural and political changes that Mr Blair had been advocating.

The fast-moving politics of law and order

Many writers (including a number of the contributors to this volume) have commented on the speed with which the particular 'ASB problem' came to be defined and the 'ASBO solution' came to be adopted in the UK (Squires and Stephen, 2005; Burney, 2006; Squires, 2006). Such phenomena apparently run in cycles and, for our present purposes, clearly demonstrate the salience of crime, disorder and 'moral decline' (however these concerns might be said to have come about) in the British public consciousness (Grier and Thomas, 2004). After all, the mid-1990s saw a rapid sequence of government-led CCTV investment 'challenge' competitions in which, on the basis of virtually no reliable evidence of effectiveness (Goold, 2004), we saw, in a matter of a few years, every major town centre going live 'on camera'. No other country saw such a massive public investment in surveillance technology. Likewise, no other country has created the kind of 'ASBO industry' we know today, nor embarked upon such a wholesale process of ambitious civic and moral renewal through quasi-criminal enforcement mechanisms.

And yet, barely a decade following this extensive British CCTV 'experiment', its ASB management successor, John Carvel, writing in the *Guardian* newspaper, reporting on the latest Office of National Statistics *Social Trends* analysis, noted that 'Britain has become a more anti-social and less tolerant society' (Carvel, 2007). One comparative international analysis goes so far as to suggest that ASB problems – judged by public surveys – are significantly worse in the UK than anywhere else in Europe (ADT Europe, 2006), whereas a comparative survey of cost-effectiveness in measures to tackle anti-social behaviour notes, rather tellingly, that 'the concept of anti-social behaviour is not widely used outside of the United Kingdom' (Rubin et al, 2006: 2). It is not immediately obvious where one should break into this cycle of problem definition: not only does the particular concept of ASB seem fairly specific to the UK, but the series of problems comprising the phenomenon is reportedly worse here, although the British are also, seemingly, less tolerant. Furthermore, despite over a decade of, first CCTV and later ASB, policy measures, the problems are, if the Office of National Statistics *Social Trends* analysis is to be believed, no nearer a solution. The more that has been done about ASB (what has been done, the ways it has been done and the language used to describe it – '*mindless yobs*', '*neighbours from hell*'), the more the anti-social behaviour problem has become a major preoccupation. Tonry (2004), for one, has argued that, in its high-profile focus on anti-social behaviour, New Labour has made a small problem worse, 'thereby making more people aware of it and more dissatisfied with their lives and their government' (Tonry, 2004: 57). Other commentators, including some of the contributors to this volume, would agree, concurring with Turner (2006) that tough measures to tackle ASB may well prove counterproductive, tending to further alienate and isolate marginalised social groups and ASB perpetrators.

Other commentators, of course, have pointedly disagreed about ASB being a small problem (Field, 2003; Blair, 2004c), a point we shall develop shortly, while government representatives and official publications alike seldom allow much in the way of doubt to tarnish official evaluations of the ASB/Respect strategy's effectiveness. As the Government Office for London, typical of many similar announcements, headlined the launch of the Respect Action Plan in January 2006:

> The Government's *Respect Action Plan* ... is building on the successful drive to tackle anti-social behaviour and is taking the work to a new level, seeking to address the deeper underlying causes of unacceptable behaviour. (www.gos.gov.uk/gol/Community_safety/Anti_social_behaviour/)

However, what become obvious in these discussions of ASB, notwithstanding the empirical areas of disagreement about the scale of the problems or how best to tackle them, are some wider although equally vital questions about what ASB represents – and to whom (those 'deeper underlying causes') – in contemporary Britain. In putting this volume together, a key objective was precisely to explore such questions and to sketch the various positions that different commentators have taken up vis-à-vis the anti-social behaviour question.

Addressing these more interpretative issues brings us back to the CCTV and ASB connection, for the two areas of policy development are closely related in a number of ways: the top-down nature of the policy making, the preoccupation with urban crime and disorder, the 'solution' preceding the evidence, and the importance of local implementation partnerships. Yet, significant though these issues are, both CCTV installation and ASB management were also important for the ways in which they constructed the problems that each sought to manage and for how they erected new systems of central–local governance, accountability and legitimation (leading to some commentators to speak of a new process of 'governing through crime' (Simon, 2007) or through 'crime and disorder' (Garland, 2000; Crawford, 2002)). For example when, in 1996, and still prior to the advent of New Labour in national government, the Local Government Management Board (LGMB) undertook its own survey of the activities being undertaken by local authorities under the banner of 'community safety', the following list of most frequently occurring priorities was arrived at:

1. CCTV installation
2. Young people
3. Alcohol and substance misuse
4. Fear of crime
5. Victims and communities

Presented as a simple list, these priorities are both familiar and mundane, but reconfigured through a *politics* of law and order into which ideas about culture and difference – and political interests – are factored, the simple list then begins to resemble the following diagram (Figure i.2) in which the LGMB's priorities have been more appropriately reconfigured.

Such a reordering of the priorities of localised governance through crime and disorder instantly reminds us just how explicitly 'ideological' this exercise in social controlling always was. Even before the widespread adoption of the label 'anti-social behaviour' and still two years before the 'Anti-Social Behaviour Order' came into being, it is abundantly clear that certain community interests were deemed to be at risk, that certain rights (to safety and to the quiet enjoyment of a given quality of life) were thought to be in jeopardy. Likewise, there seems little

Figure i.2: Local Government Management Board community safety priorities (reconfigured)

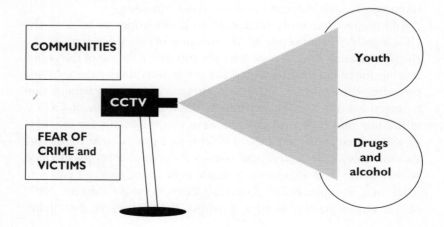

doubt that, at the level of popular perceptions at least, young people (and their lifestyles and behaviour) were especially targeted as a cause of concern.

Figure i.3: Same priorities, same political culture: dispersal of discipline

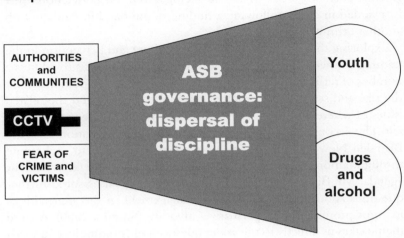

Explicit reference to 'popular perceptions' of crime and disorder is no accident either. For while the surveillance made possible by CCTV allowed the *authorities* to observe the illegalities and incivilities as they were played out on the streets of our towns and cities (leaving intervention to the police), the principles of ASB management were intended to empower *communities* by enabling residents to become more proactive in the designation of ASB and in initiating a response. The very definition of anti-social behaviour, after all, is founded upon a perception – of 'behaviour which causes or *is likely to cause* harassment, alarm or distress to one or more people who are not in the same household as the perpetrator' (Home Office, 2003: 5; emphasis added). As Burney (2006: 201) has argued, this catch-all phrase, first appearing in the 1986 Public Order Act, occupies a particular place in the modern history of the changing, even expanding, rationales of criminalisation. While critical criminologists urge the need to refocus criminology more consistently around more demonstrably calculable notions of 'social harm' (Hillyard et al, 2004) the formulation of ASB as 'alarm or distress' leads us into the rather more selective, flexible, relative and reciprocal terrain of 'offensiveness'.

Some commentators (see Flint et al, 2003, and this volume) have seen something positive in the accountability and empowerment conferred upon communities to initiate such complaints. However, there may still be some argument about the extent to which anti-social behaviour actions are genuinely initiated by 'ordinary' members of the public, especially in the light of the evidence now accumulating (see Burney, Chapter Seven in this volume) that almost two-thirds of new ASBOs currently being made are being given 'on conviction', that is, awarded in court, following a finding of guilt and in tandem with another criminal penalty.

Exploring the significance of politics, culture and perception in the framing of the anti-social behaviour problem requires us to address a number of related issues. A first involves the empirical questions about the size and scale of the problem referred to already and the related issues of where, and for whom, the problems of ASB are most acutely felt. The second question concerns the 'cultural revolution' that the Blair-led New Labour governments were attempting to orchestrate through, among other policy measures, their anti-social behaviour agenda. Mr Blair's departure from government raises some further questions about the future of ASB management in the aftermath of its most prominent and persuasive advocate (Squires, 2006). A third theme takes us directly to the wider questions of community and social inclusion, social capital and respect which, at a philosophical level, underpinned many of the values of New Labour. Significantly, many of the (broadly) social democratic commentators engaging in these debates appear to have been motivated to do so by a belief that the values of community, reciprocity and respect to which they were committed appeared to be imperilled by globalising social and economic changes, patterns of social and geographical mobility, cultural differences, inequalities, scarcities and conflicts (Findlay, 1999; Young, 1999). Finally, a fourth theme requires us to question the role of government and the law – or, more specifically, how a government should seek to influence (in particular, to improve) social behaviour. And this in the light of the familiar liberal caution that 'fraternity cannot be created by Act of Parliament' or, more simply put, that men and women cannot be made good by law alone (George, 1993). As we address these themes in turn, it will become clear that they are far from unrelated.

'Anti-social': what, how much and for whom?

Although the ASBO rapidly came to be seen as a specific response to youth problems and anti-social behaviour, the government had originally suggested that young people were not intended to be the chief recipients of the new orders. And, as Burney (2006) has shown, concern about offensive behaviour surfaced first in legislation dealing with public order, public housing management and environmental protection. All this was to change, however, as the ASBO moved to the forefront of the government's efforts to manage youth crime and disorder more effectively, reassure the public and streamline youth justice enforcement processes (Squires and Stephen, 2005). By the end of 2005, over 40% of ASBOs had been issued in respect of persons aged under 18 and evidence from the British Crime Survey began to suggest a concentration of concern about young people and anti-social behaviour (specifically 'youths hanging around') especially in the most economically deprived residential areas (Wood, 2004).

Of course concern about the behaviour of young people, especially the behaviour of young males from the poorest social groups, is scarcely original. Pearson's wonderfully illuminating 'history of respectable fears' (1983) charts the recurring historical concerns with the behaviour of those groups against whom, today, the charge of 'anti-social behaviour' would undoubtedly be laid. One imagines that, if an updated edition of the book were to be produced for today's market and today's applied social science students, contemporary concerns about anti-social behaviour would feature prominently within it. In a similar sense, a trawl through the writings of a wide array of prominent social scientists and criminologists will reveal many of the forerunners of our current concerns: in juvenile delinquency, street crime, crude and licentious behaviour, drunkenness, begging and vagrancy and violent disorder. Almost without exception, these are the behaviours associated with a particular social class, and most especially with its young males. Clearly, this is not the whole of the picture but it marks a sufficiently important historical continuity that should not be overlooked.

From the perspective of the 'respectable fears' referred to earlier, society has always been plagued by such behaviours, although the immediate problems they present and the deeper issues that they may *represent* may well be framed differently at different times and places. With this in mind, it seems fair to suggest that the contemporary significance of ASB derives more from the social contexts in which it is perceived than from anything qualitatively different about the behaviour itself. Again, there seems little new in this, either. Just as Turner (2006: 219) has defined his interest in ASB as concerning the 'symbolic affront' that such behaviour poses to the rest of the community, so juvenile offending has long intrigued scholars as much for what it was taken to represent as for the harm it caused (Bottoms, 1974).

That said, it is necessary to be aware of precisely what is being complained of, by whom, and how prevalent these concerns are. Despite the polemical tone of much of his book, Frank Field's *Neighbours from hell* (2003) left little doubt that the outward manifestation of the 'collapse in standards of personal behaviour' (p 76) of which he complained involved the outrageous behaviour of young lads and youths. Behind this, of course, lay parents who 'cannot or will not control their children' (p 84). Such comments immediately locate the behaviour for us while capturing something of its intolerable character. The context is one of close residential proximity in areas of social housing, where housing allocation decisions have (predictably but inadvertently) concentrated disproportionate numbers of 'difficult' but insufficiently supported families into areas where their reluctant neighbours lack the opportunities or resources to move out or away. Such areas virtually define the concept 'communities of fate' (Hope, 2000). From here it is but a short step to the claim made by a CDRP partner to a team of researchers exploring perceptions in a London Borough: 'Anti-social behaviour only occurs in social housing estates' (reported in Squires et al, 2004). The suggestion was palpable nonsense and, to be fair, was hotly disputed by other members of the partnership, but it is important to understand what shapes this perception – *and* that it is one that is still widely shared. Compounding the sense of entrapment and powerlessness defining the essential nature of ASB, as conveyed by Field, is its persistence. Hansen et al (2003) also drew attention to this feature, what they refer to as a mismatch between the accumulating and distressful impact of (perhaps) individually trivial anti-social acts experienced by victims, as compared with the non-accumulating consequences for offenders. Thus the persistent and 'accumulating' character of ASB endured disproportionately by vulnerable social groups was what defined its especial nuisance, thereby justifying a distinctive form of intervention that took this problem more seriously.

This rough characterisation of the phenomenon can be related to the emerging empirical evidence on ASB produced by the British Crime Survey (BCS). While overall perceptions of ASB indicated that concerns about 'teenagers hanging around' were only mentioned by just over a quarter of BCS respondents, the survey also found that those living in disadvantaged areas were significantly more likely to report high levels of concern about ASB in general, and especially likely to regard youths 'hanging around' as a big problem (Bottoms, 2006). Over 40% of respondents in such areas considered youth ASB in public areas a big problem (Wood, 2004). In effect, the picture that emerged suggested a particularly unequal distribution of perceived youth-related anti-social behaviour – a picture corresponding closely to the patterns resulting from the redistribution of criminal victimisation since the early 1980s (see Hope, 2000, 2001). It was this evidence of the concentration of victimisation in the poorest neighbourhoods (produced by 'left realist' criminology), compounding and entrenching the disadvantages of the poorest communities, that had fired New Labour's commitment to tackling social exclusion by synthesising its strategies on social and criminal justice.

Before exploring the policies, institutions, interventions and instruments arising from this newly 'joined-up' policy making – not least the hybrid new orders and quasi-criminal controls, with their shifting registers of prevention, discipline and support (Stephen and Squires, 2007) – it is instructive to comment further on the broader ambitions at the heart of all this political creativity and how they sought to engage with the 'deeper underlying causes of unacceptable behaviour' referred to above.

The cultural politics of anti-social behaviour

We have already noted how 'ideological' that New Labour's anti-social behaviour' project always was, led, very much from the front, by Prime Minister Blair (Squires, 2006).As the advent of the 'Respect Agenda' has made even more obvious, the problem of anti-social behaviour is very broadly drawn. It encompasses civic renewal, economic regeneration, personal morality, new forms of governing and the elimination of criminal and public nuisances. New Labour has sought to achieve a dramatic sea-change in public attitudes and behaviour, by exhortation, moral and community rearmament and the selective use of new sanctions and enforcement powers (see Jacobson et al in this volume for a discussion of these varying policy rationales).

A number of persuasive discourses fed into this field of policy making, with many of its roots reaching back to the Social Justice Commission Report of 1993, especially its conception of social exclusion as a question of injustice – a 'justice gap'. This connected the government's social inclusion agenda (SEU, 1998; 2000) to its more generic 'responsibilisation' strategy (Garland, 2001) leading ultimately to the 2003 Anti-Social Behaviour Act. Beginning with ambitions to 'strengthen communities' by rebalancing rights and responsibilities, to 'nip youth crime in the bud' and enforce more effectively the obligations of parents, the strategy became, in the words of its foremost spokesman, an ambitious cultural challenge to society at large and a profound assault on management, administration and professional practice in the criminal justice system. As the then prime minister argued in a speech in January 2006, marking the launch of the Respect Action Plan:

> The important thing about debating ASB, and the measures we are proposing, is not to debate it at the crude level of 'tough' or 'not tough'; populist or not. But, instead, to regard it as a genuine intellectual debate about the nature of liberty in a modern developed society. (Blair, 2006)

Blair's inclination to embrace grand philosophical principles of freedom and justice as the cardinal values underpinning his policy agenda certainly points to an ambitious cultural programme:

> It is about respect for other people. It's about decency. It's about hard-working families who play by the rules ... It's everything that strong communities should stand for, protecting the vulnerable, sticking up for what is right. (Blair, 2004c)

Even so, earlier the same year he had been rather more directive and practical, committing the government to providing the local authorities responsible for managing ASB with:

> the right legal framework to give you the power to take tough action, and ... the resources to ensure that you can enforce those powers. (Blair, 2004a)

Despite, as we have seen, the prime minister's later rejection of the 'toughness' rhetoric, these enforcement resources were subsequently described as a 'tough package of measures to give the police, housing officers, local authorities and courts the powers to tip the balance firmly in favour of the law-abiding majority' (2004c). Blair's description of this political agenda as something of a personal crusade (2004b) reinforces the broadly cultural and ideological dimension to this issue. The effective containment of anti-social behaviour, disrespect and prolific and persistent offending is heralded as:

> the culmination of a journey of change both for progressive politics and for the country. It marks the end of the 1960s' liberal, social consensus on law and order. (Blair, 2004b)

While embracing wholeheartedly the rejection of the many forms of anti-social discrimination associated with the years prior to the liberal, progressive and permissive 1960s, the prime minister confirmed a new resolution to crack down on those whom he saw to be exploiting their new-found freedoms and the criminogenic opportunities arising from the rapid social changes of late modernity.

There is a potential inconsistency here, at the heart of this governmental strategy – and it has not gone unremarked (see Norris and Williams [Chapter Fourteen], Measham and Moore [Chapter Fifteen] and Phoenix [Chapter Sixteen]) in discussions of recent government policies. These have concerned, in particular, the liberalisation of alcohol licensing (Measham, 1996, 2004; Hadfield, 2006), the revitalisation of urban night-time economies (Hobbs et al, 2005) and the advent of 24-hour cities (Coleman, 2004; Hall and Winlow, 2006), the selective liberalisation of the commercial sex industry – although with the notable exception of street prostitution (Phoenix and Oerton, 2005, 2007; Sanders, 2007; Scoular et al, 2007) – and the much debated (and much criticised) issue of 'casino led economic regeneration'. As David Garland (2001) has argued, it is characteristic of liberal criminal justice regimes to criminalise illegal opportunity *takers* (for example, those who drive too fast) rather than illegal opportunity *makers* (those who design and build the kinds of vehicles that can be driven too fast). From the mainstream liberal perspective, of course, the issue comes down to one of rational and responsible people exercising choices *not to offend*, a position that connects us directly with contemporary notions of responsibilisation and the neoclassical criminological paradigm upon which it stands: criminal actions have consequences – know them, avoid them.

To nudge this argument a little further we can also go on to define a conception of 'advanced liberalism' (or libertarianism) where even greater opportunity to offend is placed (very literally) in the hands of individuals, who are, accordingly, presumed to bear even greater responsibility, and more dire consequences, for any harm or offence they cause. The 'test case' of this perspective, which also reveals its rather obvious flaws, could well be the supposed right of American private citizens to own and carry firearms, a fairly direct consequence of which is the US's lethal homicide and firearm violence rates, which far exceed those of comparable developed societies (Cook and Ludwig, 2000; Squires, 2000). The right to carry a firearm, to live peacefully while armed and dangerous to one another, implies a very heavy burden of responsibility. Unfortunately for the US, a significant minority of citizens seem unable to exercise this responsibility and, although many Americans seem prepared to accept this as a 'price to be paid' for the values and lifestyle they prefer, it also tends to confirm that the abstractions of neoclassical legalism offer us a rather incomplete purchase on our efforts to manage disorder, prevent crime and promote good behaviour (Squires, 2006). As today's more informed social-scientific, cultural and psycho-social criminologies (Katz, 1988; Jefferson, 2002) confirm, human behaviour responds to far more disparate influences than simply the dictates of duty and conscience (these varied influences — desire, fear, ambition, excitement, revenge and so on — may even profoundly reshape our conscience or our sense of duty). None of this implies a rejection of choices, simply the need to contextualise and understand them.

It follows that the processes of rapid social change that liberalism has both welcomed and facilitated unleash potentially criminogenic influences to which the government responded by introducing a number of, at face value, very illiberal-seeming measures. Without necessarily wanting to argue, in the 'grand narrative' tradition, that liberalism appears to be destined to undermine its own conditions of existence, we are forced at least to consider how Mr Blair's famous slogan 'tough on crime, tough on the causes of crime' measures up to Garland's implied critique. To what extent is a consumer-driven, youth-oriented and alcohol-fuelled night-time economy a driver of criminal opportunities and, therefore, a cause of crime? To turn the issue around, to what extent are we prepared to tolerate the CCTV, the ID cards, the visible security, the zero tolerance of public drunkenness and the police presence, curfews, banning orders and on-the-spot fines as a consequence of our 'freedom'?

Perhaps, it will be objected, to refer to our earlier discussion, the night-time economy is largely a 'community of choice' (Hope, 2000); we are more concerned with the intolerable levels of anti-social behaviour, harassment and intimidation in the deprived 'communities of fate' (Hope, 2000). Here too we need to appreciate the importance of social context for socialisation and the factors impinging upon and influencing people's behaviour, sometimes making it virtually impossible for people to meet all their responsibilities (thereby raising questions of social support: see Stephen and Squires, 2003, 2007). But here the freedom of some is substantially undermined by the inconsiderate behaviour of others: loud music, intimidating people, drunken parties, uncontrolled dogs, dangerous driving and inconsiderate parking and challenging and abusive children and young people. Such outcomes should certainly not be read as a simple consequence of supposedly failing and neglectful parents (as Holt's Chapter Eleven in this volume argues). Indeed, the very idea that community decline can be attributed to the anti-social behaviour of individuals rather than the anti-social consequences of more fundamental social changes (Burney, 2002) – economic processes, market changes, public policies – is one of the fallacies that the notion of ASB has made more plausible (Squires, 1990). Although this is hardly a new fallacy, blaming the poorest for their own predicament is a familiar British predilection (Golding and Middleton, 1982; Novak, 1988). Undoubtedly, the deprivation, exclusion and discrimination experienced in poorer communities is immeasurably exacerbated by the depredations of criminality, the daily experiences of harassment and intimidation, and the sense of powerlessness that nothing much will be done about these issues. Yet along the way, the notion of ASB has allowed left-realist ideas of causation to flip over, holding individuals as responsible for anti-social behaviour, and ASB as the root cause of community decline. By definition, targeting anti-social individuals eclipses all other solutions (arguably, another aspect of the 'mission drift' associated with the ASB policy). Above all, such approaches neglect the accumulating weight of evidence that:

> Tackling ASB does not have to focus on the individual as the cause of the problem.... A more holistic problem-solving approach would look also for patterns of ASB and points of intervention that are a function of opportunities for and facilitators of ASB, rather than the individuals taking advantage of them. (Hodgkinson and Tilley, 2007: 394)

The contexts and the influences arising in 'communities of fate' produce fairly predictable and well-understood responses among their populations. So in addressing the 'criminal opportunity making' here, we should ask why such environments have come to be. Just as we considered the development of the alcohol-based night-time economy, so we need to see the configurations of housing, employment, education, social services, youth and criminal justice *policies* as having exacerbated these criminogenic environments. For if such communities are to continue to exist, with their all too foreseeable consequences for residents, then ASBOs and ABCs (Acceptable Behaviour Contracts), curfews and Dispersal Orders, Parenting Orders, closure notices, injunctions and evictions would appear to be the price that some people will have to pay (just as others pay it in criminal victimisation, racism, violence and fear). It is worth reiterating that this is a price paid only by some – these are communities of fate after all, not communities of choice, although not everyone is equally trapped in them.

The point opens up an inconsistency in the Blairite liberalism, for wrapped up in the comment we considered earlier, that 'anti-social behaviour only occurs in social housing estates', is an acknowledgement of the potential discrimination of ASB enforcement processes. For it was in social housing areas, and initially through housing management policies and the threat of eviction, that authorities had the greatest leverage over families. The postcoded differentiation in enforcement practice was reinforced by the prioritisation of community safety initiatives, particularly the additional surveillance and intervention tools and resources at their disposal, within New Deal for Communities areas. From the discipline of legal philosophy, commentators (see Simester and von Hirsch, 2006) have objected to the ASBO (or what they call a 'two-step prohibition') for its creation of an individually tailored (personalised) system of justice for particular people. In effect, this involves the de facto creation of a formal category of 'convenient suspects' whose future transgressions (or even merely technical breaches of orders) render them liable to some potentially severe penalties with a modicum of criminal due process – all in disregard of the founding liberal principle that the law should treat everyone as equal.

This 'majestic equality' of the law,[1] which has, in any event, been much disputed by those criminologists who have paid close attention to its actual enforcement, arguably, not only impacts on a personal and individual basis by legal measures such as the ASBO, but is undermined by the intelligence-led targeting of groups of persistent and prolific offenders within each Crime and Disorder Reduction Partnership (and what has been referred to as pre-emptive criminalisation, or 'precautionary injustice': Squires and Stephen, 2005) as the government's new criminal justice measures have been deployed in what Prime Minister Blair called 'the most radical overhaul of criminal justice law and procedure in a generation' (Blair, 2004a). Relatedly, the bold claim, subsequently voiced by the prime minister, that Britain was 'fighting 21st-century crime with 19th-century methods' (Blair, 2006) and the suggestion, from no less a person than a Home Secretary, that the Home Office was 'not fit for purpose' underpin both the centrality of 'law and order' to the Blairite cultural revolution and the scale of the changes envisaged.

Along this journey towards '21st-century criminal justice' many subsidiary themes surfaced, each playing its 'bit part' in the overall production:

- the idea that the police, courts and local authorities felt powerless to tackle the rising tide of crime and disorder, and so, often, did not really try (Faulkner, 2001);
- the idea that, partly as a result of the above, young people in particular appeared to believe they could offend with impunity (see Campbell, 2002; Squires and Stephen, 2005);
- the idea that a 'zero tolerance' of minor incivilities – underpinned by the Wilson and Kelling 'broken windows' hypothesis (1982) – could provide an appropriate enforcement-led framework to accompany regeneration efforts by taking apparently minor crime and disorder (or 'signal crimes') more seriously (Hopkins-Burke, 1998; Innes, 1999; Stenson, 2000);
- the idea that early indications of youth crime needed 'nipping in the bud' (Audit Commission, 1996) because adolescent anti-social behaviour was a reliable predictor of a criminal career (Home Office, 1997) and young people were not growing out of crime as they once had (Squires and Stephen, 2005, chapters 3 and 4), and that this reflected a much wider 'crisis of youth' that was still deepening (Furlong and Cartmel, 1997; MacDonald, 1997).

But while such discursive themes certainly sketched in many of the details for us, the big ideas revolved around questions of community, order and inclusion (especially the breakdown of 'traditional' communities – and the ensuing consequences), and the concepts of social capital and 'respect'.

We will turn to these issues shortly. But first, what of the future of this ideological crusade? With Tony Blair's resignation as prime minister announced in the weeks during which the manuscript for this book was being finalised, a question must arise as to how the ASB agenda (and the wider cultural and political changes of which it was a part) will fare with the departure of its most prominent advocate. Given how deeply embedded in public consciousness the notion of ASB has become, and how much both central and local government policy making and policy practice is preoccupied with anti-social behaviour, then it is difficult to see the issues fading, although this is not to suggest there will not be some important changes in emphasis (as already noted).

As we have already seen, the most important legacy of ASB could well be the way in which it has become the foundation upon which a whole new range of hybrid, and semi-criminal, enforcement powers has been brought into being. Across a wide range of government action against problems of crime and disorder – from the control of troublesome youth, the management of sex offenders, the targeting of gang members, the surveillance of terrorists, the focusing of multi-layered interventions on street prostitutes and substance misusers, to criminal asset recovery and anti-social behaviour management – loosely defined 'offences', streamlined due process, peremptory evidential scrutiny, pre-emptive criminalisation and inclusive net-widening sketch the parameters of an essentially new risk- and perception-driven approach to crime control and security management. Ironically, the very factors that led critics to question the focus on anti-social behaviour as a crime and disorder *strategy* – the imprecise definition, its relativity and flexibility, its low-key and, at times, almost routine nature and its close relation to youthful behaviour in public – are precisely the keys to its utility.

The new interventions – ASBOs, curfews, Dispersal Orders, Parenting Orders, policing methods and partnership practices, and so on – have achieved such a professional and administrative utility that it is hard to imagine them dismantled. If this redefinition of the purposes and procedures of criminal justice has been the government's objective in its 'modernisation' strategy, then what commentators have come to call the 'new policing' (McLaughlin, 2007) has been accompanied by a 'new criminal justice'. Likewise, if an enforcement deficit existed, the government has gone some way towards filling it. Paradoxically, this has coincided with the emergence of the first substantial waves of empirical evidence on 'what works' and 'effectiveness' in ASB management, precisely questioning the merits of an exclusively enforcement-led approach to these issues (Millie et al, 2005; Bottoms, 2006; Hodgkinson and Tilley, 2007).

Communities, social capital, respect and tolerance

It is here that some of the specific work evaluating ASBOs and enforcement issues connects to the much wider debate about society, culture, supposed moral decline, irresponsible parenting and disrespect that the government has launched. At the heart of this discussion lie a number of fundamental questions concerning:

1. how we understand the social changes that have given rise to the (familiar and historically recurring) complaint about 'moral decline', the breakdown of families and, in particular, the behaviour of youth;
2. the purchase of the criminal justice system upon crime and disorder in society in its most general sense;

3. whether, and how, a government-led 'cultural revolution' of the kind seemingly aspired to by the New Labour project might be mobilised; and

4. the range of tools and resources that governments might deploy to influence opinion and change behaviour. Implicitly, here lies a recognition that enforcement alone will never be sufficient (any aspiring golfer requires more than a single club).

Many of these issues are implicated in a news item that broke during the late summer of 2007. Merseyrail, the company responsible for operating trains in the Merseyside area had prosecuted a young woman for resting her feet on the seats facing her in a train carriage. When asked to refrain from this, she complied with the ticket inspector's request but, along with over 800 other similar 'offenders' was prosecuted anyway (her case was not the first, and over 600 cases were still pending). When the case was heard by magistrates in Chester, the court awarded an absolute discharge, suggesting also that the train company's response had been 'draconian … and ill-advised'. Magistrates suggested a 'fixed penalty' system of fines might be a better response. The train company was, however, unrepentant saying that there would be no change in policy. It was argued that the new zero-tolerance policy was designed to achieve a 'world class public transport network, free from anti-social behaviour' (Ward, 2007).

Apart from what this incident reveals about the all-consuming discourse of ASB and its seemingly limitless application, it raises a fundamental question (often seen as the true preserve of legal philosophers) about what the real *purpose* of the criminal law is and what should be its *extent*. Finally, in line with the fourth issue outlined above, it raises the question of how the goals of the criminal law might best be achieved. In the Merseyrail case, even the magistrates were only suggesting a different (probably more low-key and efficient) style of enforcement, they were not really disputing the anti-social label.

It may be no mere coincidence that this particular case captures so neatly so many of these issues. The eminent American legal philosopher Joel Feinberg devotes volume two of his quartet of books, *The moral limits of the criminal law*, to the question of *Offense to others* (Feinberg, 1985). The opening sequence of the book depicts a bus journey in which one luckless passenger is trapped and forced to endure the variously offensive, noisy, smelly, disorderly, unsanitary, crude and inappropriate behaviours of his fellow passengers (none of whom, it must be admitted, indulged in behaviour so tame as merely resting their feet on the seats). Perhaps there is something about public transport: passengers are caught together in a moment of common public purpose, travel to a given destination, and are required to rub along together according to a set of commonly understood rules (or are they?) of civility. In Stuart Waiton's terms (see Chapter Nineteen in this volume), perhaps, in the confines of the railway carriage or the bus, our respective 'bubbles' of personal space are required to jostle alongside one another in much closer proximity than we would normally prefer. In Kathryn Hughes' phrase (echoing Sartre) 'yobbery is other people' (Hughes, 2007). In this sense, perhaps the railway company is doing us all a favour in trying to set down a marker as to what is or is not acceptable: keep your feet off the seats! Perhaps a few well-publicised prosecutions will encourage other passengers to keep their feet down. This 'demonstration effect' of criminal law has long been a favourite of authoritarians, rationalists, neoconservatives and the classical school of criminology and maybe this explains some of the potency of the anti-social behaviour and Respect strategies. Many people share a common sense that something needs to be done: so something *is* being done. This brings us back to the key questions identified earlier: have we 'lost the plot' (Hughes, 2007) on anti-social behaviour? What is going on and has it all gone too far? Does ASB lie entirely within the eye of the beholder? Are we asking too much of the criminal law? What can the government do? And are there other ways of getting where we want to go (unlike Feinberg's bus, we cannot just get off)?

However, it is just at this point, where the more specific question of anti-social behaviour transforms into a much wider complaint about the moral decay of society and the 'state of the nation', that a number of contrary ideas begin to join forces. That there is widespread perception of moral decline is hardly new; the issue, especially the supposed moral decline of the young, has featured prominently among the 'respectable fears' of middle-class middle England for decades (Pearson, 1983). Perhaps the latest exponent of this is John O'Sullivan, writing in the *Sunday Telegraph* in August 2007 of a 'social acid' that has 'burnt away at the heart of Britain' (O'Sullivan, 2007). Perhaps he meant 'anti-social' acid. In an at times amusing article (for example, the police have become deflected from their main purpose of tackling serious crime and have become instead 'little more than the paramilitary wing of the *Guardian* [newspaper]' he follows Tony Blair's 2004 'new consensus' speech (Blair, 2004b) in locating the cause of our current concerns in the tolerant liberalism of the 1960s. Multiculturalism, social diversity and the BBC are also lined up for criticism.

For his solution O'Sullivan looks (much like Mrs Thatcher some 25 years earlier: Walvin, 1988; Himmelfarb, 1995) towards the supposedly confident authoritarianism of the Victorian age (although rather neglecting the dark side of the Victorian imaginary, for example see Marcus, 1969; Stedman-Jones, 1971). To address today's deepening moral decay, O'Sullivan calls for a toughening of our resolve and implicitly lends his support to the Civitas think-tank report (Green et al, 2005), calling for a robust programme of moral and situational reform and an expansion of penal capacity to incarcerate the most recalcitrant of offenders. Sweeping aside any concerns that (in European terms) Britain has an unusually high prison population, the report's authors argue instead that, judged against the levels of crime in Britain, our imprisonment rate is relatively low.

This resort to Victorian solutions (the Victorian period witnessed the establishment of the modern prison system in Britain) also draws upon more recent American practice, where penal expansion and mass incarceration are seen in the US as *solutions* to contemporary crime problems (Parenti, 1999; Garland, 2001; Wacquant, 2005). Nevertheless, as Reiner argues (2007: 160), in order to work, based upon existing knowledge and assumptions about population, crime trends and recidivism, this 'penal solution' will require the *continuing expansion* of the prison system. This potential flaw in their proposals has not, however, escaped Green and his colleagues and, as the subtitle of their report makes clear (*Can we become a more law-abiding people?*), their programme of social reform contains two further elements: (i) proposals to improve the effectiveness of imprisonment and reduce reoffending, and (ii) (of more direct concern to us here) proposals for lowering the underlying crime rate by reducing the apparent predilection of the British to offend and, in effect, making us more law-abiding. In this regard, a comment by the conservative criminologist Norman Dennis while introducing the Civitas report is rather instructive. Dennis is concerned with what he calls the continual 'dismantling' of 'the basic structure of a crime free society' and he refers to the 'religious, familial, educational, recreational and other institutions that created and sustained ... a largely crime free England during the hundred years from, say, 1855 to 1955' (Dennis, 2005: xix–xx).

Eighteen fifty-five to 1955, those years again, from the mid-Victorian period to the post-Second World War consensus; PC Dixon and the 'golden age of policing'; the new 'affluent' society when, apparently, according to Harold MacMillan, we had 'never had it so good'. But the century that saw the end of empire, the Crimean war, the Boer War, two World Wars, the General Strike and the great depression was hardly 'crime free'. Nor did it feel 'crime free' to contemporaries. There were, admittedly fewer crimes on the statute book and, probably, rather fewer opportunities to commit them anyway (the motor car and the mass-consumer economy had scarcely yet dawned). Furthermore, in any event, a rather less efficient system of policing and criminal justice still failed to record most of those offences that did occur, and consequently the media failed to report them. Finally, just as it is today, those groups and communities most frequently victimised were those least inclined, or least able, to report it (and least likely to be taken seriously if they did). Yet it is still a strange kind of historical amnesia to see this as a 'largely crime free England'.

Yet where this whole account becomes particularly interesting is where it refers to the 'religious, familial, educational, recreational and other institutions' and to the community ties that sustained a commitment to forms of morality and order. However, even this social cohesion provides no panacea for our modern sensibilities, the very same tight-knit, hierarchical, masculine, employment-based, traditional communities could well be communities in which wives, mothers and daughters had little alternative but to suffer domestic violence and abuse in privacy and silence.

Nevertheless, Dennis and the moral authoritarians are not the only commentators to argue the case for a more sustained scrutiny of the sources of social order and of the social fabric that binds us together. And, even as they argue for tougher penalties as a necessary (but not necessarily sufficient) means for reinforcing moral orthodoxy, they also recognise (in terms of our earlier four questions) that government cannot (or even should not) do it alone; that limits should be imposed on the 'reach' of the criminal law; and that enforcement action alone is unlikely to be effective – there have to be carrots as well as sticks. Other commentators talk about these issues in terms of 'social capital', collective efficacy, respect and tolerance – in other words, the social and cultural dimensions of inclusion and community cohesion, and a great deal of research, scholarship and advocacy has been devoted to understanding, establishing and nurturing these vital resources.

A substantial foundation of the government's communities and social inclusion strategy was founded on the 'communitarian' philosophy. In its more specifically criminological applications, this work presumed a relationship between community fragmentation, human behaviour and motivation, and criminality. However, researchers seeking to identify the constituent elements of 'law-abidingness' in a culture produced only the rather unsurprising and somewhat circular argument that untrustworthy people commit more crime, disintegrating societies have more crime, and crime itself promotes distrust and erodes social capital (Halpern, 2001; Turner, 2006). By contrast, 'higher levels of social capital are associated with significantly lower crime rates', whereas, 'it may be that social distrust – or mutual disrespect – plays a much stronger role in violent crime' (Halpern, 2001: 237, 247). If nothing else, shifting the focus of explanation to social values, relationships and community cohesion reiterated a sense that 'crime and antisocial behaviour is at least as strongly affected by the values and behaviour of individuals and communities as by the activities of the police and criminal justice system' (Halpern et al, 2004: 6).

Full circle: ASBOs, social change and the future

In many respects, these points return us, full circle, to some of our earlier observations about the cultural politics of anti-social behaviour. Since the 1960s there has been a significant liberalisation of attitudes and behaviour consequent upon important shifts in the economy, labour market and media. These changes have resulted in new criminal challenges and new criminal opportunities. Commentators from both left and right have disputed both the causes and the consequences of these changes, while the selective economic liberalism of recent government policy has sought to contain some of the worst of the criminogenic consequences of our new ways of life. A resurrected notion of social contract – rights and duties – has been advanced as the basis of modern citizenship and new rules of civility – 'respect and responsibility' (the title of the Home Office White Paper of 2003, the precursor to the Anti-Social Behaviour Act of that year) – have been articulated.

Turning these rather general claims about duty, behaviour and responsibility into policy and practice has, in part, fallen to the various agencies forming our new ASB management industry at both central and local government levels, to the Respect Action Team, the pathfinder authorities, the pilot projects, community safety teams and the new cadres of anti-social behaviour practitioners. Here, however, our questions about the role of government, its capacity to achieve the culture change aspired to and the tools at its disposal have become especially pertinent.

In a 2004 report for the Prime Minister's Strategy Unit, Halpern and his colleagues set out the challenge:

> Governments employ many tools, including laws, punishments and regulations, taxes and subsidies, the provision of public services, and information and persuasion. Many of these tools are designed to influence changes in

public behaviour. In some areas they work well. However, in others their effectiveness is limited. As a result policy-makers have sought out more sophisticated means of building more effective relationships between citizens and government which can influence public behaviour, particularly with a view to increasing personal responsibility. (Halpern et al, 2004: 3)

This broad outline of a wide-ranging responsibilisation and engagement strategy scarcely describes the ways in which, thus far, anti-social behaviour has actually been addressed. While agencies of government may have been energised, connected, resourced in new ways, and even selected community interests incorporated into the process within a rubric of accountability, alleged perpetrators of ASB (until recently) have found themselves to be almost exclusively the recipients of warnings, restrictions and enforcement action. Furthermore, the enthusiasm for attaching public 'name and shame' prescriptions (justified in terms of making the enforcement more effective) to ASBOs has added an extra dimension of (counterproductive) stigmatising exclusion to the orders even though, in some areas, it is claimed that young people are reinterpreting their orders as 'badges of honour' or 'street diplomas'. But how else could they respond: a defiant, self-destructive, masculine bravado in the face of hopelessness, the only resource left?

The changing contours of public expectations about governmental intervention define, for Halpern and his colleagues, the arrival of a new philosophy of government, somewhere between the self-interestedness of neoliberalism and the collective paternalism of traditional social democracy (Squires, 1990). This new 'libertarian collectivism' allows an individual the freedom to consume, enjoy, experience and take opportunities but these are invariably hedged with contractuality and conditionality. Failure to heed these rules and conditions will lead to consequences for the individual: the effect is to create a largely individualistic frame for understanding personal morality and behaviour, and in matters of law, order and morality (where government has invested so much) these 'lines not to be crossed' are ever more firmly set. The overall arrangement is not unlike a more selective version of the 'free economy and strong state' described by Gamble (1988), for public opinion, on the whole, quickly reverts to a largely punitive mindset whenever the behaviour of the lower social classes is concerned. That said, however, aligning the more philosophically inspired perspectives of Halpern and his colleagues with the developing professional practice of the ASB workforce we can, perhaps, begin to discern a sense in which behaviour change and compliance, rather than traditional enforcement strategies, emerge as the operating principles of the ASBO industry. It may be worth considering what we are to make of this new 'ASBO revisionism' and, not least, trying to assess whether it makes any difference to those on the receiving end.

Turning to the application of these ideas in professional community safety practice we find, perhaps inevitably, some inconsistency. While the language of personal responsibility, social capital, collective efficacy and, especially, 'respect' dominate the rhetoric of ASBO policy, actual practice varies (as chapters in this volume by Goldsmith [Chapter Twelve] and McIntosh [Chapter Thirteen] relate). The Respect strategy itself seems to comprehend behaviour change through the lens of a motivational self-help programme that the virtuous or committed might choose to ascend (though no doubt prompted by the threat of enforcement sanctions) (Stephen and Squires, 2007). Only relatively recently has serious attention been shifted away from an 'enforcement' focus and directed instead towards the circumstances and conditions in which individuals might attempt to address their behaviour issues. The contributions in this volume by Edwards and Hughes (Chapter Two), by McIntosh (Chapter Thirteen) and by Mayfield and Mills (Chapter Three) describe either 'stepped', 'mixed' or 'last resort' approaches to ASBO enforcement (see also Hodgkinson and Tilley, 2007; and Pawson's [2007] informative review of ASBOs in Scotland) and the growing recognition that a balance needs to be struck between enforcement action and the support necessary to ensure that ASBO subjects have a reasonable chance of complying with, and therefore completing, their orders satisfactorily (Millie et al, 2005; Solanki et al, 2006). Such approaches seem some advance from the earlier government rhetoric in which ASBO 'success' seemed little more than a numbers game. Although, to be fair, Burney rather punctured this myth in 2002, revealing that, initially, ASBO numbers were well down on government expectations (Burney, 2002), indicating some reluctance on the part of community safety practitioners to fully embrace the 'ASBO solution'. The government response to this, after 2004, included increasing pressure on local authorities to expand ASBO usage (Squires, 2006), and subsequently the Respect campaign and Respect Action Zones. In fact, however, as Burney demonstrates in Chapter Seven in this volume, the greater part of the increase in the number of ASBOs now awarded concerns ASBOs 'on conviction' rather than free-standing orders (that is, post-conviction rather than pre-conviction).

Nevertheless, further evidence of a kind of practical 'ASBO revisionism' may be glimpsed in some of the support given to the use of Acceptable Behaviour Contracts rather than ASBOs, for, in the words of Duff and Marshall, we 'can see … a possibly more fruitful role for a version of ABCs that takes much more seriously the idea that they are contracts' (2006: 88). Such arrangements may conform more closely to the rhetoric of contract that recent government policy has voiced, but for some commentators at least, there still remain questions about just how voluntarily and freely entered into these contracts really are (Stephen and Squires, 2003; Squires and Stephen, 2005). To some degree similar considerations apply to the Individual Support Orders (ISOs) introduced by the 2003 Anti-Social Behaviour Act and in force since May 2004. Such orders are in part a reflection of concern about rates of ASBO breach and also an attempt to help young people address the causes of their offending behaviour (likewise in Scotland the ASBO enforcement requirements for young people are subordinated to issues of child welfare and justice in that ASB management interventions remain part of the Children's Hearings process). In England and Wales, an ISO has to be made in the case of any 10- to 17-year-old on whom the court is intending to impose a free-standing ASBO. Although breach of an ISO, like breach of an ASBO, is a criminal offence, these ostensibly supportive interventions are intended to help young people to address their troublesome behaviour. They also provide for a broad continuum of flexible interventions running from the more punitive to the more supportive to be adjusted according to the circumstances of individual cases. In this sense, these measures correspond more closely to an older 'care and control' dualism that has long underpinned youth justice policies and that, as some of the contributors to this volume suggest (see also Smith, 2004), still features as a key element of the operating philosophy of a significant proportion of the community safety and youth justice workforce.

At face value, the attempt to support young people responsible for anti-social behaviour and to help them deal with the issues that influence their ASB – and thereby help prevent the behaviour itself – would appear to indicate an approach to these problems offering a greater chance of success than enforcement action alone. At the same time such interventions suggest a policy more consistent with the philosophy of contractuality, mutual consent and, above all, 'respect' to which the government subscribes (Sennett, 2003; Bottoms, 2006; Turner, 2006). Whether government alone can engineer the cultural revolution to which the Blair government aspired must remain an open question. In truth, our policies for ASB have more the feel of the man with the bucket following the Lord Mayor's parade: the splendid vehicles of social, cultural and economic change passed by some time ago. Public policy merely picks up the pieces. If this suggests an essentially residual model of public policy making and a still relatively detached and backward-looking conception of criminal justice, this may not be far from the truth. Even, to paraphrase Tony Blair, as the problems of crime and disorder remain at the forefront of our 21st-century political agenda, our law and order culture remains stuck in the 19th century.

With the departure of Tony Blair, the ASB question's most prominent advocate, from the UK domestic scene many of these issues are still up for grabs. One phase of the ASBO story draws to a close and, in the chapters that follow, commentators from a wide variety of perspectives evaluate the evidence and debate the meaning and significance of this fascinating phase of rapid public policy making. The problems of ASB are unlikely to go away, the ASBO genie, as it were, is well and truly out of its bottle. The very utility of the hybrid legal powers reflected in the ASBO is likely to ensure their continuing appeal to governments of all political complexions, even in the face of profound objections from civil libertarians, and it will fall to policy makers and practitioners to make these powers and interventions effective, workable, legal and humane.

By way of conclusion it may be worth reflecting, finally, on our culture and its symbolic politics of crime and disorder. These issues, of crime, violence, ASB and immorality and behavioural impropriety in all its forms, have truly dominated a great part of the domestic political agenda of the Blair decade. We have become thoroughly preoccupied by other people's behaviour and especially by our sense that other people's standards are slipping. Like Mark Twain, we seem inclined to believe that 'nothing so needs reforming as other people's behaviour'. And yet, there remains an important sense, as Garside has argued (2006), that criminal justice policy has only a relatively small purchase on illegality and disorder and, we might add, still less of a grasp on the whole of immorality and offensiveness. In this fashion, in a supposedly liberal society – even one as preoccupied by crime as our own – the criminal justice system confronts immorality, offensiveness and illegality like King Cnut faced the incoming tide. To continue this metaphor, arguably the culture change we really need is not someone to order back a selection of the most offensive waves (punitive authoritarianism) but better planning of our flood defences, help in learning to swim, courses in boat building and advice on coping with the damp. Whether the combined effect of recent legislation, recent crime and disorder management strategies included, undermines our society's liberal credentials may be a question for another time. In this volume, the chapters by Chakrabarti and Russell (Chapter Seventeen)

Stephen (Chapter Eighteen) and Waiton (Chapter Nineteen) offer some wider reflections on these issues.

Note
[1] According to Anatole France, 'The law, in its majestic equality, forbids rich and poor alike to sleep under bridges, to beg in the streets, and to steal their bread' (*The Red Lily*, 1908).

References
ADT Europe (2006) *Anti-social behaviour across Europe*, TNS Survey for ADT (www.adt.co.uk/antisocial.html).

Ashworth, A., Gardner, J., Morgan, R., Smith, A., von Hirsch, A. and Wasik, M. (1998) 'Neighbouring on the oppression: the government's anti-social behaviour proposals', *Criminal Justice*, vol 16, no 1, pp 7–14.

Audit Commission (1996) *Misspent youth*, London: Audit Commission.

Blair, T. (2004a) Speech on crime reduction, 30 March.

Blair, T. (2004b) Speech on the launch of the five-year strategy for crime, 19 July.

Blair, T. (2004c) Speech on anti-social behaviour, 28 October.

Blair, T. (2006) Speech on the launch of the Respect Action Plan, 10 January.

Bottoms, A.E. (1974) 'On the decriminalisation of English juvenile courts', in R. Hood (ed), *Essays in honour of Sir Leon Radzinowicz*, London: Heinemann.

Bottoms, A.E. (2006) 'Incivilities, offence and social order in residential communities', in A. von Hirsch and A.P. Simester (eds), *Incivilities: Regulating offensive behaviour*, Oxford: Hart Publishing.

Burney, E. (2002) 'Talking tough, acting coy: What happened to the Anti-Social Behaviour Order?' *Howard Journal of Criminal Justice*, vol 45, no 1, pp 469–84.

Burney, E. (2006) '"No spitting": regulation of offensive behaviour in England and Wales', in A. von Hirsch and A.P. Simester (eds), *Incivilities: Regulating offensive behaviour*, Oxford: Hart Publishing.

Campbell, S. (2002) *A review of anti-social behaviour orders*, Research Study 236, London: The Home Office.

Carvel, J. (2007) 'Fivefold rise in rows over noise marks less tolerant society', *Guardian*, 11 April.

Chakrabarti, S. (2006) 'Asbomania: from social and moral justice to mob rule?', BIHR lunchtime lecture, 10 January, London (www.liberty.org.uk).

Coleman, R. (2004) *Reclaiming the streets: Surveillance, social control and the city*, Cullompton: Willan Publishing.

Cook, P. and Ludwig, J. (2000) *Gun violence: The real costs*, New York: Oxford University Press.

Crawford, A. (2002) 'The governance of crime and insecurity in an anxious age: the trans–Euopean and the local', in A. Crawford (ed) *Crime and insecurity: The governance of safety in Europe*, Cullompton: Willan Publishing.

Dennis, N. (2005) 'Understanding and the social sciences', foreword to D.G. Green, E. Grove and N.A. Martin, *Crime and civil society: Can we become a more law-abiding people?* London: Civitas, Institute for the Study of Civil Society.

Duff, R.A. and Marshall, S.E. (2006) 'How offensive can you get?', in A. von Hirsch and A.P. Simester (eds), *Incivilities: Regulating offensive behaviour*, Oxford: Hart Publishing.

Faulkner, D. (2001) *Crime, state and citizen*, Winchester: Waterside Press.

Feinberg, J. (1985) *Offense to others*, volume 2: *The moral limits of the criminal law*, Oxford: Oxford University Press.

Field, F. (2003) *Neighbours from hell: The politics of behaviour*, London: Politico's Publishing.

Findlay, M. (1994) *The globalisation of crime*, Cambridge: Cambridge University Press.

Flint, J., Atkinson, R. and Scott, S. (2003) *A report on consultation responses to 'Putting our communities first: A Strategy for tackling anti-social behaviour'*, Glasgow: University of Glasgow, Department of Urban Studies.

Furlong, A. and Cartmel, F. (1997) *Young people and social change: Individualisation and risk in late modernity*, Buckingham: Open University Press.

Gamble, A. (1988) *The free economy and the strong state*, Basingstoke: MacMillan.

Garland, D. (2000) 'The culture of high crime societies', *British Journal of Criminology*, vol 40, pp 347–75.

Garland, D. (ed), (2001) *Mass imprisonment: Causes and consequences*, London: Sage.

Garside, R. (2006) 'Right for the wrong reasons: making sense of criminal justice failure', in R. Garside and W. McMahon, *Does criminal justice work? The 'Right for the wrong reasons' debate*, London: Crime and Society Foundation.

George, R.P. (1993) *Making men moral: civil liberties and public morality*, Oxford: Clarendon Paperbacks.

Golding, P. and Middleton, S. (1982) *Images of welfare: Press and public attitudes to poverty*, Oxford: Martin Robertson.

Goold, B. (2004) *CCTV and policing: Public area surveillance and police practices in Britain*, Oxford: Oxford University Press, Clarendon Studies in Criminology.

Green, D.G., Grove, E. and Martin, N.A. (2005) *Crime and civil society: Can we become a more law-abiding people?*, London: Civitas, Institute for the Study of Civil Society.

Grier, A. and Thomas, S. (2004) 'A war for civilisation as we know it: some observations on tackling anti-social behaviour', *Youth and Policy*, vol 82 (Winter), pp 1–15.

Hadfield, P. (2006) *Bar wars: Contesting the night in contemporay Bristish cities*, Oxford: Oxford University Press.

Hall, S. and Winlow, S. (2006) *Violent night: Urban leisure and contemporary culture*, Oxford: Berg Publishers.

Halpern, D. (2001) 'Moral values, social trust and inequality: can values explain crime?', *British Journal of Criminology*, vol 41, no 2, pp 236–51.

Hansen, R., Bill, L. and Pease, K. (2003) 'Nuisance offenders: scoping the public policy problems', in M. Tonry (ed), *Confronting crime: Crime control policy under New Labour*, Cullompton: Willan Publishing.

Hillyard, P., Pantazis, C., Tombs, S. and Gordon, D. (2004) *Beyond criminology: Taking harm seriously*, London: Pluto Press.

Himmelfarb, G. (1995) *The demoralisation of society: From Victorian virtues to modern values*, New York: Knopf.

Hobbs, D., Hadfield, P., Lister, S. and Winlow, S. (2005) *Bouncers: Violence and governance in the night time economy*, Oxford: Oxford University Press, Clarendon Studies in Criminology.

Hodgkinson, S. and Tilley, N. (2007) 'Policing anti-social behaviour: constraints, dilemmas and opportunities', *Howard Journal of Criminal Justice*, vol 46, no 4, pp 385–400.

Home Office (1997) *No more excuses*, Cm 3809, London: HMSO.

Home Office (2003) *A guide to Anti-Social Behaviour Orders and Acceptable Behaviour Contracts*, London: ACPO and the Youth Justice Board, Home Office Communications Directorate.

Hope, T. (2000) 'Inequality and the clubbing of private security', in T. Hope and R. Sparks (eds), *Crime, risk and insecurity*, London: Routledge.

Hope, T. (2001) 'Crime victimisation and inequality in risk society', in R. Matthews and J. Pitts (eds), *Crime, disorder and community safety*, London: Routledge.

Hopkins-Burke, R. (ed) (1998) *Zero tolerance policing*, Leicester: Perpetuity Press.

House of Commons Home Affairs Select Committee (2005) *Anti-social behaviour*, Fifth Report of Session 2004–05, HC 80–1, London: The Stationery Office.

Hughes, K. (2007) 'Yobbery is other people', *Guardian*, 4 September.

Innes, M. (1999) 'An iron fist in an iron glove: the zero-tolerance policing debate', *The Howard Journal of Criminal Justice*, vol 38, no 4, pp 397–410.

Jefferson, T. (2002) 'For a psychosocial criminology', in K. Carrington and R. Hogg (eds), *Critical criminology: Issues, debates, challenges*, Cullompton: Willan Publishing.

Katz, J. (1988) *Seductions of crime: Moral and sensual attractions in doing evil*, New York: Basic Books.

MacDonald, R. (ed) (1997) *Youth, the underclass and social exclusion*, London: Routledge.

McLaughlin, E. (2007) *The new policing*, London: Sage.

Marcus, S. (1969) *The other Victorians*, New York: Basic Books.

Measham, F. (1996) 'The "Big Bang" approach to sessional drinking: changing patterns of alcohol consumption amongst young people in North West England', *Addiction Research*, vol 4, no 3, pp 283–94.

Measham, F. (2004) 'Play space: historical and socio-cultural reflections on drugs, licensed leisure locations, commercialism and control', *International Journal of Drug Policy*, vol 15, pp 337–45.

Millie, A., Jacobson, J., McDonald, E. and Hough, M. (2005) *Anti-social behaviour strategies: Finding a balance*, York: Joseph Rowntree Foundation/The Policy Press.

Novak, T. (1988) *Poverty and the state*, Milton Keynes: Open University Press.

Parenti, C. (1999) *Lockdown America: Police and prisons in the age of crisis*, London: Verso.

Pawson, H. (2007) 'The use of Antisocial Behaviour Orders in Scotland', DTZ and Herriot Watt University, Scottish Government Social Research website (www.scotland.gov.uk/socialresearch).

Pearson, G. (1983) *Hooligan: A history of respectable fears*, Basingstoke: Macmillan.

Phoenix, J. (2007) 'Regulating prostitution: different problems, different solutions, same old story', *Community Safety Journal*, vol 6, no 1, pp 7–11.

Phoenix, J. and Oerton, S. (2005) *Illicit and illegal: Sex, regulation and social control*, Cullompton: Willan Publishing.

Reiner, R. (2007) *Law and order: An honest citizen's guide to crime and control*, Oxford: Polity Press.

Rubin, J., Rabinovich, L., Hallsworth, M. and Nason, E. (2006) *Interventions to reduce anti-social behaviour and crime: A review of effectiveness and costs*, London: RAND Europe, prepared for the National Audit Office.

Sanders, T. (2007) 'No room for a regulated market? The implications of the co-ordinated prostitution strategy for the indoor sex industries', *Community Safety Journal*, vol 6, no 1, pp 34–45.

Scoular, J., Pitcher, J., Campbell, R., Hubbard, P. and O'Neill, M. (2007) 'What's anti-social about sex work? The changing representation of prostitution's incivility', *Community Safety Journal*, vol 6, no 1, pp 11–18.

Sennett, R. (2003) *Respect: The formation of character in an age of inequality*, London: Penguin/Allen Lane.

SEU (Social Exclusion Unit) (1998) *Bringing Britain together: A national strategy for neighbourhood renewal*, Cm 4045, London: The Stationery Office.

SEU (2000) *Policy Action Team 8: Anti-Social Behaviour*, London: Office of the Deputy Prime Minister.

Simester, A.P. and von Hirsch, A. (2006) 'Regulating offensive conduct through two-step prohibitions', in A. von Hirsch and A.P. Simester (eds), *Incivilities: Regulating offensive behaviour*, Oxford: Hart Publishing.

Simon, J. (2007) *Governing through crime*, Oxford: Oxford University Press.

Smith, R. (2004) *Youth justice: Ideas, policy, practice*, Cullompton: Willan Publishing.

Solanki, A.R., Bateman, T., Boswell, G. and Hill, E. (2006) *Anti-Social Behaviour Orders*, London: Youth Justice Board, Policy Research Bureau and NACRO.

Squires, P. (1990) *Anti-social policy: Welfare, ideology and the disciplinary state*, Hemel Hempstead: Harvester/Wheatsheaf.

Squires, P. (2000) *Gun culture or gun control? Firearms and violence – Safety and society*, London: Routledge.

Squires, P. (2006) 'Anti-social behaviour and New Labour', *Critical Social Policy*, vol 26, no 1, pp 144–68.

Squires, P., Cunningham, L. and Fyvie-Gauld, M. (2004) *Perceptions of anti-social behaviour in the London Borough of Sutton*, Brighton: Health and Social Policy Research Centre, University of Brighton.

Squires, P. and Stephen, D.E. (2005) *Rougher justice: Anti-social behaviour and young people*, Cullompton: Willan Publishing.

Stedman-Jones, G. (1971) *Outcast London*, Oxford: Oxford University Press.

Stenson, K. (2000) 'Some day our prince will come: zero tolerance policing and liberal government', in T. Hope and R. Sparks (eds), *Crime, risk and insecurity*, pp 215–37.

Stephen, D. and Squires, P. (2003) *Community safety, enforcement and Acceptable Behaviour Contracts*, Brighton: Health and Social Policy Research Centre, University of Brighton.

Stephen, D. and Squires, P. (2007) 'Rough justice, enforcement or support: young people and their families in the community', in S. Balloch and M. Hill (eds), *Care, community and citizenship: Research and practice in a changing policy context*, Bristol: The Policy Press.

Tonry, M. (2004) *Punishment and politics: Evidence and emulation in the making of English crime control policy*, Cullompton: Willan Publishing.

Turner, B. (2006) 'Social capital, trust and offensive behaviour', in A. von Hirsch and A.P. Simester (eds), *Incivilities: Regulating offensive behaviour*, Oxford: Hart Publishing.

Wacquant, L. (2005) 'The great penal leap backward: incarceration in America from Nixon to Clinton', in J. Pratt, D. Brown, S. Hallsworth, M. Brown and W. Morrison (eds), *The new punitiveness*, Cullompton: Willan Publishing.

Walvin, J. (1988) *Victorian values*, London: Andre Deutsch.

Ward, D. (2007) '"Feet on Seats" train firm defiant', *Guardian*, 6 September.

Wilson, J.Q. and Kelling, G.L. (1982) 'Broken windows: the police and neighbourhood safety', *Atlantic Monthly*, March, pp 29–38.

Wood, M. (2004) *Perceptions and experiences of anti-social behaviour: Findings from the 2003–04 British Crime Survey*, London: Home Office.

Young, J. (1999) *The exclusion society*, London: Sage.

Part One
Managing anti-social behaviour: priorities and approaches

ONE

Why tackle anti-social behaviour?

Jessica Jacobson, Andrew Millie and Mike Hough

The question addressed by this chapter may seem naive. For many, especially those who advocate firm action against anti-social behaviour (ASB), it is self-evident that the central and local state should be engaged as vigorously as possible in efforts to crack down on anti-social behaviour. However, governments vary over place and time in their enthusiasm for doing so (cf Burney, 2005), and it is reasonable to ask why they should take on this responsibility, and why they should do so now.

The government's 'Respect' website[1] provides a succinct answer: 'Anti-social behaviour ruins lives. It doesn't just make life unpleasant; it prevents the renewal of disadvantaged areas and creates an environment where more serious crime can take hold.' In fact, it has provided *three* answers in a single sentence. This alone may suggest that there is room to take a critical view of rationales for tackling ASB. The concept of ASB is a slippery one to define, of course, and governments tend to duck the issue. We can all agree that ASB falls somewhere on the continuum between mere bad manners, on the one hand, and serious criminality, on the other. Precisely where the boundaries fall is a contentious issue, because any behaviour labelled as ASB implicitly falls within the scope of the state apparatus for tackling it.[2]

In this chapter we have drawn on the results of a study that combined empirical research in five areas with a review of policy and research literature.[3] One of the aims of the study was to examine the rationales offered by policy documents and by local officials for tackling ASB. The empirical element of the study involved interviews with key officials responsible for tackling ASB, and reviews of policy documents in five Crime and Disorder Reduction Partnerships (CDRPs) in England and Wales. Although the research was conducted in 2003/04, its findings are still relevant to contemporary debate about ASB. We have anonymised the five participating sites as Lonborough, Newtown, Northport, Prospertown and Westerncity. All were cities or large local authority districts within cities. The study found, both in the policy and research literature and in officials' accounts of their work, four main rationales for tackling ASB:

- the quality of life rationale: ASB should be tackled because it is a serious problem that makes people miserable and fearful;
- the 'broken windows' rationale: ASB should be tackled because, left unattended, it leads to serious crime;
- the crime-fighting or zero-tolerance rationale: ASB strategies are useful and practical crime-fighting tools;
- the regeneration rationale: action on ASB should contribute to the social and economic regeneration of local areas.

We shall discuss each of these rationales in turn – examining the nuances of people's explanations and examining how these do (or do not) reflect theory and research on ASB.

The quality of life rationale

Perhaps the most straightforward rationale for tackling ASB is that ASB has a severe impact on the quality of life of those most affected by it: it can make people unhappy in a general sense and, more specifically, it can create or exacerbate fear of crime. This is the primary rationale for tackling ASB to be found in government literature – to use the language of Respect, ASB 'ruins lives'.

The quality of life rationale: theoretical perspectives

Some of the earliest American research literature on disorder focused on the links between disorder and fear of crime. According to Taylor (1999), an early version of what he terms the 'incivilities thesis' was developed by Wilson (1975) and Garofalo and Laub (1978), who argued that various incidents of minor disorder can inspire fear of crime among urban residents. The key idea here was that 'urban conditions, not just crime, are troublesome and inspire residents' concern for safety' (Taylor, 1999: 66).

The particular impact of disorder on people's sense of insecurity is a theme with which Innes and colleagues are concerned (Innes et al, 2002; Innes, 2004a; 2004b; Innes et al, 2005). This relationship between disorder and fear of crime is at the heart of their work on 'signal crimes', which posits that certain crimes or *disorderly incidents* may be 'disproportionately influential in terms of causing a person or persons to perceive themselves to be at risk in some sense' (Innes and

Fielding, 2002: 17). Incidents that have 'signal value' may include both 'high profile serious crimes where the public reaction to the event is based upon mediated information', and also 'less serious events which are nonetheless significant due to them being experienced directly' (Innes et al, 2002: 19).

The quality of life rationale: policy perspectives

The impact of ASB on quality of life is a theme that frequently emerges in current policy thinking on ASB. The relationship between ASB and fear of crime is emphasised in the policy literature. Fear of crime is assumed to have a great significance in itself, since 'it is fear of crime – rather than actually being a victim – that can so often limit people's lives, making them feel afraid of going out or even afraid in their own homes' (Home Office, 2003: 13). In the UK the concern with fear of crime has informed the reassurance policing agenda,[4] which recognises 'that people are not reassured by crime reduction alone and look for credible control of their environment, in addition to safety from crime and incivility' (ACPO, 2002: 8).

The quality of life rationale: local perspectives

Many of our respondents in the case study sites argued that ASB must be addressed because of the unhappiness it causes. While some suggested that a sizeable proportion of public complaints about ASB might be regarded as evidence of the increasing 'intolerance' of older people towards children and young people, they nevertheless pointed out that many lives are being made increasingly unpleasant and difficult by the thoughtlessness or malice of others. The head of the Anti-Social Behaviour Unit in Lonborough, for example, argued that 'the greatest harm [of ASB] is that it makes vulnerable members of society more vulnerable, and more excluded'. And a manager of the local warden schemes in Lonborough spoke at some length about how problems such as neighbour disputes over noise can, in the long term, cause serious damage to physical and mental health. Ultimately, she said, such problems can make people feel extremely unhappy and insecure even within the four walls of their own homes.

More specifically, the impact of ASB on fear of crime was frequently discussed in the CDRP interviews. This issue was strongly emphasised in Prospertown, for example, a low crime area in which anxieties about crime nevertheless remain high. A Prospertown police officer commented on: 'their actual perception that, by the fact they see graffiti they think that cars are getting broken into, there's burglary, it's like a city of crime really'. It was also pointed out that not only do incidents of ASB provoke fear of crime but, conversely, existing fear and anxiety can shape perceptions of ASB. This is particularly true with regard to older people's reactions to young people congregating in public places. A local Councillor in Newtown commented:

> I've done it myself – you see a group of youths standing about … and they're laughing and talking, and they're being loud the way young people are, and you immediately see them as threatening. And for people a lot older than myself they find young people today … very, very intimidating, and then they think they're going to be following them home and they're going to attack them. The fact that it very rarely happens is neither here nor there.

The ways in which public concerns about crime and ASB feed into and reinforce each other were highlighted also by the ASB coordinator in Westerncity. He commented that the preoccupation of the public with ASB is such that the concept of criminality has broadened and become all-encompassing:

> they [young people] are sitting in a park at night – they've got to be doing something, they've got to be causing damage, they've got to be littering. They can't just be sitting there. So I think anti-social behaviour is altering perceptions of crime.

The 'broken windows' rationale

The 'broken windows' rationale for tackling ASB assumes that there is a particular causal link between disorder, or ASB, and crime in that, if left unattended, minor disorder leads to major crime. This has proved a highly popular view within policy circles in both the United States and Britain.

The 'broken windows' rationale: theoretical perspectives

In the United States, earlier ideas about the links between disorder and fear of crime were developed into the 'broken windows' thesis outlined by Wilson and Kelling in their famous 1982 article in *Atlantic Monthly*. Wilson and Kelling argue that disorder can provoke fear; and, further, that the fear can itself help to create the physical and social environment in which real crime will flourish. This is because residents who are fearful are likely to withdraw from public spaces and will not intervene when they observe disorderly or criminal behaviour. Informal social controls over an area are thus relaxed; local troublemakers and offenders become bolder in their actions; and offenders from outside the area are attracted to it. Wilson and Kelling's thinking on these issues was clearly influenced by Jacobs (1961), who wrote of the need for 'casual enforcement of civilisation' if the streets are to remain safe, and by Newman's work on defensible space (1972).

Hence, 'disorder and crime are usually inextricably linked, in a kind of developmental sequence' (Wilson and Kelling, 1982). The process by which disorder leads to fear *and* crime is symbolised by the broken window. Wilson and Kelling argue that if a broken window in a building remains unrepaired, all the other windows in the building will soon also be broken, because 'one unrepaired broken window is a signal that no one cares, and so breaking more windows costs nothing. (It has always been fun)'.

The 'broken windows' rationale: policy perspectives

Over the 25 years since the *Atlantic Monthly* article was first published, the relationship between disorder and crime posited by Wilson and Kelling has been extensively explored and debated by criminologists – with results that, when viewed as a whole, are inconclusive. There is little question that areas with high levels of crime also suffer from ASB. At issue, however, is whether the latter triggers the former in the way claimed by Wilson and Kelling. Despite only weak evidence to this effect, the theory has been highly influential in policy as well as research circles – largely as a result of its intuitive appeal. In terms of its impact on policing, it has proved to be 'a coat of many colors' (Taylor, 2005), that is, subject to differing interpretations and used to justify a range of approaches to crime and disorder.

In Britain, 'broken windows' theory is cited with great frequency as a rationale – or indeed an almost irrefutable justification – for a host of policing and crime-prevention measures that target ASB. At the start of the chapter, we quoted from the Respect website, which claims that ASB 'creates an environment where more serious crime can take hold'. This line of argument was prominent in the (2003) government White Paper on ASB, under the heading 'The spiral of anti-social behaviour', directly echoing 'broken windows' theory:

If a window is broken or a wall is covered in graffiti it can contribute to an environment in which crimes takes hold, particularly if intervention is not prompt and effective. An abandoned car, left for days on end, soon becomes a burnt-out car; it is not long before more damage and vandalism takes place. Environmental decline, anti-social behaviour and crime go hand in hand and create a sense of helplessness that nothing can be done. (Home Office, 2003: 14)

The 'broken windows' rationale: local perspectives

Despite the enthusiasm for the 'broken windows' thesis at national policy level, its endorsement was less than wholehearted in our five case study sites. For example, in Prospertown one local authority officer cited 'broken windows' theory with only qualified approval, arguing that the link between ASB and crime is not always clear. In Northport, some respondents did make reference to the need to tackle ASB in order to break the cycle of fear of crime, crime and neighbourhood decline. Others, however, argued that they did not regard ASB work as a means of crime reduction; rather, they wanted to tackle ASB in response to public demand, and also as part of a much wider and longer-term programme of social and economic regeneration.

It was in Westerncity that there was the clearest articulation of a 'broken windows' type of agenda. Here, a police superintendent directly referred to 'broken windows' theory and talked about the way in which serious crime can take hold in a community following minor incidents of criminal damage and ASB. A police sergeant highlighted the role played by fear of crime in this kind of cycle of decline, arguing that ASB can provoke fear of crime, which in turn keeps people away from an area and weakens natural surveillance.

In Lonborough and, to a lesser extent, in Newtown, Westerncity and Prospertown, various respondents spoke about links between ASB and crime in terms of the development of *criminal careers* rather than in terms of neighbourhood change (see for example Farrington, 1992). They argued that many people – particularly children and young people – who engage in relatively minor ASB are likely to move on to more serious forms of misbehaviour, and ultimately criminal behaviour, in the absence of intervention.

This 'criminal careers' perspective on the links between crime and ASB does not necessarily contradict the central tenets of 'broken windows' theory; but the latter theory is much more concerned with changing patterns of crime in neighbourhoods than with the evolution of criminal behaviour in individuals. Additionally, in charting the process by which an area becomes crime-ridden, 'broken windows' theory places a heavier emphasis on the role played by offenders who *move into* the area (hence Wilson and Kelling refer, for example, to 'criminal invasion') than on the contribution of existing residents who may increasingly turn to criminality.

The crime-fighting (zero-tolerance) rationale

The 'broken windows' rationale is about tackling ASB in order to reduce crime. Another crime-prevention rationale for tackling ASB does not focus on the ways in which ASB can lead to crime, but on the usefulness of ASB strategies as crime-fighting tools. From this perspective, the reduction of ASB is not necessarily an important outcome in itself: the main objective is the apprehension, disruption or deterrence of serious criminals.

The crime-fighting rationale: theoretical perspectives

There are a number of ways in which efforts to tackle ASB can be directed towards crime-fighting goals. Most obviously, where these efforts entail robust enforcement against incivilities and minor crime – or what is often described as 'zero-tolerance' policing – this creates opportunities for arrests and surveillance of serious offenders. The concept of zero tolerance is most commonly associated with policing in New York City under Police Commissioner William Bratton. The 'broken windows' thesis is often said to have 'theoretically informed' zero tolerance (Burke, 1998: 12); and Kelling himself writes that 'broken windows' was given 'unprecedented publicity when it was implemented as policy and practice in New York City' (2001: 120).

From a critical perspective, Harcourt (2001) argues that these apprehension and surveillance aspects of order-maintenance policing are the primary mechanism by which such initiatives contribute to reductions in crime. In his view, therefore, the claim of 'broken windows' theory that greater orderliness will, in itself, have a positive knock-on effect on crime is misplaced: it is the *process* of imposing order, rather than the existence of that order, that can impact on crime (see Matthews and Briggs' discussion of the 'enforcement deficit' argument, Chapter Four in this volume).

Despite the associations commonly made between 'broken windows' theory and zero-tolerance policing, the relationship between the two is not clear-cut. This is partly because 'zero tolerance' is an ambiguous and contentious term, used more readily by the media and politicians than by the police and policy makers.[5] The ambiguity is illustrated by the fact that Kelling (1998), despite his close association with the New York experience, argues that the general concept of zero tolerance pulls in quite the opposite direction to 'broken windows'. He asserts that the former implies the imposition of order from outside a community and denies the importance of police discretion in *negotiating* order. Writing from a British perspective, Pollard (1997) stresses the distinction between zero tolerance, which is a narrow, enforcement-oriented solution to crime and disorder, and 'broken windows', which is about understanding the problems and envisaging wide-ranging solutions.

The crime-fighting rationale: policy and local perspectives

The use of ASB strategies for the apprehension and surveillance of serious offenders is not a theme that is discussed in the British policy literature on ASB;[6] and it was not strongly emphasised in the CDRP sites. Possibly, this is due in part to the very different context of policing and nature of criminality in Britain as compared to the US.

However, a different but related understanding of how ASB work can be used to target serious offenders emerged in an interview with the head of the Anti-Social Behaviour Unit in Lonborough. One of the main functions of this unit is to make use of civil remedies such as injunctions, evictions and Anti-Social Behaviour Orders (ASBOs) against the perpetrators of ASB. The head of the unit argued that the availability of these civil options usefully extends the range of potential responses by the statutory agencies to serious criminal behaviour. An ASBO, for example, may be used against a serious offender where there is insufficient evidence for criminal prosecution – as the evidential requirements (as well as requirements under the 1998 Human Rights Act relating to the process of law) are less strict with respect to actions under the civil as compared with the criminal law. This flexibility of civil remedies also means that there is ample scope for using them alongside criminal prosecution when an offender has been engaged in a variety of criminal and anti-social activities. And, since the introduction of the 2002 Police Reform Act, ASBO applications can be granted following a criminal conviction (commonly known as 'criminal ASBOs', or 'CrASBOs').

Similar points were made by a local authority director in Newtown. She said that on some occasions, when a perpetrator of ASB was appearing in court on more serious charges, they would continue to proceed with a CrASBO application as an additional sanction:

because we actually want to use this crisis as a point at which to effect some change in their behaviour. And we can sort of bargain within the shadow of the law, if you like, about getting them to agree to behave in a certain way.

In Lonborough, the manager of the local authority-run warden schemes highlighted another way in which ASB work can contribute to crime fighting. The local warden schemes carry out high-visibility patrols, with the aim of reducing ASB and related problems through deterrence, passing on information about problems to the relevant agencies, and community engagement. The manager said that in carrying out this work the wardens are also able to undertake a substantial amount of intelligence gathering about local crime for the police. The wardens are cleared by the local force headquarters to receive restricted information and, thanks to an information-sharing protocol between the police and local authority, are well briefed about local people and problems. With this information to hand, and because they are on the streets for seven hours a day, the wardens are in a prime position to observe or hear about local criminal activity.

The regeneration rationale

The regeneration rationale has various dimensions (see also Hancock, 2006; Millie, 2007). In part, this is about tackling ASB to reverse cycles of economic decline. Tackling ASB is also seen as a necessary component of cultural change. Finally, ASB strategies are frequently linked to the aim of generating or restoring a sense of 'community'. The Respect website is clear that ASB 'prevents the renewal of disadvantaged areas'.

The regeneration rationale: theoretical perspectives

Among the many US researchers who have elaborated on the basic tenets of 'broken windows' theory, Skogan (1986, 1990)[7] has been particularly influential. He took the 'broken windows' thesis further by looking at the ways in which disorder contributes to the broader social and economic decline of entire neighbourhoods. According to Skogan, disorder sparks fear of crime and may increase levels of serious crime; his most pressing concern, however, is with the process by which disorder 'is an instrument of destabilization and neighborhood decline'. This occurs because:

> Disorder erodes what control neighborhood residents can maintain over local events and conditions. It drives out those for whom stable community life is important, and discourages people with similar values, from moving in. It threatens house prices and discourages investment. (Skogan, 1990: 3)[8]

For Skogan, problems of disorder, crime and neighbourhood decline are closely linked also to broader structural conditions such as poverty and instability. He is also concerned with the part that 'social disorganisation' and the associated lack of informal social control play in spirals of neighbourhood decline.[9] Other researchers have also focused on social disorganisation, which is generally defined as a community's inability to achieve shared goals and exercise social control (see, for example, Bursik, 1988). Dating back to the work of Shaw and McKay (1942) on juvenile delinquency, the relationship between social disorganisation and crime has long been a concern of criminologists. This relationship was the focus of research by Sampson and Grove, which used the British Crime Survey. This research found that 'communities characterized by sparse friendship networks, unsupervised teenage peer groups, and low organisational participation had disproportionately high rates of crime and delinquency' (1989: 799).

More specifically, the idea that *disorderly* neighbourhoods are also socially disorganised is a theme that runs through much of the research on disorder. As observed by Hancock (2001), the term 'collective efficacy' has gained prominence in research in this field, because this concept, unlike the term 'social disorganisation', conveys the sense that 'socially heterogeneous communities are, in some circumstances, able to assert common goals' (Hancock, 2001: 79).

The concept of collective efficacy has been examined in some depth by Sampson and colleagues. There are two elements to their definition: it is about the existence of mutual trust and solidarity among residents of a local area, and the consequent capacity of residents to intervene in social situations for the common good. Hence collective efficacy is defined as 'social cohesion among neighbors combined with their willingness to intervene on behalf of the common good' (Sampson et al, 1997: 918). Accordingly, areas with high collective efficacy are areas in which informal social control can be exercised over potentially criminal or disorderly behaviour. Sampson and Raudenbusch (1999) conducted extensive research in Chicago that explored the links between crime, disorder and collective efficacy. They conclude that a lack of collective efficacy is associated with high levels of both disorder and crime.

The idea of collective efficacy is a close relative of the concept of *social capital*. Social capital is a term that refers to the capacity for cooperative action that is inherent in social networks. Putnam, whose work is most closely associated with the concept, defines social capital as 'networks, norms and trust that facilitate coordination and cooperation for mutal benefit' (Putnam, 2000: 19). Communities with dense social networks may be rich in social capital, and this richness may give them the capacity to ward off various threats. Putnam has made the important distinction between 'bridging capital' and 'bonding capital'. Bonding social capital refers to the close networks that often exist within stable, homogeneous communities – the social cohesion that is an element of the definition of collective efficacy. Bridging capital refers to the capacity to mobilise community and other resources. Bonding capital, he argues, is good for 'getting by', while bridging capital is crucial for enabling communities to 'get ahead'. It is the latter that communities need if they are to develop their capacity to respond to ASB.

The regeneration rationale: policy perspectives

The possibility that social capital has been – or is being – dangerously depleted is what explains political interest in communities and in ways of nurturing them. A great deal of the political preoccupation with ASB can be traced to the belief that it may be corrosive of communities. Thus, in much of the British policy literature the task of tackling ASB is presented as one aspect of a much broader process of social and economic regeneration. The expectation is that action to reduce ASB will ultimately contribute to the formation of neighbourhoods and communities that are more integrated, cohesive and economically viable. Indeed, regeneration – however understood – is often presented as the overarching aim of all ASB work, in relation to which other aims are subsidiary.

Hence, in line with the theory expounded in the US by Skogan, among others, it is sometimes suggested in the policy literature that reducing ASB not only has a knock-on effect on crime rates in local neighbourhoods, but can also prevent or reverse a general process of economic decline. The Home Office ASB 'Toolkit', for example, refers to the aim of 'creating sustainable areas, in which people wish to live, work and stay' (Home Office, 2001). And the Social Exclusion Unit (SEU) report on ASB observes that one of the costs of failing to tackle ASB in a local area is that residents who can move quickly will do so, with the result that 'whole communities can be decimated in months'. Owner-occupiers, meanwhile, will be unable to move and will therefore 'face plummeting property prices, pushing them into negative equity, and rising insurance costs' (SEU, 2000: 33).

Cultural rather than economic revitalisation is another common theme in the policy literature. For example, the Respect website says:

> We need to create stronger communities – ones where people are informed about what action is happening to address their concerns, where people feel it is worth them taking the time to pick up the phone, go to a residents' meeting or put a youth night on for the local kids ...

The regeneration rationale: local perspectives

The regeneration rationale for ASB work – with regeneration viewed in economic, cultural and community terms – was articulated by several of our respondents in the case study sites.

For example, on the economic theme, it was stressed in Westerncity, Newtown and Northport alike that efforts to reduce ASB can potentially have a positive impact on local economic conditions. A Westerncity police superintendent commented that areas with high levels of ASB may be seen as unfavourable places to live – as demonstrated by large numbers of empty properties. On the other hand, a local initiative involving visible policing of a parade of shops where there had been problems of ASB led to an upturn in profits. In Newtown, respondents commented that ASB contributes to the sense that an area is neglected, encourages upwardly mobile residents to move out and businesses to relocate, and has negative repercussions for local schools and other services. And in Northport, respondents spoke of the need to tackle ASB in order to break the cycle of fear of crime, crime and, ultimately, population drift away from the city.

Community engagement was also frequently mentioned by respondents as a vital aspect of work on ASB. For example, a Westerncity police sergeant spoke of the need for 'community ownership' of problems, which means that 'people take care of their backyard'. Another Westerncity respondent talked of how local communities have become more 'disparate', meaning that neighbours do not necessarily know each other and are therefore disinclined or unable to act against unruly children and others. Tackling ASB therefore depends on greater 'inter-involvement' within neighbourhoods. A Prospertown police respondent, similarly, spoke of the need for neighbourhoods 'to take some responsibility for themselves'. Neighbourhood Watch and residents' associations can play an important role in this, he argued.

However, although some respondents voiced the opinion that local ASB work can play an important part in economic and social regeneration, others questioned this rationale and pointed to the complexities of the relationship between ASB and wider social or structural problems. Some respondents, for example, were more concerned with how deprivation can generate ASB than with the potential impact of ASB strategies on economic problems. A local authority officer in Westerncity, for example, commented that problems such as graffiti are not so much a trigger of neighbourhood decline as 'a sign of the decline of a neighbourhood'. In Newtown, a local authority officer spoke of the need to 'tackle social inequality on a number of fronts' in order to 'eliminate the causes of anti-social behaviour and crime'.

Two of the Northport respondents noted that those areas of the city with particular problems of ASB are neighbourhoods in which there is a concentration of privately rented properties and a high turnover of tenants. They regard ASB work as an integral part of a wider programme aiming at economic regeneration, but recognise that the linkages between problems of ASB, crime and decline are complex and work in all directions. Northport respondents also highlighted some of the (related) difficulties associated with the task of community renewal. They commented that the city's deprived neighbourhoods have limited capacity to solve their own problems and high levels of dependency on public services. Because of these deeply rooted problems, the current generation of socially excluded people involved in crime and ASB are viewed as difficult to retrieve.[10] Thus, Northport's programme of regeneration has as one of its primary aims the social inclusion of the next generation at risk; and community building is viewed as a long-term goal.

In both Westerncity and Lonborough, it was argued that structural problems – such as unemployment, low income levels and an education system that overemphasises academic attainment and fails many children according to that criterion – need to be addressed before a sense of community can start to emerge in certain neighbourhoods. It was also pointed out that broader cultural changes have, over the past decades, undermined community feeling – and can hardly be reversed simply at the will of the government. For example, as was observed by a Westerncity local authority officer, the trends towards more people living alone, and the privatisation of leisure activities, have played a large part in the decline of community. In Lonborough, a local authority respondent said that, with the emergence of a much more individualistic society, many of the 'traditional community structures' have been destroyed; and since the culture that supported them has dissipated, these structures cannot be put back into place. She also pointed to the discrepancies in government thinking about community,[11] which stresses the need for working-class communities to be strengthened and empowered to run their own affairs, but accepts the individualism of the middle classes.

Echoing issues raised in the ASB policy literature, a few of our respondents called for cultural change. In both Westerncity and Newtown, for example, there was discussion of the need for greater social responsibility and of the role that parents and schools should play in instilling self-discipline in children and young people. However, some respondents made the case for a different kind of cultural shift – arguing that attitudes among ASB complainants, as well as among ASB perpetrators, need to change. It was suggested that older people should be more 'tolerant' of youth: that dealing with ASB is, in part, about confronting the wishes of some adults to 'tidy [children] off the streets' (as argued by a Westerncity respondent). A local authority officer in Lonborough talked about the need for more 'shared understandings' of what behaviour is and is not acceptable, and about the difficulties of achieving this within neighbourhoods that are socially and ethnically diverse. One of her colleagues discussed the need for cultural change that involves selling young people the message that they are important and that their contribution to society is appreciated. This, she argued, will play a much more significant part in reducing ASB and accompanying problems than the kinds of enforcement-oriented 'quick fixes' favoured by government.

Conclusions: competing rationales?

How are we to weigh up these competing rationales? Indeed, are they actually competing or do they all offer complementary support for policies to tackle ASB?

Perhaps the first point to stress is that the first – quality of life – rationale is that ASB should be tackled as a social harm *in its own right*, while the other three regard ASB strategies as instrumental in securing wider social objectives, such as crime reduction and neighbourhood regeneration.

Let us consider the instrumental arguments first. In principle, at least, the claims embedded in these rationales can be empirically tested – although, as we have seen, research has made only limited progress in doing so. In our view the evidence remains quite weak that robust enforcement action against ASB will yield benefits downstream in terms of reductions in serious crime. On the other hand, we are more optimistic that supporting neighbourhoods' collective efficacy – or efforts to nurture the social capital necessary for self-regulation – will pay off. However, one should have realistic expectations. Skogan's warning about the limits to social engineering at neighbourhood level probably applies to Britain just as much as to the United States:

> There are no 'silver bullets' in social policy because ... the political system deflects them, the social system rejects them, and the legal system protects us against them. Our nation's cultural and political diversity, coupled with its strong orientation toward individual rights rather than collective responsibilities, should deter us from expecting too much in the way of engineered social change. (1990: 18)

How should one assess the argument that the state should tackle ASB as a social harm in its own right? Should ASB be regarded simply as behaviour that offends against manners or morals,[12] falling outside of the regulatory frameworks of the state? Or has the state a proper interest in containing the social harms caused by ASB? These are important political questions. For most of its life the current New Labour administration has not engaged with them, however. Instead, it has supported its ASB policies using political rhetoric and a depressing form of anti-intellectualism. There has not even been any government attempt to define in practical terms what forms of ASB fall within the scope of the new powers that have been created. Official statements often imply that anyone of good sense can recognise ASB when they see it. 'Yob behaviour' and 'neighbours from hell' are not terms that invite critical scrutiny.

Despite this, we think that it is of great importance to identify what it is about the social harms associated with ASB that justifies state intervention – and, where perpetrators are given ASBOs, the potential imposition of a five-year prison sentence. In our view it is the *persistence* of ASB that can justify state action. Offences against manners and morals should remain beyond the reach of the state – unless there is a pattern of persistent targeted behaviour that renders it as serious in its impact as conventional crimes against the person. We do not necessarily expect readers to accept this particular attempt to say what it is about some forms of ASB that justifies a state response. But we think it incumbent on the government to provide a definition of some sort – that both justifies and sets limits to state intervention (a view shared by many of the contributors to von Hirsch and Simester, 2006).

Notes

[1] www.respect.gov.uk

[2] For our own attempt at a definition, see Millie et al (2005: 2).

[3] We are very grateful to the Nuffield Foundation for funding the study. Further details are available at www.kcl.ac.uk/icpr

[4] Since evolved into 'Neighbourhood Policing' (Home Office, 2005).

[5] Pease (1998) observes of the book *Zero tolerance: Policing a free society* (Dennis, 1997), which includes articles by William Bratton and officers involved in 'zero-tolerance'-type initiatives in the UK, that 'every single contributor distances himself from the phrase [zero tolerance] and its overtones, either explicitly or by never using the phrase'.

[6] Although similar arguments have been made about the value of enforcing traffic legislation.

[7] See also, among others, Taub et al (1984), Lewis and Salem (1986), Kelling and Coles (1996), Meares and Kahan (1998).

[8] In the British context, the work of Skogan and others has influenced researchers interested in the relationship between housing markets and crime patterns, and the development of 'residential community crime careers' in urban areas undergoing decline (see Hancock (2001) for a review of British studies in this field).

[9] Skogan has a particular interest in how community policing can help to address the intersecting problems of disorder, crime and neighbourhood decline. He heads the ongoing evaluation of Chicago's community policing programme, known as the Chicago Alternative Policing Strategy, which was launched in 1993. (See, for example, Skogan and Hartnett (1997) and Skogan et al (2002) for overviews of the work and impact of this programme.)

[10] As noted by Johnston and Mooney (2007), there is a danger of labelling all those who live in areas of accentuated ASB concern – such as council estates – as 'problem people'.

[11] Presumably the communitarian-type ideas taken on by New Labour (see for example Burney, 2005).

[12] For a detailed discussion of anti-social behaviour, incivility and offence, see von Hirsch and Simester (2006).

References

ACPO (Association of Chief Police Officers) (2002) *Annual Report 2002*, London: ACPO.

Burke, R.H. (1998) 'A contextualisation of zero tolerance policing strategies', in R.H. Burke (ed), *Zero tolerance policing*, Cambridge: Perpetuity Press.

Burney, E. (2005) *Making people behave: Anti-social behaviour, politics and policy*, Cullompton: Willan Publishing.

Bursik, R.J. (1988) 'Social disorganization and theories of crime and delinquency', *Criminology*, vol 26, pp 519–51.

Dennis, N. (ed) (1997) *Zero tolerance: Policing a free society*, London: IEA.

Farrington, D. (1992) 'Criminal career research in the United Kingdom', *British Journal of Criminology*, vol 32, no 4, pp 521–36.

Garofalo, J. and Laub, J. (1978), 'The fear of crime: broadening our perspective', *Victimology*, vol 3, pp 242–53.

Hancock, L. (2001) *Community, crime and disorder: Safety and regeneration in urban neighbourhoods*, Basingstoke: Palgrave.

Hancock, L. (2006) 'Urban regeneration, young people, crime and criminalisation', in B. Goldson and J. Muncie (eds), *Youth crime and justice*, London: Sage.

Harcourt, B.E. (2001) *Illusion of order: The false promise of broken windows policing*, Cambridge, MA: Harvard University Press.

Home Office (2001) *Crime reduction toolkits: Anti-social behaviour*, www.crimereduction.gov.uk/toolkits/as00.htm.

Home Office (2003) *Respect and responsibility – taking a stand against anti-social behaviour* (the Anti-Social Behaviour White Paper), London: The Stationery Office.

Home Office (2005) *Neighbourhood policing – your police; your community; our commitment*, London: Home Office.

Innes, M. (2004a) 'Signal crimes and signal disorders: notes on deviance as communicative action', *British Journal of Sociology*, vol 55, no 3, pp 335–56.

Innes, M. (2004b) 'Reinventing tradition? Reassurance, neighbourhood security and policing', *Criminal Justice*, vol 4, no 2, pp 151–71.

Innes, M. and Fielding, N. (2002) 'From community to communicative policing: "signal crimes" and the problem of public reassurance', *Sociological Research Online*, vol 7, no 2, www.socresonline.org.uk/7/2/innes.html.

Innes, M., Fielding, N. and Langan, S. (2002) *Signal crimes and control signals: Towards an evidence-based conceptual framework for reassurance policing – A report for Surrey Police*, Guildford: University of Surrey.

Innes, M., Hayden, S., Lowe, T., Roberts, C. and Twyman, L. (2005) *Signal crimes and reassurance policing: Volumes 1 and 2*, Guildford: Surrey Police.

Jacobs, J. (1961) *The death and life of the American city*, New York: Vintage.

Johnston, C. and Mooney, G. (2007) '"Problem" people, "problem" spaces?: New Labour and council estates', in R. Atkinson and G. Helms (eds), *Securing an urban renaissance: Crime, community and British urban policy*, Bristol: The Policy Press.

Kelling, G.L. (1998) 'The evolution of broken windows', in M. Weatheritt (ed), *Zero tolerance policing: What does it mean and is it right for policing in Britain?*, London: Police Foundation.

Kelling, G.L. (2001) '"Broken windows" and the culture wars: A response to selected critiques', in R. Matthews and J. Pitts (eds), *Crime, disorder and community safety: A new agenda?*, London: Routledge.

Kelling, G.L. and Coles, C.M. (1996) *Fixing broken windows: Restoring order and reducing crime in our communities*, New York: Free Press.

Lewis, D.A. and Salem, G. (1986) *Fear of crime*, New Brunswick: Transaction Books.

Meares, T. and Kahan, T. (1998) 'Law and (norms of) order in the inner city', *Law and Society Review*, vol 32, no 4, pp 805–38.

Millie, A. (2007) 'Tackling anti-social behaviour and regenerating neighbourhoods', in R. Atkinson and G. Helms (eds), *Securing an urban renaissance: Crime, community and British urban policy*, Bristol: The Policy Press.

Millie, A., Jacobson, J., McDonald, E. and Hough, M. (2005b) *Anti-social behaviour strategies: Finding a balance*, Bristol: The Policy Press.

Newman, O. (1972) *Defensible space: People and design in the violent city*, London: Architectural Press.

Pease, K. (1998) 'What shall we count when measuring zero tolerance?' in M. Weatheritt (ed), *Zero tolerance policing: What does it mean and is it right for policing in Britain?*, London: Police Foundation.

Pollard, C. (1997) 'Zero tolerance: short-term fix, long-term liability?' in N. Dennis (ed), *Zero tolerance: Policing a free society*, London: IEA.

Putnam, R.D. (2000) *Bowling alone. The collapse and revival of American community*, New York: Simon and Schuster.

Sampson, R. and Grove, B. (1989) 'Community structure and crime', *American Journal of Sociology*, vol 94, pp 774–802.

Sampson, R.J. and Raudenbush, S.W. (1999) 'Systematic social observation of public spaces: a new look at disorder in urban neighbourhoods', *American Journal of Sociology*, vol 105, no 3, pp 603–51.

Sampson, R.J., Raudenbush, S.W. and Earls, F. (1997) 'Neighbourhoods and violent crime: a multilevel study of collective efficacy', *Science*, vol 277, pp 918–24.

SEU (Social Exclusion Unit) (2000) *Report of Policy Action Team 8: Anti-social behaviour*, London: SEU.

Shaw, C.R. and McKay, H.D. (1942) *Juvenile delinquency and urban areas*, Chicago: University of Chicago Press.

Skogan, W. (1986) 'Fear of crime and neighbourhood change', in A.J. Reiss and M. Tonry (eds), *Communities and crime*, Chicago: University of Chicago Press.

Skogan, W. (1990) *Disorder and decline: Crime and the spiral of decay in American neighbourhoods*, New York: Free Press.

Skogan, W. and Hartnett, S.M. (1997) *Community policing, Chicago style*, New York: Oxford University Press.

Skogan, W., Steiner, L., Dubois, J., Gudell, J.E. and Fagan, A. (2002) *Taking stock: Community policing in Chicago*, Washington, DC: National Institute of Justice.

Taub, R.P., Taylor, D.G. and Dunham, J.D. (1984) *Paths of neighbourhood change: Race and crime in urban America*, Chicago: Chicago University Press.

Taylor, R.B. (1999) 'The incivilities thesis: theory, measurement, and policy', in R.H. Langworthy (ed), *Measuring what matters: Proceedings from the Policing Research Institute meetings*, Washington, DC: National Institute of Justice.

Taylor, R.B. (2005) 'The incivilities or "broken windows" thesis', in L.E. Sullivan (ed), *Encyclopedia of law enforcement*, Thousand Oaks, CA: Sage.

von Hirsch, A. and Simester, A.P. (eds) (2006) *Incivilities: Regulating offensive behaviour*, Oxford: Hart Publishing.

Wilson, J.Q. (1975) *Thinking about crime*, New York: Basic Books.

Wilson, J.Q. and Kelling, G.L. (1982) 'Broken windows: the police and neighbourhood safety', *Atlantic Monthly*, March, vol 249, pp 29-38.

TWO

Resilient Fabians? Anti-social behaviour and community safety work in Wales

Adam Edwards and Gordon Hughes

The proper subject of criminal anthropology is the anti-social individual in his tendencies and in his activity. (Ferri, 1917: 79)

Anti-social behaviour was the hydra-headed monster that represented a spectrum of bad behaviour, from serious to merely irritating, afflicting neighbourhoods. (Burney, 2005: 16)

Introduction

Central to the public debate opened up by the contemporary sensitivity to, and seeming obsession with, anti-social behaviour among politicians, policy makers, the media and, in turn, growing numbers of the population, is why this 'new' social problem of anti-social behaviour (but see Ferri, 1917) has achieved such a widespread salience in the popular imagination in the last decade. Few can have failed to notice the incessant chatter about, panic over and clamour for 'tough' solutions to a growing array of potentially dangerous 'anti-social outcasts', arguably outstripping longer-established concerns over crime per se. The contemporary crusade against the anti-social in the UK is characterised by an array of representational forms, from the villains' gallery of noisy neighbours, disrespectful youth in gangs, persistent and aggressive beggars, prostitutes and drug users to environmental signs of disorder such as the polluting acts arising from dog fouling, graffiti, abandoned vehicles and fly-tipping. It is now impossible to discuss contemporary modes of governance across the spectrum of crime control and community safety measures without reference to the threat of the anti-social.

The rhetorical power of what has been called a 'moral authoritarian communitarian' discourse (Hughes, 1996) is palpable in the daily diet of tabloid media and populist political representations of the 'broken society'. In turn, it is widely speculated in critical criminological and human rights literature on the subject (including contributions to this volume) that profoundly exclusionary and damaging consequences for specific categories of 'at risk' populations are resulting from interventions such as the use of Anti-Social Behaviour Orders (ASBOs). Research on ASBOs and their consequences is, however, at an early stage and this suggests a certain caution over too precipitous a judgement on the government of a policy issue that is of intense concern to the general public. In this chapter, findings from research undertaken by the authors into the work of community safety managers in Wales, entailing responses to anti-social behaviour in each of the 22 community safety partnerships in this country, are used to question prevailing assumptions about the problematisation of this signal issue in popular concerns about crime and disorder. We question the validity of two diametrically opposed but equally 'smooth' narratives: that governing anti-social behaviour is either a morally righteous, enlightened and commonsensical campaign against a feral minority, or else that it represents a moral panic manufactured to support an increasingly punitive and intolerant state. In contrast to both of these positions, attention is paid throughout this chapter to the simultaneous governmental strategies of 'conditional inclusions and exclusions' in the management and control of people designated as anti-social.

It is suggested that there is a dominant national state project towards the punitive exclusion of specific categories of youth, often the most marginalised, already 'outcast' and angry, together with both damaged and damaging adults. At the same time, when the actual practice of governing this problem is examined in specific local contexts, the picture is far from uniform. Both compromise and contestation are present in the institutional realities of delivering community safety strategies, especially with regard to the problem of anti-social youth. As a site of contested government, we contend that partnership work in the UK around the theme of the 'anti-social' is likely to remain 'unstable' and the actions of key actors are to varying degrees 'unpredictable' (Stenson and Edwards, 2003; Clarke, 2004). Despite the national project to 'roll out' a common approach to anti-social behaviour across England and Wales, the uneven development of policy and practice in particular localities should not be underestimated by social scientists, as it indicates both the resilience of established political rationalities of rule and opportunities for political invention and creativity (Edwards and Hughes, 2005). Our contention is that, far from being 'eclipsed' (Garland, 1996) or 'dead' (Rose, 2000), social democratic or 'Fabian' rationalities are not only alive but are often predominant in the thinking of many community safety managers charged with formulating and coordinating the implementation of strategies for the reduction of crime and disorder. In turn, this suggests a messy complexity to the government of anti-social behaviour, which is obfuscated by the abstract and reductive narratives found in both official policy-making circles and much critical academic commentary.[1]

In the substantive sections that follow, we outline in brief some of the key findings generated from a research project focused on the work of managers in all 22 community safety partnerships (CSPs) in Wales. Following a methodological note on this research project, we outline some salient features of the specific context of community safety work in the devolved polity of Wales. We argue these features need to be foregrounded in any understanding of the local unfolding of the policy and practice of controlling anti-social behaviour in CSPs. The complex and hybrid narratives of disorder which underpin the problem-solving work undertaken by community safety practitioners are then considered and in conclusion we explore the implications of these narratives for the prospective conceptualisation of anti-social behaviour and research into policy responses.

Welsh matters

A methodological note

The empirical basis for the discussion that follows arises out of a research project undertaken by the authors for the network of community safety practitioners in Wales, the Welsh Association of Community Safety Officers (WACSO). WACSO commissioned an independent review of the changing role of local community safety practitioners and their teams (where applicable). Vital to the success of the project was the depth of access to key players enabled by WACSO's sponsorship of the research and its independence from both the Home Office and the Welsh Assembly Government (WAG). The research relevant to this chapter was undertaken between February and June 2007. It comprised a questionnaire-based survey sent to all community safety managers in CSPs in Wales, textual analysis of each CSP's community safety strategy and audit for 2005–08, and in-depth semi-structured interviews with community safety managers in each local authority area.

The project is unique in that it is the first time community safety managers from every CSP in Wales have been surveyed and interviewed, providing the basis for an intra-national comparative study of control practices in the country. The study also enabled a detailed dialogue with community safety managers about the challenges encountered in governing safer communities, which many defined as an open-ended 'problem-solving' activity rather than a precisely delineated profession. The findings associated with this central theme of the research will be published subsequently (Edwards and Hughes, 2007, 2008). For the purposes of this chapter, and given the key aims of this edited collection, we focus specifically on what can be learnt about the purported rise of an 'ASBO nation' from the narratives of community safety managers reflecting on their own practices and experiences of working in partnerships charged with tackling anti-social behaviour.

Community safety in a devolved polity

To fully appreciate these narratives, it is necessary to contextualise them in terms of the particularities of undertaking community safety work in the devolved Welsh polity. The WAG has a range of statutory powers relating to the policy and practice of community safety, including local government, health and social services, and education. At present, its powers do not extend to policing and criminal justice per se but crime prevention, through tackling substance misuse and promoting 'youth inclusion', do fall within the Assembly's remit. Considered as a distinct policy area, community safety has been a responsibility of the Assembly Government's Department of Social Justice and Regeneration,[2] emphasising the Assembly Government's interest in locating issues of crime and disorder within a problematic of social rather than criminal justice. That local partnerships in Wales have retained the prefix 'community safety' rather than the officially designated Crime and Disorder Reduction Partnerships (CDRPs) in England is also more than a semantic difference. The distinction between CSPs in Wales and CDRPs in England has performed an important symbolic political function in, as one of our respondents put it, 'Dragonising'[3] the policy area as well as further emphasising the social policy orientation of responses to crime and disorder (see also Drakeford, 2005).

Whether such symbolic differences translate into radically different practices of control between England and Wales remains a moot point for the kind of comparative research that we would advocate but that, to our knowledge, has yet to be undertaken. Pressures for convergence clearly include the role of the Home Office in establishing certain performance targets for CDRPs and CSPs and linking the two main funding budgets hitherto dedicated to partnership work and dispensed from Whitehall, the Basic Command Unit Fund and the Building Safer Communities Fund, to success or failure in meeting these targets. Findings from our survey of CSPs suggest, however, that WAG provides the overwhelming proportion of funding received by the Welsh partnerships, accounting for between 60% and 80% of their annual budgets and this funding is allied to a very particular post-devolutionary politics in Wales that is suggestive of an important break with the direction of crime and disorder reduction in England. The WAG Substance Misuse Action Fund and Safer Communities Fund are dedicated to reducing problems of substance misuse and promoting youth inclusion, objectives of an 'old' social democratic impulse to engineer social integration through more intensive welfare state interventions.

Indeed, broader commentaries on post-devolution government in Wales have emphasised the political goal of reasserting the importance of social democracy and creating a 'high-trust' polity in which disillusioned citizens are reconnected to more accountable and responsive public authorities through the democratisation rather than commercialisation of public services (WAG, 2006). The Beecham Inquiry into public service delivery in Wales noted that the commercial conception of citizens in England, as consumers of services delivered through quasi-market competition, could not be replicated in Wales, both because of political opposition to the very idea of commercialising public services and because of its impracticality, given the problems of sustaining alternative competitors in a country with a highly dispersed demography, particularly in the rural and valley areas (Beecham, 2006: para 2.13). This broader political context is significant for a discussion of any putative 'ASBO nation', because ASBOs have been routinely regarded by elite decision makers in the Welsh polity as the epitome of low-trust state–citizen relations, inimical to the post-devolutionary project of building a more inclusive society (Drakeford, 2005) and to be used only as a last resort.

Variation and uneven development in Welsh localities

As emphasised by the Beecham Inquiry, an important feature of Wales as a country is the variation in ecological, demographic, economic and political features between its regions and towns and cities. At one extreme, there are the deindustrialised coalfields alongside commercial cities of the south, as against the generally sparsely populated farmlands and wildernesses, alongside tourist towns, in north, west and mid-Wales. It also remains a dual-language country, characterised by continuing unevenness in the cultural significance of the Welsh language. In our research across this area, these factors were significant in the tensions expressed between meeting national targets around both community safety and crime and disorder reduction set by both the Home Office and the Welsh Assembly as the principal funding bodies.

Community safety priorities in Wales

The evidence from our three main sources of data (documentary text, questionnaire and interview) suggested that the local priorities in Wales, as with local CDRP priorities in England (Hughes, 2007), were in large measure derived from national government policy priorities, though in this case from both the Home Office and the Welsh Assembly Government. For example, the main purpose of community safety work, according to our respondents, in order of significance, was:

1. to promote social justice and regeneration (WAG)
2. to tackle ASB in accordance with the Home Office Respect Agenda (HO)
3. to achieve the objectives of the Home Office's Public Service Agreement (PSA) on crime reduction (HO)
4. to rebuild trust between citizens and public authorities (WAG)
5. to achieve WAG's objectives to prevent youth crime and reduce substance misuse (WAG).[4]

When we explored what community safety managers in Wales perceived to be the most important priorities for community safety for the local population they served, dealing with anti-social behaviour was unanimously ranked as the top priority, with substance misuse a very close second. Fear of crime and violence were equally ranked as the next key local priorities, followed by measures to address domestic abuse, prolific and other priority offenders, vehicle crime, youth offending and burglary. It should be noted, however, that managers in two of the most rural CSPs noted that road safety was also a top priority. Interestingly, neither terrorism nor serious organised crime was viewed as a local priority and hate crime was also ranked as a low priority. It is evident that these categories are not always easily distinguishable from each other (for example, violence and domestic abuse, or youth offending and anti-social behaviour). That said, we were struck by the overwhelming concern expressed in strategy documents, in questionnaire responses and, most significantly, in many of the in-depth interviews over anti-social behaviour and its connections to substance misuse, from illegal drug and particularly alcohol consumption, and to young people. Volume crime such as property crimes associated with car theft, burglary, robbery and so on were surprisingly low if not absent from community safety managers' concerns.

What are we to make of this preoccupation, among practitioners whose orientation to their work is one informed primarily by principles of social democratic inclusion rather than neoconservative exclusion, prevention rather than enforcement and repression, social crime prevention rather than situational measures, and adaptive problem solving rather than symbolic repression, with controlling anti-social behaviour (Hughes and Gilling, 2004; Hughes, 2007; Edwards and Hughes, 2007b)?

The complex conceptions of anti-social behaviour revealed in interviews with our respondents question the relatively 'smooth' narratives found in academic and public policy commentaries on this phenomenon. The concept of smooth narratives has been employed by some sociologists of scientific knowledge as a pejorative reference to the tendency, often found in academic and governmental accounts of social problems, to provide abstract, reductive explanations that belie the complex, messy, variable and contingent qualities of social relations (Law, 2004). This mess is further complicated by the interpretations that social actors, such as community safety managers, place upon the social problems they apprehend and, in turn, the interpretations that social scientists place upon these. In deciphering the doubly hermeneutic explanation of social problems, it has been argued that commentators should be more suspicious of the 'grand narrative themes' that have animated governmental and academic discourse than of the mundane narratives of everyday life (Clegg, 1993). While social research cannot afford to be subservient to the accounts of its respondents, it needs to find ways of taking what they say about their own practices seriously, or else claim an ontologically privileged position from which only *ex cathedra* judgements can be advanced (Clegg, 1993: 42). It is in this spirit that we suggest it is productive to contrast grand narrative themes about anti-social behaviour, found in the academic and official literature on the subject, with accounts provided by community safety managers about their everyday experiences of governing this problem.

Resilient Fabians? Narratives from the coalface

Taken as a whole, the community safety managers we interviewed were unapologetic about trying to 'crack down' on 'youth annoyance'[5] in particular places and at particular times. Young people and anti-social behaviour was commonly expressed as a particular blight on the lives of other members of the most marginalised neighbourhoods in their locality. Property crime itself was less of an issue, especially in those areas such as the South Wales valleys where, it was only half-jokingly remarked, there was not that much left to steal. Knowledge, however partial, of Wilson and Kellings' (1982) 'broken windows' thesis was marked and few questioned the logic of 'nipping' minor incivilities in the bud before things became worse. This appears part and parcel of the problem-solving work of community safety managers, few of whom felt the need to be apologetic about what some critics of ASBOs have interpreted as the selective labelling, stigmatisation and excessive repression of 'normal' adolescent misbehaviour. However, the same actors also consistently expressed the view that the causes of breakdowns in civility and public order required more profound explanation and remediation in both the short and long term. Our respondents accepted that controlling 'youth annoyance' can entail the displacement, even exclusion, of anti-social people in the short term. It was felt, however, that such measures need to be complemented by interventions aimed at repairing relations across the generations, particularly through forms of social prevention addressing the causes of disorder in the boredom of many young people and their alienation from key institutions of social integration.

For example, one community safety manager in South Wales argued that anti-social behaviour was a clearly expressed priority for the local population he served, stimulating far greater interest and concern than the crime reduction targets established by the main funding bodies of his CSP:

> The majority of people here, in this place alone ... I'll tell you what they're affected by – kids on bikes, off-road biking, and the environmental damage they cause ... pain in the arse. Setting fire to the trees, hanging around, throwing stones, making a general nuisance of themselves, taking booze, drugs and stuff, those quality of life things ... they're not incidental. They are disorder crimes and yet in terms of what we get measured by ... we never get acknowledged about that. But people who get involved in those crimes

gradually gravitate to higher levels of crime that government then picks up on like criminal damage, like violence.

I'm not saying it's a zero-tolerance approach but going back to that concept ... the causes of crime and where you start to pick that up and start to address that. It's a hinterland between education and trying ... and get the kids to understand and appreciate their place in society and what it is like to be responsible ... and before they become a branded criminal. It's how we need to be getting into that gap. (CSM, Locality 18; emphasis added [6])

This same manager, when pressed about the tension between responding to popular democratic concerns about public order – potentially misguided and reflecting particularistic interests themselves – and that of top-down, rational, bureaucratic expertise (from both public authorities and the social-scientific research community), acknowledged this difficulty but thought it arose largely because of the limited datasets available beyond that of police intelligence. In particular, he argued that the main tension between tolerance and intolerance of certain behaviours was mostly an issue at the margins, which were of course in need of careful monitoring. The CSM suggested, and noted that this might be controversial for an academic audience, that there is a bedrock of local 'common sense' about 'things that are patently unacceptable' and where the hot spots of worst disorder and incivilities were. For all this, however, youth annoyance was seen by this manager as a complex rather than a simple, homogeneous, thing:

It ranges from good kids chilling out on a Friday night, just being with friends and associates, having a drink, some going over the top, doing drugs, some do criminal damage, and some who are complete criminals and so on. So that's quite a complex issue and of course then you add to it some of the spatial dimensions and add to it some of the social and cultural dimensions because they are all different in this particular area and some of the other influences. And we started doing that [ie, targeting particular areas and times for interventions from the CSP] and it's been a sort of testing ground to see if we can pull together the idea of a multi-agency tactical team. (CSM, Locality 18)

According to this commonly held viewpoint among CSMs in Wales, 'multi-agency tactical problem solving' was presented as the way forward, an 'intelligent approach', for getting behind 'surface' concerns about youth annoyance to address social causes, acknowledging:

> we already know here where we get the highest proportion of youth annoyance and criminal damage will be undoubtedly the places where we have the greatest incidence of social exclusion, economic deficiencies etc., etc. (CSM, Locality 18)

In apparent accord with the 'broken windows' thesis, another community safety manager in South Wales identified 'quality of life' issues as the core concerns of the local population rather than crime reduction. Commenting on the contents of the postbags that elected members receive routinely, this manager argued:

> If you [as an elected councillor] want to stay in the bunker, you won't see ... But if you go knocking on doors around the streets or go to public meetings of constituents ... or go and do their own visual audit of their ward, they will see and then have to involve themselves in community safety issues. It will be in your face whether it be litter, abandoned cars, graffiti, or a general ambience that that is a nice environment. Or why is it a nice environment: because people work well together. (CSM, Locality 3)

This manager argued for the vital role of a dedicated coordinator acting as a catalyst for the kind of multi-agency interventions needed to address the multifarious causes of anti-social behaviour:

> We have more positive interventions at times than the rest of SE Wales put together [ie a 'four-strike staged process' from initial warning letter to ASBO] ... What matters to us is the level of support we offer to the individual and to the community. It is about making those positive interventions early on and in such a way that people moderate their behaviour ... It is about all parties coming to the table together with their own professional view, their professional tool-bag if you like to assist in making things better for the community. It is about consistency of attendance by the different groups, individuals who can make decisions and bring resources. And it is also about strategic leads making

funding lines available to make things happen on the ground.
(CSM, Locality 3)

When pressed to say whether this was a harmonious consensus, the respondent accepted there were conflicting views, particularly regarding conceptions of anti-social youth, often reflecting the differing occupational subcultures of particular partner agencies and competing interpretations of statutory law. The conflict between community safety teams and the social services departments of local authorities was identified by some of our respondents as a key issue shaping the policy response to anti-social behaviour among young people, not least because of apparently competing statutory obligations. Whereas section 37 of the 1998 Crime and Disorder Act places a statutory duty on CSPs, and on allied youth offending teams supporting the aim of the youth justice system, to prioritise the prevention of offending behaviour by children and young persons, section 1 of the 1989 Children Act places a statutory duty on any court to treat the 'welfare of the child' as paramount. In a minority of localities the issuing of Anti-Social Behaviour Orders has even been contested by social services departments – sometimes in the courts – against other wings of their own local authority allied to the CSPs, as counter to the welfare of those children subject to these orders and, therefore, in contravention of section 1 of the 1989 Children Act. Respondents also made reference to the welfare ethos of social and youth workers and their focus on casework with particular individuals. This was counterpoised to the control orientation of other partners, particularly the police and municipal housing managers, under pressure from residents and tenants to discipline entire cohorts of young people through the use of ASBOs, Parenting and Curfew Orders, criminal sanctioning and other, more immediate measures for reducing offending behaviour and restoring public order. Many of our respondents acknowledged that their role as community safety managers was to broker *satisficing* deals between these competing agencies, recognising the various statutory, occupational and populist pressures to which they are subject while seeking to expedite responses to particular problems of public disorder.

This brokerage role is central to the work of community safety managers, the discipline of which compels an understanding of the multifaceted definition and causes of anti-social behaviour and the breadth of possible policy responses. In contrast to police-led responses to troublesome youth hanging around on street corners, namely 'the nonsense' of simply moving them on, it was argued that:

We need to identify what young people's requirements are as citizens and what is this whole national pastime we have in this country of demonising young people. The vast majority of young people are hard working, conscientious, good citizens and the future. But we know there is only a hard core of people … also police are increasingly saying we can't deal with these people. 'They are not doing anything' and the other responsible authorities have to listen. (CSM, Locality 3)

This manager argued for the central importance of joint work across agencies to divert young people away from much problematic behaviour and the crucially important contribution that detached youth workers can make relative to the more symbolic role of police patrols or the deployment of Police Community Support Officers (PCSOs). It became clear, through many of the interviews with our respondents, that the occupation of community safety manager was often a tortuous process of bargaining between implacable partners, especially with regard to the political and culturally emotive issue of governing young people's use of public space.

In occupying this position, community safety managers were not in a position – even if so minded – to act as simple interlocutors for the Home Office's Respect Agenda, or footsoldiers for the government's ASBO tsar, if they wanted to retain the involvement of those partners primarily concerned with the welfare of children and young people. As noted earlier, there has been substantial political investment, financial as well as symbolic, in a more social democratic welfarist approach to crime and disorder in Wales, allied to a citizen-centred model of public service, for which the prolific use of 'low-trust' measures such as ASBOs is anathema. This broader, post-devolutionary project places a considerable pressure on community safety managers, reinforced by funding streams from the Welsh Assembly Government that account for a significant share of their annual budgets, to counterbalance the 'Manchester tendency'[7] with strategies that place a premium on the social inclusion of young people. Nonetheless, in keeping with our broader thesis on the importance of contextualising debates over public safety, there is evidence of variation in local CSPs' adherence to this Fabian project, with some notable advocates of ASBOs as an economic and highly effective means of restoring order.

Conclusion

Such contestation emphasises the political agency of community safety managers and the partnerships they coordinate, the consequences of which cannot be articulated within the smooth narratives of disorder that have predominated in both official and academic discourse. The conception and government of anti-social behaviour is a messy practice, both in its doing and in its apprehension by social researchers. The greater concerns of community safety managers across many localities in Wales are focused on efforts to prevent or, at best, to manage disorder and local feelings of fear and insecurity. Much of this work is profoundly influenced by a social democratic ethos that belies seductive but simplistic official narratives of ASBOs as a progressive palliative for 'feral' populations.

The resilient Fabianism of community safety managers' accounts of their own work also disturbs narratives of social control in critical social science, which are in danger of believing the hype of the very political projects they seek to challenge. The distinction between the neoliberal and neoconservative impulses constituting the 'free economy, strong state' project of 'New Right' politics (King, 1987; Gamble, 1988) has animated critical commentary on British government for too long, obfuscating the complex interdependencies between state and civil society that both necessitate political agency and enable local resistance (Marsh and Rhodes, 1992). The incorporation of this distinction into criminological research, notably through the work of David Garland (1996, 2001) and Nikolas Rose (1999, 2000), has further obscured an understanding of social control as an emergent, necessarily contingent, product of the struggle for sovereignty over territories and populations (Stenson and Edwards, 2003).

As such, grand narrative themes such as the 'eclipse', even 'death', of social democratic criminology overestimate the complex interplay between local priorities over social order and those emanating from both Whitehall and the Welsh Assembly Government. In this way, our research suggests that it is both conceptually flawed and empirically misleading to speak of a unitary 'British model' or 'ASBO nation' that governs populations through sanctioning against anti-social behaviour, particularly when the impact of the devolved polities of the UK on policy responses to crime and disorder is recognised.

A larger challenge for research and policy in this field is to explore both the broader conditions of social integration that explain the generation of these new forms of disorder and their anti-social consequences, as lived experiences, for the populations most ravaged by the loss of old stabilities around previous divisions of labour at the workplace and in the home. To paraphrase Paul Willis (1977), what does it mean, especially for young men, to 'learn *not* to labour', given their actual and prospective ejection from stable, full-time employment? Such a project lies beyond the traditional scope of criminology and requires the reinvigoration of a political-sociological imagination within criticisms of anti-social behaviour.

Notes

[1] The limited space available here precludes a detailed description of these abstract and reductive narratives but see Hughes (2007) for a fuller discussion and critique.

[2] Following the Assembly election in May 2007, the Department was restructured and renamed the Department of Social Justice and Local Government. Community safety remains within this department. The emphasis on social rather than criminal justice approaches to reducing crime and disorder is, if anything, likely to be further enhanced following the agreement, in July 2007, between the Labour Party and Plaid Cymru (the nationalist party of Wales that adopts a relatively left-wing stance on social policy issues, including those of crime and disorder) to form a coalition government.

[3] A reference to *Y Ddraig Goch* or the Red Dragon that is the national symbol of Wales.

[4] HO designates Home Office policy priorities, and WAG designates Welsh Assembly policy priorities

[5] The term 'youth annoyance' was often used interchangeably with that of 'anti-social behaviour' to depict the priorities of those local people who communicated their concerns to community safety managers via various public meetings, elected councillors and the media.

[6] For purposes of anonymity we have coded responses from community safety managers (CSMs) in terms of the 22 local government areas in which they work (Locality *n*).

[7] A reference to Manchester City Council, which has become synonymous with the prolific use of ASBOs as a measure of first recourse in establishing public order, accounting for a sixth of all ASBOs issued in England and Wales during the first five years of their availability as a civil sanction (Hughes and Follett, 2006).

References

Beecham, J. (2006) *Beyond boundaries: Citizen-centred local services for Wales*, Cardiff: Welsh Assembly Government.

Burney, E. (2005) *Making people behave*, Cullompton: Willan Publishing.

Clarke, J. (2004) *Changing welfare, changing states*, London: Sage.

Clegg, S. (1993) 'Narrative, power and social theory', in D.K. Mumby (ed), *Narrative and social control: Critical perspectives*, London: Sage.

Drakeford, M. (2005) 'Wales and the third term of New Labour: devolution and the development of difference', *Critical Social Policy*, vol 25, no 4, pp 497–506.

Edwards, A. and Hughes, G. (2005) 'Comparing the governance of safety in Europe: a geo-historical approach', *Theoretical Criminology*, vol 9, no 3, pp 345–63.

Edwards, A. and Hughes, G. (2007) 'Community safety work in Wales: governing (dis)order in a devolved polity', paper presented at BSC Conference, London School of Economics, London, 18-20 September.

Edwards, A. and Hughes, G. (2008) 'The role of the Community Safety Officer within Wales: challenges and opportunities', Final report of the WACSO Research Project.

Ferri, E. (1917) *Criminal sociology*, Boston: Little Brown.

Gamble, A. (1988) *The free economy and the strong state*, London: Macmillan.

Garland, D. (1996) 'The limits to the sovereign state: strategies of crime control in contemporary society', *British Journal of Criminology*, vol 36, no 4, pp 445–71.

Garland, D. (2001) *The culture of control: Crime and social order in contemporary society*, Oxford: Oxford University Press.

Hughes, G. (1996) 'Communitarianism and law and order', *Critical Social Policy*, vol 16, no 4, pp 17–41.

Hughes, G. (2007) *The politics of crime and community*, Basingstoke: Palgrave Macmillan.

Hughes, G. and Follett, M. (2006) 'Community safety, youth and the "anti-social"', in B. Goldson and J. Muncie (eds), *Youth justice: Policy, practice and politics*, London: Sage.

Hughes, G. and Gilling, D. (2004) 'Mission impossible: the habitus of the community safety manager', *Criminal Justice*, vol 4, no 2, pp 129–49.

King, D.S. (1987) *The New Right: Politics, markets and citizenship*, London: Macmillan.

Law, J. (2004) *After method: Mess in social science research*, London: Routledge.

Marsh, D. and Rhodes, R.A.W. (eds), (1992) *Policy networks in British government*, Oxford: Clarendon Press.

Rose, N. (1999) *The powers of freedom*, Cambridge: Cambridge University Press.

Rose, N. (2000) 'Government and control', *British Journal of Criminology*, vol 40, no 2, pp 321–39.

Stenson, K. and Edwards, A. (2003) 'Crime control and local governance: the struggle for sovereignty in advanced liberal polities', *Contemporary Politics*, vol 9, no 2, pp 203–17.

WAG (Welsh Assembly Government) (2006) *Making the connections – Delivering beyond the boundaries*, Cardiff: WAG.

Willis, P. (1977) *Learning to labour: How working class kids get working class jobs*, Farnborough: Saxon House.

Wilson, J.Q. and Kelling, G. (1982) 'Broken windows: the police and neighbourhood safety', *Atlantic Monthly*, vol 249, no 3, pp 29–38.

THREE

Towards a balanced and practical approach to anti-social behaviour management

Gillian Mayfield and Andy Mills

Introduction

This chapter approaches the issue of tackling anti-social behaviour from the perspective of practitioners and policy makers operating at a local level. It focuses on three aspects:

- practice and policy as applied in one local authority area (Leeds, the second-largest English local authority);
- the key issues for practitioners around the country (as identified by research undertaken by the National Community Safety Network); and
- new moves to address the causes, as well as the symptoms, of anti-social behaviour (the government's Respect Agenda and the Positive Approaches group).

The first section examines the strategic approach to anti-social behaviour adopted by Leeds and the establishment and operation of policies and interventions to address anti-social behaviour through a dedicated unit and multi-agency problem-solving panels. It describes briefly the experiment in multiple Anti-Social Behaviour Orders (ASBOs) of Operation Cape and its mutation into smaller, rolling multi-agency programmes (latterly promoted as 'weeks of action' by the government for its 44 'critical partnerships').

The second section examines the findings of the National Community Safety Network's research (*Anti-social behaviour: Key issues and recommendations – a practitioners' perspective*). This considered the difficulties 'on the ground' concerning: priorities and target-setting; resources and costs; definitions and information gathering, analysis and sharing; and the consistent management of anti-social behaviour (ASB).

The third section looks at the proposals coming out of the Positive Approaches alliance, which argues for resources and emphasis to be placed on prevention and early intervention, and the development of Respect and its combination of support, intervention and enforcement.

Tackling ASB at a local level – the Leeds approach

We must preface this section by being clear that we are making no particular claims for Leeds either having a superlative approach to tackling ASB or being especially representative of other authorities around the country. On the first count, there will always be some area that has progressed at least one of the elements of its strategy to a significant degree; on the second, making comparisons with other districts is always very difficult. Having said that, we suggest that there are similar approaches adopted elsewhere in England. And, as everywhere else, we are always trying to improve what we do and to respond to new initiatives in what is a fast-developing field of policy and practice. So by the time you read this chapter, it is inevitable that changes will have happened, in Leeds as elsewhere.

ASB has emerged as a key issue for the city, as evidenced in all the surveys the council and the Crime and Disorder Reduction Partnership (CDRP) undertake. Successive political administrations have demanded and supported a vigorous approach to tackling ASB. It is a serious issue, and it can have a tremendous impact on those individuals and communities that suffer from it.

One question that we are always asked – and that we frequently pose ourselves – is whether or not the problem of ASB has become worse. It is a very difficult question to answer. It is certainly now easier to report incidences of ASB and crime, and people may be more encouraged to do so in the knowledge that nowadays agencies have more powers to tackle problems than hitherto. Perhaps people's tolerance levels have declined; equally, perhaps people are not as considerate as they used to be. One thing is clear – people want something done about ASB and the view of the city council is that people should not be expected to suffer from the poor behaviour of others.

In 2001 we created the Leeds Anti-Social Behaviour Unit (ASBU), building on a small tenancy enforcement team within housing services. The ASBU, which has 40 staff and provides a service across all types of tenure, now resides within Leeds Community Safety, a council division that includes service delivery elements as well as the partnership support and commissioning functions for community safety and drugs.

The strategic approach we adopted – and have continued to maintain – was recommended by the government and consists of:

- prevention
- enforcement
- resettlement and support.

All of these aspects of our work are supported by a partnership approach, with case management, investigation and overall coordination being the responsibility of the ASBU. We deal with about 1,000 cases per year. The partnership approach is evidenced by the use of multi-agency area ASB panels, consisting of the key relevant senior managers for that area.[1] The role of the panels is to share information on their areas' problems and on individuals, to reduce ASB through using a problem-solving approach, and to agree resources to target diversionary activity as well as enforcement activity. On the latter point, the panels are the means by which we undertake the statutory consultation for ASBOs if these are deemed necessary (and, with this, the risk assessment for any publicity of the order as well as identifying any support, such as is available through Individual Support Orders).

For *prevention* a wide range of options is available to the panels. We can refer young people – and almost half of the perpetrators of ASB referred to us are relatively young – to the city-wide Positive Activities for Young People scheme, and to the Positive Futures sports-based social inclusion programme. Depending on the area, we may also be able to refer into one of the senior or junior Youth Inclusion Programmes. The Youth Service offers a range of diversion and intervention programmes and we may also deploy detached youth workers. Mediation may be used, also warning letters and Acceptable Behaviour Contracts (ABCs). The latter are often employed in conjunction with support programmes to help those with contracts to successfully complete them. In addition, we should not overlook the wider prevention and early intervention agenda, such as preventing truancy and exclusion from school, which does have a significant impact on ASB.

If such interventions fail – or if the behaviour is such that immediate legal action is deemed necessary – we employ a range of enforcement powers, including Dispersal Orders, injunctions and, of course, ASBOs. The authority has not been shy of using ASBOs (we will discuss the use of multiple ASBOs shortly), but they are really only the tip of the iceberg so far as the Leeds Anti-Social Behaviour Unit's overall activities are concerned.

There is a keen debate – hence this book – about whether or not ASBOs work, and whether breach of an ASBO represents failure. We can point to ASBOs that have had a significant impact on the recipient and have proved the impetus for them to turn their lives around – likewise, for others they have been like water off a duck's back. Trying to draw lessons from what factors have to be in place to make an ASBO effective is not easy, because each order has several facets and individuals' circumstances are so very different, but we can safely say that there has to be some willingness on each individual's behalf to change behaviour. Breaches, we feel, should not necessarily be deemed a failure. When we examined the situation in Leeds we found that in one year – 2004/05 – there was an ASBO breach rate of 63%; however, 68% of these had been for two or fewer breaches. Some level of breach is to be expected and many people who are committing behaviour serious enough to warrant an ASBO are likely to 'test' the system at least once. Each order is different and therefore the seriousness of the breach is a factor that should also be considered alongside the breach behaviour as compared to the level and types of behaviour occurring prior to the order being made. It is worth noting that the average number of breaches across all orders was two.

Does this level of breach make ASBOs a failure? We think not. If it does, how does the criminal justice system (CJS) as a whole compare? How many people convicted of a crime go on to reoffend? Should that mean we abandon the CJS? If nothing else, the use of ASBOs and other enforcement measures lets the community know that the authorities take their concerns seriously and sends a clear message out as to what is deemed unacceptable behaviour. On the other hand, neither should the number of ASBOs awarded be seen as the mark of a successful strategy even if, at times, a rather different impression may be given by the Home Office.

The attention focused by the press and politicians on ASBOs does disguise the fact that these are actually the tip of the iceberg so far as action against ASB is concerned. Our belief is that interventions should be early and at as low a level as possible to be effective. Earlier we mentioned Acceptable Behaviour Contracts. These are voluntary agreements between the authorities and (usually) a young person and the parents regarding the behaviour of the young person. Recent research conducted by the ASBU showed that, out of over 500 people who had ABCs in Leeds, only 5% went on to receive an ASBO. There is a danger in getting hung up on number crunching, seeking to increase the number of enforcement measures such as ASBOs, but this really should not be the point of an ASB strategy – the key aim should be to *resolve the problems causing the troublesome behaviour.*

Resettlement and support is the final aspect of our strategy, and this applies to both victims and offenders. Dedicated outreach Victim Support Officers work with the ASBU, giving complainants access to a specialist service that is not generally available for victims of ASB. We have promoted the Taking a Stand award and several winners have emerged from the area. The Youth Offending Service works with young people subject to ASBOs to help them maintain the terms of the order. Using both Respect and Department for Education and Skills (now Department of Children, Schools and Families) funding, the service has also established the all relative project, targeting the parents of at-risk young people; this is showing some early indications of success. Our Signpost Project works with families whose children are involved in ASB to tackle the factors that contribute to poor behaviour – bad parenting, poor school attendance and so on. More recently, Signpost has expanded to include the Family Intervention Project, targeting those families that face eviction because of serious ASB. Other treatment and housing support services may also be deployed. Both all relative and Signpost, it should be noted, have been externally evaluated, with positive results.

Multiple ASBOs

Leeds's first experiment in multiple ASBOs came about in 2003 with Operation Cape, a police-led operation with council support. Operation Cape used 66 interim ASBOs, leading to a substantial number of full ASBOs, to reduce street crime in the Little London area of Leeds. The rationale was to use the orders to challenge and tightly manage drug dealing in an 'open' drug market. (An 'open' market is one where class A drugs are easily available on the streets; such markets typically attract increased crime and anti-social behaviour.) In this case the driver for change was the pressure to reduce street crime, but the benefits of the intervention spread wider than this, with a significant reduction in crime and disorder in that area and an equally significant increase in public satisfaction and reassurance. Many residents commented that they could now live in peace and free from fear of anti-social behaviour, crime and drug dealing and threats from drug dealers (including a telling comment from one person that 'the ice-cream man calls here now' – before he had been too afraid). Crime statistics for the area improved: robbery was reduced by 77%, burglary by 44% and vehicle crime by 14%. Operation Cape won a National Home Office Award for reducing class A drug availability.

Notwithstanding the obvious success of Operation Cape, there were significant difficulties with adopting this approach, which made it impossible to sustain further operations on such a scale: the cost of policing operations (both during and – in the form of increased reassurance patrols – afterwards), the legal costs to the council, the difficulty of producing evidence packages in such numbers in the available timescale, the difficulty in providing complementary activity such as drugs outreach workers, and the stress on the capacity of the courts and the council's legal services and ASBU. Cape has thus mutated into a succession of 'small bang' multi-agency operations in residential areas, with coordinated work by a number of statutory and voluntary agencies in a small target area to maximise impact. One example of these in East Leeds – Operation Banrock – was shortlisted for a Tilley Crime Prevention Award. These operations (since standardised across the city under the umbrella of the CDRP as Operation Champion) still use ASBOs and other enforcement measures, but are part of a package of measures including environmental improvements. They have resulted in improved agency working as well as reductions in ASB and crime.

Another example of multi-agency operations using ASBOs, but in a different setting, is Operation Chariot. Chariot showed how prevention and diversion can work to reduce enforcement action while having a positive impact on reducing ASB. It took place during the summer/ autumn of 2004 and targeted aggressive beggars and rough sleepers in the city centre. The operation saw a concerted effort to support individuals into drug or alcohol treatment and to provide support with housing and welfare issues before enforcement action was taken. Enforcement action was subsequently only taken against a minority hard core of individuals who refused support and treatment. Many of those who eventually received ASBOs subsequently went into treatment. The operation demonstrated that even difficult cases, where behaviour is chaotic, can be dealt with successfully if agencies work together and measures are available to support and divert individuals.

Issues for practitioners nationally

In the previous section we made no claims for the Leeds approach to dealing with ASB being particularly representative of the rest of England, but we are on more certain ground with the research from the National Community Safety Network (*Anti-social behaviour: Key issues and recommendations – a practitioners' perspective*) published in 2005.

The National Community Safety Network (NCSN) is a practitioner-led organisation supporting those involved in promoting community safety/crime reduction throughout the UK. Its mission is:

- to give a national voice to practitioners
- to influence national policy and practice
- to support the professional development of practitioners
- to promote joint working in the UK and Europe.

The NCSN represents over 400 members and organisations in both the statutory and voluntary sectors, all with a common interest in promoting safer communities. Its research was based on extensive consultation with community safety and ASB practitioners[2] and, while time has moved on, its findings are still applicable. The findings of barriers that practitioners were encountering when dealing with ASB were categorised into four sections:

- priorities and target setting
- resources and costs
- definitions and information gathering, analysis and sharing
- the consistent management of anti-social behaviour.

Here we will select the most important and pertinent findings from the survey, although since the report was published many of the recommendations have since been progressed, at least to some degree.

Priorities and target setting

In priorities and target setting, the problem of instituting a strategy and a performance management system that recognised the role of preventive measures was raised. There is little doubt that the government has had a primary focus on enforcement and, until the advent of the Respect Agenda, little emphasis was placed on prevention and early intervention. Instead, partnerships were – and still are – exhorted to increase the number of enforcement measures such as ASBOs. In the performance-focused culture in which we live this has meant that whatever is easy to count gets done, while whatever is far less clear and not always easy to measure – the impact of mediation, conflict resolution, positive activities with young people and so on – receives less emphasis.

Resources and costs

Ask any Community Safety Officer about their biggest grumbles, and they will at some stage, probably sooner rather than later, bring up the problem of time-limited funding. Despite crime and disorder being major public concerns, funding for community safety within many, if not most, areas is heavily reliant on external funding. The section of the NCSN report that deals with resources and costs remains as relevant now as when it was written.

Much community safety and ASB activity is not mainstreamed into council budgets, but relies on government funding (for instance, the Neighbourhood Renewal Fund, Safer and Stronger Communities Fund), most of which now goes into the Local Area Agreement pot. These resources are then subject to more bureaucracy, and less reliability, than core funding. For practitioners, that means many are on time-limited contracts. Staff recruitment and retention become more difficult and external funding tends to drive a conveyor belt of temporary initiatives. Trailblazer and Respect are funding much valuable ASB work, but it is difficult to predict how much of this will survive the cessation of their respective funding.

Another unknown factor is the real costs of dealing with ASB. There are various models for costing work, but even legal costs are calculated very differently across different areas (because legal provision for ASB within local authorities varies enormously). More problematic is the cost of prevention and early intervention, which may be delivered by a number of organisations in both the statutory and voluntary sector. Without a comprehensive understanding of the costs involved in different methods of intervening in ASB, we are not in a position to properly assess the cost–effectiveness (and therefore the sustainability) of each intervention.

Definitions and information gathering, analysis and sharing

The question of definitions in relation to ASB has been thrown into sharper focus by the inclusion of questions about ASB in public surveys on which the performance of local authorities and partnerships will be judged. But when we ask people about ASB and the performance of agencies, what are we asking them about? ASB means different things to different people – different both in scale and in type. It can range from *leylandii* hedges growing too high for a neighbour's liking to threats of and actual violence and intimidation, taking in on the way kids hanging around on street corners, rubbish, noise, graffiti, abandoned vehicles, loud parties and so on.

What is acceptable to one person is unacceptable to another; behaviour that is acceptable or tolerated in one setting is not acceptable somewhere else. For instance, children playing rowdily in a school playground at lunchtime is a different matter from raucous behaviour outside a sheltered housing complex at night; language used by spectators at a football match would be deemed abusive and unacceptable in a shopping mall. No doubt there are growing generational differences too, and more opportunities for 'anti-social behaviour' occasioned by new technology – playing music through a mobile phone on a bus will be seen as the norm by many young people but as intrusive by their elders. The lower levels of 'ASB' are actually about different perceptions of reasonableness rather than simply about perpetrators and victims. Where this is the case an authority that can deploy low-level interventions such as mediation may prevent disputes escalating to a more serious stage; in an area where such interventions are not deployed the situation may deteriorate until an ASBO may be required – but this still raises questions about how the problem has been defined in the first place in the minds of members of the public. And then also we face questions of how best to encourage low-level and acceptable solutions while at the same time reassuring members of the public that more threatening problems will be dealt with promptly and seriously.

The government is now beginning to disaggregate the category of violent crime, because it has rightly recognised the problem of lumping together serious and minor assaults and of having a target that combines reduction of incidents with increased reporting. The same, alas, has yet to happen with ASB. In our performance-indicator culture, partnerships need to be able to compare like with like to be able to say how they are doing in relation to other authorities. At present, with ASB there is no way we can do this. So, as we intimated earlier in this chapter, while we can compare Leeds' performance on burglary and other crimes with, say, Birmingham or Manchester, we cannot say the same for ASB. We need to agree definitions and categories of ASB across the country if we are all to record and measure in the same way, and then the performance framework needs to be incorporated into the overall local government–police–partnerships frameworks for the comparisons to be valid.

Consistent management of anti-social behaviour

We are slowly moving towards a more consistent management of anti-social behaviour. Presently there is a plethora of approaches, and the service that someone suffering from ASB receives and the way in which someone causing ASB is treated will be very different depending on where one lives. Do communities have access to community mediation? How are witnesses and victims supported? Are ABCs used in all areas? What behaviour is likely to trigger an ASBO in different places – and why?

This patchwork quilt of provision does not seem very satisfactory, but its existence is perhaps not surprising. The legislation on ASB is new and the work to address ASB under the legislation is new. Every district has been developing its responses to anti-social behaviour in a different way.

The lack of a prevention focus on ASB was the single most widespread concern among practitioners. The Respect Agenda, developed since the report, goes a long way to redressing the balance. Combined with the Every Child Matters agenda, in the long term we should see a diminishing focus on enforcement as greater emphasis and resources are given to early interventions. What each district needs to develop is a spectrum of services and interventions to tackle ASB at different stages:

- work to prevent crime and ASB occurring in the first place by addressing risk factors;
- intervention at the early stages of ASB to prevent continuation and escalation;
- intervention at the serious and/or persistent stage.

If this spectrum of provision were in place in each district we would start to see greater consistency across the country in responses to ASB, instead of the postcode lottery we have now.

Positive approaches and respect

At the same time as the NCSN report was being written up in 2005, a range of organisations were coming together as the Positive Approaches group. These organisations[3] were concerned about the imbalance in public policy (in particular, the overemphasis on enforcement solutions at the expense of investment in preventive and early intervention initiatives) on anti-social behaviour.

In August 2006 the group published as a parliamentary briefing paper its '10-Point Plan for Change'. The paper's recommendations were formulated after debate and consideration of the organisations' experiences and evidence of work in the field of dealing with anti-social behaviour, and were focused on three areas – the use of Anti-Social Behaviour Orders, the value of preventive and positive approaches, and the need for research and analysis.

The first recommendation called for a comprehensive independent review of Anti-Social Behaviour Orders, arguing that ASBOs should be used, as they are in some areas, as the top of a pyramid of responses and only when other options have not worked or where the behaviour is so serious that only this option will provide the necessary controls.[4]

The main focus of the paper was on the vital need for a new emphasis on preventive and positive approaches. The group called for an early extension, and a mainstreaming, of early intervention initiatives: in all areas it should be normal practice for preventive work to have been done within families before a resort to enforcement measures. Mediation could play a much bigger part in responses to anti-social behaviour and community cohesion than its funding currently allows. The group argued for constructive work with young people, that CDRPs should be expected to have a range of suitable options available, pooling resources and provision from the range of different statutory and voluntary agencies. The success of these initiatives should be promoted to the public as a key confidence-building activity. The principle of individual support, established in the Individual Support Order for ASBOs, should be extended to work at an earlier stage.

Similarly, restorative and reparative approaches should be at the heart of local strategies for responding to anti-social behaviour and both CDRPs and criminal justice agencies should work together to ensure that this happens on the ground. The development of community resilience, community cohesion and neighbourhood policing were seen as important: neighbourhood management can contribute a great deal to the successful tackling of anti-social behaviour. But realistic timescales for its implementation, greater employment of community development practitioners and an approach that is based as much on prevention as on response are critical elements, as is a clear framework for involvement of the voluntary and community sector. Although the Police Community Support Officer role is a very important one in engaging local people, other approaches, including specialist community development skills and conflict resolution, are also vital. The issue of people with mental health problems being caught up in the ASB system (as either victims or perpetrators) led to a recommendation that, to address this imbalance, improved community mental health and adolescent services are required and that health providers need to be regarded as key players in the development of preventive packages for tackling anti-social behaviour.

Finally, Positive Approaches argued for a more radically joined-up approach to research and analysis – not only within different units of the Home Office but also with other government departments – to tackle the current morass of overlapping partnerships and agendas.

The Positive Approaches paper complemented the work of the NCSN and widened the perspective of the latter's report from community safety and ASB practitioners to a broader range of organisations, including researchers who were also engaged in responding to the issue of ASB. It is doubtful whether the concerns and recommendations of the two reports influenced the Respect Agenda, but this initiative has gone part of the way at least in trying to address the issue of interventions. The Respect Action Plan builds upon the government's previous work to tackle anti-social behaviour by attempting to broaden the approach to tackling ASB. The plan is split into six sections:

• young people
• schools
• support for parents and families
• housing
• neighbourhoods
• enforcement.

There are some basic principles in the plan: implementation cannot be achieved by government alone; every citizen has a responsibility to behave in a respectful way; the public is concerned that the values of the majority are not shared by the selfish minority; to effectively tackle disadvantage we must offer the support and the challenges needed to address anti-social behaviour and its causes; we must pass on decent values and standards of behaviour to our children.

The plan has its detractors, partly because of its name and the 'hyped-up' approach to selling it, partly because of a suspicion that it is anti-young people, partly because it fails to grasp some key issues such as alcohol and community cohesion. Nonetheless, it has made great strides, at least in the pilot Respect Areas, of promoting and developing parenting programmes and family intervention programmes. These programmes have the potential to make a significant impact on the quality of life both for families whose members are engaged in anti-social behaviour and for the communities that suffer from such behaviour.

These and other Respect initiatives go a long way to meeting the call from the NCSN and Positive Approaches for early intervention and prevention. More than this, Respect's assertive approach has demanded of local authorities and their partners in the pilot areas full commitment to the agenda – hence multi-agency buy-in to Respect has been achieved. It is a useful lesson when considering other aspects of the community safety agenda for which commitment may be less forthcoming.

Conclusion

We have tried to give a flavour of our approach to anti-social behaviour in Leeds and also give some insight into the problems identified by those involved in this field around the country. If the issue of anti-social behaviour is not a new one, then some of the approaches, powers and tools are, and it is worth remembering that we are not in a mature stage of their use. In dealing with ASB, there is agreement that early intervention and prevention are best, and ideally the resources and services will be stemming behavioural problems at a very early stage. Alas, reality is somewhat different, and it is important to the communities we serve that we put a stop to the poor behaviour that impinges on their lives. When it comes to this stage, our belief is that the key is to intervene in a way that resolves the problem. If that means enforcement, so be it.

Notes

[1] Core membership is drawn from the ASBU, West Yorkshire Police, the relevant housing ALMO (Arm's Length Management Organisation), Social Services, Youth Offending Service, Youth Service, Education Leeds and the community safety coordinator for the locality.

[2] Led by Andy Mills as NCSN Board director with the ASB portfolio, the report (National Community Safety Network [2005] *Anti-social behaviour: Key issues and recommendations – a practitioners' perspective*, Chester: NCSN) was based on an e-mail survey with all members, followed by a participative workshop at the NCSN's 2004 annual conference and the creation of a time-limited policy working group. Jean Chinery and John Hedge pulled the final report together. It can be found at www.community-safety.net.

[3] The Positive Approaches group included Mediation UK, the Local Government Information Unit, the Runnymede Trust, Revolving

Doors, the Thames Valley Partnership and the National Association of Probation Officers as well as the NCSN.

[4] While there was full agreement within the group about the value of preventive and positive approaches, the same could not be said regarding the debate on ASBOs, and opinions ranged from those who were essentially opposed to their use at all to those who were supportive of their effective deployment.

FOUR

Lost in translation: interpreting and implementing anti-social behaviour policies

Roger Matthews and Daniel Briggs

Introduction

Tackling anti-social behaviour has, over the last decade, become a government priority. The establishment of the Anti-Social Behaviour Unit in the Home Office in 2003 and, more recently, the formation of the Respect Task Force signal the strategic shift in official policy on law and order. As the officially recorded crime rate continues to drop there has been no let-up in government pressure to maintain 'law and order', with the passing of a number of pieces of legislation designed to control the range of activities that have become identified as anti-social behaviour.

In this process, there has been a shift in terminology and in the meaning of key terms such as 'disorder', 'crime' and 'anti-social behaviour', with a blurring of the distinctions between them. These terms are increasingly coming to be used interchangeably, while terms such as 'disorder', which once referred mainly to physical disorder such as vandalism, are now more readily applied to the definition of social and behavioural problems, such as street drinkers, youths or vagrants and prostitutes. There is also a growing belief that these social forms of disorder should and can be controlled through law enforcement (Hope, 1999). The conceptual slippage involved in current debates about crime, disorder and anti-social behaviour does not, however, detract from the significance given to these various activities, but rather serves as a self-reinforcing discourse that increases their profile and allows inflated claims to be made about their cumulative impact.

However, a discernible shift in emphasis is taking place, involving a decreased concentration on crimes as specific events and a focus on anti-social behaviour and disorder as low-level continual activities that extend beyond the established crime-control framework and that require a form of control that extends beyond conventional forms of policing. It necessarily requires a series of agencies working in combination, involving forms of regulation that transcend the established boundaries of criminal justice. James Q. Wilson and George Kelling (1982) have provided the most effective rationale for linking disorder and anti-social behaviour to crime in their influential and widely referenced 'broken windows' thesis, which posits an 'inextricable link' between disorder and crime (see Matthews, 1992; Kelling, 2001). In official circles, this thesis has been used consistently to justify the need to 'get tough' on anti-social behaviour and to 'nip' low-level incidents 'in the bud' before they become more serious (Squires and Stephen, 2005).

The growing focus on anti-social behaviour by the government has not occurred without critical comment from academics and journalists. Leading academic commentators on these issues have seen the increased focus on anti-social behaviour as signalling a shift in a more punitive direction. One of the main reasons given for this increased focus has been the 'perceived inefficiency of the criminal justice system' (Burney, 2005). Similarly, Squires and Stephen (2005) claim that the increased preoccupation with anti-social behaviour is a function of the perceived 'enforcement deficit':

> This 'enforcement deficit' concerns the fact that traditional criminal justice interventions tend to individualise their response around particular incidents and offenders and have no mechanism for addressing the collective and accumulating impact of harm and distress across a community. (Squires and Stephen, 2005: 3)

Squires and Stephen argue that this new focus has involved a shift away from attempts to address the conditions of the disadvantaged through welfare policies and strategies of social inclusion and replaced them with an over-reliance on discipline, punishment and containment.

In this chapter, we seek to examine the ways in which those ostensibly punitive and disciplinary policies have been interpreted and implemented in the past few years in England and Wales. Drawing on the research conducted in three London boroughs in 2006, we aim to explore the gaps between rhetoric and reality and between interventions and outcomes.[1] In doing so, we aim to argue that there are substantial difficulties and inconsistencies in the implementation of anti-social behaviour strategies. Although this chapter focuses on a relatively small number of boroughs that were seen to be 'failing', many of the issues discussed here are relevant to many other boroughs that we have recently visited.

The main problems that arose in the process of translating government policy into local authority agendas included:

- variations in the use and reliability of data collected
- problems of definition and overlapping of categories
- different perceptions of anti-social behaviour among different agencies
- problems of formulating intervention strategies
- limited use of anti-social behaviour sanctions
- lack of community involvement.

In a press release issued in January 2007, the Home Office claimed that: 'One year on from the launch of the Government's Respect Action Plan, major progress is being made in the drive to tackle anti-social behaviour and create a modern culture of respect' (Home Office, 2007). The press release pointed to the increased use of Acceptable Behaviour Contracts (ABCs), Anti-Social Behaviour Orders (ASBOs) and Parenting Orders. It also included a quote from Tony Blair in which he claimed that:

> We have seen real progress with communities across the country making full use of the powers we have put in place with councils, police, courts and local people working in partnership to make neighbourhoods safer and better places to live.

While not denying that the millions of pounds, the substantial growth of anti-social behaviour personnel and the prioritisation of anti-social behaviour as an issue have all had some impact on anti-social behaviour, we want to suggest that in a number of areas the rate of progress is exaggerated and the campaign against anti-social behaviour is being driven forward by a myopic and messianic vision that indicates little awareness of the real obstacles to the implementation of this programme.

Variations in the use and reliability of collected data

The starting point for understanding the nature of, and trends in, anti-social behaviour in any borough involves the gathering and collating of the appropriate data. In the three boroughs we examined, the quality of data collected ranged from poor to very poor. Typically, different agencies operated with different databases which drew data from different sources and employed different categories that were often incompatable and inconsistent. One borough, for example, used a combination of FLARE, CADMIS, iQuanta, and CRIS.[2] Some data was collected by the police and some by the housing departments, while other data was gleaned from calls received from members of the community.

The data received from members of the community was not sifted or 'cleaned', with the result that one incident might have involved 10 or 20 calls by different residents. Despite the fact that there was often duplication of calls, it is also widely known that some groups of residents are more active and vocal than others. Anti-Social Behaviour Units, however, tend to use calls rather than incidents as their point of reference in deciding on interventions and the formation of policy. Because calls rather than incidents were used it was very difficult to assess the clear-up rate and effectiveness of different interventions. It is, however, almost certainly the case that 'hard-to-reach', marginalised and transient groups, who are predictably those most likely to be victims of anti-social behaviour, are also those less likely to report incidents.

None of the anti-social behaviour officers in the three boroughs was very clear about the type of data they required to develop anything resembling a problem-solving or strategic approach to anti-social behaviour. Instead, they relied uncritically on whatever datasets were available and drew on whatever forms of data on anti-social behaviour were most readily available from the data analysts. The data analysts, for their part, tended to supply the data that were the easiest to access, despite any limitations they might have. In one borough, responses to anti-social behaviour were decided on by anti-social behaviour officers walking around the borough and talking to local residents. While this indicated a commendable desire to keep in touch with the experiences of local residents, it hardly provided the basis for developing a rational policy programme.

Since data were being collected on all three boroughs by different agencies using different data systems there was a high likelihood that many incidents were being double or triple counted. Although we did not trace through specific incidents in order to identify how they appeared on the different data systems, there was a very high likelihood that those incidents that cut across the crime, disorder and anti-social behaviour divide were recorded in different ways by different agencies using different data systems. Where this process is pronounced it makes a virtual nonsense of the datasets produced by each borough for its audit.

The problems of definition and the overlapping of categories

Much has been written on the problem of definition in relation to anti-social behaviour. Commentators have repeatedly pointed to the vagueness of the wording of anti-social behaviour legislation and policy programmes and the overlap with the categories of crime and disorder (Burney, 2005; Squires and Stephen, 2005). The Home Office has made a feeble and unconvincing attempt to 'refine' the categories of anti-social behaviour, reducing them from a ragbag of 16 categories to a typology of four general categories:

- misuse of public space
- disregard for community/personal well-being
- acts directed at people, and
- environmental damage (Home Office, 2004).

While this fourfold typology serves to differentiate acts directed at people such as abuse, bullying, intimidation and the like from environmental issues such as graffiti and litter, other offences such as 'harassment of neighbours' and inconvenient/illegal parking that are grouped under 'misuse of public space' could just as easily be grouped under other headings. Indeed the fourfold typology does not provide a level of consistency and clarity that makes better sense of the standard list of the sixteen offences. Whereas the 16 offences are too specific and inflexible, the fourfold typology is too general and imprecise for categorising data, undertaking analysis, or developing interventionist strategies.

While it is the case that the vagueness of the standard definitions of anti-social behaviour makes it difficult to clearly delineate what is meant by anti-social behaviour, the imprecise nature of the definition has the benefit that it can be widely interpreted and, consequently, considerable discretion can be exercised by those agencies that are charged with addressing the issue.

We should note, however, that the problem of definition is not specific to anti-social behaviour. The categories of crime, for example, are no more or less robust than many of the anti-social behaviour categories. The term 'violence', for example, is extremely broad and subject to considerable degrees of interpretation. The same can be said of other categories, such as robbery and theft (Young, 1988; Matthews, 2001). It is just that we have become familiar with these crime categories and attribute to them a sense of solidity and precision that in fact they do not have.

It could be argued that some of the anti-social behaviour categories are more reliable and easier to measure than certain categories of crime. The number of youths 'hanging around', the number of cars abandoned and incidents of graffiti, as well as the number of beggars on the street, can be counted with relative ease. Despite this, even the Respect Task Force and those who carry out research on its behalf have shied away from measuring incidents of anti-social behaviour and claim that 'the scale and impact of anti-social behaviour can only be measured by grouping the perceptions of those whose lives are affected by such behaviour' (Ipsos MORI, 2007). In presenting a review of trends in anti-social behaviour MORI engages in an interesting slippage between 'perceptions' and the 'reality' of anti-social behaviour. It states:

> Much is written about the Perception Gap in relation to crime; i.e. the perception of crime as measured by surveys is much greater than the reality (as measured by official police records). However, when it comes to many of the issues which make up anti-social behaviour, then in the absence of 'official' records, *perceptions are the only measure of reality. Indeed, by definition, this should be the case.* If we are defining anti-social behaviour as 'behaviour which causes or is likely to cause harassment, alarm or distress to one or more persons not in the same household', then the critical measure is that of the negative impact on others. (Ipsos MORI, 2007: 7; emphasis added)

This statement is as extraordinary as it is disingenuous. There is no objective reality and the type of empirical surveys on anti-social behaviour (that MORI have themselves frequently conducted) are apparently redundant. Although 'anti-social behaviour', like 'crime', is a social construction, this does not mean that it has no objectivity.

In our study, however, the main issue that arose in relation to the problem of definition concerned which agency was to take primary responsibility for addressing the issue. Without clear lines of responsibility and accountability there is a real danger that the issue falls between a number of stools.

Different perceptions of anti-social behaviour among different agencies

The significance that different agencies attach to different forms of anti-social behaviour was found to vary considerably. There were two major divisions in the three boroughs reviewed. The first was between the community safety teams and the housing departments. The other was between what were identified as enforcement agencies on one hand and welfare or caring agencies on the other.

The division between housing departments and community safety teams is a product of a historical shift from identifying anti-social behaviour as a form of activity located mainly in local authority housing estates, involving noisy neighbours and the like, to an increasing focus on the regulation of public space. Indeed, there is a deep division in some boroughs between the housing departments and community safety teams in terms of areas of responsibility, management structures and the forms of anti-social behaviour that are prioritised. In one borough that was visited the housing department and community safety team shared little common ground, exchanged virtually no information, used different datasets and worked in completely different buildings.

The split between housing departments and community safety teams is reflected in the schism that runs through many partnerships, and divides anti-social behaviour between that which occurs in public spaces (streets, parks and so on) and that which takes place in 'private' spaces such as housing estates.

There is also a pronounced difference in the attitudes towards anti-social behaviour among youth services, social services and education departments on one hand and the police on the other. In general, the former group argues for predominantly welfare responses to people in trouble and objects to the 'criminalisation' by the police of certain activities. Although each borough formally signed up to a 'partnership approach' and inter-agency working, the partnerships tended to gravitate towards a 'stick and carrot' approach that satisfied neither the welfarists nor the police. The police often expressed frustration at what they saw as 'soft' policies of the welfarists, while these groups complained of the 'heavy-handed and insensitive' ways in which the police and anti-social behaviour officers responded to what were seen as generally low-level incidents perpetrated by young, disadvantaged and marginalised groups (see Matthews et al, 2007).

Problems of formulating interventionist strategies

The lack of accurate and reliable data, as well as the difficulties in partnership working, created problems in developing effective interventionist policies. Consequently, many of the policies that were developed in the three boroughs were reactive. Alternatively, they were easily swayed by political imperatives and priorities. Because each borough lacked a robust and objective dataset that could form the basis of a rational policy programme, issues that were highlighted by the media, the Home Office or local politicians could all too easily change the direction of policy. Consequently, policy programmes were rarely sustained or consistent. Although routine procedures were established for dealing with things such as litter, graffiti and abandoned cars, policies on most other forms of anti-social behaviour varied immensely over time, with issues that were priorities at one time moving down the agenda at other times, irrespective of the objective prevalence of the issue.

Responses in each of the boroughs were therefore inconsistent and patchy. For many issues, there was a lack of clear strategy or tactics, and instead policies were proposed because they fitted with the general council objectives and priorities or because they were seen to be politically correct. Thus, forms of anti-social behaviour that were known to have a relatively low number of victims or offenders in the borough were given priority whether or not they reflected the real concerns of residents.

Because interventions were largely reactive, inconsistent, patchy and based on 'feel-good' factors, the impact was often short term. There was little consideration of the causes of anti-social behaviour in each of the boroughs and the focus was mainly on achieving government targets or realising local government priorities. Potential central government funding was always a consideration and, while there were some attempts to respond to local concerns, reference to actual or potential funding possibilities was a significant element in the discursive exchanges between practitioners.

Limited use of anti-social behaviour sanctions

Over the past few years, an impressive array of sanctions has been developed to deal with anti-social behaviour, including Acceptable Behaviour Contracts/Agreements (ABCs/ABAs), Anti-Social Behaviour Orders, Parenting Orders, Housing Injunctions, Fixed Penalty Notices, Penalty Notices for Disorder, Closure Orders (crack houses), Dispersal

Orders, Demoted Tenancies, Individual Support Orders (ISOs), as well as the introduction of special powers for tackling witness intimidation and drug-related civil orders to attach to ASBOs.

In the boroughs we visited in the course of our research, it was apparent that the development of the various sanctions available was uneven and very selective. As the recent report by the Youth Justice Board has indicated, the use of sanctions tended to be more a function of the attitudes and preferences of the agencies involved rather than tailored to the specific situation or context of the offenders involved (Solanki et al, 2006).

In the three boroughs, there were found to be considerable variations in the forms of anti-social behaviour that were targeted and in the sanctions used. In one borough, sanctions were developed against street prostitutes, while in other boroughs such sanctions were felt to be inappropriate for this group (see Sagar, 2007, and see the discussion by Phoenix in Chapter Sixteen in this volume). Aggressive and persistent beggars were found to be dealt with in differing ways in the three boroughs, with two boroughs using a combination of ASBOs and Dispersal Orders, while in another they were simply moved on by the police and neighbourhood wardens.

The available range of sanctions, however, was not fully deployed in the three boroughs. Although ABCs and ASBOs were becoming more widely used, with two boroughs having issued 17 and 20 ASBOs respectively, the third borough had issued only eight ASBOs. One borough had issued ten Dispersal Orders, while the other two had issued none and one. Similarly, one borough had issued eight times as many Parenting Orders as the other two boroughs together had issued over the previous 12-month period (see Table 4.1)

It was also the case that there were considerable perceived variations in the level and types of anti-social behaviour in the different boroughs, however these incidents were recorded. Consequently, the types of sanctions used varied greatly, and because different agencies often had a different view on the seriousness and impact of different forms of anti-social behaviour, different approaches were often recommended.

The lack of clear strategy, together with staff turnover and long-term absences, in one borough, created problems of deploying and implementing sanctions. Certain agencies were criticised within the three boroughs for not 'signing up' to the partnership approach and did not regularly attend meetings or engage in the types of intervention that were recommended. Although continued reference was made to section 17 of the 1998 Crime and Disorder Act (which established a statutory duty upon local agencies to work in partnership to tackle

Table 4.1 Number of anti-social behaviour sanctions used in each borough, 31 March 2005 to 1 April 2006

ASB sanctions	Borough 1	Borough 2	Borough 3
ASBOs	17	8	20
Crack house closures	6	18[1]	4
Dispersal Orders	1	0	10
Evictions	5	0	6
Injunctions	10	3	3
Parenting Orders	40	3	2
Curfews	6	0	23
Supervision Orders	42	0	45
ABCs/ABAs	94	188	36
ISOs	2	Not available	0
YISP	40	200[2]	100[3]
ISSP	40	Not available	Not available

Notes:

[1] The term used in Borough 2 is 'drugs warrants' rather than 'crack house closures'.
[2] The figure represents referrals from only seven wards funded for the YISP programme.
[3] This figure includes those who have received an 'onset', which is an assessment used for those not in the criminal justice system (normally 8- to 13-year-olds).

crime and disorder issues), key agencies were conspicuously absent from meetings concerned with addressing anti-social behaviour.

The major deficiency, however, was the very low level of monitoring and evaluation of anti-social behaviour sanctions. In one borough there was virtually no evaluation of interventions and in the other two the level of monitoring and evaluation was poor. In many cases, interventions were deemed to have worked if the particular issue that they related to decreased, although, in the majority of cases, the causal links were never examined. If, following the deployment of certain sanctions, such as ABCs or ASBOs, the level of anti-social behaviour increased in the areas where they were issued, this was not seen as a sign of failure but often provided the rationale for even greater or more extensive use of these measures. The combination of a lack of adequate data, the limitations of data analysis and the minimal level of monitoring and evaluation meant that it was almost impossible to identify 'what worked' let alone 'why it worked'.

There were, no doubt, some interventions that had some impact. One borough had used Dispersal Orders to address anti-social behaviour around train stations, which was generally considered to be successful. Another borough introduced an alcohol ban in the town centre that was enforced by the police with support from pub landlords and off-licence managers, which appeared to reduce the problems of street drinking in the area, particularly by underage youths, although there was no examination of displacement.

However, the lack of monitoring and evaluation at the local level reflected the lack of monitoring and evaluation of anti-social measures by the Home Office. The Home Office has not focused on the extent to which different local areas are using different interventions, with the exception of ASBOs and Dispersal Orders, although there is some evidence that local Crime and Disorder Reduction Partnerships (CDRPs) are making increased use of the sanctions available. The National Audit Office, in its review of anti-social behaviour, concluded that:

> The absence of formal evaluation by the Home Office and the impact of providing support services in conjunction with interventions prevents local areas targeting interventions in the most efficient way to achieve the best outcome for the least cost. (National Audit Office, 2006: 5)

Whether the responsibility for evaluating interventions designed to reduce anti-social behaviour is primarily the responsibility of the Home Office or of local CDRPs is a moot point. What is clear, however, is that there is little clear idea of what works and, more importantly, why and how it works. The limited evaluation of different measures, however, becomes even more significant when we recognise that measures to reduce anti-social behaviour are often used in combination with and, in some cases, overlap with criminal sanctions.

Lack of community involvement

The relationship between the CDRP and the local communities in the three boroughs examined was found to be, at best, patchy. Although reference was frequently made to 'community engagement', such engagement was often token and short-lived. An event was organised in one borough, for example, at which members of the community were invited to participate in a discussion on crime and anti-social behaviour – but no one turned up. This was mainly because the event was poorly organised and local residents were not properly informed. It may also be the case that members of the community are less concerned about anti-social behaviour than we are led to believe. In another borough, several anti-social behaviour community panels were organised in four different areas. In all, 20,000 leaflets and letters were sent out and advertisements were placed in the local press. An average of 25 people turned up to each event.

There was also evidence that anti-social behaviour coordinators were preoccupied with achieving set targets, organising presentations to the CDRP (designed to show how well they were doing) and writing strategy documents (although they had very little understanding of 'what worked' on which to base a strategy). There was also a prevailing sense in which the practitioners implied that *they* knew what the 'real' problems were and, informally, members of the partnerships expressed disparaging remarks about local 'busybodies' and those members of the community who persistently complained about incidents that the practitioners felt were trivial.

At the same time, members of the community in the three areas had high expectations of the local authorities to combat anti-social behaviour, and were very critical of what they saw as the limited effectiveness of different interventions. Local and national media campaigns had no doubt increased their expectations and they often expressed frustration at what they saw as the inability of the local authority to address these issues and improve their quality of life. Residents clearly expected a response to their anti-social behaviour concerns but they frequently considered interventions to be too slow, inadequate or misdirected. One fairly typical comment by a resident from one of the boroughs claimed:

> We suffer in the long term. The council response is far too slow, inefficient and not direct enough. The residents are left in 'limbo' and sometimes we feel we have to take the law into our own hands. The Council are supposed to be given all these new powers, but they are scared of their own shadow. They won't do anything. They keep sending letters saying 'we'll do this, we'll do that' but they never act on it.

Residents were critical of what they saw as uncoordinated, short-term interventions. They reported that they were 'bored and tired' of receiving strategy newsletters. There were complaints about the anti-social behaviour 'hotlines' that simply recorded messages without necessarily triggering an intervention. Some residents described how they resorted to using the 999 emergency number in order to get a response to anti-social behaviour, and even then they reported long delays or limited police action. One resident put it thus:

> We had a lot of hassle from people on the estate, they vandalised our car, we called the police, and one time we called there were about 16 kids outside, and they didn't come. These people were threatening my son and I called the police. They didn't come. About an hour later, the police car drives into the car park, and leaves. They don't come to my door and ask, 'Are you ok?'. Nothing. I have got no confidence in the police.

Conclusion

It is evident, when we 'drill down' into the workings of local partnerships that, there is a considerable gap between the 'rhetoric' of government-led anti-social behaviour campaigns and their actual interpretation and implementation. The major problem with these campaigns is the quality of the data on which they are mobilised, coupled with a lack of analysis and evaluation.

Policies do not generally reflect objective problems, because it is far from clear exactly what the problems are, and there is little understanding of 'what works'. There are also issues about the management and sharing of the data that is available, with all its limitations. The introduction of new 'hotlines' and single non-emergency numbers will predictably compound rather than solve the problems of data gathering.

In place of a rigorous and detailed understanding of anti-social behaviour there is a great deal of creative accounting taking place, with many of those involved making exaggerated and unfounded claims about 'success'. Where 'success' in whatever form can be reasonably claimed to have occurred, we do not know whether it could have been better achieved in other ways and at less personal and economic cost. As the machinery of anti-social behaviour grows in scale it is becoming evident that this is not the smooth-running, efficient and effective machine that it is often presented as being.

Notes
[1] This research was funded by the Government Office for London.
[2] Call and Dispatch Management Information System (CADMIS); Crime Reporting Information System (CRIS). FLARE and iQuanta are not acronyms.

References

Burney, E. (2005) *Making people behave: Anti-social behaviour politics and policy*, Cullompton: Willan Publishing.

Home Office (2004) *Defining and measuring anti-social behaviour*, London: Home Office.

Home Office (2007) 'Forty areas appointed to lead the respect programme', Press release, 22 January, (http://press.homeoffice.gov.uk/).

Hope, T. (1999) 'Crime, community and inequality: the rise of disorder in British public policy', Inaugural professorial lecture, University of Keele, October.

Ipsos MORI (2007) *Anti-social behaviour: People, place and perception*, London: Ipsos MORI.

Kelling, G. (2001) 'Broken windows and the culture wars: a response to selected critiques', in R. Matthews and J. Pitts (eds), *Crime, disorder and community safety*, London: Routledge.

Matthews, R. (1992) 'Replacing broken windows', in R. Matthews and J. Young (eds), *Issues in realist criminology*, London: Sage.

Matthews, R. (2001) *Armed robbery*, Cullompton: Willan Publishing.

Matthews, R., Easton, H., Briggs, D. and Pease, K. (2007) *Assessing the use and impact of Anti-Social Behaviour Orders*, Bristol: The Policy Press.

National Audit Office (2006) *Tackling anti-social behaviour*, London: The Stationery Office.

Sagar, T. (2007) 'Tackling on-street sex work: Anti-Social Behaviour Orders, sex workers and inclusive inter-agency initiatives', *Criminology and Criminal Justice*, vol 7, pp 153–68.

Solanki, A., Bateman, T., Boswell, G. and Hill, E. (2006) *Anti-Social Behaviour Orders*, London: Youth Justice Board.

Squires, P. and Stephen, D. (2005) *Rougher justice: Anti-social behaviour and young people*, Cullompton: Willan Publishing.

Wilson, J. and Kelling, G. (1982) 'Broken windows: the police and neighbourhood safety', *Atlantic Monthly*, March, pp 29–38.

Young, J. (1988) 'Risks of crime and fear of crime: A realist critique of survey-based assumptions', in M. McGuire and J. Pointing (eds), *Victims of crime*, Milton Keynes: Open University Press.

Part Two
Anti-social behaviour management:
emerging issues

Governing through localism, contract and community: evidence from anti-social behaviour strategies in Scotland

Rionach Casey and John Flint

Introduction

The Scottish Executive's anti-social behaviour strategy is primarily being delivered at the local authority level, with a particular emphasis on the worst-affected neighbourhoods (Scottish Executive, 2003). The 2004 Anti-social Behaviour (Scotland) Act required each local authority and police chief constable to prepare and implement an anti-social behaviour strategy within their area, supported by additional Scottish Executive funding.

This chapter explores how forms of accountability, partnership and contract play out within anti-social behaviour strategies. Two key dimensions are examined: the dual and simultaneous processes of centralisation and localism within governance frameworks; and the contested concepts of citizenship and responsibility for governing anti-social behaviour, mediated by the interface between formal and informal mechanisms of social control. The chapter concludes by arguing that the ambiguities of roles, the limited scales of intervention and the resistance of actors create a disjunction between strategy rationales and actual delivery of policies on the ground.

The chapter is based on the findings of two research studies: a Scottish Executive-funded assessment of the impact of anti-social behaviour strategies at the neighbourhood level in four Scottish local authorities (Edinburgh, Fife, North Lanarkshire and the Scottish Borders); and an evaluation of the Neighbour Relations policy and practice of the Glasgow Housing Association, which manages 75,000 homes in the city. (For the full findings from these studies and a detailed account of the research methodologies, see Flint et al, 2007a, 2007b).

Multi-level governance, neighbourhood and community

Policy programmes within Scotland are characterised by mechanisms of multi-level governance, through which attempts are made to generate a cohesive government response to social problems at national and local scales (Kearns and Forrest, 2000). These contemporary forms of multi-level governance are based on networks and nodes of multi-agency partnerships, involving state and non-state actors delivering interventions at the local level within a national legislative, regulatory and funding framework. This framework cedes some powers and responsibilities to local agencies while locking them into increasingly transparent forms of accountability, audit and performance measurement, including a revitalised concept of professional responsibility in which front-line officers and organisations are subject to visible accountability from both central government and local citizens (Faulkner, 2003; Scottish Executive, 2005a). This is manifested through the use of contract as a mechanism for regulating partnership relationships between actors. The use of contractual forms of governance is evident in crime and anti-social behaviour policy and practice, ranging from outcome agreements between national government and local strategic partnerships, the use of formal protocols between local organisations and the development of Acceptable Behaviour Contracts and Good Neighbour Agreements between individual citizens and local agencies (Crawford, 2003; Flint, 2006a).

Local neighbourhoods have been given increasing prominence within multi-level governance structures and are identified as the site within which policy interventions will be targeted and delivered, based on a new 'localism'. This involves the devolution and decentralisation of powers, responsibilities and resources to front-line agency officers and neighbourhood-based offices and partnerships, epitomised in the concept of neighbourhood management (Kearns and Forrest, 2000; Flint, 2006a). This focus on neighbourhoods is strongly linked to the prominence of notions of 'community' within contemporary rationales of governance as providing both the arena and mechanics of government. In other words, the social processes within local neighbourhoods, civic engagement and communal interaction arising within 'communities' are to be harnessed to deliver policy objectives, manifested in the attempts to build *social capital* and *collective efficacy* within neighbourhoods as a response to crime and anti-social behaviour (Amin, 2002; Faulkner, 2003; Flint, 2006a). This conceptualisation has resulted in the needs of 'communities' being prioritised over those of individual perpetrators of anti-social behaviour, while local residents are given increasing powers *and* responsibilities to actively engage in the governance of anti-social behaviour. Thus, the Scottish Executive anti-social behaviour strategy is aimed at 'Putting our communities first' and argues that 'communities have a responsibility for tackling anti-social behaviour' and 'must be involved in the solutions' (Scottish Executive, 2003: 2–7).

However, these forms of multi-level governance are problematic (Kearns and Forrest, 2000; Crawford, 2006). As Stenson (2005) describes, there are continual struggles within and between state and non-state agencies for sovereign control over populations and territories, with agency officers and citizens having their own agendas for governance and their own forms of knowledge and expertise. Central policies and commands are therefore tempered by local differences in community governance, resulting in a gap between policy and implementation. Anti-social behaviour policy and practice is characterised by such plurality and contradictions (Hughes, 2006). Recent studies of neighbourhood anti-social behaviour strategies have revealed the complexities and challenges facing multi-agency partnership interventions, and the disjunctions and instabilities between strategic rationales and aims and the reality of interventions in different localities (Prior et al, 2005; Hughes, 2006). The discontinuities between strategy and front-line delivery arise from the 'revisions, resistances and refusals' of agency officers and residents to 'play their allotted role in governmental processes' (Prior, 2007: 30–1).

Innes and Jones (2006) provide a useful analytical framework for conceptualising how anti-social behaviour, governmental interventions and residents' perceptions shape neighbourhood change. They develop a typology of *risk*, *resilience* and *recovery* factors to describe dimensions of neighbourhood dynamics. Innes and Jones describe how *risk* factors (comprising both actual and perceived anti-social behaviour) generate insecurity, but also argue that these risks may be ameliorated by *resilience* factors within neighbourhoods, including the presence of *collective efficacy*. This refers to the ability of local communities to engage in forms of social control that challenge anti-social behaviour. *Recovery* factors lead to enhanced security and longer-term sustainable improvements in local neighbourhood dynamics, environments and material circumstances. Innes and Jones focus in particular on the relationship between formal social control, including the presence of official authority figures such as police officers and wardens, and informal social control (the collective efficacy arising from the daily interactions between residents), and argue that sustainable improvements to neighbourhoods often require interventions aimed at generating both forms of social control. However, the relationship between them is often ambiguous and problematic (Faulkner, 2003; Flint, 2006b; Prior, 2007). We now turn to exploring our research evidence about processes of centralisation and localism within anti-social behaviour strategies in Scotland, followed by a discussion about the relationships between formal and informal social control within local neighbourhoods.

The dual processes of centralisation and localism

The Scottish Executive's national anti-social behaviour strategy epitomises the forms of multi-level governance described above. The strategy is delivered on three geographical levels: national, local authority and neighbourhood. The Scottish Executive envisages the strategy as primarily being delivered at the local level, based on multi-agency partnerships and empowering front-line officers and residents: 'It is only local agencies, working in a co-ordinated way with local people that can tackle anti-social behaviour effectively' (Scottish Executive, 2004: 3). This neighbourhood-level activity is to be coordinated by local authority-led anti-social behaviour strategies that are responsive to local needs and priorities and 'must take into account differences between communities' (Scottish Executive, 2004: 3). Local authorities are required to identify the particular problems within local communities and to encourage the development of dedicated 'community-based teams with a clear focus upon tackling anti-social behaviour' (Scottish Executive, 2003: 17). This approach suggests considerable autonomy and differentiation between and within local authorities. However, the Scottish Executive also argues that 'action needs to fit with national priorities', based on 'joined up action at the local level within a national framework' (Scottish Executive, 2004: 3). Local authorities are therefore subject to nationally collated performance indicators and new accountability frameworks and outcome agreements that link the additional funding provided to them for tackling anti-social behaviour to Scottish Executive priorities – for example, focusing upon the most deprived neighbourhoods.

Our research identified a number of local-level tensions and policy dilemmas resulting from the dual processes of centralism and localism. These included:

- gaps between policy and implementation
- tensions between local autonomy and holistic and consistent strategic interventions

- different priorities and formalised partnership arrangements
- contested roles and responsibilities
- the distribution of skills and expertise
- targeting versus universal 'reassurance'
- displacement and equity.

Both of our studies confirmed the gap that exists between policy aims and implementation, arising from the different priorities, interpretation and capacity of agencies and officers. A consistent finding was that, while there was an evident consensus and improved partnership working at strategic partnership levels, this was not necessarily replicated on local neighbourhood scales. For example, the Glasgow Housing Association (GHA) has very clear policies and procedures for tackling anti-social behaviour, supported by good practice guidance. However, these are delivered through a devolved network of 63 local housing organisations (LHOs). This resulted in differentiated localised responses to anti-social behaviour, manifested in divergent responses to incidents and contrasting levels of partnership working between LHOs and other agencies. In addition, the numbers of anti-social behaviour cases referred by LHOs to the central GHA Neighbour Relations Team for further action varied considerably, with the rate of referrals not coinciding with the extent of anti-social behaviour in local neighbourhoods. Similarly, local authority anti-social behaviour strategies were being interpreted very differently in the case-study neighbourhoods in our Scottish Executive-funded study. One factor underlying this was the relatively limited awareness of the strategies among practitioners at the neighbourhood level. While increased funding and improved local partnership working were widely reported, this was not usually attributed to improved coordination between local authority- and neighbourhood-level strategies. Indeed, there was considerable confusion about how neighbourhood approaches fitted into wider strategies, exacerbated by the plethora of new initiatives and funding streams.

These decentralised structures often promoted innovation and strong local partnership working. We found evidence in both studies of local agencies taking greater risks in terms of sharing information, working together and implementing new initiatives. For example, in some neighbourhoods, agencies were now able to share information on a weekly basis at the level of individual households and thereby to develop targeted and coordinated responses to micro-level problems. One important consequence of the new anti-social behaviour strategies did appear to be a 'green light' being given for local practitioners to become more flexible in entering partnership approaches with other local organisations. However, this also created challenges for ensuring holistic and consistent interventions across local authority areas. In other words, despite attempts to ensure greater consistency in the governance of anti-social behaviour, centralised strategy teams were unable to enforce it. Rather, central policies and processes were subject to local interpretation that ranged from competing definitions of what constituted anti-social behaviour to divergent views about when action was appropriate and what interventions should be used. The decentralisation of governance also made it difficult to ensure that local actions were linked into wider strategic objectives operating at the local authority or city level. Attempts to ensure holistic approaches to addressing anti-social behaviour that include prevention, early intervention, enforcement and support depend on local agencies being connected to the networks that facilitate this; for example, making referrals to mediation, addiction, victim support or social work services. In reality, the extent to which local agencies use these services varies considerably.

However, this variation is also the manifestation of more substantial differences in the priorities of different organisations within multi-level governance structures. For example, the immediate imperative for local neighbourhood management partnerships or individual LHOs is to resolve anti-social behaviour within their own locality, including the use of enforcement actions such as eviction or restricted allocation policies. However, for the GHA or local authorities, the priority is to reduce *overall* levels of anti-social behaviour in their areas, rather than merely to shift its geography, which suggests a priority on prevention and sustainable solutions. Our research found that, while prevention, early intervention and support for perpetrators were increasingly the focus of strategic-level interventions, the majority of neighbourhood-level interventions have, to date, been enforcement based. In part, this reflects the emphasis on enforcement that characterised earlier manifestations of national anti-social behaviour strategies. However, it also highlights the difficulties that front-line officers have in developing time-consuming partnership arrangements and expanding the range of partners, for instance to include local youth organisations that are often dependent on volunteers. Furthermore, while enhanced partnership working and a 'uniform' approach to tackling anti-social behaviour may be desirable at the strategic level, it is precisely the perceived difference between the roles and priorities of local agencies that often underpins their legitimacy and therefore effectiveness at the neighbourhood level. For example, the fact that neighbourhood wardens are not the police, or that youth projects do not engage in enforcement action, enables them to engage effectively with particular groups within communities. There is therefore a challenge in facilitating the continuing differentiation of front-line services within more coordinated strategies.

Our research found evidence of increasingly formalised partnership arrangements, including protocols for information exchange and joint outcome agreements. This had clearly resulted in enhanced information sharing and improved intelligence, enabling more refined and targeted interventions and also ensuring that data protection requirements were adhered to. However, we also found that neighbourhood-level information sharing was often not explicitly linked into these more formalised structures. Some practitioners also suggested that the increased contractualisation, formalisation and accountability governing relations between agencies such as the police and local authorities risked 'commercialising' processes of information exchange and the deployment of resources that might undermine developing informal networks at the neighbourhood level.

Both our studies supported the arguments of Stenson (2005) about contested roles and responsibilities for tackling anti-social behaviour. Again, while at the strategic level there was acceptance and 'buy-in' from agencies about their involvement in anti-social behaviour strategies, this was not replicated consistently at the neighbourhood level, where there were ongoing disputes between police, housing and social work officers about what forms of anti-social or criminal behaviour they were respectively responsible for resolving. One of the main features of anti-social behaviour strategies in Scotland has been the development of centralised, dedicated anti-social behaviour units that are staffed by officers from a range of professional backgrounds and deal with the most serious cases, including those involving legal action. All four of our case-study local authorities and the GHA had introduced these units. It was evident that these units had become very important and highly regarded resources within their localities. However, this centralisation of expertise and responsibility had implications for the attempts to develop localised capacity to tackle anti-social behaviour. While the concentration and coordination of expertise in these units was welcomed and enabled team officers to become increasingly effective in resolving serious cases, there was widespread concern that this was resulting in the units replacing, rather than complementing, skills, action and responsibilities at the neighbourhood level. For example, GHA's Neighbour Relations Team argued that LHOs should retain primary responsibility for resolving all but the most serious cases. The danger is that a dynamic develops whereby front-line officers cede responsibility to centralised units. This results in these units being unable to cope with the levels of demand and reduces further the skills and knowledge among front-line officers, who consequently refer even more cases to the centralised units. A major challenge within anti-social behaviour strategies is therefore to ensure that knowledge and expertise, including awareness of both enforcement and support mechanisms, is distributed adequately across and within neighbourhood teams. However, the generic workload of front-line officers, rapid staff turnover and the geographical variations in anti-social behaviour caseloads between individual officers makes this dissemination of capacity very problematic.

The constraints on local actors within multi-level governance structures, noted above, are evident in anti-social behaviour strategies. Local authorities are required to target the worst-affected and most deprived neighbourhoods and to link funding, for example for community wardens, to interventions within defined localities. This targeting is justifiable on the grounds of both effectiveness and equality, as is the increasing use of 'hot spot' interventions that involve short-term, intensive multi-agency interventions in areas experiencing particularly severe forms of anti-social behaviour. However, local authorities and other agencies have to balance this targeting with managing the political imperatives to provide reassurance to all communities through, for example, wardens and policing. They also need to be able to be flexible and responsive to change, and this explains why a range of interventions, including wardens, community police officers, environmental clean-up squads and CCTV units, are being deployed on a mobile and reactive basis, rather than being tied to specific neighbourhoods.

Decentralised neighbourhood management structures, as this research has found, lead to considerable variation in policy interpretation, agency practice and intervention outcomes, often linked to considerable resources being allocated to some localities. We found robust evidence that this had led to significant improvements in some of the worst-affected neighbourhoods. However, there is also evidence that some of these successes displace problems elsewhere, and that the levels of resources deployed to achieve these localised improvements are not replicable or sustainable for all neighbourhoods experiencing serious anti-social behaviour problems. Processes of localism create, as well as ameliorate, inequalities between communities, while centralised strategic partnerships find it increasingly difficult to impose more consistent and equitable anti-social behaviour outcomes across neighbourhoods.

Defining the responsibilities of citizenship: formal and informal social control

Our research found evidence of significant improvements in agency responses to anti-social behaviour, arising from more effective deployment of available mechanisms and enhanced partnership working, resulting in improved intelligence, targeting and holistic interventions at individual household and neighbourhood levels. However, there was considerable disparity between perceptions of improvement reported by agency officers and the views of local residents. The majority of agency officers believed that anti-social behaviour had stabilised and that some of the most serious forms of anti-social behaviour had reduced in the last two years. In sharp contrast, a significant proportion of residents perceived that most forms of anti-social behaviour continued to be common or very common. Only a minority of residents were of the opinion that anti-social behaviour had decreased and the performance of local agencies had improved over the last 12 months, although where improvements were identified, these did relate to the most prevalent forms of anti-social behaviour in the case-study neighbourhoods.

Residents' knowledge of the tools being deployed to tackle anti-social behaviour varied widely. Where residents were aware of initiatives such as wardens, concierges and environmental hit squads, their assessment was usually very positive. Similarly, awareness of a heightened police presence was important in providing reassurance and symbolising local agencies' willingness to address anti-social behaviour, and in facilitating residents' engagement with local agencies. Community police officers were particularly positively perceived, especially when they operated in an area for a significant period of time, enabling them to be on first-name terms with residents. However, in all of our research neighbourhoods, there were residents who were entirely unaware of such measures. There was also widespread uncertainty among residents about how they could engage in active citizenship: about what constituted an 'appropriate' complaint; to whom they should report; what telephone numbers they should use; and the procedures and actions that would follow. This lack of awareness extended to measures such as Anti-Social Behaviour Orders (ASBOs), with residents being unsure which individuals were subject to them, the conditions attached to the orders and to whom alleged breaches should be reported. The official presence of additional police on the streets also became normalised and there was a widespread feeling among residents that there needed to be yet more police in order to effectively tackle the scale of the problem. In addition, there was continued frustration regarding police response times and in particular the lack of a police presence in the evenings and at weekends, when anti-social behaviour was perceived to occur most frequently.

The increased presence of official agencies in tackling anti-social behaviour raises an issue about the 'contract' to be struck between the responsibilities of local agencies and the citizenship responsibilities of residents. It is uncertain whether the increased presence of police, wardens and concierges supplements the role of local residents, or merely replaces resident engagement, resulting in residents 'abdicating' responsibility to 'officialdom' and hence losing any sense of informal social control over, or responsibility for, anti-social behaviour in their neighbourhood. This appeared to be particularly true of responses to the behaviour of young people, as articulated by one youth worker:

> What happens is that adults retreat behind their closed doors
> and then complain about the kids outside kicking a ball. The
> police then arrive with flashing blue lights and then other
> adults see this and think there are frequent serious incidents
> so they better not risk informally challenging kids.

The idea that anti-social behaviour is 'someone else's responsibility' may also be a factor in the under-reporting of such incidents to official agencies, which was a major issue in the two studies, although reporting levels were increasing. Fewer than a third of residents in the Scottish Executive study reported incidences of anti-social behaviour that they had experienced, while a third of GHA tenants did not report a neighbour relations incident directly affecting them. There were four factors underlying this under-reporting problem. The first was the impression among residents that there was no point in reporting problems because 'nothing could be done' to address the offending behaviour. Second, there was concern that reporting an incident would exacerbate the problem and 'make things even worse'. Third, there was a widespread fear of retaliation arising from either direct confrontation with alleged perpetrators or reporting incidents. Fourth, there was a deep-rooted culture of 'keeping yourself to yourself', that in some cases was linked to distrust of and non-cooperation with the police. The reasons for under-reporting were also, in some cases, linked to poor police (and other agencies') practices, which did not instil confidence that residents' complaints would be sensitively handled – for example, making overt visits to complainants and immediate follow-up visits to alleged perpetrators. In a cyclical process, under-reporting or unwillingness to act as a witness prevents agencies gathering sufficient evidence to take action, which consequently further reduces residents' proclivity to engage with officialdom.

When residents did make an official complaint, there was no clear pattern in levels of satisfaction or dissatisfaction between different agencies. A satisfactory response was more likely when complaints were handled quickly and sympathetically and when victims and witnesses were kept informed of developments. However, although support for victims and witnesses are areas of growing priority for the agencies concerned, our research points to the generally poor experiences of, and lack of initial support to, those who proceed to make a complaint. We found that only a minority of victims and witnesses were offered any advice and support (usually in the form of contact numbers), advice on how to avoid the alleged perpetrators, and mediation and victim support services. The lack of support to victims and witnesses was compounded by the lack of ongoing contact with agencies and lack of information regarding their particular complaints. Only half of the victims and witnesses we interviewed reported being kept informed of further actions and developments, and this was a source of considerable frustration. There are clear implications here for the reporting of anti-social behaviour and addressing the culture of under-reporting. Our research points to the need for close contact with residents who have made a complaint, better information about support services and more robust referrals processes at a local level, including to mediation and victim support services.

Innes and Jones' (2006) study, which points to the important relationship between informal and formal social control mechanisms in neighbourhood security, resonates with the research reported in this chapter. In particular, it provides evidence that communities in neighbourhoods perceived to be 'at risk' need the support of agencies such as the police in developing a collective efficacy to address anti-social behaviour. Key to this is the idea of 'voice', which is defined as the ability and capacity to articulate a community's self-defined needs, and to have those listened to and taken seriously by those in authority (Innes and Jones, 2006: 41). They assert that the police and other agencies of formal social control are not the primary guarantors of neighbourhood security, but that they can influence and structure the capacity for informal social control that resides within communities (Innes and Jones, 2006: 49). In terms of our own research, then, it is clear that the police and other agencies of social control need to think about how their interventions can have a positive impact on the capacity of local communities to practise formal and informal social control over the longer term. Empowering residents individually through facilitating and supporting individuals to report incidents, and collectively through community mediation techniques and community consultation, as used in 'hot spot' initiatives in some of our study areas, to identify residents' knowledge and priorities, are important mechanisms here. It is also essential to recognise that agency interventions do not occur in a social vacuum, but rather compete for legitimacy and dominance with other forms of power and informal social control regimes within neighbourhoods (Stenson, 2005), which results in resistance or non-engagement with local anti-social behaviour strategies.

Conclusions

The anti-social behaviour strategies of the Scottish Executive, Scottish local authorities and the Glasgow Housing Association epitomise the rationales, processes and dilemmas of contemporary multi-level networked governance. Our research found that, while these strategies have delivered improved agency performance and some localised reductions in anti-social behaviour, there is a gap between policy aims and implementation. This arises from the tensions between centralisation and localism, contested roles and responsibilities between actors and the deployment of limited resources to tackle complex and multi-factored problems. It is evident that effective formal social control mechanisms, including policing and the use of ASBOs, are an important component of anti-social behaviour strategies, but that their impact in terms of providing reassurance is limited. However, our research suggests that the extent to which increasing the local responsibilities and 'powers' of practitioners and residents can deliver reductions in anti-social behaviour (as argued by Innes and Jones, 2006, and Faulkner, 2003) is also limited. We would argue, rather, that three main factors are important.

First, there is a need for some stability within anti-social behaviour strategies, including assured longer-term funding and a cessation of continual new legislation, directives and partnership restructuring. This would enable strategies to bed in, to become more accessible and understood by practitioners and residents, and their longer-term effectiveness to be properly evaluated.

Second, there is a need for reframing how resident empowerment is conceptualised within anti-social behaviour strategies. This includes defining what residents' roles and the expectations of citizenship should be, underpinned by more accurate and comprehensive information about the capacities, but also limitations, of available services. It also requires a more nuanced empowerment of particular groups, such as young people, within local communities, which will necessitate challenging tolerance levels among other sections of the community and encouraging more informal interaction rather than reliance on formal agencies to resolve lower-level disputes and tensions.

Third, there is a need for a more explicit account within policy narratives of the priorities and trade-offs inherent in the governance of anti-social behaviour. This includes recognising the tensions between centralising and localising processes, rather than searching for a seamless and synergy-generating relationship. It also requires a debate about the extent of the ambitions of government and active citizenship. If the holistic and multifaceted interventions that are required to effectively tackle anti-social behaviour (Millie et al, 2005) are to be delivered in all of the neighbourhoods experiencing serious problems, then this will require significant and sustained additional resources and the addressing of the wider economic and social forces impacting on deprived neighbourhoods.

References

Amin, A. (2005) 'Local community on trial', *Economy and Society*, vol 34, no 4, pp 612–33.

Crawford, A. (2003) '"Contractual governance" of deviant behaviour', *Journal of Law and Society*, vol 30, no 4, pp 479–505.

Crawford, A. (2006) 'Networked governance and the post-regulatory state? Steering, rowing and anchoring the provision of policing and security', *Theoretical Criminology*, vol 10, no 4, pp 449–79.

Faulkner, D. (2003) 'Taking citizenship seriously: social capital and criminal justice in a changing world', *Criminal Justice*, vol 3, no 3, pp 287–315.

Flint, J. (2006a) 'Active responsible citizens? Changing neighbourhoods, changing order', in A. Dearling, T. Newburn and P. Sommerville (eds), *Supporting safer communities: Housing, crime and neighbourhoods*, Coventry: Chartered Institute of Housing, pp 29–44.

Flint, J. (2006b) 'Citizen empowerment strategies and anti-social behaviour policy in the UK', *Géographie, Economie et Société*, vol 8, no 1, pp 17–36.

Flint, J., Casey, R., Davidson, E., Pawson, H. and McCoulough, E. (2007a) *Tackling anti-social behaviour in Glasgow: An evaluation of policy and practice in the Glasgow Housing Association*, Glasgow: Glasgow Housing Association (available at: http://www.gha.org.uk).

Flint, J., Green, S., Hunter, C., Nixon, J., Parr, S., Manning, J., Wilson, I., Pawson, H., Davidson, E. and Sanderson, D. (2007b) *Evaluation of the implementation and impact of local anti-social behaviour strategies at the neighbourhood level*, Edinburgh: Scottish Executive.

Hughes, G. (2006) *The politics of crime and community*, London: Sage.

Innes, M. and Jones, V. (2006) *Neighbourhood security and urban change: Risk, resilience and recovery*, York: Joseph Rowntree Foundation.

Kearns, A. and Forrest, R. (2000) 'Social cohesion and multilevel governance', *Urban Studies*, vol 37, nos 5/6, pp 995–1017.

Millie, A., Jacobson, J., McDonald, E. and Hough, M. (2005) *Anti-social behaviour strategies: Finding a balance*, York: Joseph Rowntree Foundation.

Prior, D. (2007) *Continuities and discontinuities in governing anti-social behaviour*, Birmingham: University of Birmingham.

Prior, D., Farrow, K., Spalek, B. and Barnes, M. (2005) *Anti-social behaviour and civil renewal: A study of the Hodge Hill district of Birmingham*, Birmingham: University of Birmingham.

Scottish Executive (2003) *Putting our communities first: A strategy for tackling anti-social behaviour*, Edinburgh: Scottish Executive.

Scottish Executive (2004) *Guidance on anti-social behaviour strategies*, Edinburgh: Scottish Executive.

Scottish Executive (2005a) *Guidance on accountability framework and outcome agreements*, Edinburgh: Scottish Executive.

Scottish Executive (2005b) *Standing up to anti-social behaviour: First anniversary report*, Edinburgh: Scottish Executive.

Stenson, K. (2005) 'Sovereignty, biopolitics and the local government of crime in Britain', *Theoretical Criminology*, vol 9, no 3, pp 265–87.

SIX

Anti-social behaviour and minority ethnic populations

David Prior and Basia Spalek

Introduction

Criminal justice issues in relation to 'race' and ethnicity have generated substantial research and policy interest. The experiences of minority ethnic groups as offenders/suspects have been examined and direct, indirect and institutional forms of racism have been explored, particularly in relation to police stop-and-search patterns, court processes (including sentencing) and custody. At the same time, substantial research has been generated in relation to minority ethnic groups and victimisation, in particular their experiences of racist crime. In contrast, the specific issue of anti-social behaviour (ASB) and minority ethnic populations has not attracted much research attention, perhaps due to the traditional focus on criminal, rather than social, justice within accounts of 'race'/ethnicity and crime/victimisation.

Anti-social behaviour, while overlapping with criminal behaviour, widens the lens of criminological research to focus on social harms rather than only on those events defined as criminal by the state. A focus on anti-social behaviour with respect to minority ethnic groups therefore raises a broader question about whether responses to ASB can potentially help to achieve social justice for minority ethnic communities, particularly as these communities experience racist victimisation as a social process rather than a criminal event. Thus, given the government's desire to encourage citizens to 'take a stand' and make use of the ASB powers to tackle unacceptable behaviour in their neighbourhoods and communities, there is a general question about the response of minority ethnic citizens: to what extent are minority ethnic citizens and communities adding their voices to the demands for action to be taken against anti-social elements? More specific questions concern the extent to which the post-1998 ASB policies and powers create opportunities for minority populations by providing further means of addressing forms of racial harassment and abuse, thereby offering significant additional protection to minority ethnic individuals and communities.

However, given that agencies of the criminal justice system have been accused of direct, indirect and institutional forms of racism involving the criminalisation of particular minority ethnic groups, there is the potential for responses to anti-social behaviour to result in the further criminalisation of these groups. This chapter therefore also examines the question whether the post-1998 ASB policies and powers pose a threat to minority populations in enabling people whose behaviours are perceived as 'different' to be labelled anti-social and subjected to further discriminatory interventions: are ASB powers being used disproportionately to regulate and penalise members of minority ethnic groups?

A second group of questions explored in this chapter concerns the ways in which cultural factors (including the occupational/professional cultures of practitioners) influence the construction of the ASB 'problem' itself in relation to minority ethnic populations. Given the open-ended and subjective definition of anti-social behaviour in policy and practice (refer to other contributions, especially by Squires [Introduction and Chapter Twenty], Matthews and Briggs [Chapter Four], and Burney [Chapter Seven], in this volume), it is important to try to understand both how perceptions of ethnicity and faith may influence official approaches to addressing ASB *and* the relevance of, and meanings attached to, the phenomenon of ASB by minority ethnic populations. Do policy makers and practitioners define ASB in different ways according to the ethnicity or faith affiliation of individuals or groups? If so, what is the effect of this? Conversely, do different ethnic or faith minorities hold different conceptions of what constitutes ASB and different expectations of what should be done about it? Other research has shown that cultural factors that may be linked to particular ethnicities can shape and significantly influence the process of victimisation (Spalek, 2004, 2006).

However, both these sets of issues need to be set in a broader analysis of current policy discourse. We therefore begin by briefly considering the key concepts and definitions we shall be using – particularly the ideas of 'race', ethnicity, religion and identity – before discussing the significance of the current 'law and order' policy context in which constructions of and responses to anti-social behaviour in relation to minority ethnic populations need to be understood.

Concepts and definitions and their policy implications

One of our aims in this chapter is to distinguish between, and to assert the separate significance of, concepts of 'race', 'ethnicity' and 'religion'. To the extent that it refers to the social, cultural or behavioural characteristics of individuals and groups deriving from common biological or genetic factors, 'race' is now largely discredited as an acceptable or useful concept, although the Home Office and agencies of the criminal justice system (CJS) continue to use what are essentially racialised categorisations for data collection purposes (Garland et al, 2006). Moreover, 'race' still has substantial currency in everyday popular discourse, most obviously to denote people of different skin colour and other physical characteristics, and in official discourse, where it is often used to denote negative phenomena, in phrases such as 'racial discrimination', 'racism' or 'race hate crimes', or very broad areas of policy or legal concern such as 'race relations' and 'race equality'. Other than when we refer directly to such uses, in this chapter we will use the terms 'ethnicity' and 'ethnic' rather than 'race' or 'racial'. In contrast to these descriptive categories, 'racialisation' refers to a process of social construction whereby people are assigned to a social group defined by alleged biological or cultural characteristics (Webster, 2007), and this is likely to be an important concept in relation to perceptions of ASB.

Ethnicity we take to refer to a form of identity based on a shared body of social and cultural norms, beliefs and practices shaped by a common linguistic, religious, geographical and historical heritage. Religion is therefore one of the factors that contributes to an ethnic identity, but research increasingly shows that 'faith identity' is of major significance in its own right. Religious identification is a more important aspect of self-identity for individuals belonging to minority ethnic groups than for white groups. For example, the 1994 National Survey of Ethnic Minorities revealed that 95% of Muslims, 89% of Hindus and 86% of Sikhs surveyed considered religion to be 'very' or 'fairly' important to the way that they lead their lives, in contrast to 46% of white members of the Church of England and 69% of white Roman Catholics (Modood et al, 1997: 301). According to findings from the Home Office Citizenship Survey in 2001, in contrast to the 17% of white respondents who said that religion was important to their self-identity, 44% of black and 61% of Asian respondents said that religion was important. For Muslims, religion was ranked second, after family, in terms of importance to their self-identity (Home Office, 2003).

The relationship between ethnicity and faith cannot easily be fixed. Different ethnic groups may share the same religion, and for some people, at certain times, religious or faith-based identity may be experienced as more significant than ethnic identity. The legal implications of this have been a contentious issue for British Muslims, in particular, with the creation of new categories of 'racially aggravated offences' under the 1998 Crime and Disorder Act, based on a notion of 'racial group' that specifically excluded religion as a defining feature. This had the effect of providing protection to Sikhs and Jews, who were recognised as distinct 'racial groups', but not to Muslims, who were classed as a religious not a 'racial' group. This anomaly was addressed in the 2001 Anti-Terrorism Crime and Security Act, which introduced a 'religiously aggravated' element to the categorisation of crimes, enabling higher penalties to be imposed on offenders who are motivated by religious hatred. Subsequently, in 2004–05, two thirds of the 34 prosecutions for religiously aggravated crime involved Muslims as victims.

The significance of religion or faith as a factor in understanding criminal motivation is also highlighted by monitoring reports from community groups. For example, the Community Security Trust (CST), which represents the Jewish community on matters of anti-Semitism in the UK, recorded 455 anti-Semitic incidents in 2005, this being the second-highest annual total since the CST started recording incidents in 1984 (CST, 2006: 4). According to the Islamic Human Rights Organisation (IHRO), attacks on Muslims increase during periods of more overt faith-based activity, such as the month of Ramadan (IHRO, 2006). And evidence from the Metropolitan Police revealed a sharp increase in faith-related hate crimes, including verbal abuse and physical assaults, following the 7 July 2005 bombings in London (European Monitoring Centre on Racism and Xenophobia, 2005). The message here is that, in understanding the different forms that anti-social behaviour can take and the reasons why it occurs, it is vital that policy makers and practitioners are aware of the potential for the faith identities of individuals to become the trigger for acts of ASB. This suggests, in turn, that there is indeed a vital role for the ASB legal powers to be used to provide protection to minority groups from harassment based on either ethnic or religious intolerance.

As well as drawing attention to the importance of recognising the distinction between 'ethnicity' and 'faith' as separate bases for social identity (and for attracting the hostility of others), it is necessary to acknowledge the differences that exist within ethnic or faith-based populations. This is particularly important, given the tendency for policy discourse to use simple labels to categorise minority groups:

'blacks', 'Asians', 'Muslims', etc. There is increasing recognition that the populations covered by these labels are far from homogeneous; that 'Asians', for instance, includes people with widely varied national and regional identities and distinct faiths; or that 'Muslims' includes people from quite different parts of the world and quite different traditions of Islam. The wide variety of Muslim groups and the diverse nature of Muslim communities pose particular challenges for strategies of engagement. For example, the voices of Muslim women and youth are likely to be marginalised through conventional consultation processes that target their efforts on 'community leaders'. At the same time, it is important to explore which religious strands within Islam are represented in engagement processes, and what are the ethnicities of Muslim individuals who are participating in engagement processes.[1]

But beyond that, it is also important that policies and those who implement them are sensitive to differences within minority ethnic or religious populations relating to distinctive patterns of family life, the role of women, the significance of social networks and attitudes, and expectations regarding crime and social order. Again, we need to emphasise that because the identification of and response to ASB rests so much upon subjective interpretations of aspects of everyday social interaction, an understanding of – or at least a willingness to engage with – the many factors that can influence such interactions and the meanings attached to them is crucial to the implementation of ASB policy.

Ethnicity in law and order policies

It is also important to look at the wider law and order policy context when examining questions about perceptions of and responses to anti-social behaviour in relation to minority ethnic communities. Two key factors are especially important: responses to ethnic minorities within mainstream crime reduction practices, especially in tactics such as 'stop and search' and the use of prison sentences; and the growth in 'anti-terror' operations specifically targeting minority individuals and groups (FitzGerald and Hale, 2006).

The over-representation of black people in prison, particularly those of African/Caribbean heritage, has generated much research attention. Questions have been raised about the extent to which black people's offending rates can be explained by discriminatory treatment within the criminal justice process (Webster, 2007). Thus, police stop-and-search patterns consistently show an over-representation of particular ethnic groups and have generated considerable discussion about police attitudes and assumptions that may underpin this. According to critical race perspectives, high arrest rates should be viewed as the result of police prejudice rather than high criminality (Gilroy, 1987). More recent analyses conclude that there appears to be no general pattern of racial bias in stop-and-search tactics (Rowe, 2004; Waddington et al, 2004). Nonetheless, the issue of racism in the CJS is significant, particularly given the finding of the Macpherson report that the Metropolitan Police Service was institutionally racist (Macpherson, 1999: para 6.34).

More recently, Asian men, in particular young Muslim men, have attracted political, social and research attention. While Asian men have traditionally been viewed by the authorities, as well as by wider society, as law-abiding and peaceful, a series of terrorist attacks has led young Muslim men to be viewed as constituting a 'problem group' (Poynting et al, 2004; Poynting and Mason, 2006). Ethnic minorities associated with Islam have therefore experienced increased attention from the police and security forces (as well as from policy makers and academics), so that there has been ethnic and religious targeting and, indeed, racial profiling of individuals, invoking an 'othering' of the communities concerned and a racialisation of security threats (Poynting and Mason, 2006).

It might be argued that, similar to crime, anti-social behaviour has the potential to constitute a site through which political debates about 'race' issues emerge and through which power struggles are played out, and so ASB powers may be used disproportionately against particular minority ethnic communities. However, there is an absence of empirical data in relation to ASB and ethnicity. It is both curious and worrying that, in contrast to the extent of ethnic monitoring within the mainstream criminal justice system, in terms of official policy monitoring at national level no statistical data are available on the ethnicity of people who make formal complaints about ASB or of those who are the alleged perpetrators (Isal, 2006).

With regard to the use of the principal legal mechanism for controlling anti-social behaviour, the ASBO, there is a further striking absence of ethnic monitoring data (Isal, 2006). The consistent over-representation of minority ethnic people in parts of the criminal justice system provides grounds for concern that such disproportionality may also be characteristic of the use of the ASB powers (FitzGerald and Hale, 2006). However, since the ethnicity of those on whom ASBOs are imposed is not recorded, it is not possible to say, on the basis of official statistics, whether there are any variations in the extent to which members of different ethnic groups are receiving ASBOs (Isal,

2006).The disproportionate application of ASBOs to members of ethnic minorities does, nonetheless, seem to have become even more probable with the availability of the 'CrASBO' (an ASBO attached to a criminal conviction). At least 50% of the steep rise in the numbers of ASBOs being granted nationally since 2003 is accounted for by CrASBOs (see Burney, Chapter Seven in this volume) and, as FitzGerald and Hale point out, the over-representation of minority ethnic people in the criminal justice system generally 'means that they will disproportionately experience the impact of the "bolt-on" ASBO' (2006: 83). Such concerns are further fuelled by the fact that minority ethnic populations are more likely to live in disadvantaged areas or in social housing, where use of the ASB powers is prioritised (FitzGerald and Hale, 2006; Isal, 2006).

Minority ethnic communities, racist victimisation, ASB and social justice

National crime surveys suggest that minority ethnic groups experience significant levels of victimisation. Findings from the British Crime Survey show that Pakistanis and Bangladeshis are significantly more likely than white people to be the victims of household crime (Clancy et al, 2001: 2), and other studies have found that racist victimisation is an important aspect of everyday life for many minority ethnic individuals (Bowling and Phillips, 2003; Chakraborti and Garland, 2004; Rowe, 2004).The 1998 Crime and Disorder Act introduced race hate crime legislation, which provided higher penalties for offences that were racially aggravated.The definition of a racist crime as proposed by the Macpherson Report (1999) is used, this being 'any incident which is perceived to be racist by the victim or any other person'. Although this indicates a significant shift in terms of police crime-recording practices, as police officers have traditionally used an evidential approach that seeks to corroborate allegations rather than automatically accepting victims' accounts (Rowe, 2004), significant challenges remain. The definition of racist crime as an incident is itself problematic, as this views racial violence as a one-off event rather than as an insidious feature of daily life. Racist victimisation may be conceptualised more accurately as a process rather than an incident, since victims of racist violence are often repeat victims; thus individuals' everyday lives are framed by actual, or the perceived threat of, racist acts of abuse and violence (Bowling and Phillips, 2003). This highlights the potential significance of the ASB powers as a means for dealing with racist victimisation, since ASB tends to be defined in terms of its persistent nature (rather than a one-off occurrence) and as a process of cumulative harm. Tackling racist victimisation through ASB powers might therefore be a powerful mechanism through which to respond effectively to minority ethnic communities' experiences of racism, perhaps helping to achieve social justice for these communities where criminal justice has largely failed them.

Following the introduction of new questions into the British Crime Survey, we have some data about *perceptions* of ASB among different ethnic communities. Thus, according to BCS 2003/04 'black and minority ethnic communities were more at risk of perceiving anti-social behaviour (24% compared to 16% average in England and Wales)' (Isal, 2006: 7), but this is little more than a headline statement, since no information is available on differences in perception between ethnic groups nor on the types of ASB that were of particular concern to the minority ethnic respondents. Chakraborti and Garland's (2004) work sheds some light on the types of ASB that appeared to be of concern to minority ethnic communities in one rural area, with racial harassment and young people loitering perceived to be the offences that caused the highest degree of anxiety.

Moving from the 'threat' to the 'opportunity' implied in ASB policy, there is another evidential gap regarding the extent to which ASBOs are being used as a way of addressing racial harassment or other forms of racially motivated ASB. There is certainly evidence from BCS 2003/04 that racial harassment was experienced as a problem by 7% of respondents, and an early Home Office review found that racial harassment featured as a contributory factor in 20% of ASBO cases (Campbell, 2002). Isal reports evidence from some local areas that the ASB powers have been used explicitly to tackle racist behaviours and also notes that, through the Respect Action Plan, social landlords are being prompted to use their ASB powers to deal with racially motivated ASB (Isal, 2006: 8).

Summary

The discussions in the two sections above illustrate that ASB policies and powers in relation to minority ethnic communities raise important questions, particularly with regard to tackling racist victimisation, as well as in relation to the potential to criminalise particular groups. However, in the absence of comprehensive and reliable data we can only conclude that there are grounds for supposing that the application of ASB policies and powers is likely to have a contradictory impact on ethnic minority individuals and communities: providing some additional means of relief in the face of instances of racial harassment and other forms of ethnically motivated abuse, but simultaneously contributing further to the established institutional bias of the criminal justice system against ethnic minorities.

Constructions of ethnicity and ASB

The second set of issues raised in our introduction concerns the ways in which anti-social behaviour is constructed as a particular sort of problem in particular circumstances, and the influence that ethnicity or faith might have on the meanings that are attached to ASB. It appears, however, that such questions have rarely been asked by either policy makers or researchers. This may be because, as Flint has noted, 'much of the imagery and discourse around ASB has focused on white working-class communities' (Flint, 2006: 333) and published research on local accounts of and responses to ASB rarely makes explicit reference to its relevance to non-white communities, even when research was conducted in areas with substantial minority ethnic populations (for example, Burney, 2005; Millie et al, 2005).

In order to at least make a start on addressing this absence, in this section we present some ethnographic data to illustrate ways in which issues relating to ASB in the context of ethnically diverse communities are expressed. This draws on research on responses to ASB in an urban area that included some neighbourhoods where the non-white population (mostly south Asian Muslims) was in the majority, other neighbourhoods where the Asian population constituted a substantial minority and some neighbourhoods that were overwhelmingly white (for an overall account of this research, see Prior et al, 2006). The data is taken from interviews and group discussions involving officials of various agencies and adult residents from several different neighbourhoods (all place names have been fictionalised).

Perceptions of minority ethnic communities

Among officials involved in developing and delivering responses to ASB, there was recognition of differences between Asian and white communities, particularly with regard to attempts to pursue a strategy of community engagement:

> The Asian communities are often pretty active but they tend
> to be organised on ethnic lines rather than geographically.
> (Police officer)

> In Warren Hall [a majority Asian area] there are lots of small community groups linked to families, mosques or political networks. In Standen [an area of deprived white social housing tenants] we're trying to develop this – there aren't the established groups ... (Council officer)

> Moorside and Glen is one estate but they're seen locally as distinct areas and communities. What works for one won't work for the other. Then you get further differences between the different ethnic communities. (Ward councillor)

One example of difference, as noted by a senior police officer, was in the degree to which different communities were prepared to tolerate forms of official intervention designed to reduce problems of anti-social behaviour:

> We can't rely on enforcement alone, it needs a variable approach. There are different levels of tolerance in different communities. For instance in Standen we use Dispersal Orders, alcohol bans and other restrictive orders because of the perceived threat from young people. We don't do that in Barnfields [another majority Asian area] because it's not appropriate to the area, it's perceived as racist.

And this was justified by a more junior police officer with operational responsibilities in the area in question, by reference to different forms of behaviour in different communities. Thus, the police were prepared to use ASB powers to address the problem of young people in majority white areas gathering in large groups close to local shopping centres, and so deterring other people from using the shops. This contrasted with the officer's perception of young people's behaviour in Asian areas: '[There's] no call for Dispersal Orders, kids don't hang around on corners.'

Thus there is evidence here of conscious decisions being made by service providers to vary their approach to ASB issues in accordance with their understandings of the prevailing social and cultural norms and patterns of behaviour within minority ethnic communities.

However, these understandings were clearly challenged by residents in one ethnically mixed area, who cited various examples of problems caused by groups of Asian young people in public places:

> We had a gang of Asian youths who used to hang around
> a launderette [in Wade Lane, an estate of mixed white and
> Asian population]. They damaged it and other shops and
> put people off from going there. (Resident 1)

> We get lots of Asian teenagers coming here who are not
> from the estate, 50 or so of them aged 17/18. Last week
> they killed a rabbit and stood around laughing about it,
> what sorts of people do that? (Resident 2)

> The main problem is the Asian lads aged 17+ who don't
> live on the estate. It's their friends who they invite over,
> they let them into the blocks, then they cause trouble.
> (Resident 3)

But residents were equally concerned about the problems caused by
groups of young white people:

> On the Moorside and Glen estate ... youths hanging around
> in groups causes feelings of intimidation. For example,
> there's a new zebra crossing but people won't use it because
> a group of kids hang around next to it. (Resident 4)

> It's similar with the Glen estate shops, young people
> running around, deterring people from using the shops.
> (Resident 5)

Such statements would appear at least to indicate that the assumptions
of police officers that straightforward contrasts could be drawn between
the typical behaviours of white youths and Asian youths are open to
question. Indeed, responses from residents seemed much more strongly
to indicate major concerns with the behaviour of young people in
general, regardless of their ethnicity; residents complained about the
behaviours of young people in white neighbourhoods in much the
same terms as they did about some Asian youths.

Community responses to ASB issues

Although statements by officials from different agencies, as quoted
above, indicated their claims to knowledge of the social characteristics
of Asian communities, including a proliferation of community groups
and networks, the research did not reveal a clear sense of how to

work with these communities in responding to issues of ASB. Rather, it seemed as though official perceptions that Asian communities had different ways of doing things were themselves an obstacle:

> There are also difficulties within the Asian community because of the role of [an ethnically based political party] which made various promises and deals with residents, but didn't lock these deals into the resource planning and delivery process, so things didn't happen. There seem to be different processes by which proposals emerge, a lack of transparency about where ideas come from and who is promoting them. (Council officer)

Some residents, on the other hand, were less likely to be put off by such concerns and addressed issues directly with Asian 'community leaders'. Thus in relation to the problems at the launderette, referred to above:

> We got together with the mosque leaders to discuss it and they intervened and helped reduce the problem. (Resident 1)

And this kind of approach was perceived as worth persisting with even when progress was difficult:

> So we're trying with the mosque to be able to use one of their meeting rooms but it's taking a lot of negotiation. They are difficult to work with – they don't say 'no' but you just keep getting referred to a different person or a committee. (Resident 1)

There was also an example from the research of residents in one area initiating forms of community action to start to address various problems that the area was facing, including anti-social behaviour. This was recognised and applauded by officials:

> Grovelands is a good example, this is a new estate in Barnfields developed by three housing associations. They are a group of people thrown together who are now coming together to tackle anti-social behaviour. (Senior police officer)

> It wasn't a community but they've formed one to deal with
> the problems they face. (Council officer)

> It was a group of strong-minded individuals who really got
> it together and promoted it. (Housing manager)

This group, led by two white women, had set about organising small-scale activities to try to bring adult residents together and develop a sense of collective ownership of the estate and its problems, and to provide activities that would interest and engage young people. They were particularly concerned about growing incidents of vandalism by young people, the development of a violent gang culture among local boys and some instances of inter-ethnic violence. Having talked to some of the boys and established that they were interested in playing football, the women set about creating organised opportunities for this, with positive results:

> I managed to build relationships between them. The
> atmosphere on the estate changed overnight. They started
> (football) training together and formed a team so they could
> play others, and the gang fighting ended. (Resident 6)

The success of this had led them to address other needs, and, acknowledging that Barnfields is an ethnically diverse area, they had tried to put together initiatives that encouraged Asian, black and white girls and boys to take part:

> There are a number of activities where we've mixed girls
> and boys and had mixed ethnicities, Asian, black and white.
> (Resident 6)

> The homework club and the art club have had mixed
> ethnicities. (Resident 7)

> There is a difficulty getting young Asian girls involved. We
> had girls-only badminton classes, black, mixed, white girls
> came along but not Asian girls. (Resident 6)

The difficulty with Asian girls highlighted the importance of working with the parents:

With the kids, you have to build trust with the parent, to convince them we're in charge – especially to involve girls in activities. (Resident 6)

And smaller projects involving smaller groups of young people also helped to gain the involvement of Asian communities. With a small number of people you get a greater Asian involvement. Small clubs, involving 10 or 12 children are much more successful. (Resident 6)

Analysis

We recognise that the ethnographic data we have presented here is very limited, and it is primarily intended as an illustration of what such research can offer. We certainly do not wish to draw any general conclusions from it. However, we think it does highlight some interesting avenues for potential further inquiry, and we identify them here in that light: as possible topics for future research.

Thus, first, the data raises questions about the ways in which officials construct 'difference' in their accounts of local communities – the dimensions along which areas of substantial minority ethnic population are identified as being different from areas of predominantly white population. What are the processes that shape such identifications? What sources of 'knowledge' are being drawn on? What is the role of 'stereotypes' in these constructions of difference – even where, as may have been the case here, stereotypes were apparently 'benign' in that they ascribed positive characteristics to ethnic communities?

Second, the data suggests that officials build on their understandings of the differences between ethnically contrasting areas to develop different kinds of responses and interventions, making judgements about the acceptability or non-acceptability of certain interventions in certain communities. While this indicates a sensitivity about the effects of different forms of regulation on communities that seems welcome, it also prompts questions about the validity of the judgements being made if the understandings of community characteristics (such as the communal acceptability of particular interventions) may themselves be inadequate. Further, it suggests the possibility that problems that particular communities are actually experiencing go unrecognised by officials and are thus not responded to in the way that similar problems are in areas that are perceived differently.

Third, the extracts above show how 'ordinary residents' can apparently develop a level of knowledge and understanding about social and cultural differences that provides a basis for building trust and developing forms of collective action. The data does, however, illuminate only one set of perspectives on this: it would be interesting to explore the views of, say, the parents of Asian girls in the area to establish what their perceptions of the 'difficulties' are in terms of participation in community activities. And there is certainly more to be learned about the processes of dialogue and negotiation, and the discursive identification of problems and solutions, implied in the developments described.

Conclusion

Much of the discussion in this chapter has necessarily been tentative and provisional. There is, at present, simply very little by way of an evidence base about what is going on when ASB policies encounter minority ethnic communities, in terms either of statistical measures of inputs and outputs or of qualitative accounts of how people (in agencies and in communities) are constructing and deploying meanings of 'ethnicity' and 'anti-social behaviour'.

We have, however, sought to make a number of points that we think are important for future work in this area. First, the questions around perceptions of and responses to anti-social behaviour in the context of minority ethnic communities cannot be divorced from the wider law and order policy context. Here, the two key factors that impinge on the ASB issue are the response to ethnic minorities within mainstream crime reduction practices, especially in practices such as 'stop and search' and the use of prison sentences, and the growth in 'anti-terror' operations specifically targeting minority individuals and groups (FitzGerald and Hale, 2006).

Second, we have argued that the relationship between ethnic and faith-based identities needs to be better understood and, in particular, that the role of religious faith and the values, norms and practices that emerge from it should be recognised as a significant issue in shaping what is and is not viewed as anti-social behaviour in different communities and how it should be responded to. Third, it is vital to acknowledge the complex reality that is covered by the terms 'ethnicity' and 'faith'. The 'minority ethnic population' of the UK is extremely heterogeneous, embracing a multitude of different identities and racialised constructions. This is becoming a more, rather than less, complex issue as new immigrant groups arrive and settle in the UK, while the longer-established minority communities – the African-Caribbeans and the south Asians – themselves undergo social change along dimensions of class, generation and gender. And it is, of course, important to remind ourselves that the majority white population is itself complex and differentiated; arguably, much of the concern about ASB arises out of the differences between, say, the white middle and working classes or between different generations within the white population.

Finally, and following on from the previous point, it is important to be aware of the dangers of 'over-ethnicising' discussion about the impact of ASB policies. We need to be wary of implying that the issue of ASB and minority ethnic communities is always to be considered separately from 'mainstream' questions about ASB: in many areas local communities are mixed, with varying degrees of integration between ethnically different groups, including white and non-white, and the likelihood is that common concerns about ASB will be evident. One of the neighbourhoods featured in the ethnographic data we presented earlier, where a number of community initiatives had been developed, is an example of this. The message is perhaps that greater awareness and understanding is needed of the factors within minority ethnic communities that shape attitudes towards ASB and the interventions intended to tackle it, but that local policies and practices need also to avoid this becoming a rationale for wholly segregated and distinctive responses.

Note

[1] Although space limitations preclude us from exploring the issue further in this chapter, it is important to recognise other groups liable to be subject to racist abuse and discriminatory practices, such as Gypsy and Traveller communities and refugees and asylum seekers. Moreover – and of increasing significance demographically – people of mixed heritage can suffer distinct forms of victimisation and discrimination, in part because they do not fit conveniently into particular ethnic categories.

References

Bowling, B. and Phillips, C. (2003) *Racism, crime and justice*, Harlow: Longman.

Burney, E. (2005) *Making people behave: Anti-social behaviour politics and policy*, Cullompton: Willan Publishing.

Campbell, S. (2002) *Implementing Anti-Social Behaviour Orders: Messages for practitioners*, Findings 160, London: Home Office.

Chakraborti, N. and Garland, J. (eds), (2004) *Rural racism*, Cullompton: Willan Publishing.

Clancy, A., Hough, M., Aust, R. and Kershaw, C. (2001) *Ethnic minorities' experience of crime and policing: Findings from the 2000 British Crime Survey*, Findings 146, London: Home Office.

CST (Community Security Trust) (2006) *Community Security Trust: Antisemitic Incidents Report 2006* (www.thecst.org.uk/docs/Incidents%5FReport%5F06.pdf).

European Monitoring Centre on Racism and Xenophobia (2005) *The impact of the 7 July 2005 bomb attacks on Muslim communities in the EU*, November.

FitzGerald, M. and Hale, C. (2006) *Ethnic minorities: victimisation and racial harassment: Findings from the 1988 and 1992 British Crime Surveys*, Home Office Research Study 154, London: Home Office.

Flint, J. (ed) (2006) *Housing, urban governance and anti-social behaviour*, Bristol: The Policy Press.

Garland, J., Spalek, B. and Chakraborti, N. (2006) 'Hearing lost voices: issues in researching "hidden" minority ethnic communities', *British Journal of Criminology*, vol 46, no 3, pp 423–37.

Gilroy, P. (1987) 'The myth of black criminality', in P. Scraton (ed), *Law, order and the authoritarian state*, Buckingham: Open University Press.

Home Office (2003) *Survey 2001 people, families and communities*, London: Home Office Research, Development and Statistics Directorate.

IHRC (Islamic Human Rights Commission) (2006) *Law and British Muslims: Domination of the majority or process of the balance (a report)*, London: IHRC Publications.

Isal, S. (2006) *Equal respect*, London: The Runnymede Trust.

Macpherson, Sir W. (1999) *The Stephen Lawrence Inquiry: Report of an inquiry by Sir William MacPherson of Cluny*, London: HMSO.

Millie, A., Jacobson, J., McDonald, E. and Hough, M. (2005) *Anti-social behaviour strategies: Finding a balance*, York: Joseph Rowntree Foundation.

Modood, T., Berthoud, R., Lakey, J., Nazroo, J., Smith, P., Virdee, S. and Beishon, S. (1997) *Ethnic minorities in Britain: Diversity and disadvantage*, London: PSI.

Poynting S. and Mason, V. (2006) 'The resistible rise of Islamophobia: anti-Muslim racism in the UK and Australia', *Journal of Sociology*, vol 43, pp 61–86.

Poynting, S., Noble, T. and Collins, J. (2004) *Bin Laden in the suburbs: Criminalising the Arab other*, Sydney, Australia: Sydney Institute of Criminology and Federation Press.

Prior, D., Farrow, K., Spalek, B. and Barnes, M. (2006) 'Anti-social behaviour and civil renewal', in T. Brennan, P. John and G. Stoker (eds), *Re-energising citizenship: Strategies for civil renewal*, London: Palgrave Macmillan.

Rowe, M. (2004) *Policing race and racism*, Cullompton: Willan Publishing.

Spalek, B. (2004) 'Islam and criminal justice', in J. Muncie and D. Wilson (eds) *Student handbook of criminal justice and criminology*, London: Glasshouse Press, Cavendish.

Spalek, B. (2006) 'British Muslims and the criminal justice system', in T. Choudhury et al (eds), *Muslims in the UK: Policies for engaged citizens*, Budapest: Open Society Institute.

Waddington, P., Stenson, K. and Don, D. (2004) 'In proportion: race and police stop and search', *British Journal of Criminology*, vol 44, no 6, pp 889–914.

Webster, C. (2007) *Understanding race and crime*, Maidenhead: Open University Press.

SEVEN

The ASBO and the shift to punishment

Elizabeth Burney

New Labour's 'tough on crime' mantra heralded the introduction of a range of criminal justice policies intended to turn this into a reality, a tendency that has brought new instruments of punishment and control every year since 1997. The earliest and still the most controversial was the introduction of the Anti-Social Behaviour Order (ASBO) in the 1998 Crime and Disorder Act. The measure immediately attracted criticism for its legal form and for its potentially punitive reach. It stands at one end of a punitive spectrum that ranges through to a huge increase in imprisonment and indeterminate sentences that occurred under the Blair administration.

As David Downes has said: '[H]aving adopted such punitive measures as Anti-Social Behaviour Orders towards offenders at the more trivial end of the spectrum ... the government has little left in its locker, except more imprisonment, for the truly serious' (Downes, 2007: 3). As this chapter will show, the ASBO itself, in the 21st century, has acquired a more overtly punitive character, in both law and practice. First, however, some basic legal arguments concerning the punitive nature of the ASBO will be rehearsed.

In designing the instrument that was originally called the 'community safety order', the Labour government was determined to bypass the prosecution process that it considered ineffective in dealing with persistent neighbourhood nuisance, and at the same time to bind alleged perpetrators with tailor-made restrictions enforced by threat of punishment. Punishment was therefore the second of what Simester and von Hirsch (2006) have called 'two-step prohibitions', of which there are several other examples. There is technically no punishment involved in a civil order (step 1) such as the ASBO, which delivers prohibitions designed 'to protect persons ... from further anti-social acts by him' (1998 Crime and Disorder Act, section 1(1)(b)). Only if the prohibition is flouted does a criminal offence occur that can be prosecuted (step 2) and punished by up to five years' imprisonment.

The appellants in *Clingham and McCann*[1] sought to challenge the status of the ASBO, arguing that in reality and substance the nature of the process was criminal, given the content of the orders and the criminal character of breach proceedings. The issue at stake was the hearsay evidence that supported allegations of serious and persistent abuse and crime by the youths in their respective neighbourhoods. Hearsay evidence is permissible in civil cases, but the appeal claimed that, given the potential serious consequences of an ASBO, it should be disallowed and treated with criminal procedural rules of evidence and governed by Article 6 of the European Convention on Human Rights (the right to a fair trial), which includes the right to examine witnesses.

The Lords were having none of this. In statement after statement they argued that the ASBO was not a punishment or penalty, only a preventive order necessary to protect communities, and was therefore undoubtedly civil in nature. Lord Steyn (para 23) said it should be considered entirely separately from the crime of breach.

Lord Hope (para 75) expressed a general view when he said:

> The defendants say that prohibitions which banish the defendant from an area of the city where he lives, or which expose him to harsher penalties than he would normally face if he commits a crime, have all the characteristics of a penalty for the anti-social acts which he is found to have committed. An anti-social behaviour order may well restrict the freedom of the defendant to do what he wants and go where he pleases. But these restrictions are imposed for preventive reasons, not as a punishment.

In spite of this prevailing view, their Lordships decided that, in view of the seriousness of the consequences, the standard of proof of anti-social behaviour in an ASBO application should be equivalent to the criminal standard (which was the second part of the appeal). However, when it came to the need to impose prohibitions in order to prevent anti-social conduct in future, they said there was no need for such proof, as it was 'an exercise of judgment or evaluation' (Lord Steyn, para 37).

The Lords' line of reasoning concerning the non-punitive nature of the ASBO has been maintained in the courts ever since, regardless of the subjective experience and practical difficulties experienced by recipients of the orders. Many academic critics disagree (Ashworth, 2004; Macdonald, 2003, 2006; Burney, 2005; Simester and von Hirsch, 2006).

Simester and von Hirsch offer a principled critique of the legal status of the ASBO and the position that it is not punitive in character. On the latter they make four main points:

1. There is no proportionality written into the rules for ASBO prohibitions (although Home Office guidance in 2000 said they should be reasonable and proportionate).
2. The prohibitions imposed often have a very harsh effect on the lives of recipients, such as 'a curfew or an exclusion from an area (estate, suburb, shopping mall, even one's home)' (p 191). Moreover they must last at least two years, with no upper limit.
3. Orders have been imposed on self-harming persons, on people with mental disabilities, and prostitutes – all categories that have been specifically decriminalised, or at least partially so, by the will of parliament.

It soon became apparent from reported cases that these fears were well founded. For example, an ASBO imposed by Haringey magistrates on a youth in 2000 included a two-year 8pm to 7am curfew (Burney, 2002). Even if the recipient was aged over 18, this would have been still four times the permitted length of a curfew imposed as a criminal sentence. In the sample of cases examined by Campbell (2002), 9% of ASBOs had been given to people with learning disabilities, and a later example concerned a 13-year-old autistic boy, given an ASBO because his trampolining disturbed the neighbours. A much publicised case concerned a suicidal woman with an ASBO forbidding her to go near rivers, lakes or railway bridges. More commonly, as in the *McCann* case, the orders ban people, often teenagers, from family neighbourhoods, cutting them off from relatives and friends for years on end.

4. Additionally, the practice of publicising ASBOs with names, addresses, even photographs of the recipients adds an expressive, humiliating character to the punitive experience (Pratt, 2000). The practice was declared legal in *Stanley v Brent*[2] and has been promoted in the Home Office 'Together' campaign. The Youth Justice Board reported how this could rebound on families and encourage vigilantism (Solanki et al, 2006). It was strongly condemned by the Council of Europe's Commissioner for Human Rights (Gil-Robles, 2005: 83), who urged the government to:

> Reformulate Anti-Social Behaviour Order guidelines so that they neither encourage nor permit the excessive publicity of the making of orders against juveniles. In order to guarantee the right of children to privacy, reproduction

and public dissemination of posters reproducing the pictures
of children submitted to ASBOs should be prohibited.

ASBO usage has spread far beyond the original scenario of
neighbourhood troublemaking and has become an almost random tool
of control, being applied or threatened in many everyday situations
and some bizarre ones. Macdonald (2006) cites a pirate DJ who ran
his radio station from the top of a tower block, who was banned from
entering any building more than four storeys tall. He also cites a Scottish
Executive recommendation of ASBOs against people feeding gulls in
seaside towns, and the threat of ASBOs against taxi drivers in North
Wales who sound their horns when picking up customers. A Norfolk
farmer received an order forbidding him to let his pigs and geese escape.
It has been reported that a profoundly deaf girl was put in custody
when she breached an order forbidding her to spit (Burney, 2005).

Enter the CrASBO

Despite the high profile given to the ASBO legislation by the Home
Office, the orders were initially used only sparsely and were concentrated
in a few areas, notably Manchester, where the idea chimed with local
practice towards misbehaving council tenants. Many local authorities
within the new Crime and Disorder Reduction Partnerships (CDRPs)
attempted multi-agency problem solving for repeat incivilities, and/or
preferred a step-by-step approach, beginning with informal warnings,
using ASBOs as a last resort. Impatiently, Home Secretary Jack Straw
wrote to local government associations telling them that they need
not exhaust all other options before applying for an ASBO – clearly
indicating that stern action was preferred to welfarist or diversionary
solutions. However, it was his successor, David Blunkett, who eventually
provided the means for ASBO lift-off.

A late amendment to the Police Reform Bill, which received royal
assent in July 2002, was the means of achieving this. The Act permitted
'relevant authorities' (police, local authorities or social landlords[3])to
apply for ASBOs as part of proceedings in the county court (section
63) or criminal court (section 64). Following a criminal conviction, the
court may also of its own accord make an ASBO. The post-conviction
ASBO (enacted as section 1C of the 1998 Crime and Disorder Act
[CDA]) can be made if the court considers that, at any time since the
introduction of the ASBO legislation, the offender has acted in an
anti-social manner as defined in the 1998 CDA and that the order
is necessary to prevent any further anti-social behaviour. The alleged
behaviour does not have to be linked to the offence leading to the

conviction; and, unlike the original type of ASBO, no consultation with other agencies is required. These orders cannot be rescinded within less than two years, although they may be suspended while the offender is in prison, to commence on his release.

Another innovation in the 2002 Police Reform Act was the interim ASBO – orders given before a full hearing of evidence of anti-social behaviour, intended to restrain an offender immediately. These orders are short-lived and must be served personally, but they carry just the same punishment if breached as the full ASBO. Some defendants claim that they were unaware of having received their interim order.

The post-conviction ASBO, or 'CrASBO' as it became labelled, introduced an entirely new character to the orders. Now they could be simply sentencing add-ons, indistinguishable from the criminal process and effectively providing retrospective sentencing for past activities. If there had been any doubts about the punitive nature of ASBOs, this legislation removed them at a stroke.

The CrASBO quickly became popular with the courts, often at the instigation of police officers who found it a useful way of keeping tabs on persistent offenders (Burney, 2005). ASBO numbers began to climb, and while their growth was lauded by the Home Office it has never been officially acknowledged that this was almost entirely due to the use of CrASBOs. The measure was implemented at the end of 2002, and three years later CrASBOs accounted for two thirds of all orders, as Figure 7.1 shows.

Figure 7.1: Comparison of ASBOs issued on application vs those issued on conviction (CrASBOs)*

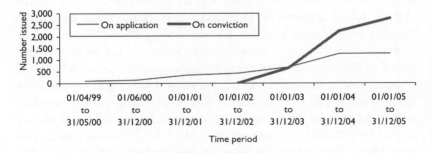

* = based on figures from Home Office RDS – OCJR (Wain, 2007)

CrASBOs are popular with police and local authorities because they are cheaper and easier to obtain than via the application route (Burney, 2005). Typically, they are sprung at the last minute. A youth of 18 told Solanki et al (2006: 82):

> I was in the court cell, waiting for sentencing, when a solicitor came in with a request from the city for an ASBO to be placed on me. The solicitor said: 'there is nothing we can do to stop them giving you this ASBO. If they put it forward, you have to have it.'

Magistrates were warned of CrASBO overuse in a hard-hitting editorial in the *Justice of the Peace*:[4]

> ASBOs on conviction have got out of hand. Offenders in their pre-teens are being prohibited from wearing 'hoodies', associating with their 'criminal' chums, going to particular places such as car parks etc. Not only does this interfere with their social development, it also operates to stigmatize them and set them against authority. Moreoover, it sets them up for punishments, often custody, for doing things that you or I take for granted. Is this really the sort of lesson that we should be teaching 'recalcitrant' and 'rebellious' youngsters? Could this turn into a social time-bomb?

The post-conviction ASBO clearly adds to the punitive weight of a sentence, even if it is technically and often factually unrelated to it. Court of Appeal cases have revealed how section 1C orders have sometimes been used deliberately to impose further punishment or to impose irrelevant prohibitions. A spate of judgments in 2005 have 'helped to set appropriate boundaries that should serve to restrain "trigger-happy" misuse of this disposal' (Stone, 2006: 196).

A key case is *Boness*,[5] in which the appeal judges pronounced a set of principles that serve to limit inappropriate use of ASBOs or inappropriate conditions. Dean Boness was an 18-year-old who received three years' young offender institution (YOI) detention for burglary, following previous convictions for a range of crimes. The detention was to be followed by a section 1C ASBO for five years which, *inter alia*, forbade him from entering any public car park within a specified area except for work reasons, entering any building or land that was educational premises except as a pupil, and wearing or carrying anything that could be used to cover the face. The court quashed the order on the grounds that, after a period of detention followed by supervision, further restraint was unnecessary. Also, many of the prohibitions were unnecessary or unclear – for example, the effect would be to prevent him using a supermarket car park, entering a teaching hospital or playing fields attached to a school where he was engaged legitimately in sport, or wearing a scarf or jumper, or even carrying a newspaper. The judges also criticised the use of ASBOs simply to increase punishment or to impose prohibitions on behaviour that was criminal but not 'anti-social' within the meaning of the 1998 Act.

Similarly, in *Starling*,[6] the offender, described in court as 'a pestilential nuisance to the public in Falmouth for quite some time', received an ASBO on top of his conviction for aggravated vehicle taking and affray. The court reduced the length from an excessive five years to two, and struck out or amended some of the prohibitions as unreasonable, too vague or unenforceable. 'Not to consume alcohol in a public place, or be under the influence of alcohol in a public place' was changed to allow him to drink on licensed premises. 'Not to be in possession of any bladed article' was deleted, as it would prevent him from using a knife to eat or prepare food.

The Court of Appeal has warned against the use of CrASBOs simply to forbid actions that are already prohibited under criminal law. Although in *R v P*[7] it had said that after a short sentence an order might serve to 'remind' the offender that certain actions were criminal, this was modified in *Boness* when the court said the test should be simply whether an ASBO was *necessary* to protect the public from further anti-social acts. This does not rule out forbidding some actions that are also offences, but can also include restrictions intended to limit opportunities for criminal acts.

Morrison[8] established that CrASBOs should not be used in cases of driving while disqualified, which in itself does not cause harassment, alarm or distress. As in *Boness*, this judgment stated the important principle that section 1C should not be used simply in order to increase the maximum penalty beyond that which was available for the substantive offence. The court pointed out that the purpose of an order was not to punish an offender and it criticised defence lawyers for sometimes suggesting an ASBO in order to avoid a custodial sentence.

In *Lonergan v Lewes Crown Court*[9] a 19-year-old had received a CrASBO that imposed a curfew from 11.30pm to 6am for two years. The argument that this was incompatible with human rights was dismissed, but the significance of the judgment lies in its reminder that:

a curfew for two years in the life of a teenager is a very considerable restriction of freedom. It may well be necessary but in many cases ... either the period of the curfew could be set at less than the full life of the order or ... in the light of behavioural progress, an application to vary the curfew under s.1(8) might well succeed.

In *Wadmore and Foreman*[10] the court summed up a long list of principles arising from earlier cases concerning the use of ASBOs including section 1C. The offenders were aged 14 and 15 when they robbed a pizza delivery man of £30 and were sentenced to a 12-month detention and training order to be followed by a five-year ASBO. It was held that the order (containing several prohibitions, including some that were criminal offences) was too long and too vague, and in any case the proper procedure had not been followed. There was no evidence of anti-social behaviour other than the robbery itself and there were no clear rules governing such applications in the Crown Court.

The principles listed in this case reiterate the reminder that ASBOs must be considered *necessary* to protect the public. The terms of an order must be recorded, precise and enforceable, and must be directed at conduct already shown to relate to this need, rather than in vague, generic terms. Not all conditions have to run for the full course of the order. Following custodial terms of more than a few months there should be only limited need to impose a suspended ASBO, and if the sentence itself is sufficient deterrent there should not be an order forbidding specific criminal offences. As *Archbold News*[11] pointed out:

> Since all offenders who receive a custodial sentence will now be released on license and are liable to recall, it is vitally important that sentencers consider the combined effect of an ASBO and license conditions before deciding that an ASBO is necessary, and that ASBOs do not simply become routine.

Most importantly, the final point made in this judgment was that:

> It was unlawful to make an order as if it were a further sentence or punishment. An order should not be used merely to increase the sentence that the offender was to receive.

So far there is no available evidence that CrASBOs have been significantly curbed by these principles – statistics later than 2005 were still awaited at the time of writing. But new Home Office guidance (2006) on the use of ASBOs has incorporated some of the caveats highlighted by the Court of Appeal.

Breaching ASBOs

A further range of legal issues has been raised by the widespread occurrence of breach of ASBO conditions. Court statistics for the period 1 June 2000 to the end of 2005 show that on average 47% of people subject to ASBOs in England and Wales breached the terms of their orders (and this does not include known multiple breaches).[12] Breach rates varied from 74% in Durham to 11% in Northamptonshire. Differences may reflect police and Crown Prosecution Service practice, and also the difficulties of enforcement. Greater Manchester, the authority with the largest number of ASBOs (1,227) had a 56% breach rate, despite its police focus on persistent offenders subject to ASBOs.

It is also obvious that many more breaches occur than are detected and prosecuted. Technical infringements, such as entering a forbidden zone, can easily occur unseen, and very widely drawn or vague prohibitions may be unenforceable. In *Boness* the Court of Appeal said that ASBOs are only appropriate where there is a practical way of policing them, and it cited an earlier case where the recipient was forbidden entry to any hotel, guesthouse or similar premises in the Greater London area.[13]

The Court of Appeal has ruled on cases of ASBO and CrASBO breach that have raised different issues. One such issue arises when the breach involves conduct that is neither criminal nor anti-social.

The case of *Lamb*[14] concerned a youth with a long criminal record who received a section 1C order forbidding him to enter the town centre, to be drunk in a public place or to use the metro system. He breached the metro rule several times, being sentenced on various occasions and receiving detention and training orders that were cancelled or reduced on appeal. Aged 18, he entered the adult court, where he was sentenced to 22 months' detention for further successive breaches of his order. The Court of Appeal held that, given the continual flouting of his order, it was right he should receive a custodial sentence. But none of his actions had involved causing harassment, alarm and distress, which might have been seen as a public order offence, and they were not crimes in themselves. Yet he was at risk of the full five-year sentence for ASBO breach because there was no limitation through linkage to a crime with a lesser penalty (see below). The court decided he should receive two months' detention for each of the three points of breach (being in the town centre, being drunk in public and using the metro), to run consecutively. In this case repeated defiance of the court was the only wrongdoing.

Things are more complicated when breach of the ASBO occurs in conjunction with other offences. As Solanki et al (2006) found, citing a case where damage had been done to a bus shelter and the culprits were charged with criminal damage and with an ASBO breach for causing criminal damage, this form of breach is much more common than a straight ASBO breach, and it is likely to be felt as a double punishment. In this court area magistrates tended to sentence concurrently in such cases, but the police were said to disagree, believing ASBO breaches should carry a distinct and separate punishment.

The Court of Appeal has had differing opinions on the question of how much punishment can be given for breach. In the case of *Morrison*, where the defendent had repeatedly driven while disqualified, the Crown Court had decided to sentence on grounds of breach alone, and gave him 12 months' imprisonment. The appeal judges pointed out that this was double the maximum for driving while disqualified and pronounced the principle that breach should not be used to increase the punishment beyond that available for the statutory offence. This point is particularly important for offences such as being drunk and disorderly, or soliciting, which can only be fined. Some prostitutes have indeed been imprisoned for breach of orders connected with their street activities. However, the strict *Morrison* principle was later challenged in *Stevens*,[15] when the Court of Appeal said proportionality, rather than substantive offence maxima, should limit breach sentences, although the current offence might affect proportionality.

How often do ASBO breaches attract custody rather than a lesser sentence? As Solanki et al (2006) found, some courts sentence breaches with custody almost automatically when other crimes are involved. They quote one magistrate as saying:

> I mean at the beginning it was, if anybody breaches it in any way – custody. That was what we were told and that was what we did. Until all the young offender institutions were full. (p 125)

Figures released by the Home Office in 2005 showed that between 1 June 2000 and 31 December 2003 nearly a quarter (23%) of all

ASBOs issued in England and Wales resulted in a custodial sentence for breach. Of the 437 cases, 179 were for juveniles, equivalent to 9% of all 10- to 17-year-olds with ASBOs. These are shocking figures that will not have improved with time. The Youth Justice Board was extremely concerned at the numbers entering YOIs with ASBO breaches – until it found out that nearly all were in receipt of criminal sentences that had triggered the breach proceedings. The YOI investigated by Neil Wain (2007) estimated that up to half of inmates had been sentenced for ASBO breach, but it was not possible to separate those in custody for stand-alone breach as distinct from breaches associated with other offences.

Adding a suspended ASBO to a young person's detention has been frowned upon (for example, see *R v P* and *Boness*) on the grounds that a period of supervision follows the detention. And, as has been pointed out, all custodial sentences are now followed by a licence or supervision period. In other words post-custody ASBOs seem an unnecessary belt-and-braces procedure, which could actually hamper rehabilitation.

The experience of ASBOs

There has been little published research on the effect of ASBOs on recipients (see contributions by Goldsmith [Chapter Twelve] and McIntosh [Chapter Thirteen] in this volume), but what there is suggests that the punitive weight can be onerous and damaging. Solanki et al (2006) interviewed 24 young people on ASBOs. Most were vague about their prohibitions, and about half of those on interim orders had received them without warning.

These youngsters acknowledged that they had been behaving badly. But they mostly felt great difficulty in adhering to the orders, especially those involving exclusion zones. The latter could impinge seriously on family life, sometimes forcing the whole household to move or obliging the young person to live elsewhere, such as with grandparents. They found it hard not to associate or communicate with forbidden friends, and some said they simply could not avoid their best friends despite the threat of breach. Being confined to the house was experienced as oppressive (see also Stephen and Squires, 2003) – some took to drink or drugs in consequence. The length of the order is particularly hard to contemplate for an adolescent; one said that he would rather be in prison. Parents also expressed this as their main concern. Few were aware that it was possible to return to court to ask for a variation of ASBO terms.

A wider sample was examined by Solanki et al (2006) for the consequences of breach. Of the 137 cases, 49% were known to have breached their ASBOs, mostly more than once. Custody was imposed only once when the breach was the sole offence, but was more common (35 cases) when associated with other convictions.

Another study (Wain, 2007) provides interviews with 23 people on ASBOs, nearly all youths. Because of difficulties accessing ASBO-holders living in the community, most of the interviews were obtained from young men in a YOI. All interviewees said they had breached their ASBOs, some many times. These interviewees, too, found the association and exclusion conditions most irksome, and sometimes devastating. One 20-year-old spoke bitterly about the effect on himself and his family. He had been made literally homeless and the exclusion area meant that he was banned from visiting his sick mother and his pregnant girlfriend, and missed seeing his little brother grow up. When he did visit his mother he was breached. 'It's a bit mad when you get sent to jail for being in your Mum's, innit?' was his comment.

The stigma of an ASBO is far reaching and conveys vicarious punishment. Several interviewees told of bad effects on their families, emotionally and socially. One said his epileptic father had suffered as a result. A woman said her children were tormented on the school bus because their parents had had leaflets through the door about her ASBO. Others spoke of the way their ASBO had tarnished their whole family following publicity.

Conclusion

The overall effect on the young people with very restrictive ASBOs was likely to be long lasting. Effectively they were deprived of what Sampson and Laub have referred to as the 'normal routes to socialisation' and desistance from offending by being cut off from family, community, friends and many job or education opportunities (Sampson and Laub, 1993). In the longer term, society would suffer as well as those whose lives had been distorted as the result of ill-considered restrictions.

The more punitive the effects of ASBOs and the more that they are used as an add-on to criminal sentences, the harder it becomes to uphold the technical position expressed in *McCann* that, because they are civil orders, the safeguards of the 1998 Human Rights Act do not apply. Article 8 (respect for private and family life) is especially relevant, as may be Article 10 (freedom of expression) and Article 11 (freedom of assembly and association). It is perhaps surprising that, by late 2006, no applications on ASBO issues had been made to the European Court of Human Rights (personal information).

The 'rights of communities', a more nebulous concept, is a way of saying that the state should uphold everybody's right to peaceful enjoyment of their property and freedom to use public space unmolested. It is time to explore ways of achieving these necessary aims other than by overuse of back-door punishment presented as 'merely' preventive.

Notes

[1] [2002] UKHL 39.

[2] [2004] EWHC 2229 (Admin).

[3] Social landlords were added to the 'relevant authorities' permitted to apply for ASBOs by the same Act, and other agencies have subsequently also been given this power.

[4] *Justice of the Peace*, vol 169, no 44, p 845, 29 October 2005.

[5] [2005] EWCA Crim 2395.

[6] [2005] EWCA Crim 2277.

[7] [2004] 2 Cr App R (S) 343.

[8] [2005] EWCA Crim 2237.

[9] [2005] EWHC Admin 457.

[10] [2006] EWCA Crim 686.

[11] *Archbold News*, 2006, issue 4, p 4.

[12] House of Commons Written Answer, 26 March 2007, col 1308W.

[13] *Werner* [2004] EWCA Crim 2931.

[14] [2005] EWCA Crim 3000.

[15] [2006] EWCA Crim 255.

References

Ashworth, A. (2004) 'Social control and "anti-social behaviour": the subversion of human rights?' *Law Quarterly Review*, vol 120, pp 263–91.

Burney, E. (2002) 'Talking tough, acting coy: what happened to the Anti-Social Behaviour Order?', *Howard Journal*, vol 41, no 5, pp 341–56.

Burney, E. (2005) *Making people behave: Anti-social behaviour, politics and policy*, Cullompton: Willan Publishing.

Campbell, S. (2002) *A review of Anti-Social Behaviour Orders*, London: Home Office.

Downes, D. (2007) 'Editorial: Ten years on', *Criminal Justice Matters*, no 67, Spring.

Gil-Robles, A. (2005) *Report by Mr Alvaro Gil-Robles, Commissioner for Human Rights, on his visit to the United Kingdom 4–12 November 2004*, Strasbourg: Office of the Commissioner for Human Rights.

Macdonald, S. (2003) 'The nature of the Anti-Social Behaviour Order – R *(McCann and others) v Crown Court at Manchester*', *Modern Law Review*, vol 66, no 4, pp 630–9.

Macdonald, S. (2006) 'A suicidal woman, roaming pigs and a noisy trampolinist: refining the ASBO's definition of "anti-social behaviour"', *Modern Law Review*, vol 69, no 2, pp 183–213.

Pratt, J. (2000) 'Emotive and ostentatious punishment: its decline and resurgence in modern society', *Punishment and Society*, vol 2, no 4, pp 417–39.

Sampson, R.J. and Laub, J.H. (1993) *Crime in the making: Pathways and turning points through life*, Harvard: Harvard University Press.

Simester, A. and von Hirsch, A. (2006) 'Regulating offensive conduct through two-step prohibitions', in A. von Hirsch and A. Simester (eds), *Incivilities: Regulating offensive behaviour*, Oxford: Hart Publishing.

Solanki, A.-R. et al (2006) *Anti-Social Behaviour Orders*, London: Youth Justice Board.

Stephen, D.E. and Squires, P. (2003) *Community safety, enforcement and Acceptable Behaviour Contracts*, Brighton: HSPRC, University of Brighton.

Stone, N. (2006) 'Legal commentary: "Enforcement of Anti-social Behaviour Orders" and "discretion in provision of secure PACE accommodation", *Youth Justice*, vol 6, no 3, pp 211-18.

Wain. N. (2007) *The ASBO: Wrong turning, dead end*, London: Howard League for Penal Reform.

EIGHT

A probation officer's story

Mike Guilfoyle

Banned from Camden

When I 'stumbled' across John in the Probation Office waiting room with his outreach worker, I remembered thinking, against a tight deadline, how I might have approached a considered assessment of this client. An earlier assessment had concluded that:

> It is clear from John's complex history over the last 15 years that he is a vulnerable individual who appears to have been as much a victim of his challenging behaviour as a victimiser of others. He is highly likely to come into contact with the Criminal Justice System in the future. It is also in my opinion [sic] clear that he will continue to represent a challenge to those Services engaged in meeting his complex needs.

John had been allocated to me initially for preparation of a Crown Court pre-sentence report. He was awaiting sentence for breaking into his former demoted flat, having recently been rehoused after a lengthy period as a street homeless person in a resettlement hostel. While I pored over the paperwork before me, I noticed that he was also in breach of an ASBO (imposed by Camden Council – widely acknowledged as London's ASBO champion – for eight years) for persistent begging while sleeping rough. It was accepted by all parties that when he attempted to break into his former flat he was 'out of it' due to a toxic combination of drink and drugs and had no proper recollection of how the offence might have occurred. When I enquired about the terms of the ASBO, he was totally vague and could only utter that he thought he was banned from entering the borough. Here was a first problem: the hostel in which he had been placed was only a short walk from the borough boundary. Furthermore the 'Camden ban' would actually prevent him from accessing some of the street-level services that might well have offered him targeted support.

I asked him whether he was concerned about the consequences of breaching his order or whether he viewed the ASBO as a deterrent. The Magistrates' Association recommended that the starting point for such breaches is custody. Unlike, according to tabloid media headlines, some of his younger counterparts, John did not appear to view his ASBO as a 'badge of honour' or 'street diploma'. No added kudos appeared to derive from what seemed a very self-destructive career path. Nor did he rail against the system; rather, he appeared bemused by the level of official attention his misdemeanours had attracted. What was the significance of Camden Council's eight-year ban? Surely the period imposed should be considered overlong by any definition? What was clear was that John was a vulnerable, confused and substance-dependent client.

His outreach worker provided the right combination of supportive concern and detached professionalism. But could she provide any corroborative information about the strictures that bound John to remain out of the London borough of Camden as a result of the ASBO? Although Camden does have an electronic database holding information about people in receipt of an ASBO, the point at issue with John was that his very vulnerability (he did in a clearer-headed moment accept that he could be 'argumentative') was entwined in his lengthy career as a homeless opiate user whose marginal lifestyle was so highly predictive of the risk of further reconviction.

He also proved to be a challenging historian when I inadvertently credited him with more offences for dishonesty on his antecedent list than he remembered being responsible for. The passage to the hostel, while seen as a 'turning point' by his outreach worker and also by John, was not without the residual reminders that his chaotic lifestyle brought with him. He missed his court dates and went into a further downward spiral, fearful that he had little to lose if he could not move ahead without the prospect of being breached for any unwitting incursion into the borough he had so many local connections with.

When he did resurface, his outreach worker was able to negotiate surrender to the warrant issued at the Crown Court. The outreach worker's ability to engage with John by breaking down some of the mistrust he showed in our interview was based on a degree of occupational flexibility that she enjoyed in being able to gain his hard-won confidence over many years. He actually asked the court that he be sent to prison rather than risk yet again being breached. For the original offence of burglary he was sentenced to 30 months' custody.

Even subsequent to this sentence, I still had difficulties obtaining a copy of the ASBO and its conditions from Camden, and remained unclear as to whether the ASBO breach was considered still outstanding (for, in passing sentence, the Crown Court had asked that all matters be resolved). Above all, I was unsure how John, who, when he can, avoids all contact with Probation, will fare when he is released on licence from prison.

My experiences and perceptions as a probation officer in a Central London Probation Office, covering an area with the highest overall crime rates in the capital, has been that an ever-increasing part of my caseload now contains those on Anti-Social Behaviour Orders. I refer to the current legal definition of anti-social behaviour (ASB) as that which is for present purposes framed within the, albeit contested, wording at the outset of section 1(1)(a) of the 1998 Crime and Disorder Act, but with further refinements in ASB legislation enacted since that time, most recently via the amendments to the 2006 Police and Justice Act. That such a definition lacks 'specificity and measurability' seems beyond question (Burney, 2005), but this is an area of analysis taken up by other contributors to this volume.

ASBO and redemption

I recently enjoyed reading about a fictionalised account of a young man on an ASBO based on the antics of a 16-year-old called 'JB', the central character in Danny Rhodes' lively debut novel *Asboville* (Rhodes, 2006). The redemptive storyline reminded me of the importance, in my own practice, of continuing to learn from the understanding of others' experiences and interactions in negotiating the new penal landscape of 'ASBOing', portrayed so well in Rhodes' novel. The challenge that I set myself is that, however stubbornly resistant some lives are to managing change, I have in mind a general working principle of 'never too early, never too late'. Yet the voices of front-line practitioners drawing on their own work-based experiences have been so often marginalised in recent policy debates. Furthermore, there is a marked absence of a positive image for probation in the popular mind – let alone the mass media. This has sapped front-line morale and made the service much more vulnerable to organisational change (Farrow, 2004). This unsympathetic environment often means that one can become so inured to the daily round of hard-pressed and demanding casework that one's own sensibilities become dented as another seemingly 'unresponsive' client is consigned to prison.

The added imposition of an ASBO (or, more particularly, the newest sentencing add-on and policing tool, the CrASBO – imposed post-conviction – under the 2002 Police Reform Act) can merely serve as yet another decontextualised risk factor to configure when putting together the initial Offender Assessment (OASys). In fact, many believe that the real risk lies in setting up offenders to fail. OASys is the national system for assessing the risks and needs of offenders. Developed jointly by the Prison and Probation Services, OASys is touted as the 'most sophisticated Offender assessment tool anywhere'. But I am ever mindful of the near inevitability of the prospect that breaches of such orders will feature in yet another soon-to-be-completed pre-sentence report. As with the enforcement of community penalties ('trapdoor to prison'), the political override seems to be to sidestep any evidence-based review that might highlight the mismatch between strict enforcement and reconviction. Added to this, there appears as an underlying characteristic of the new landscape of ASB enforcement what commentators have dubbed the 'creeping criminalisation of everyday life'. To be ASBOed (indeed the operative verb to '*slap* an ASBO' tells us plenty about how these issues are conceived) is now very much a part of the English language, and a familiar feature of probation caseloads.

I did my equivalent of the Home Office's 'one day count' and identified that no fewer than 20% of my caseload had fallen foul of the ASB legislation now or in the recent past. ASBO stories regularly flavour my colleagues' accounts of their own practice experiences, as witnessed by some of the more absurdly unrealistic and unmanageable restrictions that pepper the CrASBOs they are tasked to oversee as part of their wider supervisory remit. Humorous exchanges across the office desks often go something like:

> 'Guess what they have added to the list of blanket restrictions on this case?'
>
> 'Not to enter the area covered by the M25!'
>
> 'But how do they report to this Probation Office?'
>
> 'Or for that matter the Job Centre, GP surgery etc.'
>
> 'But conditions within orders can be appealed.'
>
> 'Yes', I say, 'but how many are successful in doing so?'

Probation practice now

How might a more constructive and less punitively inflected practice develop with those under supervision, and how can practitioners become more forward-looking and better engage with those caught up in the ASBO mire? Indeed New Labour's ambivalent hostility to probation, and the current legislative moves to abolish a public Probation Service via the Offender Management Bill, in many ways appears to mirror the febrile tabloid hostility to all forms of transgressive behaviour.

In response to this public policy onslaught, Harry Fletcher, Assistant General Secretary of the National Association of Probation Officers (NAPO), has been at the forefront of campaigning to 'Keep Probation Public' while also working with the AsboConcern Alliance. Together, they have undertaken to try to mitigate some of the more damaging effects of the ASB legislation and open up a second front to look more constructively at positive outcomes and good practice.

The impact of ASB on those local communities that often bear the brunt of many forms of multiple deprivation should be acknowledged at the outset and not left aside as a marginal consideration. As someone who for many years lived in one such high-crime neighbourhood in the 1990s (prior to the 1998 Crime and Disorder Act), one has to keep in focus that offensive behaviour and respectable fears have a long history. The 'dangerous other' has long occupied the attentions of social commentators, and criminological musings. Apparently as many as 80% of children between the ages of seven and 16 have been told off for playing outdoors (Joseph Rowntree Foundation, 2005; McMahon, 2006). Bringing ASB legislation to bear on children's play raises important issues. Just where does ASB begin and end (von Hirsch and Simester, 2006)?

I particularly recall how the need for a 'quick-fix' solution to the 'anti-social behaviour' of an especially vexed and troublesome neighbour dominated my own psyche for some time. I recollect that my own frustrations swung between angry – nothing was being done to resolve matters – and a vengeful desire for some executive action. After several momentous happenings, the 'cumulative impact of repeated incidents' and three court appearances, I moved to another part of London. At least for me the gateway to criminality was not the obvious next step!

Since then, the growth in the strategic importance of the 33 London Crime and Disorder Reduction Partnerships (Probation is a statutory partner), charged with mobilising local support for preventive action and developing reassurance policies, has been very impressive. Safer

Neighbourhoods, Civil Renewal, Community Safety (more latterly the Respect Agenda) are the neologisms that now designate – and increasingly dominate – our local initiatives. Whether community safety and security come only at the cost of producing a culture of suspicion will no doubt preoccupy other contributors to this volume. I am entirely in favour of a tiered approach to ASB, although I was quite unprepared for just how many agencies are now involved in the ASB policy, strategy and delivery industry. Until I perused Appendix 5 of the National Audit Office's report, *Tackling anti-social behaviour* (NAO, 2006), I had been fairly sceptical about the impact of these policies on the ground in some areas. However, the report does, creditably, favour a gradualist approach to ASB.

The recent pace of change, in organisational and legislative terms, facing the Probation Service has been phenomenal and the changes are still ongoing. Not the least significant of these has been the creation of NOMS (National Offender Management Service), an organisational behemoth that is geared eventually to supersede Probation. The new 'Working with Offenders' slogan proposed for Probation and based on the four tiers of the Management of Offenders model is: 'Punish, Help, Change and Control'. Any enduring humanistic ethos seems to many, in and out of the service, as increasingly anachronistic. Furthermore, the worrying retention of anti-social behaviour policies within the Home Office, with the creation of a new Ministry of Justice (in May 2007), hardly seems likely to lead to a more coordinated and integrated criminal justice system. Among the more troubling aspects of these 'modernising' changes (which are of course wider than just Probation) has been the corrosive impact of recent policies on probation casework. One obvious result has been increasing caseloads, fear-driven performance targets, macho–managerialist control strategies and actuarial standardisation. This, of course, has to be set against the time constraints allowed for any serious rehabilitative casework, estimated at 'about one third of one percent of the waking lives of offenders on supervision' (Farrall, 2002).

It is important to acknowledge that there has been a welcome revival of interest in effective one-to-one working relationships with offenders. How I try to enlist this renewed emphasis on working relationships, neatly conveyed in much of the re-energised desistance literature, is to recognise that it is as important to understand why people stop offending as it is to understand why they offend in the first place. Such issues need to be given greater professional attention. Furthermore, using good 'local knowledge' is an essential starting point in any constructive work with 'offenders'. Unfortunately, as a label, this is often eschewed by many Probation staff, concerned by the reductive and coarsening language of Probation, not least of which is the adoption of the alternative designation of Probation Officers as Offender Managers! It all rather begs a question as to whether we have given up on the eradication and prevention of offending. Maybe change and rehabilitation are no longer the primary focus of our interventions. Such are the cultural shifts in the Probation Service and the way it now sees its statutory role.

Professional judgement and intuitive feeling need to be preserved, rather than subsumed beneath the actuarial risk assessment methodology that is such a dominant feature of current probation practice. This results in a level of routinisation of practice as a way of coping with high caseloads. It also imposes greater stress on practitioners. As a counterpoint to this, John's story (referred to above) starkly calls into question the need to re-examine the possibility of any 'quick-fix' solutions. So much of what I had hurriedly read from John's accompanying paperwork left me uncertain about just how someone so clearly emotionally damaged by his early childhood experiences – the trauma of which was very vividly present in our interview – was expected to cope with an ASBO. Later experiences included cycles of bullying and withdrawal, leading to eventual exclusion from school, punctuated by choking and painful flashbacks. With his extensive care system experiences, multiple drug usage and IV-related HIV status, John, now aged 28 years, would readily qualify as a 'chronic and persistent offender'. His closest relationships with others had been for the most part bereft of any meaningful contact, as he struggled to deal with any close attachments and feared the early death that had been the fate of his 'remote' parents.

Can his effective reintegration be optimistically achieved without the restoration of full citizenship? That is, without the burden of an overly restrictive ASBO? Will John remain someone for whom enforcement and control are the only currency he knows? Yet he was an 'expert by experience' of the care/criminal justice system. The pattern of zero-tolerance policing that ensnared John and that was visited upon other parts of Kings Cross certainly disrupted local drug markets and cleansed the streets of drinkers, beggars and prostitutes, and this action certainly resulted in what appeared to be an exponential growth in requests for probation reports.

So what did I learn from this foreshortened encounter (as attempts to secure John's consent to some form of court-mandated drug treatment came to nought)? Clearly, there is some difficulty in policing and enforcing the terms of an ASBO if the recipient is altogether unclear as to what these terms actually mean. What of the issue of John's future risk management? As John is prey to so many different pressures to live within the law upon release, such complex risks must be many and diffuse.

Maybe I was trying to make too rapid a rate of progress in so short a space of time. The allotted timings for the preparation of his report and all the associated multiplicity of bureaucratic form filling are calibrated at just over six hours. Did I place too great a pressure on seeking quick real-time changes? When from my own practice experience, I am only too aware of the benefits of slowing things down so that hopes and aspirations can be realistically framed and relapses are seen as an ability to make progress rather than an automatic sign of failure. That is to say, it takes time to learn effective relapse prevention strategies before long-term recovery can be achieved. By the time people get the 'help' they need they are often in a 'bad way'. Certainly, inter-agency collaboration is a linch-pin for more effective working. This is actively promoted as the bedrock for one of the more welcome measures arising from the 1998 Crime and Disorder Act, the creation of Youth Offending Teams. But three enduring facets of good practice stand out for me as professional qualities necessary to working in partnership. Simply put, these include: effective listening, determined advocacy (rebranded as 'brokerage', as mention of advocacy is unlikely to feature in any performance management table!) and viewing people in the context of their whole lives.

Unfortunately, the strident 'we just need to bloody enforce things better' approach espoused by Louise Casey (the government's Respect Taskforce coordinator) could just as well have been uttered by many of her contemporaries in Probation. John's brief case history is, of course, just a snapshot from a practitioner's perspective, but I have calculated that my caseload, over the last 18 months, has contained over a dozen ASBO/CrASBO clients. They provide some representative features of the ways in which a collaborative approach acted as the spur to attempts to move clients towards accepting formal ameliorative treatment and/or re-engaging with other community providers, without losing sight of the need to be clear about statutory responsibilities. However, identifying personal strengths and deficits, seeing the process of change as a highly individualised one, fraught, sometimes ambivalent and contradictory, alongside the importance of shared decision making as well as recognising the salience of local situational factors and contexts, remains all important.

For clients such as John, 'criminogenic' needs such as drug treatment, accommodation, training and employment have to be addressed, and other ongoing support provided, if compliance with supervision is to have a chance to succeed and to help stabilise his lifestyle. I would not overlook non-criminogenic needs, equally important in establishing the right type of therapeutic alliance for clients such as John (Ward and Maruna, 2007), but what will result if his continuing ASB and drug usage continue unabated? The overarching policy area now lies within the Home Office remit, whereas his borderline offending is part of the Ministry of Justice apparatus. How will the much-vaunted Social Exclusion Unit's work on preventing reoffending (via its seven rehabilitative pathways for ex-prisoners) play out on the ground for John (Raynor, 2007)? If we only pursue enforcement-led policies will these exacerbate or reduce the likelihood that when John is released his own experiences of vulnerability and victimisation will be overlooked and we will continue to see him only as a troublesome offender?

Opposition to any methods seen as providing the community some respite from persistent 'low order' offenders is, at best, muted. But surely the fact that so many ASBOs are inappropriately imposed may cause people to demand a 'rethink' (NAPO, 2005)? All that I know about the work I do convinces me that, once the facts of any particular case are known, the punitive turn is not an inevitable outcome.

One's professional skills are too readily hindered by a system that too often places a low premium on such skills, while professional and experienced practitioners are constrained by ever more elaborate management mechanisms, designed to offer the public protection from certain types of offenders. As an experienced practitioner, at the heart of my professional practice is a holistic appreciation of the offender as a person in his/her social setting. This helps to shape my approach and, by dint of such experience, is more likely, in my opinion, to offer a better prospect of protecting the public by making for safer communities. Does the community that John will be returning to have a say? To the best of my knowledge the outstanding balance of John's ASBO still remains in force. Will resettlement have any meaning for him if the continuing threat of a penal sanction for the most trifling thing, such as straying accidentally into Camden, continues to govern his everyday choices? Or is it simply the case that much of the burgeoning growth in ASB legislation, with policy making running well ahead of any firm criminological evidence base, is itself deeply anti-social?

References

Burney, E. (2005) *Making people behave: Anti-social behaviour, politics and policy*, Cullompton: Willan Publishing.

Farrall, S. (2002) *Rethinking what works with offenders: Probation, social context and desistance from crime*, Cullompton: Willan Publishing.

Farrow, K. (2004) 'Still committed after all these years? Morale in the modern-day probation service', *Probation Journal*, vol 51, no 3, pp 206–20.

McMahon, W. (2006) *Bowlby's contribution for an ASBO age*, London: Crime and Society Foundation.

NAO (National Audit Office) (2006) *Tackling anti-social behaviour, House of Commons 99 session, 2006–2007*, London: National Audit Office.

NAPO (National Association of Probation Officers) (2005) *A briefing for the launch of ASBO concern: The last 6 years*, Briefing by H. Fletcher, London: NAPO.

Raynor, P. (2007) 'Community penalties: probation: "what works", and offender management', in M. Maguire, R. Morgan and R. Reiner (eds), *The Oxford Handbook of Criminology* (4th edn), Oxford: Oxford University Press.

Rhodes, D. (2006) *Asboville*, London: Maia Press.

von Hirsch, A. and Simester, A.P. (2006) *Incivilities: Regulating Offensive behaviour*, Oxford: Hart Publishing.

Ward, T. and Maruna, S. (2007) *Rehabilitation – beyond the risk paradigm, key ideas in criminology*, London and New York: Routledge.

Part Three
Anti-social behaviour case studies: particular social groups affected by anti-social behaviour policies

NINE

Rationalising family intervention projects

Sadie Parr and Judy Nixon

Introduction

As part of New Labour's drive to tackle anti-social behaviour, in January 2006 the government launched a 'new approach to the most challenging families' involving a national roll-out of 53 'Family Intervention Projects' (FIPs) (Respect Task Force, 2006a). This latest anti-social behaviour policy initiative, more commonly (and rather unhelpfully) referred to by the media as 'sin bins', provides families who are homeless or at risk of eviction (usually from social housing) as a result of anti-social behaviour with intensive support to address their often multiple and complex needs (Dillane et al, 2001; Jones et al, 2005, 2006; Nixon et al, 2006a, 2006b). Compared with alternative anti-social behaviour measures such as ASBOs or possession orders, FIPs are framed as representing a more 'sustainable' solution to anti-social behaviour, fostering the development of 'acceptable' and 'appropriate' conduct such that the landlord does not pursue legal action that may culminate in eviction and subsequent homelessness.

The particular form of support employed by FIPs varies from family to family, but commonly encompasses practical assistance in the home, provision of advice, liaison and advocacy support, signposting to other services, help in managing finances and claiming benefits, personal skills development, parenting skills training and behaviour management. Most of the projects operate an outreach-only support service to families living in their own homes, with a small number also providing an additional 'core' residential service comprising flats managed by the project. Families living in FIP core accommodation are required to adhere to a set of rules and regulations that usually includes a requirement for children and adults to be in the accommodation at a set time in the evening; restricted access in and out of the project building where the flats are located; visitors by permission only; together with specific rules deemed appropriate for particular families. Referrals to FIPs are made by a wide range of local agencies, with families' choice as to whether or not to work with the FIP highly constrained by the threat of homelessness or anxieties about the prospect of children being taken into care (Nixon et al, 2006a).

In this chapter, we draw on policy texts, newspaper reporting and rich data from a three-year qualitative study of six FIPs to explore the discursive field in which the projects are conceptualised. We begin by unpacking the political rationality that underpins and shapes FIP policy and, in so doing, make explicit the moral justifications that are employed, the way in which target families are problematised and the presupposed distribution of tasks among governing authorities (Rose and Miller, 1992). While locating our analysis within a governmentality framework, we accept that processes of governance are fraught with contradiction and discontinuities, with the outcome by no means certain (Flint, 2002; Raco, 2003; Stenson, 2005; Hughes, 2007; Prior, 2007). The focus of the second and third sections of the chapter is therefore on the ways in which the FIP political rationality is mediated, contested and challenged, by reference to media representations and the views of project staff and partner agencies on the role of FIPs in the governance of conduct.

Governmentality and political rationalities

Inspired by the work of Foucault (Burchell et al, 1991), governmentality studies seek to understand the way individuals are governed and govern themselves. The term acts as a macro-level framework for analysing how societies are governed and serves as a micro-level conceptualisation capturing the rationale of ruling and its techniques (Dean, 1999). Governmentality is therefore, in part, concerned with discourses and forms of representation that mark out the field in which problems and interventions are made 'thinkable' (Rose, 1990). The concept that we have taken from this literature is 'political rationality' (Miller and Rose, 1992), which refers to forms of calculation about political activity (Dean, 1999). These contain certain regularities and can be identified using methods of discourse analysis. In particular, attention is directed at differentiating their moral dimension (concerning the appropriate powers and distribution of tasks for different forms of authority and the ideals to which the activities of government should be directed), their epistemological character (how objects of government are conceptualised) and the distinctive idiom that translates 'reality' into a common language amenable to intervention. Political rationalities link thought with the exercise of power and are intrinsically connected to *technologies* of government. This is not simply concerned with the implementation of political programmes but involves the diverse mechanisms by which authorities enact government. With regard to political rule, governmentality thus redirects attention away from the actions of the state towards the localised settings in which power is actually exercised. As Garland suggests, within this framework of government at a distance, power is translated from one locale to another:

> power should be viewed as a matter of networks and alliances through which 'centres of calculation' exercise 'government at a distance'. Power is not a matter of imposing a sovereign will, but instead a process of enlisting the cooperation of chains of actors who 'translate' power from one locale to another. This process always entails activity on the part of the 'subjects of power' and it therefore has built into it the probability that outcomes will be shaped by the resistances or private objectives of those acting 'down the line'.
> (Garland, 1997: 182)

Such processes of 'translation' emphasise how technologies of governance devised at the centre are linked to and dependent on activities, organisations and individuals operating in a local context. However, the discursive focus of much of the work on governmentality has a tendency towards 'over-determinism', and in describing the rationalities that inform the development of FIPs we draw attention to the complex way in which central policies are mediated by local differences and forms of 'habitus' (Stenson and Edwards, 2001; Stenson, 2005) among local agents, highlighting the complexities, unintended consequences and resistance evident at a local level.

What type of political rationality informs the construction of FIPs?

Drawing on a number of official government texts, the following section addresses the question as to how the state-generated idea of FIPs has been constructed as a politically legitimate and moral policy.

As early as 2000, the government's Social Exclusion Unit urged local Crime and Disorder Reduction Partnerships to develop intensive interventions including, where appropriate, residential support for people who had been evicted or who had abandoned housing due to anti-social behaviour (SEU, 2000: 93). It took a further six years, however, for FIPs, modelled on the Dundee Families Project, to emerge as a flagship ASB initiative. After winning the 2005 general election, the then prime minister, Tony Blair, announced that a particular priority for the government would be to 'bring back a proper sense of respect' (Blair, 2005). It is in this context that, in January 2006, the Respect Action Plan (Respect Task Force, 2006a) outlined the key role FIPs were to play in the promotion of a 'twin track' approach to anti-social behaviour involving both action to address the underlying causes of problem behaviour and the use of appropriate sanctions to protect the community.

The stated primary objective of FIPs is to change the behaviour of 'a small number of highly problematic families that account for a disproportionate amount of anti-social behaviour' in order to 'restore safety to their homes and the wider community' (Respect Task Force, 2006b). A secondary objective is to 'tackle the causes of poor behaviour', defined across government texts primarily as poor parenting (Blair, 2005, 2006). This targeting of the family as the focus for intervention is not new. For over a decade, New Labour's legislative measures aimed at 'disorderly' as well as criminal behaviour have had 'problem' families at the centre (Muncie, 2002; Jamieson, 2005). The epistemological basis to the linking of ASB with the 'problem family' is complex, but essentially involves a focus on individual deficiencies rather than an acknowledgement of structural constraints, such as poverty, which make parenting harder (Hill and Wright, 2003; Gillies, 2005). On the one hand, government policy statements draw on moral underclass and risk-factor discourses to attribute causal primacy for anti-social behaviour to deficient parenting and dysfunctional families:

> I want to signal a specific new front in the government's response to anti-social behaviour. Poor parenting can lead directly through to anti-social behaviour. Bad parenting is not simply a private matter which is nothing to do with the rest of us. (Blair, 2005)

In defining 'the problem' in these terms, the discourse draws sharp distinctions between different types of people, with a minority of 'problem families' described in emotive terms as 'hard-core offenders' and while the discourse is silent on the precise nature of the 'offences' committed, it is alleged that such families 'terrorise' communities in which they live:

'Hard core' offenders are people who repeatedly act anti-socially, often in relation to different people, locations and situations. The numbers are small. However, they cause disproportionate problems for other people. In some cases it can be whole families, or groups of families, who are hard-core offenders. These families can effectively terrorise the community they live in and they may often be linked to crime and drug abuse. (SEU, 2000: 61)

On the other hand, the target families are simultaneously defined by reference to a social exclusion discourse as having 'multiple problems' requiring 'multiple solutions'. In this context, FIPs are rationalised as a response to the inability of agencies to support these families. Interestingly, this construction places the emphasis not on the failing of state and non-state agencies but on a failure of families' ability or willingness to engage with welfare agencies:

Families will often be engaged with a large number of services, many of whom are dealing with just one member of the family or one problem on a piecemeal basis – up to twenty is not uncommon. This can mean that agencies, like anti-social behaviour teams and support services, can be played off against each other, or that the families are confused as to which agency they need to listen to. (Respect Task Force, 2007a: 32)

In setting out the object of governance in these terms, the political rationality defines the fitting relationship between responsible authorities and promotes multi-agency assemblages of state, local authorities and voluntary organisations. Moreover, and as is emblematic of wider processes of governance, the policy creates new identities for agencies as they become responsible for the regulation of anti-social behaviour. In so doing, FIPs are constructed as a new brokering service enlisted to 'grip' both families and agencies involved with them: 'We will roll out schemes which "grip" problem households and the array of services involved with them and change their behaviour' (Respect Task Force, 2006a: 21).

One of the defining features of the governance of conduct is the employment of a moralising discourse emphasising surveillance, classification, self-regulation, welfare conditionality and community obligations (Flint, 2006). Families are conceptualised through a normative framework that constructs them as morally deficient and denotes certain desirable subjectivities that FIPs should aim to cultivate. FIPs, like many other strategies of government, do not simply contain and control behaviour, they seek to transform the 'anti-social' subject into an active, self-governing, responsibilised citizen in accordance with the stated norms attributed to the wider community (Flint, 2004). Families must be taught to 'take their responsibilities to their families and to other people seriously and try hard to raise their children well' (Respect Task Force, 2006b). It is the responsible authorities who are rationalised as knowing what constitutes appropriate and acceptable conduct and who are responsible for proactively (re)shaping families' behaviour.

A 'twin track' approach comprising support 'backed up' by the threat of disciplining sanctions provides the basis for a distinctive idiom through which the FIP policy is articulated and families rendered governable. As the policy has evolved, with a greater emphasis placed on the disciplining role of FIPs, the discursive constructs used to describe the projects have changed. Initially they were simply referred to as 'rehabilitation' or 'resettlement' projects, they subsequently became known as 'intensive family *support* projects' reflecting the novel supportive dimension of the intervention. More recently, however, they have been relabelled 'family *intervention* projects', with an associated repositioning of their role, in which support is reinforced by coercive sanctions. The nature of the sanctions to be employed if families fail to engage with FIP interventions has become ever more punitive, culminating in measures introduced in the 2007 Welfare Reform Act to withhold housing benefit from those who decline to work with family support projects. Indeed, as the then home secretary, John Reid, made clear, where families will not or cannot engage, disciplinary power in the form of sanctions will be used:

> A network of intensive projects will be created to work with the most difficult families and challenge them to change their behaviour. For those who refuse to take this help and continue to ruin the quality of people's lives, I believe it is right that the tax payer says enough is enough and stops funding their housing benefit ... (DWP, 2006)

The promotion of FIPs as a flagship policy of New Labour's third term reflects a move away from the employment of punitive disciplinary mechanisms to 'governance at a distance', involving a more diffuse set of governance technologies enacted through non-state agencies (Flint, 2003). Through the application of a normative gaze in which 'responsible' behaviour is defined in relation to shared values and expectations, FIPs can be seen to mirror wider trends in governance, combining proactive interventions with the sanction of disciplining power if families fail to improve their capacity for self-regulation. In the next section, we examine how the political rationality that informs the construction of FIPs is reflected and reinforced by media reporting.

How are Family Intervention Projects constructed in the media?

The issue of anti-social behaviour attracts a high level of media attention and there has been a proliferation of articles, radio and television programmes commenting on and reviewing the varied measures that have been introduced to control behaviour. It is to the complex, interdependent and dialectical relationship between policy making and news reporting (McLaughlin, 2002) that we now turn. Drawing on an analysis of articles published in the UK national press and in local newspapers operating in areas where FIPs are located (Nixon et al, 2008), we examine the ways in which FIPs have been portrayed in the news media and 'communicated' to the public.

Across the diverse range of reporting of FIPs, three (overlapping) dominant narratives are identified. We have labelled these as a 'not in my backyard' argument associated with 'demands from below' (Stenson, 2005) that resist the policy in protest that FIPs will harm the quality of life of local residents and are a 'soft option' for dangerous and disorderly 'others'; a 'rights-based critique' in which FIPs are portrayed as punitive and stigmatising; and, reflecting the political rationality that underpins government policy, a 'sustainable solutions' argument in favour of the projects. Although more common in the tabloid press, prominence and priority has been given to presuppositions and discourses associated with the 'not in my backyard' narrative and this is variously evidenced by the way in which articles sensationalise the public reaction.

The origins of this discourse can be located in the press coverage of the pioneering Dundee Families Project when the core residential unit was established in 1996. The negative construction of FIPs and families who work with them has, however, endured, as is illustrated in the selection of headlines collected over the period 2003–07 (Table 9.1).

As the headlines outlined in Table 9.1 indicate, at both national and local levels the majority of newspaper reports have historically tended to construct FIPs in pejorative terms, with the labels used to describe them carrying a host of negative connotations. As the emphasis is often on the nature of the core units, with their strict rules and regulations to which

Table 9.1: New media headline constructions of FIPs, 2003–07

Newspaper	Date	Headline
Star	16 October 2003	Hell Neighbours Caged
Express	16 October 2003	Problem Families to be Caged in Council Effort to Sort Out their Bad Attitudes: Yobs Sin Bin
Daily Star	20 October 2003	Scum in: Sin Bins are Open
Guardian	18 February 2004	Peace process: Manchester has just, very quietly, opened the doors to England's first unit for housing 'neighbours from hell'
Sunday Express	5 November 2006	New War on Yob Families: 50 secure units planned for neighbours from hell
Independent on Sunday	5 November 2006	The 'sin bin' society
Daily Mail	11 April 2007	Disruptive families are threatened with sin-bins
Daily Telegraph	12 April 2007	State Sin Bins for Britain's Worst Families
Express	12 April 2007	Asbo families face sin bins

the families must adhere, the projects are most commonly labelled as 'sin bins'. Derived from sports parlance, when applied to FIPs, 'sin bin' connotes a place where outcast families must be relegated following 'offences' of bad behaviour. This construction firmly establishes projects not as a supportive intervention but as a form of punishment where families are penalised.

A similarly pejorative discourse is apparent in the ways in which families working with FIPs are constructed. Media articles commonly draw on discourses which view 'the anti-social' as a distinct and homogeneous category. Indeed, families are viewed through the prism of terms such as 'scum', 'neighbours from hell', 'troublemakers', 'yob families', 'nightmare neighbours', 'nightmare families', 'hell families' and 'yobs'. The labels are unmistakably divisive and construct families in ways that perpetuate an 'us and them' mentality. The following extract demonstrates these points: 'Neighbours from hell will be caged in a real-life ghetto of grief in a scheme to crack down on antisocial behaviour. Problem families will be moved into fenced housing under the 24-hour gaze of attitude experts' (*The Star*, 16 October 2003).

As the government's commitment to family support interventions has increased, there has, however, been a corresponding shift in the discursive representations of the projects, with the gradual emergence of a 'sustainable solution' discourse that enables supporters of projects to take centre stage in newspaper articles:

> The trouble is, there is no cage, and the only bars of any height around the unit are to protect the cars of staff and residents. Furthermore, the project is not compulsory and residents will be free to come and go as they like. The media hype and ensuing news blackout is overshadowing what could become one of the most positive and progressive initiatives of recent years. (*Guardian*, 18 February 2004)

This suggests that New Labour as well as local political actors may be better at 'communicating' their policies to the public (McLaughlin, 2002), yet the term 'sin bin' has endured as a ubiquitous label for FIPs in both the tabloid and the broadsheet press.

This exploration of news media portrayals of FIPs highlights two key issues. First, the media are by no means neutral commentators but are active participants in the governmental apparatus, playing an important role in influencing and even driving political discourse and public opinion. Journalists employ symbolically powerful terms to depict FIPs and families referred to them. Some of these slang and crude terms such as 'neighbours from hell' and 'yob' promulgated by the mass media have been embraced and reproduced by unflinching politicians as standard (for example, Respect Task Force, 2007b). This demonstrates the unstable and unfinished nature of political rationalities. Second, public understandings of government policies are derived chiefly through the reporting and commentary of journalists and, in turn, such discourses potentially impact on the efficacy of FIPs. Not only do negative portrayals fuel public fear, leading to disputes about the location of FIPs (Nixon et al, 2008) but they also influence families who may decline the opportunity to become involved with an FIP as a refusal of and resistance to the stigmatising mentalities of governance invested in them by the media (and government).

Practitioners' construction of family intervention projects

Drawing on rich qualitative data derived from semi-structured interviews with FIP staff and partner agencies, in the final section of this chapter we highlight how political rationalities deployed 'on the ground' acquire fresh meaning in their processes of translation. Stenson (2005) and Hughes (2007) point to the important role that professional habitus, 'the cultural, emotional and instrumental repertoires and dispositions for cognition and action' (Stenson, 2005: 274), plays in the mediation and contestation of the political rationalities that shape policy frameworks. These 'discontinuities' have the potential to disrupt the logical unfolding of the governmental project (Prior, 2007: 3). At a micro-level the way such discontinuities are played out is illustrated by reference to the varied and contested way in which local stakeholders constructed the role of the FIPs together with the anti-social subject.

Within political rationalities, FIPs are portrayed as quasi-disciplining mechanisms designed to 'grip' both families and agencies. This was not a construction shared by practitioners, who expressed a different view of the role of the projects, seeing them not so much as 'gripping' services but rather as 'plugging' a gap resulting from the structural constraints welfare support agencies are subject to:

> often support and intervention would be missing because social services criteria for what they will accept and deal with is so high due to their resources so, yeah, I think there was, there was a gap and this was partly about plugging that gap. (Project manager)

Further, it was also clearly recognised that working practices in some FIPs have the potential to undermine established professional identities and modes of operation, as one social worker acutely pointed out: '[FIP workers] are not professionally trained, they are cheaper to employ and they're easier to control' (social worker).

Notwithstanding such criticisms, local stakeholders' views on the role of the FIP strongly reflected a 'sustainable solutions' discourse, with the projects constructed as providing a welcome alternative to more overtly disciplining interventions such as Anti-Social Behaviour Orders or possession action together with valuable additional resources in an under-resourced welfare sector. Many participants described how the development of the FIP reflected a sea-change in local responses to anti-social behaviour, involving greater recognition of the need to address the underlying causes of problematic behaviour. This change in approach was summed up by one respondent who had recently taken up a post with responsibility for the local authority anti-social behaviour strategy:

> When I was in housing, I dealt with all the problems and the anti-social bit, and I was always pushing for 'let's evict them'. You know, they're causing me problems on my estate and causing this and that, 'get them out'. But now, I deal solely with neighbour nuisance, now I'm on a different side of the fence now and I can accept how and why some families are falling apart. (Community safety officer)

A similar change of approach to dealing with anti-social behaviour in some communities was strengthened by growing support for FIPs among local residents:

> I think people recognised that it was a good way to be taking action and working with them … and most people are quite happy to give someone a second chance to let, you know, see what they do, let's see what this unit can do, let's see what outreach can do for them. (ASB officer)

With regard to the problematisation of target families, the subjectivities of families are constructed by project staff in a more nuanced manner than is reflected in political and media representations of the anti-social subject. While acknowledging that an individual's or family's behaviour was often disruptive and problematic, it was recognised that families were often living under extreme stress caused by complex and mitigating factors arising from their personal histories, often compounded by economic hardship:

> I think at the last count, something like thirty to forty per cent, I think it was about thirty-seven per cent of our families have a mental health problem that was, that was either a parent, or a child or more than one member of the family, and poor school attendance is prevalent in that forty per cent of cases, so those are big issues. Poverty is also a major player, benefits and being a single parent. (Project manager)

In talking about underlying factors that contribute to anti-social behaviour, poor parenting was frequently given causal primacy by project staff, who often described it in terms of repeat cycles of deficient parenting and instability in families, and technologies of government often focused on the improvement of parenting skills. However, in contrast to the state-generated political rationality, poor parenting was not viewed as a single and simple cause of anti-social behaviour – the two were not correlated in a straightforward manner. Rather, service users were seen as individuals who were facing a host of problems and pressures that had left them with limited personal resources, which, in turn, had made good parenting difficult. Poor parenting was linked to other vulnerabilities present within families' lives, such as poverty, mental health problems and unstable housing histories. Moreover, parents were not constructed as uncaring, wilfully irresponsible or neglectful, and project staff indicated that it was difficult to blame parents as the sole cause of their children's behaviour:

> It could go on down to anything to make poor parenting. Health, mental health issues with parents is a strong one that we've got at the moment, that's affecting the way they're parenting the children. Area which they're living in, the area's very deprived so there's nothing for them anyway, that's a strong one. (Project worker)

Whereas the 'problem family' and the 'neighbours from hell' form a distinct category in government and media rhetoric, local agents suggested that displays of anti-social behaviour exhibited by families were often symptoms of underlying complex problems that could just as well be manifested as depression or alcohol misuse. A number of project managers and key stakeholders felt that the multiple support needs identified in the families supported by the projects were no different from those found in families receiving other kinds of welfare provision. Rather, it was the fact that a family's problems had manifested themselves in such a way that their behaviour had been interpreted and labelled 'anti-social' that triggered intervention from an FIP:

> In practice a lot of the families that we work with are very, very similar – in terms of their presenting issues – to families that may use other family support services and what have you. The difference is the way some of those problems manifest themselves, is considered anti-social. (Project manager)

Consequently, a common thread running through descriptions of families was a reluctance to label families as 'anti-social' (or indeed 'neighbours from hell'), feeling that it was counterproductive in achieving change (Nixon et al, 2006a: 33). Indeed, project staff were very aware of the demonising impact of negative portrayals of families in political and media discourses and, as a result, stated that they tried to avoid the use of stigmatising labels: 'It's just youth nuisance problems; but the family, no I wouldn't say they were anti-social' (project worker).

At the same time, however, it was readily acknowledged that most families referred to the project had been involved in behaviour that was disturbing and distressing, and project managers freely expressed sympathy and understanding for those in the community who had made complaints. In reconciling these two different points of view, project managers were very clear about the distinction that should be made between referring to *behaviour*, as opposed to *people*, as 'anti-social'. They described how they use the term with great care, while at the same time being alert to the need to challenge other practitioners who may be less careful in their choice of language to describe families:

> I think it's a useful label as long as people understand that we're not, not speaking to sort of demonise them in that way by saying it, it's just a description of what they're actually doing. We're not calling them, I wouldn't call them anti-social families, that kind of skews the meaning completely and I wouldn't call the kids yobs like the government like to do. (Project manager)

Such comments, evidencing local resistance to dominant narratives, are potentially very significant. They serve to remind us of the continued importance of local political cultures, which, as Hughes suggests, could 'provide a space and opportunity for creative ideological appropriation by local alliances and networks which could challenge or at least negotiate the terms of repressive local and central tendencies' (Hughes, 2002: 127).

In this section of the chapter we have sought to illustrate how political rationalities are indeed mediated by the actions of local agents who respond to central government policy in a variety of ways. The evidence from our research suggests that professionals are not being passively 'operated on' and that critical narratives remain (Hughes, 2007). Political rationalities or government intentions are not accepted unproblematically by political agents in local settings but are dependent on the way local actors translate and implement policy.

Conclusion

Governmentality is concerned with the *how* of governing, the ways in which power and knowledge are exercised. An examination of 'political rationalities' encourages us to scrutinise the discourses, forms of knowledge and subjectivities that constitute FIPs.[1] The chapter has highlighted that while the government's 'new approach to the most challenging families' restates the domestic sphere as both the source of the problem of anti-social behaviour and a site for solutions, the enactment of FIPs within a local context remains complex and ambiguous. Paying attention to the localised development and operation of policies facilitates a more nuanced understanding of the manifestation of the FIP policy and reinforces the view that to properly debate anti-social behaviour policy we need to look at the practices of those who implement policy, not just the policy text itself. It is possible that, despite the pervasive nature of government rhetoric and the popular appeal of the Respect Agenda, these projects may have the potential to provide opportunities for local agents to be creative, opening up possibilities for genuinely positive interventions built of mutual trust and respect.

Note

[1] It is, however, important to be aware of the limits of the governmentality approach. As Garland (1997) and others have suggested, rather than viewing governmentality research as an autonomous mode of enquiry, it should be developed in conjunction with other sociological theories in order to move beyond 'how' questions to ask about the conditions of governmentality and underlying social structures and processes: 'Although governmentality refers to a set of techniques, practices and institutions that pre-exist and shape agents' behaviour and in this sense can be seen as something underlying, we still need a deeper level that explains the shaping of governmentalities themselves' (Joseph, 2006: 12).

References

Blair, T. (2005) 'Improving parenting', Speech, Meridian Community Centre, Watford, 2 September.

Blair, T. (2006) 'Respect Action Plan Launch', Speech, 10 January.

Burchell, G., Gordon, C. and Miller, P. (eds) (1991) *The Foucault effect: Studies in governmentality*, London: Harvester Wheatsheaf.

Dean, M. (1990) *Governmentality: Power and rule in modern society*, London: Sage.

Dillane, J., Hill, M., Bannister, J. and Scott, S. (2001) *Evaluation of the Dundee families project – final report*, Edinburgh: Scottish Executive.

DWP (Department for Work and Pensions) (2006) 'Action to tackle nuisance neighbours', Press release, 5 June.

Flint, J. (2002) 'Social housing agencies and the governance of anti-social behaviour', *Housing Studies*, vol 17, no 4, pp 619–37.

Flint, J. (2003) 'Housing and ethnopolitics: constructing identities of active consumption and responsible communities', *Economy and Society*, vol 32 no 3, pp 611–29.

Flint, J. (2004) 'The responsible tenant: housing governance and the politics of behaviour', *Housing Studies*, vol 19, no 6, pp 893–910.

Flint, J. (2006) *Housing and anti-social behaviour: Perspectives, policy and practice*, Bristol: The Policy Press.

Garland, D. (1997) '"Governmentality" and the problems of crime', *Theoretical Criminology*, vol 1, no 2, pp 173–214.

Gillies, V. (2005) 'Raising the meritocracy: parenting and the individualisation of social class', *Sociology*, vol 39, no 5, pp 835–53.

Hill, J. and Wright, G. (2003) 'Youth, community safety and the paradox of inclusion', *Howard Journal of Criminal Justice*, vol 42, no 3, pp 282–97.

Hughes, G. (2002) 'Crime and disorder partnerships: the future of community safety?' in G. Hughes et al (eds), *Crime prevention and community safety: New directions*, London: Sage Publications.

Hughes, G. (2007) *The politics of crime and community*, London: Palgrave Macmillan.

Jamieson, J. (2005) 'New Labour, youth justice and the question of "respect"', *Youth Justice*, vol 5, no 3, pp 180–93.

Jones, A., Pleace, N. and Quilgars, D. (2005) *Shelter Inclusion Project: Two years on*, London: Shelter.

Jones, A., Pleace, N. and Quilgars, D. (2006) *Addressing antisocial behaviour – An independent evaluation of Shelter inclusion project*, London: Shelter.

Joseph, J. (2006) 'Neoliberalism, governmentality and Social Regulation', Paper presented at *Sovereignty and Its Discontents* seminar, University of Kent, 27 April.

McLaughlin, E. (2002) '"Same bed, different dreams": postmodern reflections on crime prevention and community safety', in G. Hughes and A. Edwards (eds), *Crime control and community: The new politics of public safety*, Cullompton: Willan Publishing.

Miller, P. and Rose, N. (1992) 'Political power beyond the state: problematics of government', *British Journal of Sociology*, vol 43, no 2, pp 172–205.

Muncie, J. (2002) 'A new deal for youth: early intervention and correctionalism', in G. Hughes, E. McLaughlin and J. Muncie (eds), *Crime prevention and community safety: New directions.* London: Sage.

Nixon, J., Hunter, C., Parr, S., Myers, S., Whittle, S. and Sanderson, D. (2006a) *Interim evaluation of rehabilitation projects for families at risk of losing their homes as a result of anti-social behaviour*, London: Office of the Deputy Prime Minister.

Nixon, J., Hunter, C., Parr, S., Myers, S., Whittle, S. and Sanderson, D. (2006b) *Anti-social behaviour Intensive Family Support projects: An evaluation of six pioneering projects*, London: Office of the Deputy Prime Minister.

Nixon, J., Parr, S., Hunter, C., Sanderson, D. and Whittle, S. (2008) *The longer-term outcomes for families who have worked with Intensive Family Support projects*, London: Communities and Local Government.

Prior, D. (2007) *Continuities and discontinuities in governing anti-social behaviour*, Birmingham: University of Birmingham.

Raco, M. (2003) 'Remaking place and securitising space: urban regeneration and the strategies, tactics and practices of policing in the UK', *Urban Studies*, vol 40, no 9, pp 1869–87.

Respect Task Force (2006a) *Respect action plan*, London: Home Office.

Respect Task Force (2006b) *Family Intervention Projects: Respect guide,* London: Home Office, available at www.respect.gov.uk/article. aspx?id=5846

Respect Task Force (2007a) *Respect handbook: a guide for local services*, London: Home Office, (available at www.respect.gov.uk/members/ article.aspx?id=9764).

Respect Task Force (2007b) 'Innovative new help to tackle "neighbours from hell"', News, 11 April.

Rose, N. (1990) *Governing the soul: The shaping of the private self*, London: Routledge.

Rose, N. and Miller, P. (1992) 'Political power beyond the state: problematics of government', *British Journal of Sociology*, vol 43, no 2, pp 173–205.

SEU (Social Exclusion Unit) (2000) *Report of Policy Action Team 8: Anti-social behaviour*, London: The Stationery Office.

Stenson, K. (2005) 'Sovereignty, biopolitics and the local government of crime in Britain', *Theoretical Criminology*, vol 9, no 3, pp 265–87.

Stenson, K. and Edwards, A. (2001) 'Rethinking crime control in advanced liberal government: the "third way" and the return to the local', in K. Stenson, and A. Edwards (eds), *Crime, risk and justice: The politics of crime control in liberal democracies*, Cullompton: Willan Publishing.

TEN

Street life, neighbourhood policing and 'the community'

Stephen Moore

Although street-life people (defined later) may not, at first sight, appear to be a major issue when discussing anti-social behaviour in a national context, in fact the public's response to them provides a number of interesting insights into the process by which certain groups come to be viewed as a threat and their consequent treatment by the wider community. The theoretical insights gained here can equally be applied to understanding the treatment of other groups, such as young people, new migrants and Travellers.

In this chapter I aim to discuss the mechanisms by which certain groups become increasingly *visible* as threats to public safety, and the conditions under which they become *demonised*. I then suggest that the 'default position' of communities, when asked what they want done about a problem group, is, and, historically, often has been, to seek their *elimination*. The process of 'getting rid of' or eliminating a group perceived as threatening is more likely to occur when power over decision making on the future of the 'out-groups' is handed over to communities. Neighbourhood policing, one of New Labour's major policing initiatives, may increase the likelihood of greater punitiveness and social exclusion (Squires, 1998). Finally, and briefly, I will explore the notion of 'community' and 'neighbourhood' in New Labour thinking, specifically as it applies to anti-social behaviour (ASB), and suggest that those very 'out-groups' that often appear to threaten 'the community' are arguably the communities that actually contain most of the elements that commentators and politicians tend to regard as central to their notions of community.

The basis of this chapter is research I have been conducting for over two years in what I will call Cathedral City, exploring the street-life people's relationship to local communities, the council and the police. This has been done by examining official documents on the problem, and through interviews and discussions with local council officials, members of organisations working with the street-life people and with police officers at various levels charged with organising and enforcing the regulations concerning street-life activities. I have also attended public meetings where the local community has expressed its views about the existence and activities of street-life people, and interviewed members of the public. Finally, I have both observed and spent time with the street-life people themselves.

'Street life' in the UK

No clear definition exists for people with a street lifestyle, or street-life people as I will call them here, but I would suggest they have all or most of the following characteristics:

• they choose to live out the majority of their waking hours (and sometimes sleeping ones too) in the company of others in public places;
• they perform the whole range of social and physical activities in public places, including those which are generally regarded as private and/or inappropriate;
• they are generally unwaged;
• they are often dependent on drugs and/or alcohol.

Street-life people are those clustered groups of badly dressed, rough-looking men and women of all ages whom you encounter on the marginal areas of the centres of most British cities. They are regarded as an aberration in affluent Britain, often stumbling along or swaying unsteadily on a street corner or in shop doorways. People pass them quickly, avoiding eye contact, or, as they beg for money for 'a sandwich and a cup of tea', some may pause to hand over a little loose change.

Street-life people are often confused with homeless people/rough sleepers, both by the public and in policy research, and indeed there is an overlap between the two groups. Although rough sleepers tend to be street-life people, actually the majority of people who live out their lives on the streets have accommodation – either social housing or hostels. Although figures are extremely difficult to obtain, work done for Cathedral City Council indicates that approximately 70% of those the police and council defined as having a street lifestyle were not 'homeless'.

There are no national figures available for those with a street lifestyle, nor even official estimates. In Cathedral City the numbers of street-life people actually on the streets *at any one time* is about 15 times the numbers of rough sleepers. However, as the street-life population is a fairly mobile one, with people moving in and out of the area, becoming ill or even dying, the total number is likely to be considerably higher. The Department for Communities and Local Government (DCLG) estimates that only 495 people are sleeping rough on any one evening in Britain (DCLG, 2005), although Randall and Brown (2002) suggest that the true figure is probably ten times this. One could estimate, then, that the minimum figure for street-life people in Britain may be around 7,500. However, it is not unreasonable to argue that the true figure is likely to be much higher, given that the most accurate estimate of rough sleepers in London alone is over 3,000 (CHAIN, 2005). In terms of homelessness, the charity CRISIS suggests that there are 380,000 homeless in Great Britain as a whole (CRISIS, 2006).

Street-life people are found all over Britain, as we shall see later, although in many situations they are 'invisible', that is, they exist in the run-down parts of the city centres, where they merge into the background of most people's daily lives. They are, however, most visible in tourist cities, partly because of the increased chances of earning from begging and partly because they are much more visible to the public here in the attractive and affluent city centres. So, cities such as London, Brighton, Cambridge, York, Oxford and Bath all have significant street-life issues. However, increasingly, as cities seek to regenerate the less attractive central areas, street-life people start to be an issue.

Randall and Brown found that street-life people typically spend 18 hours a day outside throughout the year. About one third of their sample had been living this way for more than five years and virtually all the people interviewed had spent some time sleeping rough. Typically, street-life people drink and use drugs and may beg to obtain funds. Randall and Brown (2006) found that:

> Some [street-life people] sleep in hostels at night, but spend much of the day and evening on the streets. However, very few hostels require residents to be out during the day. Some sleep in day centres or hostels during the day, but are out on the streets at night moving around. A few have been rehoused into a permanent home but have failed to settle properly and still have their social lives on the streets. People dependent on begging for a substantial part of their income have to spend large amounts of time on the streets, even if they have accommodation. (Randall and Brown, 2006)

The issue in Cathedral City

Cathedral City is a small city with a particularly attractive centre, situated around the historic college buildings of a university. Most relevant to street-life issues, there are a number of large green spaces throughout the city centre. The city appears to be, and is, affluent, with some of the highest house prices in the UK. It is popular with tourists and foreign visitors, as well as having a large influx of foreign students in the summer. As such, it presents an attractive locale for street-life people, who obtain much of their income by begging. It also has a well-deserved reputation for being a liberal city with a range of charities and services for rough sleepers, as well as having a comprehensive programme to try to assist street-life people and drug users/alcohol dependants. However, Cathedral City, like most UK cities, has a significant number of social problems, including a chronic housing shortage, significant pockets of poverty and a range of crimes, including theft and robberies from foreign students. It also tends to have quite high numbers of beggars, buskers and *Big Issue* sellers. Bordering the historic city centre are other, less attractive zones; one of these, the Field Road area, consists of closely packed Victorian terraces originally built for railway workers, with an outer layer of social housing developments. The road itself is about a mile long and has a drug dependency unit situated towards one end and a night shelter for homeless people at the other. There are also some hostels for homeless people located in roads off Field Road itself.

Street-life people have been a presence in Cathedral City for a considerable number of years. From 2001 onwards yearly surveys showed an increase in the levels of concern regarding street-life people – in fact, by 2003 the demand for the removal of homeless people from the streets had risen to fifth place in concerns expressed by residents. These concerns were most forcefully expressed in the Field Road area. Each day those members of the street-life community dependent on drugs attend the drug dependency unit where, after being breathalysed (methadone would not be prescribed if they had been drinking that day), they would be given their prescription. The street-life people would then buy cans of extra-strong alcohol and gather in areas of Field Road to pass the time. Every day there was a considerable presence of street-life people traversing and then congregating in the road.

During 2003/04 a vocal minority of residents made approaches to the city council using a variety of means, including petitions to the council, direct approaches to local councillors, complaints to the police and letters to the local newspaper to 'get something done' about the issue.

An image was generated of a community outraged by the behaviour of outsiders. The response of the authorities, in line with government exhortations for local councils to consult with communities (DCLG, 2006), was to undertake a series of public meetings. These meetings were generally well attended at first, with the majority of people expressing their outrage at the behaviour of the street-life people. It is not possible to know how representative of the feelings of the broader community the public meetings were, but letters to the local newspaper were overwhelmingly in support of a more aggressive approach to street-life people.

Language commonly used by both the local press and community leaders often referred to the need to 'clear up' or 'clean up' Field Road, to 'purge' the area, 'get rid of' the nuisance. One speaker referred to the street-life people as 'lepers' and suggested that they should be moved out of the area into some sort of 'colony' of their own. The tone of the meetings was that the street-life people were threatening and disrupting the community by their activity. Strongly influenced by this public pressure and central government's exhortations to use the punitive new anti-social behaviour measures introduced in 1998 and 2003, the city council and police force decided to take a harder line over the 'problem'. The adoption of a tougher line was reinforced by a frequently reiterated belief that the Cathedral City authorities had traditionally taken a 'soft' line on such issues, that this was part of the problem and that some hostels were virtually conspiring to exacerbate the problems (such claims were never substantiated).

Initially, the police argued for a ban on drinking alcohol in designated public places (DPPO), a power that was introduced in the 2001 Police and Criminal Justice Act, and this was supported by the majority of people attending the public meetings. However, the council opposed this and sought instead to introduce a local by-law. After a number of fairly heated public meetings it was finally agreed to introduce a Section 30 Dispersal Order (2003 Anti-Social Behaviour Act) for Field Road. Such orders give the power to police officers, within designated areas, to order groups of more than two people to disperse who, in the opinion of the police officer, are behaving in such a way that a member of the public feels they are being 'harassed, intimidated, alarmed or distressed'. Orders last for six months and must then be renewed.

The police also decided to be more proactive in their use of ASBOs and targeted these against a small number of street-life people. The initial results seemed very positive (at least for the area's residents). Complaints from the public dropped and the numbers of street-life people in Field Road fell considerably. The local media carried glowing reports of how successful the action had been. However, displacement then occurred and the street-life people began to gather further into the centre of the city. As a consequence, the police and council then designated a number of other Dispersal Orders to cover these new gathering places. Over a period of more than two years, the effects of the Dispersal Orders have been to displace groups of street-life people to an ever widening arc around central Cathedral City and a sort of game developed in which street-life people would be dispersed from one area, then move to just outside that area, until the police would introduce a new Dispersal Order moving them on once again. At one point, the street-life people who drank alcohol decided that the best place for them was to congregate on a large public green just outside the main police station. By the late morning there might well be up to 40 people gathering to drink and socialise. The police were pleased with this situation because they could keep an eye on them, and the street-life people felt that they would be allowed to stay there because 'the public' could easily avoid close contact. However, yet again, after complaints from councillors, tourists and members of the public, a Dispersal Order was applied here as well.

After more than two years of Dispersal Orders and ASBOs, a public meeting was demanded by Field Road residents. The constant displacement of street-life people around the city had finally driven them back to areas bordering Field Road and they had taken to gathering in a small play park just outside the original dispersal area, only half a mile from their original gathering point.

The eliminative ideal

While the ASBOs and Dispersal Orders may have temporarily placated the complainants, it subsequently became clear that residents were less concerned with controlling the behaviour of the street-life people than with getting rid of them. Indeed, the key theme that emerged over the four years was that street-life people were in the wrong place and that they should just 'go away'. *How* that was achieved represented the split between local residents, rather than *if* this should happen, as nobody put forward the argument that street-life people might have a right to spend their time on Field Road. All speakers at the public meetings shared the notion that street-life people were ruining life for the normal community and if only they were sent away things would be fine. The division among attendees was between those who called for more vigorous police action in driving the street-life people away and those who suggested that the street-life people should be able to live their lifestyle – but just not in their area. Calls were also made for the closure of the drug dependency unit.

Rutherford has referred to this desire for problematic groups to just disappear (1997) as the 'eliminative ideal'. How this happens varies across time and society and may involve extermination, imprisonment or confinement in welfare institutions (it also relates closely to the chorus of media approval for the so-called 'sin bins' for difficult families, see Parr and Nixon, Chapter Nine in this volume). However, the key point is that what actually happens to the individuals when they are 'eliminated' seems not to be of great concern to the public who are rid of them. Clearly, the eliminative ideal runs almost entirely contrary to the focus on social inclusion that has been claimed as such a central feature of recent government 'community' policy.

This eliminative community response to socially problematic groups has a long history, and can be related directly to practices and discourses that date from at least the medieval period in England and that sought to find solutions to forms of deviancy through 'pushing away' or 'clearing out' from society those considered to pose a threat to social order. According to Rutherford:

> The eliminative ideal strives to solve present and emerging problems by getting rid of troublesome and disagreeable people with methods which are lawful and widely supported. (1997: 117)

The actual form of elimination varies from the more liberal approaches (therapeutic communities) to the most savage (transportation and the Holocaust), but the underlying theme remains the same – to get rid of the problem by getting rid of the people. Moore and Scourfield (2005) have applied the notion of elimination to street-life people, arguing that this is the default position of most community meetings when it comes to groups perceived as threats.

By the 19th century, according to Rutherford, eliminative processes began to take place within a discourse the moral tone of which increasingly constructed 'vagrants' as a 'social contagion', a 'residuum', a 'plague', or as 'social contaminants' (Morris, 1998). This group, characterised by fecklessness, moral turpitude and cultural depravity, was constructed as an inferior 'race' apart and therefore had to be 'cleansed' from decent society. As McConville (1998) puts it, referring to minor criminals: '[These convicts] were seen as a national threat, people whose implacable criminal natures were compounded by an animalistic sexuality and profound immorality and who were likely to expand a dangerous subversive class' (p 121). Here we see expression of two strong recurrent themes that underpin elimination. First, there is the fear of contamination/pollution and, second, there is the essentialising, pathologising construction of the 'contaminants' (Joffe, 1999).

Those other groups that posed a threat for various reasons were also subject to eliminative processes, to be placed in closed institutions:

> The 'Great Incarcerations' of the nineteenth century
> – thieves into prisons, lunatics into asylums, conscripts into
> barracks, workers into factories, children into school – are
> to be seen as part of a grand design. Property had to be
> protected, production had to be standardized by regulations,
> the young segregated and inculcated with the ideology of
> thrift and success, the deviant subjected to discipline and
> surveillance. (Cohen, 1985: 25)

From the public perspective, then, one important consequence of this process of institutionalisation was similar to transportation in that it made deviants *invisible* in society – elimination through incarceration.

During most of the 20th century, eliminative processes were justified in medical and therapeutic discourses; people with mental illness and those with learning difficulties were placed in isolated institutions for their own good (Cohen, 1985). The increase of street-life people may be linked to the decline in large-scale institutions and the development of the alternative model of reform of community care that increasingly led to people with a range of social and mental difficulties becoming more visible in public places. Accordingly, the people of Field Road are doing nothing new in expressing their desire for the street-life people to disappear: in one sense they are simply following a long historical tradition, although it is important to appreciate the contexts in which they come to articulate these particular intolerances.

However, before the desire for elimination comes into play, there must be a process by which certain groups come to be seen as falling into the category of eligibility for elimination. There are three principal components of this process: visibility, demonisation and matter-out-of-place/pollution.

Visibility

It is not immediately obvious why the problem of street-life people rose to the top of people's concerns in Cathedral City by 2003. There was clearly a very significant increase in the numbers of street-life people gathering in the city centre and police statistics suggest that the numbers begging had increased markedly over a three-year period. This may also be partially linked to the gradual closure of residential institutions for the mentally ill and the introduction of community care in the 1990s, as a result of the Griffiths Report (Griffiths, 1988). However, the growth of the problem could also reflect a gradual reshaping of Cathedral City, with some of the traditionally working-class urban areas, in particular Field Road, becoming increasingly gentrified. Hancock (2003) has suggested that the reshaping of urban areas since the 1990s has had a significant impact on perceptions and patterns of victimisation. Middle-class areas appear to have significantly lower levels of tolerance of anti-social behaviour than working-class areas (Wood, 2004). Yet the numbers themselves are not so great that it would appear to be an obvious problem – indeed the casual visitor to the city might not even notice the presence of street-life people apart from a few people begging.

One concept that has received relatively limited attention in social science theorising and that may help in understanding how their presence came to be such a problem is that of *visibility*. The term was first used explicitly by Slovic (1992), who questioned why the public tend to react to certain perceived threats in a concerned manner, compared with the much lesser concern shown towards other problems that might be judged objectively as more harmful. Slovic argued that the key element is visibility, and that the visual impact of a threat plays a significant part in public perceptions of a risk.

This visibility thesis is particularly important for understanding the public response to anti-social behaviour because the actual amount of crime perpetrated by street-life people is in fact relatively small; the crime rate in Field Road actually rises in the evening, when they are absent. Their activities during the day are highly visible and local residents find them threatening, but the street-life people are not actually engaged in significant levels of crime. Normal social interactions, such as are carried out within all groups of people, including arguing, raised voices, laughter and socialising, are all carried out in full view of passers-by. As one resident said:

> groups of them congregating around the old John Lewis site and by the toilets – they're so loud and messy that you just don't want to … er … walk past them … and if they see you looking they can get really rude. I just walk by and ignore them, but I don't like going past them … I don't like them acting as if … they own the place. (Shop assistant)

Of course, the actions of street-life people may be more dramatic and extreme, but it is perhaps less the activities themselves that draw people's attention and disapproval than it is their being played out in full public view. But the visibility of a group does not make it necessarily perceived as a risk. Students are commonplace in Cathedral City, as are tourists – but neither group generates fear in the city. The notion of visibility also provides an explanation of why that behaviour becomes visible and interpreted as threatening. The notion of 'signal crimes' is useful here.

Innes (2004) argues that public concerns about their own level of crime risk rarely reflect the statistical reality (as is the case with the street-life people); instead, some forms of crime and disorder are 'especially visible to people and are interpreted by them as "warning signals" about the risky people, places and events that they either do, or might, encounter in their lives'. Innes suggests that certain forms of behaviour and signs (such as broken glass, faeces, graffiti) can plug into wider cultural concerns and generate a sense of fear and threat. Citing Goffman to suggest how certain forms of behaviour link to wider cultural concerns to generate this fear, he writes:

> when an individual finds persons in his presence acting improperly or appearing out of place, he can read this as evidence that although the peculiarity itself may be a threat to him, still, those who are peculiar in one regard may well be peculiar in other ways too. (Goffman, 1972, cited in Innes, 2004: 341)

Applying Innes' signal crimes analysis to street-life people, they demonstrate exactly this threat to normality. Their (apparent) unpredictable and sometimes unpleasant behaviour and their unkempt appearance frightens local residents and chimes with stereotypes of mad, dangerous offenders. As one resident put it: 'they get drunk, they poo and urinate and swear – would you want that around you?' (audience member, public meeting). And another:

> well, I don't like them particularly, though I must say I er, er feel sorry for them, sort of ... but it's more the older people and children that I worry about. You er ... just don't ever know what next, what they are going to do. I just steer clear, but, as I say, that's easy for me to do. (Resident after public meeting)

Yet not everyone is concerned about the street-life people; indeed for many students and residents of the area the street-life people do not have 'visibility'. Innes suggests just this when he refers to the 'shifts in frequency and intensity as people traverse and navigate different social situations' (2004: 337). This is a useful insight, as anti-social behaviour is something that is defined by the victim and whether people are offended by it or not – its visibility to people varies. So, for example, when a mixed group of male and female students was asked about their fears of the Field Road area, a large majority thought it was a very, or fairly, safe place. The fears they expressed were more likely to centre on groups of young males. Street-life people were not seen as an issue, and I use the word 'seen' here in two ways: first, they were not perceived as a threat, but also they were not really noticed by the students.

Interestingly, over the period of the study core groups of residents have been vocal in their concerns over the problem of street-life people, and at various times other groups have entered and left these discussions. Many of the earlier concerns were raised by traders in the area, yet by the third year their interest seems to have waned. On the other hand, in the original public meetings regarding the street-life issue, no younger mothers from the social housing estates in one part of the area attended. By 2007, when the effect of the Dispersal Orders was to force street-life people into hanging around in their area, their attendance was noticeable and they were vocal in demanding an end to the situation. This would strongly suggest that concerns over anti-social behaviour impact differently at varying times and in changing circumstances.

So, street-life people are clearly visible, clearly different and clearly frighten some but not others. Though quite why some people are less concerned than others about street-life people is a further question.

Demonisation

Visibility tends to go hand in hand with another process – that of *demonisation*, to use Young's (1999) term. Young suggests that demonisation occurs when problematic people are classified as not belonging to society, existing only as outsiders and threats. This is an accurate description of the views of residents who see street-life people as behaving irrationally and objectionably, with the only possible motivation for their actions ascribed to drugs or alcohol. There is an element of truth in this for a small minority of street-life people, although, as we shall see later, the majority of them make reasonable choices, given the hand they have to play.

According to Young, the processs of demonisation is composed of three elements. The first of these is the *ascribing of an essentialist other*, by which the person who is seen as the problem is seen as being profoundly different from the normal person. The person being demonised is viewed as failing to share common, human characteristics and therefore sacrifices the claim to reasonable treatment:

> [the street-life people] are just ... well, they are ... behave, well the only way to describe it is like almost animals sometimes... (Audience member, public meeting)

Such remarks, and others like them, allowed the local residents to cut off the street-life people from ordinary society, such that normal standards of concern were not seen as appropriate to them.

The second element consists of the *reaffirmation of normality*. This is an idea clearly borrowed from Durkheim (1982), and is the shared belief among the community that the behaviour of the problem person unambiguously steps over the line of reasonable behaviour (for example, using heroin and discarding the used needles in a children's play area). This contrasts with much marginal behaviour towards which 'ordinary' people may hold ambivalent attitudes (for example, smoking marijuana):

> It isn't possible to take children into the park any more, I mean these people and their dogs behave in a way that you know is so inconsiderate. Well, worse ... I took my children and our dog in there a few weeks ago, and their dogs just attacked ours and when ... I was perfectly polite and just asked them if they would you know get hold of their dogs and their language ... they just swore. I can never take my children in there again. (Audience member, public meeting)

Finally, there is a process of *distancing* by which people believe the anti-social behaviour is the result of personal failings in the individual and is not related to wider problems of society. Such attitudes persist despite the fact that the available evidence for street-life and homeless people is that the majority have been in care during childhood or have been in the armed forces, and/or suffer from a range of physical and mental illnesses (Diaz, 2006).

> I don't think we should blame them, they are ...
> can't help it ... the way they are is a result of drugs
> and drink and things ... but why should we suffer?
> (Audience member, public meeting)

Pollution and contamination

The final theme in social science writing that helps to understand
the attitudes of the community towards street-life people is that of
pollution and *contamination*. Earlier we saw that in the 19th century
eliminative processes began to take place within a changing discourse
that emphasised a moral tone of contagion, with 'vagrants' described
as a 'social contagion', a 'plague', or as 'social contaminants', according
to Morris (1998). They were also, according to Morris, viewed as an
inferior 'race' apart and therefore must be 'cleansed' from decent society
– a term with many frightening resonances. Similarly, the 'pollution'
of the area was a constant theme of complaints from residents, and in
particular they were concerned about discarded needles and faeces. This
was very much 'matter out of place', to use Douglas's term (1992);

> You ought to go out the back of my shop, every morning I
> come out to find it full of their muck. (Audience member,
> public meeting)

> I don't mind them as people, it's just that they shit behind the
> bushes in the park. (Audience member, public meeting)

> Three thousand needles that's how many we found. Kids
> can't play anywhere 'cos they come across these things. Parks
> are no-go areas. (Audience member, public meeting)

What we have seen so far is that the community in Field Road has *made
visible* the street-life people and in doing so has come to see them as a
problem. The process of becoming visible involves reconfiguring the
activities of the street-life people as a problem and then moving on to
a stage where, through a process of *demonisation*, the street-life people
lose the right to be in the area. Further support for the argument that
they should be sent away (*eliminated*) comes from their presence on
the streets and in other 'inappropriate places' where their activities are
likely to *contaminate* children and *pollute* the area.

Communities, policing and ASB

So far we have examined the position of the street-life people in terms of the 'problem' perceived by the local community, exploring how the situation has arisen and what the local community wants to be done about the street-life people. We now consider the impact of neighbourhood policing on this situation.

The notions of *community* and *social capital* have been extremely important in New Labour thinking and have permeated policy on a range of issues. In relation to the former, a significant influence is usually attributed to Amitai Etzioni's (1993) notion of communitarianism, which is founded in the notion of the existence of a community of interconnected people who balance their responsibilities as individuals towards their community on the one hand and on the other expect certain rights from it in return. Likewise, Putnam's (2000) concept of social capital has emphasised the importance of *social networks* that create 'norms or reciprocity and trustworthiness'.

The thrust of New Labour policy has been to attempt to reconstitute the social bonds of community that have been seen to become lost over time. Reflecting this, the White Paper *Building communities, beating crime* (Home Office, 2004), *The National Policing Plan 2005–2008* (Home Office, 2005) and the *National Community Safety Plan* (Home Office, 2006) have led to the creation of a new style of neighbourhood policing that stresses the need for the local community to engage in identifying priorities and requires the police to be responsible to 'the community' through public meetings. The police are also required to work in collaboration with a range of other agencies – broadly speaking, all those who are members of the local Crime and Disorder Reduction Partnerships.

The idea, rooted somewhere far back in the criminology of new-left realism (Lea and Young, 1993) and communitarianism (Etzioni, 1993), was that, by drawing local communities into influencing policing policies, the police force would gain greater respect and legitimacy in the eyes of the public:

> as a Government, we have a firm belief in strong, empowered and active communities ... Specifically in terms of community safety, we want to see increased policing by active *cooperation* between the public and police, not just traditional notions of *consent*. People closest to the problems in their own neighbourhoods and areas have the best ideas about how they can be addressed. They should have a

genuine opportunity to help shape and to be a part of the solutions. (Home Office, 2006: 15)

The government makes clear how the public should voice these concerns in the White Paper *Building communities, beating crime*, which states that:

> If the service that a community receives does not meet the standards set out in their local contract with the police, or if there is a particular problem associated with crime or anti-social behaviour, there will be a specific mechanism to trigger action, it will be to require attendance by the police or relevant local agency at a public meeting to discuss the issues and explain what action they are going to take. It could also lead to a specific request to take certain actions to address the problem. If the agencies decided that no action was to be taken, the agencies concerned would need to explain why. (Home Office, 2004: 41)

So, the public has been given the right, in collaboration with the police, to effectively set neighbourhood policing priorities. The requirement to hold public meetings if dissatisfied is a powerful weapon in the hands of 'the community'.

However, the Respect Action Plan places even greater control in the hands of the public. If they feel that a particular issue has not been dealt with adequately, the public have the power, through their local councillor, to demand a 'community call for action'. This involves the issue being taken to a scrutiny committee of the local authority.

Policing therefore has been drawn into the wider active citizenship remit of New Labour (Home Office, 2004). Failure to address a problem, which may have wider causes (Young, 1999; Squires, 2006), can now be laid at the door of the local authority. Linked to the increase in power given to the public in a particular neighbourhood, there is also the increase in the influence of local councillors on local policing decisions. As a result of the policy changes indicated above, Cathedral County Constabulary has established neighbourhood policing teams charged with gathering and responding to the wishes of the local community.

As we have already seen, regular public meetings over two-and-a half-years consistently produced demands from the community to crack down on street-life people and get rid of them. However, as the problem continued and police officers and council officers became aware that they were not actually resolving the problem of street-life people, merely displacing the problem from one area to another, a change in attitudes developed. It became fairly obvious to the police and officials that they were engaged in a pointless task, because the majority of the street-life people did not actually present a significant crime problem. Furthermore, there was a realisation that it was not unreasonable to see the street-life people as victims themselves – often of sexual abuse when children, of marital disharmony, of mental illness, of drug and alcohol dependency – rather than necessarily as aggressive troublemakers:

> When you look at them, most of them, you just think ... poor sods, what on earth are they doing that actually harms anyone? Yeah, there are some really nasty, messed up people ... but that's a minority and I doubt if there is anything anyone can do for them. (Police officer)

This changing attitude was reflected in the way the terminology changed. Whereas the terms 'homeless' or 'street drinkers' had routinely been used in discussions in 2003, by 2005 'street-life community' was the preferred term used in police and council discussions. Thus, over the years, those dealing with the problem felt increasingly uncomfortable with taking a punitive approach to the majority of the street-life people, which had merely excluded them from various parts of Cathedral City without actually solving the problem.

These attitudes are not shared by the local media or those who lead the protests about the presence of street-life people in the city communities in Cathedral City, where public meetings have routinely called for the expulsion of street-life people from their areas. Increasingly, police officers in these meetings are seen as defenders of the street-life community, as they seek to put forward a balanced view of the issue. This has led to accusations in the meetings of soft policing.

In one attempt to persuade the public that the authorities had been working on the problem and that the street-life community also had rights, a senior council officer asked drug agency workers, police officers and a representative of the street outreach team (who help resettle homeless people) to attend a public meeting so that a less negative view could be put forward. Once again, the overwhelming majority of the audience demanded that the street-life people be moved away. One speaker in the audience demanded far more rigorous policing and was rewarded with strong applause. Some speakers even acknowledged their understanding of the street-life people's problems, but still suggested they be dispatched elsewhere.

Since the issue was first raised, little has changed. New Labour's community-led agenda has prevented the development of more reasoned policies and the police feel constrained to continue a punitive line against the street-life people that they may privately disagree with. The outcome of handing power to the community is that punitive voices are heard (Squires, 1998) and, rather than drawing people into the community as government rhetoric would have it, processes of social exclusion develop.

Bauman's criticism of community is helpful here. Bauman argues that the communitarian idea of community refers to an ideal that has never existed nor will ever exist. Indeed, Bauman argues that the very attempt to construct a community in these terms inevitably involves a constant battle to define the boundaries of the community and to maintain it. The actual process, he argues, generates fear and hostility. It is worth quoting him in full:

> Indeed, attempts to reconstruct community will produce the very opposite of people's imagined idea of community. The really existing community will be unlike their dreams – more like the opposite – it will add to their fears and insecurity instead of quashing them or putting them to rest. It will call for twenty-four hours a day vigilance and a daily resharpening of swords; for struggle, day in and day out, to keep the aliens off the gates and to spy out and hunt down the turncoats in their midst. And to add a final touch of irony, it is only through all that pugnacity, wolf-crying and sword-brandishing that the feeling of being in a community, of being a community, may be kept lingering and protected from evaporation. Homely cosiness is to be sought, day in and day out, on the front line. (Bauman, 2001: 17–18)

This is exactly what appears to happen when the community is given power to define what is threatening and problematic. A visible out-group is chosen, demonised and then becomes the focus of what is community. In this case, the street-life people provide the 'aliens at the gate', as Bauman puts it.

And finally, the street-life people themselves – a community?

John looks like a typical street-life person – a scraggly beard and unkempt hair, roll-up and can of Special Brew in the same hand. He explains that he sees himself as a teacher to people new to street life, teaching them how to keep warm in winter and survive. He says he likes living on the streets, and makes a broad gesture at the busy marketplace full of tourists and affluent shoppers, indicating that he feels a link to all the people there. John prefers to sleep on the streets most of the year and can be found, most mornings, sitting on a bench in the Market Square or nearby, watching the world go by. He is an alcoholic and for the moment seems perfectly happy remaining one. Next to him is Jack. Jack likes to lecture passers-by on Marxism and accuse any member of the public who engages him in conversation of selling out to capitalism. Jack is also an alcoholic and intends to continue drinking for as long as he lives – which is likely to be sometime in his 40s. Jack has a flat in town and has lived there for the last ten years. He says he simply likes being on the streets:

> So, you know I'll be a good boy, you know go to fuckin' work and pay my fuckin' rent and you know watch telly at night. Like fuck I will. That's what, like ... see that is capitalism, you know ... got you. But here ... I got friends, I got a drink. This is ... obvious ... what's better. (Conversation, Cathedral City marketplace, 2006)

The assumption behind New Labour policy on neighbourhood policing is that the only community is that of the majority of decent, law-abiding people and that policing should be responsible to them. However, research on the street-life people indicates that this assumption is contestable. Hall (2003, 2005) in the south of England, Butchinsky (2007) in Oxford, Squires and Measor in Brighton (1999) and this research in Cathedral City all suggest that the street-life people too have a community, dissimilar perhaps to the residential communities of New Labour policy, but just as real.

Street-life people are strongly aware of the differences between themselves and the majority population. They are aware also that only by helping each other can they help themselves. The majority of street-life people are on the streets because they have chosen (from a limited range of options) to be there. They do not like all other street-life people – just as there are divisions and dislikes between the neighbours in a street. However, overall they recognise that they need to help one another. Anyone arriving in Cathedral City who is homeless and with no money whatsoever can have a group of friends within a couple of hours, a place to sleep, a roll-up to smoke and, most likely, a can of drink, if they know where to go. Street-life people are aware of the attitudes of the public towards them and they know that they need to look after each other. A web of favours holds them together: for example, when it gets too cold, if John and Jack have not had too big an argument, John sleeps on Jack's floor. Neither knows when it may be Jack's turn for a favour.

Does any of this qualify them as a community? What can be said for certain is that, on the whole, they do form a vibrant, dense network of interdependent people. Here, Hall's description of the young homeless can be transposed almost exactly as a description of the relationships of street-life people:

> They were an interdependent bunch: implicated in one another's daily affairs as a network of friends, acquaintances and hangers on. There was a patchy network certainly more than a little fuzzy at the edges, sparse in places and constantly refiguring; but it was extraordinarily dense elsewhere, stringing together clusters of close, intense association. (Hall, 2003: 5)

This is a perfect description of the street-life people, except that instead of 'goods' in the following comment, we might substitute 'alcohol and drugs'. What held them together is also explained eloquently by Hall.

> This was one of the things that kept them going and also one of the things that kept them together – the exchange of money and goods. One way or another directly or indirectly, sometimes very circuitously and at several removes, they all owed one another and were bound together by these threads of debt and obligation. (Hall, 2003: 5)

So, ironically, what we appear to have here, among the street-life people, is as close as one can reasonably get to a community with its overlapping web of rights and obligations, but what this community does not have is political power; instead, that lies with the imagined community of New Labour, so accurately captured by Bauman. This powerless street-life community (already victims of society) has become the means by which a sense of community is generated among the Field Road residents – apparently largely united in anger and disapproval of these 'demons'. The police and council officials, who understand the problem and have developed a degree of sympathy for the majority of street-life people, are disempowered through the policy of community and neighbourhood policing and are prevented from introducing less punitive measures. Instead, they are coerced by community feeling into a form of control about which they have significant reservations.

Conclusion

The chapter started with the claim that, although it is not seen at a national level as a significant problem, studying the street-life community provides useful insights into the relationship between New Labour's policies on community and its impact on marginal groups. The issue of visibility is an important one; certain groups emerge from the range of groups (ethnic, age, gender, religion) with which we 'rub along' (to use Bauman's term) in everyday life. These groups become visible, such that we note their presence and see them around, no longer invisible in the general mix. The more we note their presence, the more visible they become. Processes of demonisation can take hold. Demonisation is much easier for some groups, which can clearly be seen as not sharing similar characteristics to 'us', than for others. In the case of street-life people this can be their bedraggled appearance and their rather unpredictable behaviour. However, the process similarly applies to other groups.

Demonisation is linked with the notion of contamination and pollution. The very ground they use becomes tainted by their actions and their detritus. We have also seen that the community response is and has historically been to wish the outsider groups 'away'. Rutherford's notion of the 'eliminative ideal' expresses this perfectly. We do not want them here – they should go back to where they came from, be conscripted, put in prison, back to the social housing estates – whatever, just not *here*. Under conditions of high visibility and demonisation, the 'community' appears not to want social inclusion.

The chapter has also thrown light on the impact of neighbourhood policing initiatives. The government's policy of encouraging communities to engage with the police and to set priorities has, arguably, led to the translation of punitiveness, with the police becoming constrained to engage in policies that they realise are not the most appropriate, but that the public want. This links with a more general belief (encouraged by successive governments) of a decline in trust of professionals and greater stress being placed on the right of the community to 'have its say' – even where this is uninformed.

A final point was also made. One assumption behind New Labour's community-based policies is that there are communities that are threatened by small minorities of problem groups, for example nuisance neighbours and youth gangs. The policies are meant to enable the community to fight back. In the case of the Field Road residents and the street-life people, the latter have as much claim as the residents to be a functioning community – yet their community ideas and views are typically ignored.

References

Bauman, Z. (2001) *Community: Seeking safety in an insecure world*, Cambridge: Polity Press.

Butchinsky, C. (2007) 'Understanding and responding to homelessness', in M. Seal (ed), *Experiences, identities and cultures*, Lyme Regis: Russell House Publishing.

'Cathedral City' Council (2006) *Assessment of the need for wet centre provision*, 'Cathedral City' Council.

'Cathedral City' Council (2006) *The Homelessness Report*, 'Cathedral City' Council.

CHAIN (Combined Homelessness and Information Network) (2005) *Rough Sleeping Report for London 2004/05*, London: Broadway.

Cohen, S. (1985) *Visions of social control*, Cambridge: Policy Press.

CRISIS (2006) *Statistics about homelessness*, available at www.crisis. org/page.builder/infoandstatistics.html

DCLG (Department for Communities and Local Government) (2005) *Improving opportunity, strengthening society*, London: DCLG.

DCLG (2006) *Strong and prosperous communities: The local government White Paper*, London: DCLG.

Diaz, R. (2006) *Street homelessness briefing*, London: Shelter (available at http://england.shelter.org.uk/files/docs/22945/Street%20Home lessness%20factsheet.pdf) (accessed 20 July 2007).

Douglas, M. (1992) *Risk and blame: Essays in cultural theory*, London: Routledge.

Durkheim, E. (1982) *The rules of sociological method*, London: Macmillan.

Etzioni, A. (1995) *The spirit of community. Rights, responsibilities and the communitarian*, London: Fontana.

Goffman, E. (1972) *Relations in public: Microstudies of public order*, New York: Harper Colophon, cited in M. Innes (2004) 'Signal crimes and signal disorders: notes on deviance as communicative action', *British Journal of Sociology*, vol 55, no 3, p 241.

Griffith, Sir R. (1988) *Community care: Agenda for action: A report to the Secretaty of State*, London: HMSO.

Hall, T. (2003) *Better times than this: Youth homelessness in Britain*, London: Pluto Press.

Hall, T. (2005) 'Not miser, not monk, benefits and the free gift', *Sociological Research Online*, vol 10, no 4, (ww.socresonline.org. uk/10/4/hall.html).

Hancock, L. (2003) 'Urban regeneration and crime reduction: contradictions and dilemmas', in R. Matthews and J.Young (eds), *The new politics of crime and punishment*, Cullompton: Willan Publishing.

Home Office (2004) *Building communities, beating crime*, London: Home Office.

Home Office (2005) *The national policing plan 2005–2008*, London: Home Office.

Home Office Crime Reduction and Community Safety Group (2006) *National Community Safety Plan 2006 update*, London: Home Office.

Innes, M. (2004) 'Signal crimes and signal disorders: notes on deviance as communicative action', *British Journal of Sociology*, vol 55, no 3, pp 335–55.

Joffe, H. (1999) *Risk and the other*, Cambridge: Cambridge University Press.

Lea, J. and Young, J. (1993) *What is to be done about law and order? Crisis in the nineties*, London: Pluto Press.

McConville, S. (1998) 'The Victorian Prison', in N. Morris (ed),, *Oxford history of the prison*, Oxford: Oxford University Press.

Moore, S. and Scourfield, P. (2005) 'Eliminating the visible: exploring the community response to anti-social behaviour', *Crime Prevention and Community Safety*, vol 7, pp 51–61.

Morris, L. (1998) 'Dangerous classes: neglected aspects of the underclass debate', in E. Mingione (ed), *Urban poverty and the underclass*, Oxford: Blackwell.

Putnam, R. (2000) *Bowling alone: The collapse and revival of American community*, New York: Simon & Schuster.

Randall, G. and Brown, S. (2002) *Helping rough sleepers off the streets*, London: ODPM.

Rutherford, A. (1997) 'Criminal policy and the eliminative ideal', *Social Policy and Administration*, vol 31, no 5, pp 116–35.

Slovic, P. (1992) 'Perceptions of risk: reflections on the psychometric paradigm', in S. Krimsky and D. Goulding (eds), *Social theories of risk*, Westport, CT: Praeger.

Squires, P. (1998) 'Cops and customers: consumerism and the demand for police services. Is the customer always right?', *Policing and Society*, vol 8, pp 169–88.

Squires, P. (2006) 'New Labour and the politics of antisocial behaviour', *Critical Social Policy*, vol 26, no 1, pp 144–68.

Squires, P. and Measor, L. (1999) *Report on the Equinox Day Centre in Brighton*, Brighton: Health and Social Policy Research Centre, University of Brighton.

Wood, M. (2004) *Perceptions and experience of antisocial behaviour: Findings from the 2003/2004 British Crime Survey*, Home Office Online Report 49/04.

Young, J. (1999) *The exclusive society: Social exclusion, crime and difference in late modernity*, London: Sage.

ELEVEN

Room for resistance? Parenting Orders, disciplinary power and the production of 'the bad parent'

Amanda Holt

Introduction

Since their inception in the 1998 Crime and Disorder Act, Parenting Orders have provided New Labour with another tool with which to fight its battle against crime and anti-social behaviour. However, a number of issues and concerns surrounding the use of Parenting Orders have been raised. These have included: their effectiveness (including the quality of this evidence base) (see Holdaway et al, 2001; Ghate and Ramella, 2002), their likely negative psychosocial effects on parents, including issues of stigmatisation and blame (see Bowers, 2002) and concerns about the way that they act to provide for welfare needs through the courts (see Haydon, 2004). Acknowledging these issues, however, this chapter aims to provide a critique of the practice of Parenting Orders through the lens of Foucault's notion of 'disciplinary power' (1977). Such an approach will provide an analytical framework to understand why, despite the neutral term 'parent', Parenting Orders tend to be issued to mothers, lone parents and those living in the most deprived areas. This chapter will discuss how the mobilisation of the 'psy-complex' in the 20th century (Ingleby, 1985; Rose, 1985) has enabled parents to be classified on the basis of white, especially middle-class, 'norms' of parenting and how such processes of classification have informed the practices of a number of agencies, including youth justice agencies and parenting practitioners.

However, rather than capitulating to the common binary arguments of whether the use of Parenting Orders is good or bad, this chapter concludes by suggesting that, like parents themselves, Parenting Orders cannot be judged within such a simplistic dichotomous paradigm. Instead, it is argued that, while Parenting Orders may certainly position some parents in ways that may produce negative outcomes, there may also be opportunities for new subjectivities to emerge in the discursive spaces opened up by Parenting Orders. Similarly, possibilities for resistance and subversion should be recognised in the negotiations between agencies and parents, and care should be taken to avoid seeing parents only as passive objects in any analysis of youth justice policy and practice.

Parenting Orders: policy and legislation

Within the remit of youth justice, Parenting Orders can be issued to parents in cases where their child has received a Child Safety Order, an Anti-Social Behaviour Order, a Sex Offender Order, or has been convicted of an offence.[1] The 2003 Anti-Social Behaviour Act has also enabled their use against parents whose children have been engaged in anti-social behaviour 'in the interests of preventing the child or young person from engaging in further criminal conduct or anti-social behaviour'.[2] That is, *parents who have not committed any crime can receive a Parenting Order in response to their children who have not committed any crime.* Nevertheless, parents in receipt of an Order are required to attend a 'counselling or guidance programme',[3] and must also comply with any other discretionary conditions specified in the Order.[4] Although such conditions are not specified, the accompanying guidance document for police and local authorities suggests it may include 'avoids contact with disruptive and possibly older peers', 'avoids visiting certain areas, such as shopping centres, unsupervised' and 'is home during certain hours and is effectively supervised' (Home Office, 2005: 12). A Parenting Order can last for up to one year, and failure to comply with the conditions set can result in a summary conviction and a fine of up to £1,000.[5]

The legislation states that, before issuing the Parenting Order, if the child or young person is under 16 years, 'a court shall obtain and consider information about the person's family circumstances and the likely effect of the order on those circumstances'.[6] The Youth Justice Board (YJB) guidance document (2004) suggests such information will be in the form of an ASSET assessment, which is completed by a Youth Offending Team (YOT) officer although informed by other agencies (for example, police and social services). This 26-page document involves an assessment of the young person on 12 'dynamic risk factors',[7] one of which is 'Family and personal relationships'. If this initial assessment suggests that parenting 'is a significant factor in the child or young person's misbehaviour [then] a detailed assessment of the parents should be carried out' (YJB, 2004: section 2.18). This should identify, for example, parenting risk and protective factors, issues relating to culture, literacy, race, gender, disability and an appropriate support programme, as well as the individual needs and circumstances of the parent. Any recommendation for a Parenting Order made by the YOT officer after this parenting assessment will be included on the Pre-Sentence Report that is presented to the court.

Who are the parents?

Over 7,000 Parenting Orders have been issued to parents under the remit of youth justice from the period June 2000 (when they were first introduced nationwide) to December 2006.[8] However, the socio-demographic characteristics of the parents can only be explored through indirect and incomplete data, as the Home Office does not directly record such information. For example, the sample data from research that looked at the characteristics of attendees of parenting support classes found that 81% were mothers, 49% were lone parents and 56% were unemployed (Ghate and Ramella, 2002). Similarly, Lindfield (2001) surveyed 96 Youth Offending Teams during the first three-month period of the implementation of Parenting Orders and found that 79% of parents who had been issued Parenting Orders were mothers. While these data are statistically disproportionate to those of lone parents and unemployed parents in England and Wales at that time, the figures cannot be considered in isolation, because the correlations between motherhood, lone parenthood and unemployment constitute what many have termed the 'feminisation of poverty' (see Pearce, 1978). Furthermore, while 90% of attendees were white British, 3% were black Caribbean,[9] which is more than double the proportion of black Caribbean families with dependent children in England and Wales at that time, although this is still significantly less than the proportion of young black people who are involved in the youth justice system (see Prior and Spalek, Chapter Six in this volume). Further, a disproportionate 2% of attendees were refugees and asylum seekers. While it would not be wise to make assumptions about entire populations, it would be disingenuous to avoid remarking on how the parents who are issued with Orders differ so markedly in socio-demographic composition from those who issue the Orders, particularly in terms of age and occupational and social status (Morgan and Russell, 2000), or to avoid considering the implications of such structures of inequality. However, this issue is one that runs deeper than the practices of local magistrates' courts, and a brief explication of Foucault's concepts of 'disciplinary power' and 'governmentality' will illustrate this.

Disciplinary power and governmentality

Much of Foucault's later work focuses on the emergence of 'disciplinary power' in the 18th century, which gradually replaced 'sovereign power' as a more efficient form of governance (Foucault, 1991). Thus, rather than controlling the population through external measures at the site of the body (such as through public tortures and hangings), disciplinary power involves the exercise of power at the site of the 'soul' (Foucault, 1977). This necessarily involved the emergence of a number of 'technologies of the soul' (Foucault, 1977: 30) that produced a new, self-regulating kind of subject: the justice system and the social sciences were examples of two such technologies. Together with their own 'army of technicians' (Foucault, 1977: 11), such as social workers, psychiatrists and psychologists, they were involved in the processes of normalisation at the site of the soul. As Foucault explains:

> Psychiatric expertise, but also in a more general way criminal anthropology and the repetitive discourse of criminology, find one of their precise functions here: by solemnly inscribing offences in the field of objects susceptible of scientific knowledge, they provide the mechanism of legal punishment with a justifiable hold not only on offences, but on individuals: not only on what they do, but also on what they are, will be, may be. (Foucault, 1977: 18)

Thus, individuals became 'objects' that could be surveyed, measured, assessed and classified, not only in terms of their actions, but in terms of their 'selves'. Assessments were made in terms of an individual's deviance from 'normality', and normalisation prescriptions for treatment interventions were made accordingly. Thus, it was no longer the offence that was judged, but the offender, and hence the category of 'delinquent' emerged in the early 19th century at the same time as precise statistical measurements made such categorisation of individuals possible (May, 1973). Foucault refers to such objectifying practices as 'dividing practices' (1982: 208), since they involved dividing individuals into oppositional categories: the mad and the insane, the criminal and the law-abiding and, applied to today's youth justice system, 'good parents' and 'bad parents'. However, while such objectification processes produced 'totalising effects' (Lacombe, 1996), Foucault's later work also examined 'individualising effects' produced through the mechanisms of 'subjection'. This is defined by Foucault as 'the way a human being turns him or herself into a subject' (1982: 208) and concerns how individuals make sense of their self, using the discourses that are available to them to enable this. In this way, a state's regulation of its people is no longer coercive but self-regulatory, since aspects of control are internalised and are no longer experienced as originating from institutions (Mills, 2003). The result is a form of *governmentality* (Foucault, 1991) where citizens are active in constructing and governing their selves within particular disciplinary discourses. These discourses are constituted by particular decentralised expert knowledges that concern the nature of citizenship and morality. So what is the nature of these 'expert knowledges' that constitute disciplinary discourses and practices?

The objectification of 'bad parents': the role of the psy-complex

The production of expert knowledges regarding what is normal and what is not is generated by that 'army of technicians' within social science institutions. Such powerful discourses, which are embodied by the psychiatric and psychological professions, are referred to as the *psy-complex* (Ingleby, 1985; Rose, 1985) and it is this which colonises families by focusing on the new discursive space they construct between the private and public spheres: the *social* (Donzelot, 1979). Ingleby notes that the psy-complex is founded on a contradiction: 'with one hand it supports the sacredness of family relations, with the other it infiltrates them and subjects them to its management' (1985: 105), which may explain its increasing dominance in policy discourse and practices.

The psy-complex professions have achieved scientific legitimacy by producing increasingly sophisticated psychometric tools that have mobilised the concept of 'developmental milestones', enabling children to be compared against each other. This is made possible because the focus and unit of measurement of mainstream developmental psychology (which has colonised explanations and treatments of delinquency) is 'the individual'. Thus, accounts of 'development' (itself constructed as something natural and universal) are necessarily devoid of any reference to social and political contexts. As Burman states: 'instead of poverty, unemployment and frustration, we have evil children, bad mothers and broken homes' (1997: 142). The development of such measures enables the success or failure of parents, as sole 'socialisers' of their children, to be established, and provides tangible evidence of a parent's own competence. It also provides the means by which parents, particularly mothers, can (and do) define themselves in opposition to 'the incompetent parent' or the 'problem family' (Urwin, 1985).

However, these normative milestones were developed by privileged white, middle-class professionals and were founded on research studies predominantly based on white, middle-class, heterosexual mothers (Busfield, 1987; Phoenix and Wollett, 1991). Thus, black and working-class styles of child rearing tend to be pathologised as 'insensitive' (Walkerdine and Lucey, 1989), while LGBT and disabled parenting only become visibles within discussions of who is (and is not) fit to parent (Burman, 1987). This has always been the case, and has been particularly prevalent from the early 1820s, when professional experts began their investigation into delinquency. For example, May remarks on how experts' judgements were coloured by their own values and prejudices: 'throughout their writings, comparison between the realities of slum childhood and their own sense of a protected childhood is implicit' (1973: 104). Decisions made in custody, fostering and adoption cases and within fertility services are all influenced by how far the (potential) parent deviates from the norm (Burman, 1997), and it is likely that decisions made by magistrates regarding the issuing of Parenting Orders are no different.

So, the psy-complex has performed an important role in producing parents who are both objects and subjects of knowledge. However, in recent years, discourses of parenting that are founded on notions of individual responsibility, morality and blame have permeated beyond the psychological and psychiatric professions and have bled into everyday public discourse, taking a very distinct form in recent youth justice policy, as the next section discusses.

Appropriating psychology for policy: the case of risk factor models

The psy-complex has produced a number of discourses and practices that suggest that the causes of 'delinquency' can be explained by parental behaviour. A number of diverse theoretical models have supported this explanation, including early behaviourist models of learning that presented the 'criminal parent thesis', psychoanalytic models that emphasised inappropriately channelled anxieties (for example, Healy and Bronner, 1936; Friedlander, 1947) and maternal deprivation (Bowlby, 1944, 1951) and the risk factor models that dominate today. Despite their competing theoretical perspectives, all of these models effectively 'blame the parent' for the child's deviant behaviour. This blaming is made more palatable because it operates within a landscape of morality where structural factors that may affect abilities to parent (such as housing, poverty and domestic violence) are ignored while individualised 'risk factors', which are produced by isolating specific 'parental behaviours', are emphasised. This is certainly evident in recent youth justice policy, where risk-based intervention strategies, of which Parenting Orders are one example, have dramatically increased since the 1990s (Muncie, 2000; Haydon, 2004; Kirton, 2005). This focus on risk factors reflects its increasingly prominent role in psychological research, which has identified an enormous array of such factors (see Rutter et al, 1998, for a review). In particular, government-funded research by Graham and Bowling (1995), which found poor parental supervision, poor discipline and criminal parents as key risk factors, is continually cited in government consultation documents in support of the implementation of Parenting Orders (see *Tackling the causes of crime* [Straw et al, 1996]; *No more excuses* [Home Office, 1997] and the Audit Commission's *Misspent youth* [1996]). Such reductionist and causal constructions of risk factors operate within what Armstrong terms a 'morality of blame', which enables the justification of 'a whole paraphernalia of surveillance and intervention based on the assumption that youth crime is an outcome of dysfunctional individuals and communities and that these individuals can be identified through an assessment process determined by experts' (2004: 104).

However, risk factor models that do attempt to account for the relationships between individuals and settings (for example, see Pitts, 2003) nevertheless fail to acknowledge the role of social processes in the framing, construction and regulation of certain behaviours, some of which are constructed as 'criminal' and some of which are not (Armstrong, 2004). In this sense, the 'social context' cannot be isolated as just another variable, since 'biological, psychosocial and environmental explanations of criminality are not neutral scientific accounts [because they construct risk] through the categories that are used to describe it' (Armstrong, 2004:108). Thus, rather than the risk factor focusing on the processes that create risk, such as racism, risk factor models instead focus on the individual who is subject to those processes, such as being black (Furedi, 2004), resulting in certain individuals' identities becoming 'risk factors' in themselves. More than this, risk factors are calculated through statistics and probabilities (rather than through direct observation) and so, while more 'selective and precise', they are ultimately applied to far larger populations of people (and thus increases the possibilities of intervention) than earlier, more embodied, constructions of delinquents and their families, which were based on notions of 'dangerousness' (Castel, 1991). Risk factor models have also shifted how 'risk' has been conceptualised, from being something that someone does (as in 'taking risks'), to something that they are ('at risk') or that they represent to others ('risk to'), a shift that subtly repositions subjects from active agents to passive victims (Furedi, 2004). Constructions of 'normality', against which 'risk' is judged, are not value-free and objective, but are shaped by the expert's own value systems and within the context of their professional interests. Thus, the truth claims to 'value-free' and 'scientific' knowledge enable its legitimisation and acceptance. Consequently the politics and accountability of such professional knowledge (both academic and professional) remains unexamined.

So, in terms of the parents who are constructed as most 'at risk' and thus in need of a Parenting Order, the available evidence suggests that it is mothers, lone parents and those who have fewest economic resources who are deemed to be most 'at risk' by youth justice agencies. However, while the effects of structural inequalities experienced by these groups of parents may suggest that these are precisely the parents who are in most need of welfare support, many have suggested that, ultimately, the notion of *risk* has effectively replaced the notion of *need* as the founding principle of social policy (Culpitt, 1999; Kemshall, 2002; Dean, 2006). In particular, Armstrong (2004) suggests that welfarism, which would involve the redistribution of economic resources, is now replaced by individual responsibility and a micro-management of individuals through the discourse of 'risk management'. The question of how parents and families 'at risk' are micro-managed under the guise of 'support' will now be discussed.

The new parenting guidance: from deviance to everyday socialisation

As outlined in the first section, the condition common to all Parenting Orders is the parenting guidance programme, which may be residential[10] and which parents must attend for a maximum of three months.[11] Local YOTs either run the programmes in-house or 'source them out' to external agencies, and they may be in the form of one-to-one and/or group sessions. While programme aims and objectives vary in terms of being more or less 'preventive' or 'therapeutic', they all share common themes such as family conflict, boundary setting and maintenance, and supervision and monitoring (Ghate and Ramella, 2002). Further, many of the programmes are based on assumptions about childhood and development that are appropriated from developmental psychology discourse, and the techniques taught to parents are based on a number of psychological concepts and ideas that are reproduced in a 'learning setting'. However, this learning process serves a 'normalising' function, as parents are required to examine their own parenting practices and experiences within a discourse of 'bad parenting'. Such practices serve to regulate and normalise parents' own subjectivities by constituting reality in particular ways.

However, in recent years, such normalisation processes have also extended their focus from deviance to everyday socialisation. In turn, the psy-professions' relationship with parents has also shifted to being less authoritarian and more democratic, as decisions are increasingly collaborative and tasks are delegated to parents to the point where parenting has become a 'technical accomplishment' of skill acquisition (Ingleby, 1985: 103). As Ingleby explains:

> the lay person acquires the mentality of the professional, through instruction and advice or through assimilation of ideas from books and the media ... whereas previously power was maintained by keeping knowledge secret, today the professions extend their influence by publicising it. (Ingleby, 1985: 102)

Thus, the dramatic increase in parenting discourse in the media has served to psychologise the perceived problems of children and young people. This discourse lends itself well to 'reality television' in its documentation of the classification and treatment of young people within an individualised, developmental narrative, and finds its home in programmes such as *Little Angels*, *House of Tiny Tearaways*, *Driving Mum and Dad Mad* and *Supernanny*. Many commentators have voiced concerns about such programmes: aside from ethical concerns around the well-being of families who participate in such programmes, many are worried about the cultural messages they send out about 'normal' (and 'dysfunctional') families and the status that is bestowed upon professional expertise that may cultivate parental dependency on experts and create uncertainty of their own parenting abilities (see Hayes, 2006, for a review). The increasing professionalisation of parenting is also manifested in the increase in self-help books, magazines and internet forums for parents of teenagers, many of which are not produced by developmental specialists and many of which are not necessarily based on scientific evidence (Smith et al, 2003). It may indeed be that 'expertise' has replaced 'the experts' as a site of regulation (Alldred, 1996) and, as Urwin (1985) suggests, parenting literature that appears to bypass the experts is perhaps all the more subtle in its normalising effects because of this. Thus, it appears that parents can be regulated in a number of sites, whether formally and judicially, in the case of Parenting Orders, or informally and commercially, through media and publications. However, these sites have recently blurred as, in the case of *Blame the Parents* (BBC2, 2005), YOT-based parenting support becomes reality TV and, in the case of a recent government-funded research study (Sanders and Calam, 2006), reality TV (specifically, *Driving Mum and Dad Mad*) becomes a means of providing parenting support for the parents of young offenders. This suggests that any distinction between regulating 'deviance' and regulating 'everyday' practices is disappearing, making the hegemony of parenting discourse ever more difficult to resist as *all* parents are increasingly co-opted as mutual agents of scrutiny.

Furedi (2001) argues that the result of such increased 'professionalisation of parenting', whether through statutory, voluntary or commercial bodies, has resulted in parents who are increasingly infantilised. Ironically, this is at the same time that Goldson (2001: 40) has argued that increased responsibilisation strategies in youth justice policy have resulted in children who are increasingly 'adulterised'. However, given the current heterogeneous and dispersed nature of parenting regulation, its experienced effects are likely to be equally heterogeneous, as are any manifestations of resistance.

Parenting Orders: an example of disciplinary power?

A number of academics (for example, Garland [1997], Smith [2001; 2003] and Crawford [2006]) have suggested parallels between elements of New Labour's youth justice reforms and Foucault's notion of 'disciplinary power'. In particular, Smith suggests that the 1998 Crime and Disorder Act represents 'a Foucaultesque strategy for classifying and controlling the problematic behaviour of the young' (2003: 159) and identifies New Labour's key strategies as resembling the 'strategies of control' anticipated by Foucault and Donzelot, 'notably in the concept of parents as agents of intervention and the creation of an extended network of agencies with a common objective of preventing crime' (2001: 23). As well as the use of Parenting Orders, this is also true of other early intervention strategies, such as the use of whole community Curfew Orders (Smith, 2003), with the result that such strategies of control have colonised new areas of social life, including families and communities (Crawford, 1997:72). For example, an element common to compulsory (and voluntary) parenting programmes is the parent's (visible) exercise of discipline (Smith, 2003) through the learning of techniques such as enforcing curfews and operating reward–punishment systems. However, such exercises of discipline also extend to *self-discipline*, where 'parenting support' teaches parents techniques of self-control, such as focusing on body postures, leaving 'sufficient silence' and 'producing non-verbal signs, like eye contact and encouraging grunts, nods etc' (Centre for Fun and Families, 2003: 5), as found in the advice booklet for parents produced by one organisation involved in producing parenting support materials. Pitts suggests that New Labour's use of such new treatment practices, including such cognitive-behavioural techniques, 'strive to make good those deficits in the behaviour, beliefs and attitudes of individual offenders and their parents, and to instil in them a new, disciplined, capacity for self-regulation' (2000:10).

Of course, this is not to suggest that the notion of 'disciplinary power' is the only principle operating within the 1998 Crime and Disorder Act. Other commentators have stressed that principles of 'restorative justice' also feature, for example, through the use of fines and compensation. In contrast, community safety strategies that focus on the offence rather than the offender may suggest a shift away from Foucauldian processes of individualisation (Crawford, 1997), and other commentators have suggested a failure of governmentality and a return to more coercive forms of governance (for example, Flint, 2002). However, as Foucault was keen to stress, any exercise of power can never be total, because it is always contingent on competing principles or discourses: it is in the spaces between discourses that new possibilities for subversion and resistance can emerge. In this sense, a Foucauldian analysis of youth justice policy does not conceptualise power as wholly repressive, because the realisation of any 'strategy of control' will always lead to disparate and unexpected consequences. Thus, 'where there is power, there is resistance' (Foucault, 1981: 95) and the exercise of power will always liberate as well as constrain. While a parent who receives a Parenting Order may indeed be positioned as a 'bad parent', this identity may be accepted, resisted or subverted. Such resistance may come not only from parents, but also from family members and youth justice agents and practitioners.

Parenting Orders: regulation or resistance?

Discourses of parental blame regarding youth offending are not new and have circulated in political, legal and psychological fields for over a century (see May, 1973). However, the coercive element of issuing a court order to force parents to change their parenting practices certainly is new, and is especially significant when it operates within the scientific rhetoric of 'what works' (Anderson et al, 2001). However, beyond this coercive element there may be more positive possibilities.

Rose (1996) suggests that the emergence of the psy-complex over the past hundred years, and the psychological practices that it embodies, have opened up a new space for political intervention and produced a new kind of 'psychologised subject'. As well as providing a new space that can be objectified and thus regulated, this process has transformed our relationship with our selves, as we subject our selves to our own judgements and evaluations against those standardised norms produced by the psy-complex. The discourses and practices that surround Parenting Orders may certainly position parents in ways that construct them as falling short of the 'norm', and this may certainly produce negative outcomes for those parents and their families. However, as Foucault emphasised, it is here that resistance to norms can play a role, and there may be some opportunities for new subjectivities, because the discourses and practices provide new possibilities for transformation. Thus, while some parents may indeed experience Parenting Orders as oppressive, other parents may discover new ways of 'being' through the space provided by parenting programmes. This may account for the variety of experiences found by a number of researchers in their evaluation of parenting programmes (for example, Holdaway et al, 2001; Ghate and Ramella, 2002; Moran and Ghate, 2005).

From my own research, where I interviewed a number of parents who had been issued with a Parenting Order, I found many ways in which the practice of Parenting Orders might be 'productive' in creating a space for new subjectivities to emerge, although such productivity is not necessarily experienced as painless. There was evidence of subversion and resistance, and transitions from policy to practice, from rhetoric to lived experience, were not seamless. I provide two examples: the first explores the issuing of the Parenting Order in the magistrates' court, while the second looks at how parenting support, a condition of the Parenting Order, was contested and negotiated by the parent in question.

Negotiating the disposal in court: the case of Lyne

When I asked how the magistrates came to issue her a Parenting Order, Lyne explained that a fine was initially issued to her. However, Lyne refused the fine in court by arguing that she was not able to afford it (she was a lone mother who did not work). Lyne explained that the magistrates went away to discuss the situation, and returned to suggest an alternative: a Parenting Order. Thus, by her outright refusal of the fine in court, the Parenting Order came to represent to Lyne her success in resistance and the magistrates' submission to her challenge. As Lyne explained:

> I think when I stood up, and said 'I don't think so, I can't afford no fine', I think that, just that sentence alone just sort of said all I had to say and that, just, when I said that, they just retired and when they come back with that [the Parenting Order as an alternative]. And I think the expression on my face as well.

Such a practice is clearly at odds with the legislation that states that Parenting Orders should be issued 'in the interests of preventing the child or young person from engaging in further criminal conduct or anti-social behaviour'.[12] For Lyne, the issuing of the Parenting Order represented something very different than what is anticipated by the government's rhetoric of support or the academic's rhetoric of coercion. Such a difference in meaning may explain the new possibilities for subjectivity that emerged for Lyne, whereby the ensuing parenting class produced a new form of agency that Lyne then applied to a number of areas in her life:

> Yeah, it did open my eyes up to a lot of little bits and pieces I probably would have just walked past in everyday life. But it has given me enough strength to sort out a few problems I was, you know, trying to cope with myself, on my own. So yeah, I've picked up a hell of a lot really out of the sessions that we had, yeah ... Well, I sacked the chap that I was with, and I used it to stop drinking, so I conquered them two, which were, you know, big elements and I also dropped half of the friends that I thought were friends 'cos it made me see things in a different way ... So, I dropped half of my friends and that, um, I was in the process of moving and I've met new friends and that, so basically it turned my whole life around, really.

Thus, while the Parenting Order failed in the planned objective of the parenting support programme, to reduce the offending behaviour of her son, it did produce more transformative 'unexpected consequences', which a Foucauldian framework anticipates. However, the question of whether the Parenting Order in this case ultimately performed a regulative function (since Lyne certainly became a more self-governing and reflective citizen) needs to be considered.

Contesting parenting support: the case of Bee

Bee, another lone mother, was angry at being issued with a Parenting Order, specifically as she was the only parent of the five in court who was issued with one (her son was one of three teenagers in court that day for the same offence, and all three sets of parents were in court). The reason why she alone was issued with a Parenting Order was explained to her:

> Their only reason, their only excuse for that was, because I said that I feel like I've been victimised because I'm a single parent, they had to surmise that it was because I was a single parent and they felt I needed more support, whereas the other one obviously mummy could support daddy and daddy could support mummy, and the other two, step-parent daddy could support mummy and vice versa ... that's what they said, because I was a single parent, they probably felt that I needed more support than the other children's parents.

Bee's anger manifested in resistance as she continually refused to accept the terms on which the Parenting Order was based:

> I was extremely angry and I would be quite verbal in that group and I don't think that's what they wanted 'cos I could've quite easily – and I would've done and I have done – sat with my youth offending lady and said 'I know that, I've done that' ... I felt quite sorry for this [parenting practitioner] because I just sat there and said 'I ... I'm sick of this parenting order business'. She said 'you need to get over it' and I said 'I won't get over it, I will continually look at it as punishment'.

Bee's resistance subsequently enabled her to transform expected Parenting Order practice by refusing to attend a class-based programme, instead negotiating home visits from the parenting practitioner as part of her 'support programme'. However, as in the case of Lyne, what needs examination is the degree to which Bee's resistance can be construed as successful. To what extent was Bee able to resist the regulative function of Parenting Orders, and what does this mean to her, to her family and to youth justice agents?

Conclusions

This chapter has argued that Parenting Orders require a more nuanced analysis than has been offered so far. Positivist 'scientific' evaluations assume that what is suggested in policy will operate in practice and, in the main, evaluate whether they do or do not work by subjecting large samples of families to statistical analysis. However, such analyses ignore power relations operating at both a structural and a local level. They ignore how Parenting Orders only regulate certain groups of parents – predominantly lone mothers with few economic resources – by constructing them as 'at risk' and subjecting them to parenting practices where they can learn how to discipline both themselves and their family members according to standardised norms of child rearing, which are increasingly difficult to resist as parenting discourse becomes ever more dispersed and pervasive. Such analyses also ignore the 'microphysics of power' at play at the local level, and the struggle and conflicts operating between parents and youth justice agents, including magistrates and parenting practitioners. Generic reviews will never capture these conflicts, because they are rarely made visible or public: as Crewe (2007) suggests, public dissent is difficult within hegemonic power relations. This is particularly relevant to Parenting Orders, when all of the scientific, political and lay communities legitimise such interventions and claim that parents are to blame, and when such messages are combined with offers of 'support': support that has often been requested by such parents for a number of years (Haydon, 2004). If resistance operates at individualised and local levels, as the evidence above suggests, and if it seeps through the cracks of contradictory discourses and practices, which forms the basis of youth justice policy (Crawford, 2001; Muncie and Hughes, 2002), then Parenting Orders will produce unexpected consequences for parents, for their families and for youth justice agencies. Unfortunately, current risk–based analyses are looking in the wrong places.

Notes

[1] 1998 Crime and Disorder Act, section 8(1).

[2] 2003 Anti–Social Behaviour Act, section 26(3)(b).

[3] 2003 Anti–Social Behaviour Act, section 18(2)(b).

[4] 1998 Crime and Disorder Act, section 18(4)(a).

[5] 1998 Crime and Disorder Act, section 9(7).

[6] 1998 Crime and Disorder Act, section 9(2).

[7] The other 11 risk factors are 'Living arrangements', 'Education, training and employment', 'Neighbourhood', 'Lifestyle', 'Substance use', 'Physical health', 'Emotional and mental health', 'Perception of self and others', 'Thinking and behaviour', 'Attitudes to offending' and 'Motivation to change' (Youth Justice Board, 2006).

[8] 'Data regarding Parenting Orders', email from public.enquiries@ homeoffice.gsi.gov.uk to author, 6 June 2006 and 'Parenting Orders data', email from Youth Justice Board to author, 17 May 2007.

[9] Other minority ethnic groups each received less than 1% of Parenting Orders (Lindfield, 2001).

[10] 2003 Anti–Social Behaviour Act, section 18(3)(a).

[11] 1998 Crime and Disorder Act, section 8(4)(b).

[12] One might note that the magistrates' practices in this particular case may also represent an act of resistance on their part, something also found in Longstaff's (2004) research, where, in some local courts,

magistrates found ways of resisting issuing Parenting Orders, despite the requirements of legislation.

References

Alldred, P. (1996) 'Whose expertise? Conceptualising resistance to advice about childrearing', in E. Burman, G. Aitken, P. Alldred, R. Allwood, T. Billington, B. Goldberg, A.J. Gordo Lopez, C. Heenan, D. Marks and S. Warner (eds), *Psychology, discourse, practice: From regulation to resistance*, Abingdon: Taylor and Francis, pp 133–51.

Anderson, B., Beinart, S., Farrington, D.P., Longman, J., Sturgis, P. and Utting, D. (2001) *Risk and protective factors associated with youth crime and effective interventions to prevent it*, London: Youth Justice Board for England and Wales.

Armstrong, D. (2004) 'A risky business? Research, policy, governmentality and youth offending', *Youth Justice*, vol 4, no 2, pp 100–16.

Audit Commission (1996) *Misspent youth*, London: The Audit Commission.

Bowers, L. (2002) 'Unrecognised victims: the parents of child and adolescent offenders', *Issues in Forensic Psychology*, vol 3, pp 49–58.

Bowlby, J. (1944) 'Forty-four juvenile thieves: their characters and home-life', *International Journal of Psycho-Analysis*, vol 25, pp 19–53.

Bowlby, J. (1951) *Maternal care and mental health: a report prepared on behalf of the World Health Organization as a contribution to the United Nations programme for the welfare of homeless children*, Geneva: World Health Organisation.

BBC (British Broadcasting Corporation) (2005) 'Blame the parents', BBC 2, Producer, P. Tilzey, Broadcast 10, 17, 24, 31 March.

Burman, E. (1997) 'Developmental psychology and its discontents', in D. Fox and I. Prilleltensky (eds), *Critical psychology: An introduction*, London: Sage, pp 134–49.

Busfield, J. (1987) 'Parenting and parenthood', in G. Cohen (ed), *Social change and the life course*, London: Tavistick Publications, pp 67–86.

Castel, R. (1991) 'From dangerousness to risk', in G. Burchell, C. Gordon and P. Miller (eds), *The Foucault effect: Studies in governmentality*, London: Harvester Wheatsheaf, pp 281–98.

Centre for Fun and Families (2003) *Living with teenagers: A bridge over troubled waters*, Leicester: Centre for Fun and Families.

Crawford, A. (1997) *The local governance of crime: Appeals to community and partnership*, Oxford: Clarendon Press.

Crawford, A. (2001) 'Joined-up but fragmented: contradiction, ambiguity and ambivalence at the heart of New Labour's "Third Way"', in R. Matthews and J. Pitts (eds), *Crime, disorder and community safety*, London: Routledge.

Crawford, A. (2006) 'Networked governance and the post-regulatory state? Steering, rowing and anchoring the provision of policing and security', *Theoretical Criminology*, vol 10, no 4, pp 449–79.

Crewe, B. (2007) 'Power, adaptation and resistance in a late-modern men's prison', *British Journal of Criminology*, vol 47, pp 256–75.

Culpitt, I. (1999) *Social policy and risk*, London: Sage.

Dean, H. (2006) *Social policy*, Cambridge: Polity Press.

Donzelot, J. (1979) *The policing of families*, London: Hutchinson.

Flint, J. (2002) 'Return of the governors: citizenship and the new governance of neighbourhood disorder in the UK', *Citizenship Studies*, vol 6, no 3, pp 245–64.

Foucault, M. (1977) *Discipline and punish: The birth of the prison*, London: Allen Lane.

Foucault, M. (1981) *The history of sexuality. Volume 1: An introduction*, London: Pelican.

Foucault, M. (1982) 'The subject and power', in H.L. Dreyfus and P. Rabinow (eds), *Michel Foucault: Beyond structuralism and hermeneutics*, Hemel Hempstead: Harvester Wheatsheaf, pp 208–26.

Foucault, M. (1991) 'Governmentality', in G. Burchell, C. Gordon and P. Miller (eds), *The Foucault effect: Studies in governmentality*, London: Harvester Wheatsheaf, pp 87–104.

Friedlander, K. (1947) *The psycho-analytical approach to juvenile delinquency: Theory, case-studies, treatment*, London: Routledge and Kegan Paul.

Furedi, F. (2001) *Paranoid parenting*, London: Allen Lane.

Furedi, F. (2004) *Therapy culture: Creating vulnerability in an uncertain age*, London: Routledge.

Garland, D. (1997) '"Governmentality" and the problem of crime: Foucault, criminology, sociology', *Theoretical Criminology*, vol 1, pp 173–214.

Ghate, D. and Ramella, M. (2002) *Positive parenting: The national evaluation of the Youth Justice Board's parenting programme*, London: Policy Research Bureau.

Goldson, B. (2001) 'The demonization of children: from the symbolic to the institutional', in P. Foley, J. Roche and S. Tucker (eds), *Children in society: Contemporary theory, policy and practices*, Basingstoke: Palgrave, pp 34–41.

Graham, J. and Bowling, B. (1995) *Young people and crime*, London: Home Office.

Haydon, D. (2004) 'The state regulation of parenting', Paper presented at *'Tough on Crime' ... Tough on Freedoms? From Community to Global Interventions Conference*, 22–24 April, Centre for Crime and Social Justice, Chester.

Hayes, E. (2006) 'Is media coverage of parenting creating less emotionally healthy families?', Paper presented at *Parent–Child 2006: Happy Families?* 13–14 November, National Family and Parenting Institute, London.

Healy, W. and Bronner, A.F. (1936) *New light on delinquency and its treatment*, London: Greenwood Press.

Holdaway, S., Davidson, N., Dignan, J., Hammersley, R., Hine, J. and Marsh, P. (2001) 'New strategies to address youth offending: the national evaluation of the pilot Youth Offending Teams', RDS Occasional Paper No. 69, London: Home Office.

Home Office (1997) *No more excuses: A new approach to tackling youth crime in England and Wales*, London: Home Office.

Home Office (2005) *The Crime and Disorder Act guidance document: Parenting Orders*, London: Home Office.

Ingleby, D. (1985) 'Professionals as Socializers: the "Psy Complex"', *Research in Law, Deviance and Social Control*, vol 7, pp 79–109.

Kemshall, H. (2002) *Risk, social policy and welfare*, Buckingham: Open University Press.

Kirton, D. (2005) 'Young people and crime', in C. Hale, K. Hayward, A. Wahidin and E. Wincup (eds), *Criminology*, Oxford: Oxford University Press, pp 385–402.

Lacombe, D. (1996) 'Reforming Foucault: a critique of the social control thesis', *British Journal of Sociology*, vol 47, no 2, pp 332–52.

Lindfield, S. (2001) *Responses to questionnaire: parenting work in the youth justice context*, Brighton: Trust for the Study of Adolescence.

Longstaff, E. (2004) 'Good enough parenting? Youth crime and parental responsibility', PhD thesis, University of Cambridge.

May, M. (1973) 'Innocence and experience: the evolution of the concept of juvenile delinquency in the mid-nineteenth century', in J. Muncie, G. Hughes and E. McLaughlin (eds) (2002), *Youth justice: Critical readings*, London: Sage.

Mills, S. (2003) *Michel Foucault*, London: Routledge.

Moran, P. and Ghate, D. (2005) 'The effectiveness of parenting support', *Children and Society*, vol 19, pp 329–36.

Morgan, R. and Russell, N. (2000) *The judiciary in the magistrates' courts*, London: Home Office.

Muncie, J. (2000) 'Pragmatic realism: searching for criminology in the new youth justice', in B. Goldson (ed), *The new youth justice*, Lyme Regis: Russell House Publishing, pp 14–34.

Muncie, J. and Hughes, G. (2002) 'Modes of youth governance: political rationalities, criminalisation and resistance', in J. Muncie, G. Hughes and E. McLaughlin (eds), *Youth justice: Critical readings*, London: Sage, pp 1–18.

Pearce, D. (1978) 'The feminization of poverty: women, work and welfare', *Urban and Social Change Review*, vol 11, pp 28–36.

Phoenix, A. and Wollett, A. (1991) 'Social construction, politics and psychology', in A. Phoenix (ed), *Motherhood: Meanings, practices and ideologies*, London: Sage, pp 13–26.

Pitts, J. (2000) 'The new youth justice and the politics of electoral anxiety', in B. Goldson (ed), *The new youth justice*, Lyme Regis: Russell House Publishing.

Pitts, J. (2003) *The new politics of crime: Discipline or solidarity?* Lyme Regis: Russell House Publishing.

Rose, N. (1985) *The psychological complex: Psychology, politics, and society in England, 1869–1939*, London: Routledge.

Rose, N. (1996) *Inventing our selves: Psychology, power and personhood*, Cambridge: Cambridge University Press.

Rutter, M., Giller, H. and Hagell, A. (1998) *Antisocial behaviour by young people*, Cambridge: Cambridge University Press.

Sanders, M.R. and Calam, R. (2006) *Great parenting experiment: The role of television in supporting parents and preventing antisocial behaviour in children – Brief report*, Manchester: University of Manchester.

Smith, C., Vartanian, L.R., DeFrates-Densch, N., Van Loon, P.C. and Locke, S. (2003) 'Self-help books for parents of adolescents, 1980–1993', *Family Relations*, vol 52, no 2, pp 172–9.

Smith, R. (2001) 'Foucault's law: The Crime and Disorder Act 1998', *Youth Justice*, vol 1, no 2, pp 17–29.

Smith, R. (2003) *Youth justice: Ideas, policy, practice*, Cullompton: Willan Publishing.

Straw, J., Michael, A. and the Labour Party (1996) *Tackling the causes of crime: Labour's proposals to prevent crime and criminality*, London: The Labour Party.

Urwin, C. (1985) 'Constructing motherhood: the persuasion of normal development', in C. Steedman, V. Walkerdine and C. Urwin (eds), *Language, gender and childhood*, London: Routledge, pp 164–202.

Walkerdine, V. and Lucey, H. (1989) *Democracy in the kitchen: Regulating mothers and socialising daughters*, London: Virago.

Youth Justice Board (2004) *Parenting Contracts and Orders guidance*, London:Youth Justice Board for England and Wales.

Youth Justice Board (2006) *ASSET: Core profile*, London:Youth Justice Board for England and Wales.

Youth Justice Board (2007) *Parenting Orders data*, 17 May, personal communication from YJB (Performance@yjb.gov.uk) to author.

TWELVE

Cameras, cops and contracts: what anti-social behaviour management feels like to young people

Carlie Goldsmith

Introduction

The Hillside Estate is a geographically isolated area of social housing in the south of England. Like many similar areas throughout the country, it has been subject to the combination of situational and social crime prevention measures used to tackle crime and 'anti-social behaviour' since long before 1998. Yet how these various strategies, designed to penetrate neighbourhoods in order to establish 'safer communities', have impacted upon young people in particular has been the key question facing the three-year ethnographic project on which this chapter is based.

What follows will be an introduction to some of the tensions and contradictions between the management of anti-social behaviour (ASB) in Hillside and the experiences of children and young people who live there. Concerns are raised about how the broad definition of 'anti-social behaviour' is central for practitioners but often leaves children and young people exposed to intervention for a range of behaviours not necessarily identified by them as 'anti-social'. In addition, the use of surveillance cameras, targeted policing initiatives, curfews and Dispersal Orders, and a range of 'contractual' agreements established to detect and prevent ASB perpetrated by young people has resulted in those who participated in the research feeling vulnerable, angry and frustrated at their perceived inability to influence these developments, or defend themselves and their families. A particular consequence for young people of being targeted for management of ASB is their increasing spatial marginalisation within their own neighbourhood. The data suggest that this shift has been precipitated by feeling unable to control being drawn into the intervention process itself, combined with targeted ASB prevention and detection strategies, including closed-circuit television (CCTV) and policing.

Methods

All of the data for this research was generated over a 14-month period using a multi-method qualitative approach. Voluntary work was conducted at two sites regularly used by young people on the Hillside Estate: a local youth club open five nights a week and during the school holidays, and a small group for young mums between the ages of 14 and 19 that met once a week. In addition to this, the Hillside Crime Prevention Forum, a monthly partnership meeting used to discuss, monitor and take action against local crime and disorder issues, was attended for nine months. Although these meetings were open to the general public and regularly advertised in the local newspaper, they were heavily dominated by those practitioners involved in preventing crime and anti-social behaviour in the area. These included representatives from the Community Safety Team, housing services, the police, local tenants' and residents' associations, and the youth service.

Thirty young people between the ages of 14 and 17 were involved in interviews that explored their experiences of living in Hillside. Interviews were also conducted with a range of practitioners, including members of the Community Safety Team, youth workers and police officers. These interviews focused on how they felt that their work impacted on the lives of children and young people and what they felt were the major challenges faced by the young people living in the estate. Retrospective data were also generated through interviews with young adults in their mid-twenties who had experienced growing up in Hillside prior to the legislative and practice changes in the youth and criminal justice fields after 1997. Towards the end of the fieldwork period two focus groups were also conducted with young people and young adults in which some of the main themes emerging from the research were discussed.

Hillside Estate

Hillside is a relatively small area of social housing in the south of England on the outskirts of a city of approximately 250,000 residents. Built predominantly after the Second World War, it has a population of approximately 10,000, 24% of whom are children and young people under the age of 18 (Census, 2001[1]). It is a predominantly white area, with only 4% of its inhabitants describing themselves as from another ethnic background (Census, 2001); 27% belong to social class categories 6, 7 and 8 (in comparison to 14.7% more generally in the South-East) and 7.5% to category 1 (concentrated at the south end of the estate, where it merges into an area of owner-occupation) (ONS, 2003). Compared with surrounding areas, the estate has the highest proportion of lone parents with dependent children and the highest rates of teenage pregnancy but the lowest rate of terminations. The local secondary school was closed in 2005 owing to a failure to raise academic standards, and the children were dispersed to other schools in the surrounding area – exposing major issues of postcode inequality in secondary school opportunities and prompting a vital debate on educational selection at age 11.

Hillside is in the top 10% of areas listed in the Indices of Multiple Deprivation (ODPM, 2004). This index combines data from seven domains covering employment, health, income, education, living environment, barriers to services, and crime, in order to describe the level of deprivation experienced in an area (ODPM, 2004: 14). According to the same report (ODPM, 2004), the South-East as a region has 5% of the most deprived areas in the country but 40% of the least deprived, the greatest disparity in Britain. This is significant because of potential implications arising for economically deprived communities when the immediate surroundings are economically advantaged.

In 1999 Hillside was designated an area of priority urban renewal and in 2000 a New Deal for Communities initiative was established. Part of the regeneration remit was to address issues of crime and disorder and, in line with the 1998 Crime and Disorder Act, a resident Community Safety Team was established and located in Hillside. Situational crime prevention had become embedded within the national community safety strategy as part of a dual approach to tackling crime and disorder at a neighbourhood level (Crawford, 1997; Hughes, 1998). In Hillside this situational approach has been realised in four main ways. Traffic-calming measures have been used throughout the estate to address the problem of speeding cars. CCTV cameras were installed in 1998 to prevent traffic violations, crime and anti-social behaviour, the first time this strategy had been used in a residential area outside of London. The establishment of a Safer Neighbourhood Policing Team allocated specific, additional police resourcing to Hillside. Finally, in 2005 Hillside was one of a number of areas chosen to receive extra funding from the Home Office to gate up 41 pedestrian alleyways because, it was claimed – primarily by the police – they were being used by young people to intimidate older residents, conceal acts of crime and anti-social behaviour and evade the police.

Running parallel with the situational crime prevention agenda has been the implementation of anti-social behaviour legislation and, along with other services established in the area, targeted interventions into the lives of young people identified as being 'at risk' of offending have occurred. These interventions have included the use of the following tools: referral to the Youth Inclusion Programme (YIP), Acceptable Behaviour Contracts (ABCs), Anti-Social Behaviour Orders (ASBOs) and tenancy enforcement actions that can result in the demotion of a tenancy or eviction from a property owned by the local authority. Figures collated in 2005 by the Home Office show that the town in which Hillside is located came in the top 10 in England and Wales for numbers of ASBOs issued in 2004.

Who is 'anti-social' in Hillside?

The perception of those directly engaged in ASB management was that it was children and young people who posed the greatest threat to the order of the estate. In line with the analysis offered by Squires and Stephen (2005), the behaviour of young people was identified as the last criminal justice issue that needed addressing in Hillside, as crime perpetrated by adults had been, for all intents and purposes, largely tackled. The head of the Community Safety Team stated this position clearly: 'We don't have a crime problem in the area, we don't have a problem with offending by adults ... our focus is changing the behaviour of young people.'

The evidence base from which these claims were made included local crime statistics showing levels of recorded crime falling in Hillside, the number of complaints of ASB from residents involving children and young people, and the perceived levels of intimidation adult residents were reporting at the local Crime Prevention Forum concerning the behaviour of young people. Taken together, these concerns justified what the head of the Community Safety Team considered to be a reasonable focus on rigorous interventions with those young people said to be engaged in ASB – and with their parents.

During Crime Prevention Forums, whose purpose was to empower *all* residents to take a stand against crime and ASB, it quickly became clear that the same perceptions of young people were shared, almost without exception, by all those attending the meetings. Likewise, discussions of young people and their reported behaviour dominated all of the meetings attended as part of this research. Children and young people as a group were routinely portrayed as reckless, dangerous and unconcerned about the ways in which their behaviour impacted on those around them. They were undeserving of sympathy, and any efforts to try to understand them, it was argued, only reinforced their seeming attitude that they could *get away with it*. 'It' was more often than not incidents of stone throwing, petty vandalism, noisy behaviour (including playing football in the street) and hanging around in spaces that were felt to be inappropriate, such as the stairwells of flats. Discussions of specific incidents would regularly develop into a conception that *all* young people from Hillside had the potential to act 'anti-socially'. In turn, the forum became a space in which strategies were developed and a number of initiatives designed to control young people's movements, and activities were developed on the forum's behest, including the introduction of additional mobile CCTV units, new CCTV cameras surrounding the local youth club, an increase in targeted police patrols and active encouragement to residents (through the tenants' associations) to report on the movements of young people on the estate when it was felt they were acting 'anti-socially'.

What is anti-social behaviour?

> Spitting, swearing, making too much noise, intimidating neighbours or other people on the estate ... playing games ... um ... it could be anything really. It depends on who's reporting it. (Local Police and Community Support Officer)

> This woman who lives across the road ... she reported me 'cos she said that I was being loud in the street but I don't think I was. I was just mucking around with my mates. Like we were making noise but it was just *normal noise*. (Jenna, 14)

The loose definition of ASB as defined in the 1998 Crime and Disorder Act has been discussed in the academic literature as highly problematic (Bland and Read, 2000; Burney, 2002; Brown, 2004). Those practitioners who were working in ASB management in Hillside, however, felt that this definition provided the necessary scope to encourage 'victims' of ASB to report incidents – even if the incidents could be construed as trivial by others – that *they* perceived as anti-social. Perception, as intended by the legislation, was important in this equation. ASB practitioners stressed the importance of taking every report seriously, as they felt it would send a message to the 'community' and that would engender trust and cooperation between residents, the Community Safety Team and the police. There were high levels of distrust towards the police among residents who were spoken to informally as part of the research. For some, distrust was generated because they felt the police were not responding sufficiently to issues of serious crime on the estate. For others (especially those with children), there were concerns about the levels of intervention with young people. Those involved in managing ASB in Hillside, including the Safer Neighbourhoods Policing Team, were impacted by these attitudes. During a break in one Crime Prevention Forum meeting this was openly recognised by the head of the Community Safety Team as a barrier to its work: 'You see the problem is residents see us as being part of the police ... it often means they won't talk to us. People get very suspicious and blame us for what they [the police] do.'

During interviews ASB managers were aware of the importance of perceptions in reports of ASB perpetrated in Hillside. They themselves acknowledged issues with residents' tolerances of one another, and disputes between families that resulted in complaints about ASB involving young people. The overall impression, however, was one of resolute pragmatism. Hillside did have a 'problem' with ASB, it was their job to take the correct action to resolve these incidents, punitive intervention was a tool in their armoury and they would therefore take the appropriate action when a complaint was made. As reflected in the literature on ASB (Brown, 2004; Squires, 2006), the social and material conditions that underlay much of the ASB witnessed in Hillside were seldom engaged with. Young people's marginalisation, both within their own neighbourhoods and in their wider local experiences, was not recognised as a significant issue. Any attempt to engage with those wider debates was closed down and interpreted as if excusing the behaviour of children and young people.

In this climate, young people reported feeling confused about exactly what ASB was and how they could avoid getting into trouble for it. The types of behaviour they had seen generate interventions were generally activities that they felt 'were part of growing up'. Being outside with friends, playing games, chatting and socialising were activities that, when they were asked about them, the young people emphasised were important to their lives, friendships and social networks. Research going back many years suggests that such activities are important to young people everywhere (Morse, 1965; Corrigan, 1974; Childress, 1994; Matthews et al, 1998; Katz, 1998; Matthews et al, 2000; Skelton, 2000;

Kearns and Parkinson, 2001; Malone, 2002; Elsley, 2004). There was awareness that for some residents these activities could be, and were being, construed as 'anti-social' but that in young people's minds the exact opposite was true. That some adults perceived their presence on the street as intimidating was something they claimed to not really understand. Some of the older boys, in particular, described situations in which, irrespective of what was going on, older residents would eye them with considerable suspicion but resolutely avoid engaging with them. Like some of the other older boys who participated in the research, Toby (age 16) was troubled by this:

> We just get singled out all the time. I just think that people forget what it was like when they were kids. I'd like to know how they'd feel if people crossed the road just to avoid you when all you're doing is standing there with your mates. It bothers me; I hate it.

The extent to which young people articulated a real sense of anger and injustice at how they felt singled out and blamed for the problems Hillside was experiencing was surprising. In contrast to the assumption that Hillside did not have a problem with offending by adults, many of the young people interviewed were experiencing tough situations in the home or neighbourhood, involving problematic adult behaviour. Domestic violence at home, the devastating effects of drug and alcohol abuse, getting caught up in arguments between rival families, and exposure to adult violence on the street were common experiences among the children and young people who participated in the research. This apparent contradiction always raised questions about the extent to which young people acted as a diversion for wider socio-economic uncertainties experienced by some residents, and were an 'easy target' for those involved in ASB management on the estate.

The process of intervention

Finding yourself the subject of an intervention did not appear to be that hard. Having the opportunity to defend yourself against any allegations being made about you proved much more difficult. As Stephen and Squires (2003) argue, for 'soft' interventions such as ABCs there is no process for assessing the guilt or innocence of those accused of acting 'anti-socially'. Although the young people who were subject to ABCs throughout the time this fieldwork was being conducted had the support of at least one parent, they felt that any attempt they made to 'tell their side of the story' would be dismissed. Asking ASB practitioners to take their word against another party was a very difficult thing either to decide to do or to execute. This left many masking uncertainty behind the front of 'not really giving a shit' and thereby entrenching the perception that they were unmoved or unconcerned about what they had been accused of, or dismissive of the consequences of an intervention for themselves or their families. Dave, a 14-year-old boy for whom ABC proceedings began in the autumn of the fieldwork, illustrated this. Having spoken to me at great length at the Youth Centre about how he did not care about getting an ABC, how it was not going to mean anything anyway, he told a very different story in our interview. He was really worried, particularly about his mum and potentially being evicted from their house. He felt that the complaints made against him arose from a situation far more complex than what was being presented. Overall, however, he did not feel able to discuss this with the community safety officer dealing with the intervention:

> **Interviewer**: Are you going to tell them that it's more complicated than what they've said?

> **Dave**: No. There's no point ... why would they believe me? As far as they're concerned I've done what they said in the letter. End of.

The 'voluntary' nature of ABCs also posed a problem for young people and practitioners. When explored, it was evident that, far from being a mutual arrangement between parents, practitioners and young people, this was not always the case. Young people were aware that, when it came down to it, they had no choice but to agree to the intervention and the conditions attached to it. Practitioners were also aware of this and acknowledged that the refusal to sign would lead to parents being 'strenuously reminded' of their tenancy obligations and, if that was ineffective, of the 'more serious action' that might follow.

ASB practitioners were also accused of not understanding the realities of life in Hillside for young people and how these could be different from the experiences of young people in other areas. In a sense, they were asking practitioners to understand their situation both within the neighbourhood and in the more localised social context. This was something that they felt *was* understood by the management and staff of the local youth club, for they were all long-term residents of the estate:

> It's different with Bec and Dave. 'Cos they know us it's like
> they take care of us. (Roxy, aged 15)

For those who attended the youth club there was a palpable feeling
of being protected and understood, sometimes irrespective of their
behaviour. There appeared to be a complexity to their understandings
of the young people in Hillside that did not appear to be the case with
those engaged in official ASB management activity. How important
this was in generating trust with young people was discussed in an
interview with Dave, the club manager:

> They know that we're [club workers] in the same boat as
> them. They know that if I wasn't in this job it would be
> hard to get work because I live in Hillside. They know that
> I have to put up with the same crap as them about being a
> Hillsider. They see me having to keep my cool at football
> tournaments when managers refuse to play us because the
> immediate assumption is that we're trouble. That's why
> they trust us.

Overall, young people felt exposed to ASB management in ways that
they were unable to anticipate or control. In addition to this there
were conflicts over other ways in which ASB was being targeted on
the estate. A brief discussion of two of these forms of intervention,
CCTV and policing, now follows.

Surveillance and policing

The presence of CCTV on the estate was identified by the local District
Commander as an essential tool in the fight against crime and ASB
in Hillside. For the police and the Community Safety Team this was a
relatively straightforward relationship. CCTV could help them evidence
reports of crime and ASB and could provide supporting evidence for
them to use in the enforcement process. The fact that there had been
a residents' vote back in 1998 that supported the introduction of ten
CCTV cameras on the estate was taken as a mandate for its introduction
and continued use. Currently in Hillside there are ten static cameras,
a variable number of police mobile CCTV units, and an undisclosed
number of cameras being used to collect evidence against those
accused of ASB. There is also an unknown number of private cameras
that residents suggest are being used increasingly by householders to
protect their homes, and cameras in the local shops.

Some young people reported that they were not really bothered by the presence of the cameras, that they had become used to them and did not really notice them any more. These opinions were usually expressed by some of the younger members of the club who, by virtue of their ages, were still closely monitored by parents. They were more likely to spend most of their time at organised activities and youth groups and did not, or were not allowed to, spend their leisure time using the streets. This was not the same for some of the older group, those between the ages of 15 and 17, who wanted the freedom and autonomy that they felt the street provided. Cameras for them were perceived to be another way in which their activities could be monitored. Kathy, who is 16, suggested the following:

> The cameras are meant to be for speeding cars but if you watch them they move and follow you when you walk up the street. If a couple of you meet, say up by the flats, the camera swivels round really quickly and stays on you. It just watches what's going on.

In response to this it was usual for them to 'test' this theory by 'acting up' in front of the cameras and seeing if there would be a response:

> They're not meant to be for us right? OK. So we think what'll happen if we have like a pretend fight? They've been watching us walk around for weeks all being mates and that, but the minute this pretend fight kicks off two police cars come flying up onto the estate. It was mental. (Louis, age 16)

Young people openly resented the extent to which they were a target of surveillance. It appeared to compromise their ability to use public space and it was a real concern that they did not know how many cameras were being used to monitor their activities. At times the static cameras became identified as legitimate targets on which their frustration could be focused. During the autumn of the fieldwork there was a tangible rise in tension due to the increase in targeted police patrols on the estate aimed specifically at young people. Cameras were smashed, areas around them vandalised and young people arrested. The following excerpt from the fieldwork diary highlights how these events were connected for the young people involved:

Things feel very tense at the moment. When I came onto the estate tonight there was a visible police presence. Police were parked up sitting in the wagons. The kids seemed really jumpy. Some of those involved were talking to me and saying that they were sick of the police being everywhere. I asked them what was going to happen later and they said there would be more trouble. They were going to do the cameras again. I said they should just go home and avoid getting into trouble but they were adamant, they wanted to do something. They said it was unfair that the police could stop and search them all the time without really having a reason.

The frustrations voiced by the young people and the youth workers at the frequency of stop and search litters the data. Club workers did not understand the purpose of an evidently counterproductive stop-and-search strategy that they knew actively created resentment among young people – especially as police managers were vocal about their lack of general support in the community. In response, the police were adamant that this was a legitimate crime- and ASB-prevention strategy. One small group of approximately eight boys, who engaged with the research only after a long period spent relationship building, highlighted the extent to which this was a problem for them and how powerless they were to deal with the situation:

> **Interviewer**: Do you have a lot to do with them [the police]?
>
> **John** (age 15): They stopped us yesterday. Well ... how many times did we get stopped around that period?
>
> **Mark**: About three times a day.
>
> **John**: Yeah it must have been three times a day at least, probably even more and they'd like ask us if we'd been in trouble and then 'cos they know what we're like they wouldn't leave us. They'd radio through.
>
> **Mark**: And then the camera up the top would move onto us.

> **John**: There was actually one point where, do you know Ernie? He got stopped literally as he walked out of his house and he got stopped straight away and we were all actually thinking about doing ... like ... getting a campaign together to sue them because we couldn't ... literally it was so bad we'd be getting stopped every five minutes. But we just couldn't do it because we didn't know how and we can't pay.

Mark and John were open about the fact that they had been reported for incidents of ASB and were engaged in behaviour that could be perceived as 'anti-social'. Experience on the estate highlighted that this was not just a problem for those who had been in trouble. Every young person who participated in the interviews reported being fairly regularly stopped and searched by the police. Routine stops were often made to take names and check that young people were not in possession of alcohol. Police suspicion was aroused by a variety of innocuous behaviours such as running down the street, as two 13-year-old girls found when they were stopped, running home from a youth work session. When asked about this incident at a forum meeting the local District Commander stated that 'running was a legitimate reason to stop a young person on this estate'.

Intensive surveillance and policing, justified as preventing crime and ASB, appeared to combine to create a climate of resentment and fear among some young people in Hillside. Concerns raised by youth workers about this strategy potentially criminalising, and certainly disenchanting, many young people were entirely dismissed by those involved in managing ASB. In response, they argued that it sent clear signals to young people that ASB would not be tolerated in any form, acted as a deterrent for young people thinking of engaging in such behaviour, provided a mechanism through which evidence could be collected, and reinforced to the 'community' that something was being done about ASB. On reflection, however, this policy and practice, by damaging relationships with young people who would grow up to be adults on the estate, appeared deeply flawed.

Use of space

When comparing the data generated in conversations with the young people, in their mid-teens, and with the young adults, in their mid-twenties, a number of significant differences were noted. The young adults reported using space much more freely. Large mixed-sex groups would congregate in spaces of which they had claimed 'ownership'. It was in these spaces that friendships were developed and their leisure time was spent. The importance of this was recognised as providing time away from adult supervision and/or complex home environments. Today's young people by contrast, appear to have a much more compromised and circumscribed relationship with public space. Although they, too, acknowledge that time away from adult supervision is important, in the same way as the older group, they did not feel able to use the space within their neighbourhood in the same ways. Instead, their friendship groups appeared much smaller and were predominantly single-sex. Some of the younger girls articulated a reluctance to spend time with boys because of what they perceived as the increased likelihood of police intervention. Boys articulated resentment towards girls, who they felt were treated differently by the police. 'Hidden' spaces such as stairwells of flats and isolated park areas were increasingly being used to avoid surveillance by the cameras and contact with the police. It was generally agreed that congregating in a group in a public space would immediately attract the attention of the police and cameras. Young people suggested that, in addition to their own concerns, parents were also placing extra restrictions on their movements because of the likelihood of police intervention.

The potential long-term consequences of these shifts are important to consider. The young adults recognised the importance of strong friendship groups, not only as a source of immediate support but also taking on the role of substitute family. As Rachel (age 23), now a youth worker in the area, remembered:

> We were like a family because loads of us didn't really have any parents, well, we did have parents but they weren't really there ... so if you needed something, like somewhere to sleep, or you wanted advice about something you would have to rely on your friends. They were really all you had.

These sources of support appeared to have lasted into adulthood, with employment and housing opportunities being generated through them. It was a way, they recognised, of overcoming discrimination from local employers who still appeared reluctant to offer jobs to people from Hillside. Removing these opportunities from young people growing up in Hillside today in an economic climate of increasing competition for jobs and housing could have potentially long-term disadvantaging consequences.

Conclusion

Young people were identified and targeted as the main perpetrators of ASB in Hillside, resulting in increased surveillance and contact with the police. Concerns raised about this strategy by those who worked closely with them were construed as excusing behaviour, and there was no attempt to address the wider socio-economic challenges faced by them. As a result, young people were an increasingly marginalised group within their own neighbourhood, raising questions about the extent to which they were an 'easy target' for ASB management in comparison to the (often more problematic and serious) behaviour of adults. Shifting patterns of the use of public neighbourhood space to incorporate increasingly 'hidden' spaces were acknowledged as consequences of the developments in ASB management. Potential longer-term consequences could arise from these changes, including making the transition from young person to young adult more difficult in already challenging circumstances.

Note

[1] The figures given from the Census are slightly distorted because of the inclusion of data from a small but more affluent area that forms part of the council ward that is dominated by the Hillside Estate.

References

Bland, N. and Read, T. (2000) *Policing anti-social behaviour*, Police Research Series 123, London: Home Office Police Research Group.

Brown, A.P. (2004) 'Anti-social behaviour, crime control and social control', *Howard Journal of Criminal Justice*, vol 43, no 2, pp 203–11.

Burney, E. (2002) 'Talking tough, acting coy: What happened to the anti-social behaviour order?', *Howard Journal of Criminal Justice*, vol 41, no 5, pp 469–84.

Census (2001) *Population by age in three bands 0–18, 19–64 and 65 and over*, London: Office for National Statistics.

Childress, H. (1994) 'No loitering: some thoughts on small town teenage hangouts', *Small Town*, vol 24, no 11, pp 20–5.

Corrigan, P. (1974) *Schooling the Smash Street kids*, Basingstoke: Macmillan.

Crawford, A. (1997) *Crime prevention and community safety: Politics, policies and practice*, Harlow: Longman.

Elsley, S. (2004) 'Children's experience of public space', *Children and Society*, vol 18, pp 155–64.

Hughes, G. (1998) *Understanding crime prevention, social control, risk and late modernity*, Buckingham: Open University Press.

Katz, C. (1998) 'Disintegrating developments: global economic restructuring and the eroding ecologies of youth', in T. Skelton and G. Valentine (eds), *Cool places: Geographies of youth culture*, London: Routledge.

Kearns, A. and Parkinson, M. (2001) 'The significance of neighbourhood', *Urban Studies*, vol 38, no 12, pp 2103–10.

Malone, K. (2002) 'Street life: youth, culture and competing uses of public space', *Environment and Urbanization*, vol 14, no 2, pp 157–68.

Matthews, H., Limb, M. and Percy-Smith, M. (1998) 'Changing worlds: the microgeographies of young teenagers', *Tijdschrift voor Economische en Sociale Geografie*, vol 89, no 2, pp 193–202.

Matthews, H., Lamb, M. and Taylor, M. (2000) 'The street as "thirdspace"', in S.L. Holloway and G. Valentine (eds), *Children's geographies*, London: Routledge.

Morse, M. (1965) *The Unattached*, Harmondsworth: Penguin.

ODPM (Office of the Deputy Prime Minister) (2004) *The English indices of deprivation 2004 (revised)* (available at www.communities.gov.uk/pub/446/Indicesofdeprivation2004revised_id1128446.pdf).

ONS (Office for National Statistics) (2003) *Socio-economic classification: All people*, London: ONS.

Skelton, T. (2000) 'Nothing to do, nowhere to go: teenage girls and "public" space in the Rhondda Valleys, South Wales', in S.L. Holloway and G. Valentine (eds), *Children's geographies*, London: Routledge.

Squires, P. (2006) 'New Labour and the politics of anti-social behaviour', *Critical Social Policy*, vol 26, no 1, pp 144–68.

Squires, P. and Stephen, D.E. (2005) *Rougher justice: Anti-social behaviour and young people*, Cullompton: Willan Publishing.

Stephen, D.E. and Squires, P. (2003) *Community safety, enforcement and Acceptable Behaviour Contracts*, Brighton: Health and Social Policy Research Centre, University of Brighton.

THIRTEEN

ASBO youth: rhetoric and realities

Brian McIntosh

Introduction

Under New Labour, the problem of anti-social behaviour (ASB) has become, and continues to be, a central policy issue. The introduction of a raft of new legislation to deal with this social problem has seen the creation of a variety of behaviour regulation instruments ranging from night curfews to the Anti-Social Behaviour Order (ASBO). However, alongside these new sanctions, one target group of such interventions is distinctly familiar: troublesome *young people*. Within the current political climate, youths identified as anti-social currently wear the mantle of society's contemporary folk devils. However, despite such symbolic prominence, what is striking is the near-total absence, in both official and more critical research, of the 'anti-social' youth perpetrator's perspective. This chapter draws upon the findings of an Economic and Social Research Council-funded exploratory pilot study that was undertaken in 2005 and draws upon in-depth interviews with two youths (both subject to ASBOs) in one locality. The interviews sought to explore the perception and impact of various anti-social behaviour interventions upon the respondents. After presenting the findings, this chapter concludes by advocating the importance of both acknowledging and listening to the 'anti-social youth perpetrator perspective' for the purposes of more holistic understandings of anti-social behaviour and the impact and consequences of its regulation.

Anti-social youth

'Troublesome' young people feature prominently in the current ASB agenda, from national policy rhetoric through to individual locales where 'anti-social youth behaviour management [is] a priority in almost all local community safety strategies' (Hughes, 2007: 126). Within both of these spheres, however, it has been argued that such youths occupy a very narrow yet specific role whereby they are seen primarily as a group from which communities need protecting (Hill and Wright, 2003; Squires and Stephen, 2005b; Hughes and Follett, 2006; Stephen, 2006). Such positioning consolidates the point whereby the problem of ASB is seen as synonymous with the problem of anti-social youth.

The broader consequence of this particular construction of the problem is that 'Anti-social behaviour has become a convenient peg on which to hang generalised prejudices about young people and their activities which make restrictive policies popular' (Burney, 2005: 67). This targeted focus towards anti-social youths has led to their becoming the disproportionate recipients of many of the new statutory and non-statutory interventions, such as the Acceptable Behaviour Contract (ABC) and the Anti-Social Behaviour Order (ASBO).[1] Although the latter order was not initially intended for youths (Burney, 2002: 473), it was 'designed, inter alia, with juvenile ASB in mind' (Morgan and Newburn, 2007: 1037). Furthermore, the persistence of the media, in its many forms, in constantly linking the term 'ASBO' with images of hooded adolescents consolidates the anti-social master status of such youths.

Constructing and explaining anti-social behaviour

In addition to the youth issue, New Labour's ASB agenda can be identified as having two further defining features. First, the current government has reverted to a 'moral authoritarian communitarian discourse' (Hughes, 2007: 112), drawing on right realism to locate the problem, explaining it as one of individual deficiency in relation to both respect and taking responsibility for one's own actions (Burney, 2005). This version of the problem is clearly pronounced in the following quote from the *Respect and responsibility* White Paper:

> The common element in all anti-social behaviour is that it represents a lack of respect and consideration for other people. It shows a selfish inability or unwillingness to recognise where one's individual behaviour is offensive to others and a refusal to take responsibility for it. (Home Office, 2003: 17)

The above policy statement, drawing upon populist 'common-sense' reasoning and promoting a particular explanation of the problem, leads to self-evident individualistic 'solutions', such as the ASBO

(Nixon and Parr, 2006: 85). Behaviour is reduced to a moral choice, crucially divorcing the importance of biographies, meanings and socio-structural contexts from how such behaviour must now be understood (Burney, 2005; McIntosh, 2005; Squires and Stephen, 2005a; Nixon and Parr, 2006). However, as much as the explanatory potential of such social understandings has now been repackaged as 'excuses' (Home Office, 1997), this does not mean that such interpretations should be abandoned.

The deficit of empirical research

The second defining, and widely acknowledged, feature of the ASB agenda is the current lack of both official and critical research into the effectiveness and impact of these new ASB measures (Smith, 2003; House of Commons, 2005; McIntosh, 2005; Squires and Stephen, 2005b; Hughes and Follett, 2006; Nixon, 2006; House of Commons Committee of Public Accounts, 2007; Hughes, 2007). To date, empirical research that engages with, and gives voice to, the perspectives of anti-social youths, especially in relation to how they perceive such new forms of behavioural control, is exceptionally sparse (although see Stephen and Squires, 2003; Solanki et al, 2006; Wain, 2007 as notable exceptions).

This absence not only has consequences for policy (see House of Commons Committee of Public Accounts, 2007), in terms of evaluation and impact, but also allows the current construction and explanation of both ASB and its perpetrators to go unchallenged. The wider implication of this research deficit is acknowledged by Judy Nixon, who has noted that, 'While there is a diverse and growing literature on ASBOs the absence of robust empirical research means that much of what is written is dominated by anecdote, conjecture and rhetoric' (Nixon, 2006: 22). This has obvious consequences for both official policy and critiques of its introduction, implementation and evaluation. This lack of perpetrator perspective research also manifests itself at the local level in many areas.

Local rhetoric and practice

As well as introducing a host of new behaviour control instruments, the 1998 Crime and Disorder Act placed a statutory requirement on all local authorities to create partnerships with other local agencies, with one of the major remits being to deal locally with ASB. Thus, while the national rhetoric discussed above, and its subsequent enforcement focus, may indeed have a degree of impact on local practice, at the local level such strategies for dealing with anti-social youth are instead often defined by compromise, contestation and even resistance (Hughes, 2007: 114). Such practice has given rise to diverse local ASB regulatory strategies.

Northtown

This research was undertaken in an area of Wales, UK. For the purposes of anonymity, as granted in the original thesis, the area will be referred to as 'Northtown'. Northtown's approach to anti-social behaviour is based more around problem solving rather than opting for more severe enforcement measures as a first resort. The particular strategy in place in Northtown is known as the 'four-strikes' approach and includes an incremental range of interventions which includes early warning letters, ABCs and ASBOs. This approach has been referred to by the Police Chief Constable for South Wales as a 'preventative early intervention approach' (Welsh Affairs Committee, 2004: 9), whereby the intention of such early intervention is to deflect individuals from escalating up the intervention tariff. The approach is deemed to be highly effective in its aim, and local data seem to support this view (Table 13.1).[2]

The Police Chief Constable has stated that this approach operates as such an effective filtering system that only those who have not taken 'every opportunity' to change their behaviour reach the stage of the ASBO (Welsh Affairs Committee, 2004: 13). This discourse of responsibility in relation to the local strategy has also permeated other interviews that I have undertaken with key local actors in the same area.[3] While this approach does seem to have success at the aggregate level, the official rhetoric towards those who have not responded to this incremental approach is one of failure to take responsibility for their own actions. As the findings suggest below, such responsibility is

Table 13.1 Number of interventions issued in selected areas of Northtown

	Letter 1	Letter 2	Letter 2 (1)	Letter 3	Letter 3 (1)	ABC	ASBO
Westside	47	10	11	-	-	-	-
Bayside	35	9	12	1	-	1	1
City Centre	29	2	1	-	-	-	1
Downside	167	44	3	19	-	7	2
Eastside	79	9	8	2	-	1	2

not always within the grasp of the anti-social perpetrator (Phoenix, in Chapter Sixteen in this volume, discusses similar issues in the policing of street prostitution).

Finally, it is important to draw attention to the flexible decision making that underpins the four-strikes strategy. In terms of practice, this approach has an in-built flexibility allowing for any stage to be bypassed if it is deemed to be necessary for the overriding goal of community protection. This point was stressed by Northtown's Community Safety Manager:

> The misconception if you like of the four-strikes process is that it is not necessarily chronological and in fact, in terms of an ASBO you don't even have to have gone through [all the stages] … in some cases you just know it is pointless issuing the 'first strike' letter to amend their behaviour as all you are doing is extending the period of torture for the community.

This subjective decision making is by no means unique to Northtown, as there is evidence that it also occurs in other areas that have adopted a tiered approach (Solanki et al, 2006: 45). However, within this local strategy the existence of such subjectivity is seen as a beneficial mechanism, although, as the discussion below indicates, this subjectivity can also lead to counterproductive or unanticipated outcomes.

Research method

The nature of the research undertaken necessitates a brief methodological note. In practice, making contact with and gaining access to these young people proved to be highly problematic. This was due mainly to three broad issues: (i) their status as troublesome young people, (ii) a problematic access strategy and (iii) the contingent nature of the ASBO itself (for a detailed, reflexive discussion on the methodology of this research project see McIntosh, 2005). The primary research method used was the semi-structured interview, which has numerous benefits when interviewing hard-to-reach groups, such as its flexibility (May, 1997; Noaks and Wincup, 2004). Both respondents were given a small financial reward for participation, as it was felt that this helped in somewhat rebalancing the power differential in the research process. For the purposes of anonymity the two respondents were given the pseudonyms of 'John' and 'Donald'.

Biographies of respondents

John was 16 years old on receipt of his ASBO and, owing to the absence of both parents, he and his elder brother stayed with his grandmother in one of the most economically and socially deprived areas in Northtown. He had a two-year stand-alone ASBO that contained a number of behavioural prohibitions and geographical restrictions. He had also been involved in a number of public order offences. He left education before the age of 16 and at the time of writing is currently serving an Intensive Surveillance and Supervision Programme (ISSP) with the local Youth Offending Team.

Donald was also 16 years old when given his ASBO. He lived with his mother, father and younger siblings. He had previously run away from home and was placed on a missing persons list. He had a five-year stand-alone ASBO. He also had a long history of offending, including a number of public order offences, but primarily car-related crime, leading to his serving a sentence in a Young Offenders Institution (YOI). He openly acknowledged that he had problems with controlling his temper and he believes such behaviour and the subsequent multiple exclusions that followed from both mainstream and specialist schooling were the reasons behind his non-completion of full-time education. Like John, he lived in the same economically and socially deprived area in Northtown and is also serving an ISSP.

The biographies of both respondents are important not only because they provide an essential dimension in understanding their response to the various interventions they received, but also because, unlike the pervasive, one-dimensional images of anti-social youths that permeate both policy and media, such background information provides an insight into their chaotic life styles that is often omitted in dominant ASB discourses. The fractured backgrounds of such youths are by no means unique to the respondents in this research (Campbell, 2002; Solanki et al, 2006). This adds credence to the observation that youths who end up being issued with an ASBO are as much troubled as they are troublesome.

The four-strikes process: perceptions and experiences

Both local rhetoric and data suggest that the four-strikes process is highly effective and one whereby any problem is not a problem of the tiered process itself, but one of the individual perpetrators. There seems to be no consideration that, while this strategy does divert many, it also has the potential to accelerate others towards more serious ASB sanctions, as the following findings suggest.

Early warning letters

Written warning letters are the first stage of the local incremental strategy. These letters are sent to individuals stating the nature of the ASB that individuals are accused of and warning of further action if desistance is not forthcoming. However, neither respondent seemed to take these early warnings with any degree of seriousness:

> A warning first and then they started sending out leaflets and letters and all that. (John)

> The first one [the warning] I didn't even care like, I didn't even read it like. My mum just had it like, it didn't bother me at first like. (Donald)

These attitudes, taken at face value, could be taken to validate the view that they had no desire to change their behaviour, as well as suggesting that this form of early intervention was held in contempt by these youths, especially in light of the seeming effectiveness of such letters as shown in Table 13.1. However, an uncritical acceptance of such viewpoints deflects attention from the local strategy and its intended outcomes and the problem of early warnings being expected to work irrespective of whether the individuals to whom they are issued have a previous offending history or not.

The issue of previous offending histories in relation to the stages in the four-strikes process was illuminated when Donald drew attention to the inherent confusions within this new approach to ASB regulation:

> It said [the warning letter] that 'you have been seen in X throwing a stone at a window', just one offence like, which they should have arrested me for like and given me a community service thing but they just kept on giving me warnings ... but it's not even like an excess behaviour, it's an arrestable offence anyway, innit, but they didn't, they just keep on giving me leaflets and that's what was doing my head in like. (Donald)

The suggestion here is that Donald believed ASB to be innately different from offending, and then only expected the sanctions for the former to be forthcoming when such behaviour was committed in 'excess'. His awareness, based on previous experience, that he ought to have been arrested for what he knew to be a public order offence, led to confusion when such behaviour was now being addressed by a seemingly lesser intervention. This issue of (mis)perception does pose questions for the local strategy and the individuals who are processed in this way.

Paradoxically, while the main benefit of this early approach seems to be found in diversion away from formal sanction, there is a suggestion that, for those who have previous criminal histories, and thus an awareness of how the legal system works, the letters do not deter. A criminal act that would have once brought an immediate response in the form of arrest was now initially attracting a substantially lesser sanction. This suggests that warning letters may give mixed and confusing signals which may frustrate the purposes for which they are originally sent.

The Acceptable Behaviour Contract

These warnings failed in their preventative effect on both John and Donald, which subsequently led to their being moved to the next stage of the process and issued with an ABC. The ABC is a voluntary six-month 'contract' that, when issued to young people, is a collective agreement signed by them, their parents and either the police or the local authority that outlines a number of unacceptable behaviours that the individual 'agrees' to no longer take part in (Home Office, 2002). The evolution from the ABC to the ASBO occurred in different ways for each respondent. John was quite honest when he made the simple admission that, as with the previous warnings, it had relatively little impact upon him – 'just didn't stop what I was doing really'.

However, the situation was completely different for Donald:

> When I went for that one, the Acceptable ABC thing, I were on a missing persons list 'cos I'd run away from home and then they give me that and I was calming down a bit … I signed it and I was good then. It was like not to throw stones at cars and that. There were three things and I put them on my fridge door and I didn't do none of that and then I went to jail, and they came to my door [with the ASBO].

This particular narrative provides a number of insights. First, it draws attention to the fractured and troubled background of the respondent and questions the very simplistic belief that his failure to heed previous warnings was one born of a failure to take responsibility for his actions. Running away from home is a clear indication of his chaotic background, whatever the specific reasons for doing so.

Second, Donald believed that the transition to the ASBO was not the product of his breaching the conditions of the ABC. It is very difficult to convey in writing how adamant he was that he had fulfilled the conditions of the contract and that he felt the reason for his being issued with the order was due to the commission of a separate offence that also led to his prison sentence. This point brings to the fore one of the problems of the subjective nature of the local approach. From the above, it is quite clear that Donald had a very instrumental view towards his ABC and did not seem to realise that the 'rules' of the ABC could be changed, based on involvement in other deviant or offending behaviours that were not included in the original contract. While the whole purpose of such operational subjectivity is to prioritise and provide community protection, there is surely validity in the argument that, given that the sanctions for breach are so severe, youths who find themselves within the web of ASB regulation should be fully informed of the major consequences that accompany non-compliance, in a language that is understandable to them.

The Anti-Social Behaviour Order

It can be argued that the ASBO has various purposes and justifications, with the most prominent of these being community protection. However, the ASBO can also be seen as a disciplinary instrument that places responsibility for behaviour, in terms of decisions, actions and compliance, solely on the perpetrator and thereby reduces understandings of behaviour to individual moral choices. The ASBO has the potential to penetrate deeply into the lives of those issued with them, given their ability to criminalise legal behaviours (both individual and social) as well as to impose wide-ranging geographical restriction. Yet very little is known about the realities of how ASBOs impact on the everyday lives of youth ASBO recipients. The following findings explore how the ASBO has impacted on each individual and their everyday lives.

The conditions

The type of order issued to both respondents was the 'stand-alone' ASBO. Neither of the orders was the continuation of interim ASBOs or issued as a post-conviction sentence.

Although both ASBOs share a number of similar conditions, each will be discussed separately (drawing attention to relevant similarities and differences) to provide a detailed understanding of how the orders impact on those subject to them.

John

As outlined earlier, John's ASBO was for a period of two years and it contained a number of public order prohibitions, including being banned from committing various public order offences, as well as geographical restrictions. Research has shown that these two types of condition are very commonly used, but also that they are far from being unproblematic (Solanki et al, 2006). As with the other stages, the ASBO did not initially prevent John from committing prohibited anti-social acts:

> Before I used to think, don't worry about it, but now I can't be bothered really … it's like, before I even had the ASBO I used to get into trouble, but after like, I just calmed down, just used to get warnings like, just used to hang around the streets causing trouble in a big gang … I just stay off the streets now where I normally hang around like. I just don't cause no bother at all. (John)

It emerged from John's interview that he had breached on a few occasions, but rather than receiving an immediate custodial sanction, this led to his being given more ASBOs. Again, John acknowledges that these did not prevent his behaviour, primarily because the threat of prison remained distant. It was not until this threat became both immediate and real that he began to address his behaviour:

> **BM**: How did you feel about going to court?

> **John**: I was feeling alright like, 'cos like he [the magistrate] said that if you get another ASBO you're going to jail and I just stopped it then. Just stopped it.

> **BM**: Were you anxious about going to court?

> **John**: Yeah, a bit anxious like with the thought of going to jail but I got that tag fitted and he said if you get another

ASBO then you go straight to jail so I stopped ... it's a big thing the ASBO innit? ... I don't want to go to jail.

This extract suggests that the likelihood of a custodial sentence for an ASBO breach may have a deterrent impact on some ASBO recipients. However, John was also a recipient of an ISSP sentence that had assisted him in finding employment with a local painter and decorator. His views on this are discussed later in the chapter, but it is possible to suggest that his perceived desistance was attributable not only to the threat of prison but also to his having something tangible to lose with this new employment opportunity.

Whatever the reasons behind his claimed desistance, John pointed out that he had introduced various avoidance strategies into his everyday life:

It's like when I used to hang around the top end with all the boys just getting into trouble all the time and now I just hang around with this one person who just chills in his house and plays the computer and all that.

Donald

For present purposes, discussion will focus on one of the conditions that Donald felt particularly strongly about – the non-association clause that prevents him from associating with a number of his peers. This prohibition has had far-reaching consequences for the respondent. Donald's ASBO was granted while he was already serving a prison sentence in a YOI. The conditions of his order became active upon his release and his first breach occurred within hours of his returning home, resulting in his being taken back to custody:

I was on his drive speaking to him [his friend] and his mum and they [the police] came along and arrested me and I went back on remand for two months. (Donald)

According to Donald, this breach was neither deliberate nor an act of defiance of the order, but because he had simply forgotten about the ASBO while he was in the YOI:

I hadn't seen them [his friends] for so long when I was in jail like, I just come out and completely forgot about it 'cos there's no time to think about an ASBO when you're in jail is there? … and I completely forgot about it like and I started speaking to my mates and that … then I got arrested. (Donald)

After being imprisoned for a substantial period of time, his first thoughts upon release were to see his family and his friends, and the ASBO was not at the forefront of his mind. The conditions of the ASBO, however, do not differentiate between intentional and non-intentional breaches, and this has specific implications for how Donald perceives its impact on his everyday experiences.

As discussed, while the deterrent element of going to prison seemed to play some role in John changing his behaviour, Donald believed that his ASBO, in particular, the non-association condition, had the completely opposite effect:

> It's to try and stop you getting into trouble really, like, but its not stopped me, it's getting me into trouble. It's supposed to calm you down, like, but most of mine [ASBO conditions] probably would, like, but not my friends one [the ASBO condition that banned him from associating with a number of friends]. That's the hardest. (Donald)

One of the reasons why Donald finds it so difficult to prevent himself from breaching this condition is that he finds it nearly impossible to avoid his friends, not through choice, but often due to factors beyond his control. According to Donald, his ASBO did not refer to all of his friends, which only compounds the difficulty of adherence to this condition:

> They're not banned from seeing me, I'm banned from seeing them … like just now when I was in the bus stop and I was speaking to one of my mates and one of them come along that I am not supposed to be with and if the police had seen me they would have arrested me like, and there's nothing I can do really, can I? I can hardly walk away when I'm waiting for the bus like … and they just arrest me for fuck all offence like, nothing. Its hard, like 'cos all the people I'm not supposed to be with live next door to me, round the corner from me … everywhere I'm walking.

Because of the close local nature of his friendship network it is difficult for him to associate with some of his friends without the presence of those whom he is banned from associating with. Further, such difficulties of avoidance are compounded when such association prohibitions, according to Donald, include his next-door neighbour, as well as those who live on the same street as he does. Such conditions in his ASBO have led him to feel that the order is unjust, as well as convincing him that he is being set up to fail because of what he perceives to be such insurmountable prohibitions.

More broadly, the above example points to one of the ironies of the ASBO, whereby the condition of his order that he finds most difficult is trying to avoid that which in any other instance would be perfectly legal behaviour but which, due to its having become an ASBO prohibition, now carries a criminal sanction if breached. Donald finds it almost impossible to avoid transgression, given that he lives in such close proximity to those he is banned from seeing. This raises a number of serious questions of what exactly his ASBO is meant to achieve, especially in relation to enforcement and coercing him to take responsibility in avoiding breaching his order. Put simply, he is not in full control of some of the social interactions which he is required to avoid. This has led to feelings and perceptions of injustice in relation to his ASBO. These perceptions are not without consequence and, as Smith (2003) has noted, 'Feelings that the system is unjust, and does not serve them well are intensified for young people who are identified and processed as offenders' (Smith, 2003: 184). In this sense, the ASBO can potentially be seen as counterproductive to its aims of both behaviour alteration (through responsibilisation) and community safety, because such feelings of injustice may neutralise any commitment to conform.

The ISSP

Throughout both interviews, both John and Donald made multiple references to the Intensive Supervision and Surveillance Programme (ISSP). This programme was designed specifically for persistent young offenders and is viewed as a credible alternative to a custodial sentence (Home Office, 2003: 34). Its rationale 'combines community based surveillance with a comprehensive and sustained focus on tackling the factors that contribute to a young person's offending behaviour' (Home Office, 2003: 34). In practice this involves the dual roles of electronic tagging and intensive supervision, where those sentenced are compelled to take part in a number of programmes that help them to address their offending behaviour as well as to engage them in structured activities, such as gaining work experience.

For each respondent, the ISSP did not replace the ASBO but, rather, became an additional level of control placed upon the individual. However, unlike the wholly negative view held by both respondents towards the ASBO, each spoke positively of the 'supervision' element of the ISSP, and how this played a crucial role in keeping them 'off the streets':

> **BM**: What did your ISSP involve?
>
> **John**: Working on offending, like, what you have done in the past ... training was good, like mechanics and all that. They get you to do mechanics and that keeps you off the streets like ...
>
> **BM**: So you enjoyed it?
>
> **John**: Yeah, 'cos I knew it was keeping me off the streets and I had something to do in the daytime like ...
>
> They do keep me from breaching the ASBO the ISSP does ... When I got out of jail the first time ... I didn't have nothing to do like so I was on the streets anyway so I would speak to my friends, but now I'm always in work or doing stuff or camping with these lot like [Youth Offending Team members] ... It cuts up me days and I've got to be in by seven [due to the electronic tag] ... just keeps me out of trouble really ... it's helped being at work. (Donald)

As well as helping them find employment opportunities, both respondents acknowledged that the introduction of structure into their lives helped to remove them from situations whereby they were likely to get into trouble. Without such positive activity, they are left with nothing to do other than hang around the streets, which each identifies as a factor conducive to their engaging in ASB. Such reflexivity is indicative that they know what works for them to keep them out of trouble, but also highlights that to do so is difficult without the provision of structured daily activity. However, given that each is also an ASBO recipient, there always exists the chance that if the ASBO is breached – either a technical breach or otherwise – this could undermine any progress made in attempts to re-engage the youths in mainstream opportunities.

Conclusion

This chapter has attempted to provide an alternative insight into the problem of ASB regulation by listening to and interpreting the perspectives of two youths issued with an ASBO. As each respondent was deemed an individual case study, caution must be taken when attempting to infer generalisations. However, these pilot findings do pose and provoke a number of questions about the relationship between the biographies of youth perpetrators, local ASB strategies and the emphasis on individual responsibility. Furthermore, the initial findings in this chapter have alluded to the complexity of ASB regulation while suggesting something further about the potential for unanticipated or unintended consequences. However, such contradictory outcomes are invariably rendered largely invisible within discussions of ASB policy and practice due to the substantial failure to engage with the views of young people subjected to ASB interventions.

Given the potential insights into ASB policy that such 'perpetrator perspectives' could provide, in terms of impact and effectiveness, and also in relation to critiques of such contemporary behavioural regulation, the general absence of such perspectives in much official and critical research is striking. There may be some reluctance to engage with such perspectives and the discourse of symbolic punitiveness they illustrate, but this should not be used as an excuse for maintaining an institutionalised ignorance of the views of such youths, even though their accounts may at times prove to be difficult, ambiguous, troubling, unsavoury or provoking of feelings of anger. However, as various authors (Burney, 2005; Squires and Stephen, 2005a, 2005b) have pointed out, there is sometimes a suggestion that researchers who conduct 'appreciative' research with youth perpetrators of ASB are seen as not taking the problem seriously. On the contrary, surely the inclusion and acknowledgement of the perpetrator's perspective, along with empirical research that engages with the perspectives of other actors involved, such as victims, needs to be brought together in ASB policy formulation, implementation and evaluation. At national policy level, however, taking the problem of ASB seriously seems to manifest itself through a populist lens rather than being grounded in a more holistic understanding of how youth ASB should be addressed.

Notes

[1] The issue of whether or not ASBOs target young people is a contested area. The following note is based on my own analysis of available Home Office data (Home Office, 2005), which currently provides ASBO

statistics up to December 2005. It can be argued that, of the 9,544 orders issued where age of the recipient is known, proportionately, orders issued to individuals between the ages of 10 and 17 from April 1999 up to December 2005 account for 41.9%. However, a number of qualifications need to be made on this figure. First, this national figure for England and Wales obscures regional adult/youth proportionality. For example, areas such as Greater Manchester not only have a high proportion of ASBOs but also the majority are issued to young people (50.6%), while youth ASBOs issued in Greater London only account for 30.6% of the 749 issued. Second, it should also be noted that, in terms of real numbers of orders issued, every year has seen an increase in the numbers issued to those aged 10–17, while simultaneously the proportion of youth to adult ASBOs has declined. Third, and more generally, while the national proportionality between youth and adult ASBOs shows that the majority are issued to the latter, the age range for ASBOs issued against young people covers seven years, as compared to a much broader age range for the adult population. It is therefore wholly legitimate to argue that such orders remain disproportionately targeted at the youth age group.

[2] The data provided in this table are based on a selection of areas in Northtown to illustrate the seeming effectiveness of the local incremental strategy and cover a one-year period. Therefore it does not include data for the whole of Northtown. The areas were purposely selected for the table to show that the impact of the 'four-strikes' approach seems to transcend both more affluent areas (Westside and City Centre) and areas characterised by high levels of social and economic deprivation (Downside and Eastside). The local strategy also includes different levels of early warning letters on a scale of 1 to 3 reflecting the nature and content of the warning included within them. The statistics listed under Letter 2(1) and Letter 3(1) in the table indicate the number of these sent out as the first type of warning issued.

[3] This information derives from interviews that I have undertaken for my own contemporary PhD research and will be included in the final thesis.

Postscript

Since the research that formed the basis of this chapter was undertaken, Gordon Brown has replaced Tony Blair as Prime Minister of the UK. This change in leadership has also been assocaited with a toning down of populist rhetoric in relation to ASB, with Children's Minister Ed Balls arguing that ASBOs are often a sign of failure. This is not to say that ASBOs have disappeared. They are still being used. However, it remains to be seen whether this change in tone is simply a case of 'turning down the volume' or one that has greater substance in relation to future ASB policy direction.

References

Burney, E. (2002) 'Talking tough, acting coy: whatever happened to the Anti-Social Behaviour Order?', *Howard Journal*, vol 41, no 5, pp 469–84.

Burney, E. (2005) *Making people behave: Anti-social behaviour, politics and policy*, Cullompton: Willan Publishing.

Campbell, S. (2002) *A review of Anti-social Behaviour Orders*, London: Home Office Research Series.

Hill, J. and Wright, G. (2003) 'Youth, community safety and the paradox of inclusion', *Howard Journal*, vol 42, no 3, pp 282–97.

Home Office (1997) *No more excuses*, Home Office: London.

Home Office (2002) *A guide to Anti-Social Behaviour Orders and Acceptable Behaviour Contracts*, Home Office: London.

Home Office (2003) *Respect and responsibility – Taking a stand against anti-social behaviour*, Home Office: London.

Home Office (2005) 'Anti-social Behaviour Order Statistics', (www.crimereduction.gov.uk/asbos/asbos2.htm).

House of Commons Home Affairs Select Committee (2005) *Anti-social behaviour*, Fifth Report of Session 2004–05, (www.publications. parliament.uk/pa/cm200405/cmselect/cmhaff/80/80.pdf).

House of Commons Committee of Public Accounts (2007) *Tackling anti-social behaviour*, Forty-fourth Report of Session 2006–07, HC 246, London: The Stationery Office, (www.publications.parliament. uk/pa/cm200607/cmselect/cmpubacc/246/246.pdf).

Hughes, G. (2007) *The politics of crime and community*, Basingstoke: Palgrave Macmillan.

Hughes, G. and Follett, M. (2006) 'Community safety, youth and the "anti-social"' in B. Goldson and J. Muncie (eds), *Youth crime and justice*, London: Sage.

May, T. (1997) *Social research methods: Issues, methods and process*, Buckingham: Open University Press.

McIntosh, B. (2005) *ASBO youth: A case study*, Cardiff: Cardiff University.

Morgan, R. and Newburn, T. (2007) 'Youth justice', in M. Maguire, R. Morgan and R. Reiner (eds), *The Oxford handbook of criminology* (4th edn), Oxford: Oxford University Press.

Nixon, J. (2006) 'ASBOs: more questions than answers in uses of research', *Criminal Justice Matters*, no 62, pp 24–6.

Nixon, J. and Parr, S. (2006) 'Anti-social behaviour: voices from the front line', in J. Flint (ed), *Housing, urban governance and anti-social behaviour: Perspectives, policy and practice*, Bristol: The Policy Press.

Noaks, L. and Wincup, E. (2004) *Criminological research: Understanding qualitative methods*, London: Sage.

Smith, R. (2003) *Youth justice: Ideas, policy, practice*, Cullompton: Willan Publishing.

Solanki, A.R., Bateman, T., Boswell, G. and Hill, E. (2006) *Anti-Social Behaviour Orders*, London: Youth Justice Board, Policy Research Bureau and NACRO.

Squires, P. and Stephen, D.E. (2005a) *Rougher justice: Anti-social behaviour and young people*, Cullompton: Willan Publishing.

Squires, P. and Stephen, D. (2005b) 'Rethinking ASBOs', *Critical Social Policy*, vol 25, no 4, pp 517–28.

Stephen, D.E. and Squires, P. (2003) *Community safety, enforcement and Acceptable Behaviour Contracts: An evaluation of the work of the Community Safety Team in the East Brighton 'New Deals for Communities'*, Brighton: Health and Social Policy Research Centre, University of Brighton.

Stephen, D. (2006) 'Community safety and young people: 21st-century *homo sacer* and the politics of injustice', in P. Squires (ed), *Community safety: Critical perspectives on policy and practice*, Bristol: The Policy Press, pp 219–36.

Wain, N. and Burney, E. (2007) *The ASBO: Wrong turning, dead end*, London: Howard League for Penal Reform.

Welsh Affairs Committee (2004) *Police service, crime and anti-social behaviour in Wales*, (www.publications.parliament.uk/pa/cm200304/cmselect/cmwelaf, accessed 2 February 2005).

FOURTEEN

'Binge drinking', anti-social behaviour and alcohol-related disorder: examining the 2003 Licensing Act

Paul Norris and Derek Williams

In this chapter, we locate the patterns of behaviour now routinely labelled as 'binge drinking' within spatial, economic and cultural changes associated with the growth of the night-time economy of British cities and towns since 1987 (see Taylor, 1999; Hobbs et al, 2000; Hadfield, 2006). We also explore recent policy interventions in respect of licensing hours, regulation and 'liberalisation'. Such changes are, in part, facilitated by shifts in the governance of cities, and, in part, insofar as they are deemed to create 'problems', call forth change, particularly in policing and surveillance of urban spaces.

We argue here that a failure (1) to properly contextualise 'binge drinking' within significant shifts in leisure and consumption patterns, and (2) to acknowledge the potential for long-run negative consequences (for individuals, social networks and communities) (Taylor, 1999) has led to a myopic focus in recent policies on 'harm reduction' and on seeking to limit alcohol-related disorder. This policy vacuum is illustrated in the underlying tension between competing ideologies of the 'citizen' and the 'consumer'. Within the former, appeals to 'responsible' drinking and civility figure, as does recognition of the importance of health education for citizens in the making. Within the latter, 'lifestyle choice' and identity are often the hallmark. More than ever, the consumer, especially the youthful consumer, is recognised as a 'rational' hedonist (Measham, 2004). While it is clearly viable to view participation as a hedonistic consumer within the urban night-time economy as an escape from or form of resistance to the regularities and discipline of the nine-to-five working day, the long-term impact on individuals in terms of health status, the implications of 'unsafe' sexual encounters or of violence (victim or perpetrator) and the possibilities of a criminal record highlight the limits of excess and transgression as 'escape attempts' (Cohen and Taylor, 1992; Taylor, 1999).

Binge drinking and anti-social behaviour

There is a great deal of UK media and political attention focused on alcohol consumption and its impact on public order and health, as witnessed by newspaper headlines, news reports and TV programmes such as *Booze Britain*. Nearly all local authority community safety strategies include tackling alcohol-related disorder in their plans. Tackling anti-social behaviour is one of the government's key priorities (and also a key area of public concern). However, the government definition of anti-social behaviour encompasses a wide range of behaviour, from 'noisy neighbours' and drunken yobs in town centres through to 'crack houses' and 'nuisance neighbours' (or simply answering your door in your underwear).

The 1998 Crime and Disorder Act defined acting in an 'anti-social manner' as a 'manner that caused or was likely to cause harassment, alarm or distress to one or more persons not of the same household as the perpetrator'. The government has since introduced the 2003 Anti-Social Behaviour Act, which came into force in January 2004. The Anti-Social Behaviour Unit was set up in December 2002 and the Anti-Social Behaviour Action Plan was launched in October 2003. The definition of anti-social behaviour was deliberately wide-ranging, to allow for 'ASBOs' to be used in a variety of circumstances. The issue of whether or not the government is more selectively criminalising anti-social behaviour is a matter of debate, which we will not go into here (see for example, Squires and Stephen, 2005). However, the terms 'anti-social behaviour' and 'disorder' are often used interchangeably, particularly when discussing behaviour under the influence of alcohol.

'Alcohol-related crime' is probably best defined by the Institute of Alcohol Studies. It is a popular rather than a legal term, and is normally used to refer to two main categories of offences:

(a)   alcohol-defined offences such as drunkenness offences or driving with excess alcohol;

(b)   offences in which the consumption of alcohol is thought to have played some kind of facilitating role. Examples of offences which are often committed by people under the influence are assault, breach of the peace, criminal damage and other public order offences. (IAS, 2007: 1)

The definition of binge drinking is even more problematic, with wide-ranging definitions, often using emotive language. Many commentators have noted the term's ambiguity (Measham, 2004). For example, in the case of someone dependent on alcohol, a 'binge' tends to refer to a periodic bout of continual drinking, perhaps over a period of days. Newburn and Shiner (2001) give a clinical definition, describing drinking over a day or more until unconsciousness, while Richardson and Budd (2003) define a binge drinker as someone who reports 'feeling very drunk once a month'.

In the UK, drinking surveys (and the government) usually define a 'binge drinker' as someone who drinks twice the recommended daily amount at least once a week. For men, that is 8 units (4 pints of beer or 3 pints of premium lager), for women, 6 units (3 glasses of wine). Measham (2004: 316) points out that a 'more generous quantitative measure of "binge drinking" is defined as the consumption of more than half of the recommended weekly "sensible" consumption levels on one drinking occasion: that is ten and a half units for men and seven units for women'.

The definitions are not really that helpful because they are too broad and are usually used to describe the drinking habits of the young. Eight units consumed over the course of a whole day and as an accompaniment to meals will not have the same effects as eight units consumed over a couple of hours on an empty stomach. The term 'binge' drinking is usually used to describe young people drunk and disorderly in a public place, which implies something of a 'moral panic' interpretation. But binge drinking is far from being either new or an exclusively British phenomenon.

As a northern European country, heavy sessional drinking and drinking to get drunk have been an integral part of Britain's culture for generations. Traditionally, beer and pubs have been the preserve of the industrial working-class man, as Cofield and Gofton (1994) have argued. Going out on a Friday night and getting drunk was what working-class lads did. The dominant mode of alcohol consumption in Britain was based on a stable, relatively culturally homogeneous market of male, industrial working-class beer consumers drinking in community pubs (see Measham, 2004).

But in the last 25 to 30 years there have been major economic, social and cultural transformations that have completely transformed the class and gender base of the workforce, and this has had a knock-on effect on alcohol consumption. Pub attendance fell by 11% between 1987 and

1992. In the 1980s there was a cultural revolution, with the arrival of the rave scene and an explosion in the use of recreational drugs, most notably ecstasy. Thus, at the same time that the old alcohol order was collapsing, the alcohol industry was confronted with the possibility of losing a new generation of alcohol consumers to a post-modern consumer leisure order of raves, clubs and illicit recreational drugs.

Illicit drug use increased steadily throughout the 1990s and into the 21st century. The British Crime Survey 2002/03 suggested a slight tailing off in self-reported use of ecstasy and cocaine, and the 2004/05 survey confirmed this trend. It appears that ecstasy pills are now 'a cheeky supplement to a night's drinking' (Measham, 2004: 313) (as portrayed in the Channel 4 programme *Shameless*). There was extensive media coverage of ecstasy use, ecstasy casualties and the related dance club scene in the 1990s, with the *Daily Mirror* vilifying Jarvis Cocker and calling for the record 'Sorted for Es and Wizz' to be banned. The rave scene provided the 'folk devils' of the 1990s; now it is the binge drinkers who are the 'folk devils'.

The alcohol industry strikes back

Both Measham (2004) and Brain (2000) make the point that the alcohol industry responded with recommodification of alcoholic drinks. First, in 1995 with alcopops (Hooch from Australia); then in 2000 ice lagers, white ciders and spirit mixers (Reef, Bacardi Breezers, Smirnoff Ice, WKD,VK, Shots, Shooters) aimed at a new generation of young alcohol consumers who were demographically and culturally much more varied than the traditional male industrial working-class alcohol consumers. There was also the redesign of licensed leisure venues, and changes in licensing policy (open 11am–11pm) and, finally, the 2003 Licensing Act. Measham (2004) argues that 'The liberalization of alcohol-based licensing is significant because it enabled the revival of the city centre cultural and night-time economies and was in sharp contrast to the increased regulation and criminalization of unlicensed raves and dance events' (2004: 318).

Hadfield (2006) charts the rise of the night-time high street, with the rise of branded and themed licensed premises over the last two decades, alongside what he calls the 'processes of back-door de-regulation' that 'resulted in a sharp increase in the number of licensed premises trading into the early hours' (Hadfield, 2006: 52). Therefore, as Measham (2004) and Hobbs (2003, 2005) point out, the current concerns on the part of the media, health practitioners and politicians must be tempered by the concerted development and official sanctioning of young adult drinking in the UK over the last 10 years.

Simon Jenkins, writing in *The Times* of 24 January 2005, says that 'Pressed by the pub owners before the last election, the Labour Party actually sent teenage voters text messages proclaiming, "Cldnt gve a xxxx 4 lst ordrs thn vte lbr on thrsday 4 extra time"', and goes on to argue that 'Binge drinking is virtually public policy' and that 'the government was ... singing from the industry song sheet'.

We argue that there is, at one level, a contradiction in government policy, on the one hand liberalising the licensing laws and appearing to support the marketing strategies of corporate leisure and brewing entrepreneurs to give longer opening hours, and on the other wanting to crack down on alcohol-related disorder and crime. Policies seeking to control the negative aspects of an alcohol-fuelled night-time economy through a combination of statutory regulation, enforceable penalties and an appeal to citizenship, responsibilisation and the building/ rebuilding of a civic culture are likely to break down at the frontier of the 'citizen–consumer' dichotomy.

The concept of citizenship has become central to policy debates, whether in explicit or implicit form, over the last decade or more, although the tensions between citizenship and capitalism first discussed by Marshall (1950) are rarely acknowledged now. For the latter, economic inequalities are an integral feature. The last Conservative government's 'Citizen's Charter' reprised that tension in its language; 'It is a charter for the individual, and in particular, for the individual consumer' (Connelly, 1993: 14). A recent report from the Institute for Citizenship (2005) defines citizenship in terms of 'social and moral responsibility', 'community involvement' and 'political literacy'. Attempts to square the circle of these tensions and contradictions take the form of linking 'choice' to public service provision within New Labour's version of citizenship (Jordan, 2005). Jordan sees the contradictions as cultural and social, raising questions of how to sustain a viable social order. The Respect Agenda follows a similar reasoning to be embedded in individuals, indeed the Respect website articulates that respect cannot be 'purchased'. In terms of anti-social behaviour and community justice there is a clear intent for 'tough' enforcement. Such sentiments provide a direct contrast with the consumerist identities that the drinks industry seeks to create and sustain.

This is buttressed by the acceptance of the need for a competitive night-time economy centred on leisure, the focus of which is a youth market. That market is targeted by sophisticated advertising and marketing: £181.3 million was spent on alcohol advertising in 2001;

the drinks industry itself sees 'advertising as an essential element in the competition between producers (and other suppliers) and is vital to an efficient market' (BLRA, 1999: 4). Marketing strategies draw upon the work of Edward Bernays, the founder of public relations, who linked the marketing of commodities to Freud's notion of unconscious desires in attempts of stimulate 'needs' and translate them into demands. This approach is in direct contrast to the rational approach, which is central to the promotion of citizenship.

Research with consumers in the youth market indicates an affinity with the commercial objectives of the drinks industry, namely consumption of alcohol as a lifestyle choice. A decade-old survey of university students reported in the *Lancet* found high levels of drinking that exceeded 'sensible' limits (61% male and 48% female) and 15% of the drinkers within the sample reported consumption of alcohol at 'hazardous' levels. 'The overwhelming reason given for taking alcohol or drugs was pleasure' (Webb et al, 1996: 922). Such findings for students are in line with the expressed preferences of those in the youth market for alcohol in general. Engineer et al (2003) report in their qualitative study a consistent finding that young people's objective was to get drunk, to drink quickly and to mix drinks to accelerate the process (2003: viii). The companion study from the Home Office, which comprises a large, nationally representative study of young people's drinking and lifestyle habits, similarly reports three quarters of the sample aged 18–24 years agreeing with the proposition that young people drink for the intoxication effects and that 57% of men and 59% of women in the sample gave 'feeling confident' as a reason for drinking (Richardson and Budd, 2003).

These findings are often at significant variance with European comparisons in which ethnographic studies, for example, find no reported correlation between young people's participation in night-time leisure and drinking for its own sake (see for example the MCM report, *Drinking and public disorder* [Marsh and Kibby, 1992]). It was thought that the 2003 Licensing Act would be a means of encouraging a more continental approach to the sale and consumption of alcohol, as Home Office Minister Hazel Blears defended the Act as part of a long-term cultural change. However, the youth of Britain holidaying abroad tend not to adopt a continental approach to drinking, so why should we assume that they would have such an approach at home? 'Changes purely predicated on a relaxation of licensing hours are unlikely to have a marked cultural effect as a whole' (Roberts et al, 2006: 1106).

There was plenty of opposition to the Act, from judges, the police, the medical profession and anti-alcohol pressure groups. On the other side, the Portman Group has argued that current data-recording practices, particularly by police forces, are quite inadequate to enable the nature and scale of alcohol-related violence and disorder to be assessed with any degree of accuracy (SIRC, 2002). So it could be argued that whether or not there is a binge-drinking problem depends on who is sponsoring the research – the Portman Group or Alcohol Concern.

It may be argued that what has distinguished the UK in the use of alcohol has been that it is usually separate from food intake. Alcohol consumption is less frequent, but drinking sessions will involve the use of much greater amounts of alcohol. The earlier licensing laws may have contributed to this by confining the use of alcohol to evenings and weekends. Thus, excessive consumption was far from being uncommon. The big change in the consumption of alcohol is that more women are drinking heavily. Also, with the rise in mass education, more students are drinking and the alcohol industry has targeted the 18- to 25-year-olds. This is linked to 'hedonistic consumption' and the night-time economy.

Both Loveday (2005) and Hobbs (2003; 2005) point out that the number of young people going into town/city centres at night to drink is unprecedented. In 1997, the licence capacity of Nottingham was 61,000; this had risen to 108,000 by 2004, with 30,000 people on the streets. In Reading, the local population of 143,000 is increased by 20% every weekend. In Norwich there can be up to 20,000 people on the street on a weekend night, while in Manchester it can be as many as 75,000 (Loveday, 2005).

Hobbs (2003) makes the point that we do literally have a 'thin blue line' in many cities and towns at weekends, for example, 12–15 police officers on duty in Nottingham city centre to police 30,000 people. The number of police on duty on a Saturday night is much smaller than the number of police at a football match or demonstration. The problems of numbers are exacerbated by the absence or inadequacy of transport out of the town/city centre after closing time, which can contribute significantly to problems of disorder and violence towards strangers (Loveday, 2005). Given the lack of police and transport, and the numbers of people who are supposedly drunk, perhaps we should be surprised that there is not even more trouble and that, in the circumstances, the majority, although noisy and drunk, are generally well behaved.

Hobbs (2006), in evidence to the House of Commons Home Affairs Select Committee, highlights the centrality of the leisure industry in the night-time economy, with one million people employed in the licensed trade, creating one in five of all new jobs, annual entrepreneurial investment of £1 billion and the pub and club industry turning over £23 billion or the equivalent of 3% of UK GDP (House of Commons, 2005). Globalising processes and a separation of brewers from pub and club chains, often owned by foreign companies, is also changing the nature of the drinks industry.

The market does not provide everyone with what they want. The alcohol industry does not want three or four people buying one bottle of wine for under £10 and drinking it over a 2- to 3-hour period. As in the 1990s, the alcohol industry will adapt to maximise profits. A good example is the Wetherspoons chain. One of its pubs can be a cafe during the day, a traditional pub in the early evening and a club (if a Lloyds No. 1 bar) at night. Wetherspoons installed TVs in its pubs before the 2006 World Cup, because during the 2002 World Cup and Euro 2004 it had lost customers during the games.

The 2003 Licensing Act

The alcohol industry has traditionally been a very powerful pressure group, with strong links to the Conservative Party. Now it appears that it has strong links to the Labour Party. The British Beer and Pub Association (BBPA) hosted a number of meetings with senior civil servants from the Department for Culture, Media and Sport (DCMS) who were members of the Licensing Advisory Group set up by the government to help draft the legislation for the 2003 Act, hardly neutral ground. Although the new law has a lot more regulation and bureaucracy, it has not really been used to great effect. There has been no national media information campaign undertaken by the government to ensure that members of the public are made aware of their rights to object under the 2003 Licensing Act. Now that local authorities are licensing authorities, it is their responsibility to fight the drinks industry in a court of appeal. Can they afford that? Urbium, which owns the Tiger Tiger chain and boasts David Cameron as a non-executive director, has been criticised for the way it has aggressively lobbied local authorities to obtain 3am licences, tripling its profits to £10 million in the process (Loveday, 2005).

To date there have been very few objections by the police, as it has proved difficult for them to link violent disorder to individual pubs or clubs, as cited by Hobbs in his evidence to the Home Affairs Select Committee (2006). In November 2005, when the new licensing law came into effect, the police launched a six-week campaign that focused on tackling alcohol-fuelled anti-social behaviour. This was the Alcohol Misuse Enforcement Campaign (AMEC). Two-and-a-half million pounds was spent on this specialist operation and it was conducted by 43 police forces. During this period, the police dealt with more than 30,000 incidents and made over 25,000 arrests (Home Office, 2006). The Alcohol Harm Reduction Strategy is also working to reduce alcohol-related crime. This is a five-year strategy for protecting the public and reducing offending.

The AMEC press release of 8 February 2006 revealed that:

- serious violent crime fell by 21%
- all violent crime fell by 11%
- other acts endangering life fell by 14%
- during the six-week campaign police dealt with 33,358 offences
- 25,486 arrests were made
- police issued 8,179 fixed penalty notices
  - 38% for drunk and disorderly behaviour
  - 37% for public order offences and harassment
  - 10% for selling to minors
- 649 summonses were issued as a result of test purchase operations or visits: 593 for selling to minors and 17 for selling to drunks. Thirty-nine were for other alcohol offences. (Home Office, 2006)

The Association of Chief Police Officers lead for AMEC, Chief Constable Michael Craik of Northumbria Police, said: 'This AMEC Campaign has shown just what can be achieved when the police and their partners focus on an issue of major concern' (Home Office, 2006). But this was just a six-week campaign, which cost £2.5 million, so a real question concerns the resources available for enforcement operations. A year-long campaign would cost over £20 million and would leave police resources lacking in other areas. The government used the above statistics to claim that the new licensing laws were working in relation to alcohol disorder.

Will the 2003 Licensing Act change our pattern of consumption and behaviour? It is hoped that it will, and that it will also 'reduce the problems of disorder and disturbance associated with fixed universal closing times' (DCMS, 2005). The DCMS believes that the Act will decrease crime and disorder as 'The Act abolishes fixed and artificially early closing times which we believe encouraged binge drinking and resulted in large numbers of young people hitting the streets simultaneously causing the police enormous difficulties.' However, from early research in three cities (of varying size) in the south of England, most pubs that have applied for and been granted extensions are open until midnight Sunday–Wednesday, and until 2am (or 3am) Thursday–Saturday. Therefore, we still have uniform extension and closing times. Also, these establishments are catering for the 18–25 age group. It is still difficult to come out of the theatre, cinema or a concert and go to have a drink and a chat afterwards, as the pubs that are open are more like nightclubs, with loud music and dance areas.

It is perhaps too early to say what effect the 2003 Licensing Act will have, but as of the time of writing, one year after the Act came into force, the picture is mixed. Critics of the Act warned that there would be an increase in anti-social behaviour, crime and alcohol-related health problems. Supporters said it would offer greater freedom and 'European'-style drinking. But it appears that drinking habits have not really changed. In Winchester there have been no applications for 24-hour licences, but some extensions. There has been no change in arrests/cautions for alcohol-related disorder. In Salisbury there are no 24-hour extensions, but several pubs open until 2am (Thursday–Saturday) and police say they have noticed no change in behaviour or arrests/cautions.

One establishment that was open until midnight and is now open until 2am has reported its takings down £1,000 a week because of competition from other establishments. In Southampton, where 627 establishments have a premises licence, 242 have applied to vary, including newsagents, supermarkets and casinos. One in four pubs has a variation licence, but no pubs or clubs are open for 24 hours. The police in Southampton say it is business as usual. Inspector Lisa Stevens said:

> What the change in the licensing law was intended for was to tackle binge drinking and some of the violent crime we see on our streets, but unfortunately I don't think it's tackled that at all. In all honesty in the first couple of months we saw a slight improvement, but it doesn't take long for changes to become the norm. Only now the fights are at gone three in the morning, not half past eleven. (BBC News, 2006)

However, consider Bournemouth and Reading, two towns where some establishments obtained 24-hour licences. In Bournemouth alcohol crime increased 15% and in Reading common assaults were up 50% in the year. The police argued that the increases reflected better incident management (BBC News, 2006). Elsewhere, alcohol-related violence in Yorkshire's cities has fallen by almost 40%, but there have been more complaints about late-night noise nuisance (Jeeves, 2007). So no definite answer can be given on whether the 2003 Licensing Act has increased or decreased alcohol-related crime and disorder. But there has not been the massive increase in incidents predicted by some people. One reason for this may be that 24-hour drinking is barely happening at all. A survey of licensing authorities by the DCMS suggests that about 3,000 out of the 200,000 premises that applied for licences under the Act can now serve alcohol 24 hours a day. Supermarkets make up 25%, pubs, bars and clubs 20% and convenience stores 20%. The remaining licences are held by venues such as hotels.

There has been a huge amount of research focusing on the medical and social consequences of alcohol on the body in recent years. The main finding is that 'the pattern of consumption matters as much, or more, than the overall amount consumed' (McNeill, 2005: 21). However, health issues have been relegated to second place in this debate. There is perhaps a need here for the disparate policy community on alcohol to create a broader coalition between crime and disorder-related alcohol use and individual and public health. Some commentators have pointed to the absence of public health considerations from debates around the current licensing legislation. Light (2005), for example, notes that liberalising of the licensing laws was debated in the 1970s but rejected on the risks associated with increased consumption.

Policy in the main has focused on harm reduction and the central belief that the problem of alcohol-related disorder can be laid at the door of 'irresponsible individuals and individual premises' (House of Commons Home Affairs Select Committee, 2005). The Alcohol Harm Reduction Strategy (Prime Minister's Strategy Unit, 2004) argues for the application of rationality in its strategy, identifying the responsibility of individuals in making choices about behaviour and the need for accurate information (presumably about the risks and negative consequences of excessive alcohol consumption). The role of the government in this context is to ensure the provision of information and to protect individuals and communities, 'ensuring a fair balance between the interests of stakeholders' (House of Commons Home Affairs Select Committee, 2005: 2). The language neatly combines bureaucratic and market rationality, emphasising the need for adherence to rules and procedures while making an appeal to stakeholders in the alcohol industry, calling for balance while safeguarding the rights of profit seekers.

Our argument here is that policies in the area of alcohol consumption, regulation, licensing and alcohol-related disorder may be seen, at worst, as 'symbolic' (Edelman, 1971, cited in Ham and Hill, 1984: 103), carrying very little attempt at meaningful implementation or, at best, failing to acknowledge the extent to which successful implementation and, indeed, cultural change in relation to the consumption of alcohol, rest upon complex processes of negotiation and compromise with key interests and underlying economic forces (Ham and Hill, 1984: 103).

Thus this policy sidelines the consequences for communities and for the wider society and does not consider the longer-term effects and the difficulties arising for the policing of night-time economies of towns and cities. Of significance here is the long-standing disconnection between health policy and the criminal justice system. As one commentator has recently argued, little attention has been paid to the linkages between health policy and criminal justice (Knepper, 2007). Knepper argues that there is a danger that the analysis of alcohol use has become a 'criminal problem rather than an under-appreciated health problem' (2007: 79).

Elsewhere, Deehan et al (2002) refer, in their study of those arrested for drink-related offences, to the regular use of forensic medical examiners, qualified doctors whose job it is to judge whether or not the person taken into custody, is (a) fit to be questioned and (b) so intoxicated that they pose a risk to themselves and need to be kept under regular (15-minute interval) surveillance while in the cells. In such settings, medical personnel function only as adjuncts to practices that process those arrested in terms of custody, release and prosecution. This draws attention to the resources needed to deal effectively with significant numbers of individuals who may have consumed large quantities of alcohol, in order to process them in police cells while ensuring their health and safety. When female arrestees are processed, it has been necessary for a female officer to be in attendance. Such considerations have often been rendered invisible in recent policy debates and are at odds with key government assumptions that the problem is reducible to behavioural change in a minority of individuals and licensed premises.

We contend that the social and political implications have also been played down in policy debates. In many other areas of public policy the cultural, ethnic and faith diversity of communities is acknowledged, but alcohol use, advertising and marketing and related policy approaches fail to acknowledge the mono-cultural, age-specific nature of Britain's drinking culture within the night-time economy of towns and cities. Cultural differences and reactions to alcohol consumption in public spaces may be seen to threaten the agenda of mutual tolerance and respect within multi-faith communities, which is an integral part of the government's focus on social order and cohesion.

Conclusions

We have argued that the concept of 'binge drinking', while being a media-generated concept within a long line of 'moral panics' such as the 'lager lout' of the late 1980s and ecstasy associated with the rave scene in the 1990s, obscure important ambiguities and contradictions within the policy debates surrounding excessive consumption of alcohol by (particularly) young people in the context of the reconfigured night–time economies of British towns and cities. We agree with Measham and Brain (2005) that 'the government appears to have been caught in the consequences of its own seemingly contradictory policies' (2005: 263).

Those contradictions and 'silences' include the health risks to future generations of rising per capita consumption of alcohol and the associated healthcare costs, and the unproven evidential base that changes to licensing reduce alcohol-related disorder and/or that current police strength and strategy will effectively cope; but the contradiction at the heart of the policy is the dichotomy of the 'consumer' (or 'customer') in opposition to the 'citizen', and the corollary of the 'civic culture', respect, tolerance and civility. The contradictions flow, we believe, from the primacy given to the drinks and leisure industry at the levels of policy formulation and implementation and a tacit acceptance that advertising and marketing strategies effectively secure and sustain a youth market in excessive alcohol consumption even where such strategies carry a 'responsible' tag. The 2003 Licensing Act, in line with other New Labour policy making, 'is couched in the language of "rights" and "responsibilities". In the context of night spaces, this means that rights will be afforded to consumers and businesses that behave responsibly' (Talbot, 2006: 161).

We have not had time here to explore other important issues related to excessive alcohol consumption, such as sexual violence (see Finney, 2004). The focus on 'binge drinking' and alcohol use in public spaces misses deeper cultural concerns over the nature of violence, mental health issues and wider questions of community building and regeneration.

It is difficult to make a complete evaluation of the 2003 Act, as it has only been in operation for a relatively short period, but also because in many urban areas processes of liberalisation have been in motion for many years. The main emphasis of the Act was on crime and disorder, and the Home Office report *Crime in England and Wales 2005/06* (Walker et al, 2006) concludes that levels remain relatively static. However, the 23 police forces that provided the data are not named; but more extraordinary is that the research limits its analyses to offences occurring before 2am, while the new law means that many establishments close after this time. The extension in licensing hours has had resource implications for a range of public services, including the police and other emergency services, transport, cleaning, environmental health and licensing and inspection personnel.

It is not surprising that the 2003 Licensing Act should produce a broad range of short-, medium- and long-term impacts, but the government needs to be more transparent in relation to crime figures and should follow the lead of Australia and New Zealand in funding independent evaluation of the effects of changes in licensing hours. The 2003 Licensing Act will not result in Britain becoming more continental. As Roberts et al point out:

> Changing the regulations that govern alcohol consumption in order to change behaviour is a complex task, a task that requires more rigorous and detailed analysis than has been applied hitherto in a British context. How a continental café culture might be achieved within the framework of British law is neither obvious nor straightforward. (Roberts et al, 2006: 1123)

We echo Jordan (2005), that the current focus on individual choice remains wedded to an individualist agenda, to the neglect of the collective issues around 'community'.

References

BBC News (2006) 'New laws and "same old trouble"', 24 November, (news.bbc.co.uk/go/pr/fr/-/1/hi/uk/6177380.stm).

BLRA (Brewers and Licensed Retailers Association) (1999) *Submission to the Department of Health on a strategy to combat alcohol misuse from the alcoholic drinks industry*, London: BLRA

Brain, K.J. (2000) *Youth, alcohol, and the emergence of the post-modern alcohol order*, Occasional Paper No. 1, London: IAS.

Cofield, F. and Gofton, L. (1994) *Drugs and young people*, London: IPPR.

Cohen, S. and Taylor, L. (1992) *Escape attempts: The theory and practice of resistance to everyday life*, London: Routledge.

Connelly, J. (1993) *Citizens, charters and consumers*, Occasional Paper series no 2, Southampton: Southampton Institute of Higher Education.

DCMS (Department of Culture, Media and Sport) (2005) 'Licensing Act 2003 explained', (available at www.culture.gov.uk/what_we_do/Alcohol_entertainment/licensing_act2003_explained).

Deehan, A., Marshall, E. and Saville, E. (2002) *Drunks and disorder: Processing intoxicated arrestees in two city centre custody suites*, Police Research Series Paper 150, London: Home Office.

Edelman, M. (1971) *Politics as symbolic action*, Chicago, IL: Markham.

Engineer, R., Phillips, A., Thompson, J. and Nicholls, J. (2003) *Drunk and disorderly: A qualitative study of binge drinking among 18–24 year olds*, Home Office Research Study 262, London: Home Office.

Finney, A. (2004) *Violence in the night-time economy: Key findings from the research*, London: Home Office.

Hadfield, P. (2006) *Bar wars: Contesting the night in contemporary British cities*, Oxford: Oxford University Press.

Ham, C. and Hill, M. (1984) *The policy process in the modern capitalist society*, Hemel Hempstead: Harvester Wheatsheaf.

Hobbs, D. (2003) *The night-time economy*, Alcohol Concern Research Forum Papers.

Hobbs, D. (2005) 'Gluttony: binge drinking and the binge economy', in *Seven deadly sins: A new look at society through an old lens*, London: ESRC (available at http://www.esrc.ac.uk/ESRCInfoCentre/ Images/seven_deadly_Sins_report_tcm6-11033.pdf).

Hobbs, D., Lister, S., Hadfield, P., Winlow, S. and Hall, S. (2000) 'Receiving shadows: governance and limitality in the night-time economy', *British Journal of Sociology*, vol 51, no 4, pp 701–17.

Home Office (2006) 'Violent crime falls following blitz on alcohol-related disorder', Press release, 8 February.

House of Commons Home Affairs Select Committee (2005) *Anti-social behaviour: Fifth report of session 2004–05, volume 1*, London: The Stationery Office.

IAS (Institute of Alcohol Studies) (2007) *Alcohol-related crime and disorder*, London: IAS.

Institute for Citizenship (2005) *Democracy through citizenship*, London: Institute for Citizenship.

Jeeves, P. (2007) 'Alcohol violence falls after pub hours shake-up', *Yorkshire Post*, 26 January.

Jenkins, S. (2005) 'Binge drinking is virtually public policy', *The Times*, 24 January.

Jordan, B. (2005) 'New Labour: choice and values', *Critical Social Policy*, vol 25, no 4, pp 427–46.

Knepper, P. (2007) *Criminology and social policy*, London: Sage.

Light, R. (2005) 'The Licensing Act 2003: liberal constraint?' *Modern Law Review*, vol 68, no 2, pp 268–85.

Loveday, B. (2005) 'The 2003) Licensing Act: alcohol use and anti-social behaviour in England and Wales', *Police Journal*, vol 78, no 3, pp 178–91.

McNeill, A. (2005) 'Binge drinking as an issue of concern', *Alcohol Alert*, no 2.

Marsh, P. and Kibby, K. (1992) *Drinking and public disorder: A report of research conducted for the Portman Group by MCM Research*, London: The Portman Group.

Marshall, T.H. (1950) *Citizenship and social class, and other essays*, Cambridge: Cambridge University Press.

Measham, F. (2004) 'The decline of ecstasy, the rise of "binge" drinking and the persistence of pleasure', *Probation Journal*, vol 51, no 4, pp 309–26.

Measham, F. and Brain, K. (2005) 'Binge drinking, British alcohol policy and the new culture of intoxication', *Crime Media Culture*, vol 1, no 3, pp 262–83.

Newburn, T. and Shiner, M. (2001) *Teenage kicks? Young people and alcohol: A review of the literature*, London: Public Policy Research Unit.

Prime Minister's Strategy Unit (2004) *Alcohol harm reduction strategy for England*, London: Cabinet Office.

Richardson, A. and Budd, T. (2003) *Alcohol, crime and disorder: A study of young adults*, Home Office Research Study 263, London: Home Office.

Roberts, M., Turner, C., Greenfield, S. and Osborn, G. (2006) 'A continental ambience? Lessons in managing alcohol-related evening and night-time entertainment from four European capitals', *Urban Studies*, vol 43, no 7, pp 1105–25.

SIRC (Social Issues Research Centre) (2002) *Alcohol and violence*, Oxford: SIRC.

Squires, P. and Stephen, D.E. (2005) *Rougher justice: Anti-social behaviour and young people*, Cullompton: Willan Publishing.

Talbot, D. (2006) 'The Licensing Act 2003 and the problematization of the night-time economy: planning, licensing and subcultural closure in the UK', *International Journal of Urban and Regional Research*, vol 30, no 1, pp 159–71.

Taylor, I. (1999) *Crime in context*, Cambridge: Polity Press.

Walker, A., Kershaw, C. and Nicholas, S. (2006) *Crime in England and Wales 2005/06*, Home Office Statistical Bulletin, London: Home Office.

Webb, E., Ashton, H., Kelly, P. and Kamali, F. (1996) 'Alcohol and drug use in UK university students', *Lancet*, vol 348, pp 922–5.

FIFTEEN

The criminalisation of intoxication[1]

Fiona Measham and Karenza Moore

There should be safe and enjoyable drinking for
the majority, but zero tolerance of the anti-social
minority. (Blair, 2004)

Introduction

At the heart of British drug policy lies a prohibitionist stance that
prioritises the relationship between drugs and crime, resulting in both
increased medicalisation based on outdated notions of addiction and
compulsion, and increased criminalisation dominated by 'war on drugs'
and 'law and order' discourses. Medicalisation through the potentially
compassionate treatment of problem users is based on an exaggeration
of the drugs–crime relationship that is used to justify coercion into
abstinence-oriented treatment.

However, the majority of young adult drinkers and drug takers fit
neither the medical model of addiction nor the discourses of crime and
compulsion. This chapter argues that this policy vacuum is being filled
by a new wave of proactive prohibition of pharmacological intoxication
(through both alcohol and illicit drug use), bolstering an enduring
'official' ambivalence to leisure, pleasure and intoxication. Four aspects
of this new wave of criminalisation are considered: first, the extension of
the 1971 Misuse of Drugs Act to criminalise emergent drugs used for
recreational purposes; second, changes to the burden of proof regarding
drug supply offences; third, the increased regulation of young-adult
drunkenness and drink-related disorder; and, fourth, the continued
rejection by the British government of repeated calls to overhaul the
drug classification system. We suggest that young people's involvement
in vibrant and diverse local leisure 'scenes' provides the target for a new
wave of stigmatisation and criminalisation of contemporary cultures
of intoxication, at odds with official policy supporting the expansion
of the night-time economy.

The relationship between the individual, the state and the market reflects tensions between leisure-time pursuits in a consumption and profit-oriented society on the one hand, and the criminal justice-driven 'law and order' agenda of the government on the other. At its heart is a process of identifying and criminalising certain transgressive practices (in the UK, for example, with illicit drug use, smoking tobacco in enclosed public places, certain adult consensual sexual practices, drunkenness and drink-related disorder) while facilitating and commercially exploiting others (such as gambling, attending sex clubs and moderate drinking), illustrated in three recent pieces of British legislation: the 2003 Licensing Act, the 2005 Drugs Act and the 2005 Gambling Act.

The British government appears to be pulling in opposite directions in terms of the deregulation and liberalisation of certain aspects of legal leisure, alongside which there has been the increased criminalisation of 'alternative' pharmacological and sexual pleasures evident in a widening net of outlawed drugs and sexual practices. David Garland (2001: 127) has referred to this as the liberalisation of 'criminal opportunity makers' alongside the criminalisation of 'criminal opportunity takers' (see Squires, Introduction, this volume). The government has embraced a somewhat arbitrary distinction between problematic and unproblematic leisure, between pleasure and addiction, between the 'sensible majority' of consumers and an apparently flawed minority, in order to justify the liberalisation of licensing and gambling laws and the consequent increased access to alcohol and gambling. In support of the Licensing Act's extension of trading hours, the Department for Culture, Media and Sport has characterised most British drinkers as 'sensible', for example, in their desire for a glass of wine after the theatre. 'The vast majority of people should be treated like the adults they are. It is ridiculous that the government should deny the entire population the right to a drink after 11pm. We will give adults the freedom they deserve and yobs the tough treatment they deserve' (Tessa Jowell, Culture Secretary, 2005). While moderate consumption of alcohol is condoned, excessive consumption is condemned and drunkenness is increasingly criticised, as outlined in the recently revised National Alcohol Strategy (HM Government, 2007). Such change may disproportionately criminalise certain socio-demographic and cultural groupings such as the under-age and young-adult pub and club goers considered below. Before this, however, we ask what is the British government's position on the regulation of leisure and the governance of pleasure? Is there a coherent political, moral or intellectual position behind current British government policy on leisure, pleasure and intoxication?

The government position

The range of policy options from prohibition, through regulation, to libertarianism in relation to drinking alcohol, smoking tobacco, gambling and consuming illicit drugs (and even regarding the liberalisation of the licensing of the 'upmarket' sex industry) has been variously embraced in each case. Assuming that total prohibition and total libertarianism are both unworkable and unlikely, the government has opted for the 'third way' in alcohol and gambling policy, the middle ground between freedom and restriction, termed 'better regulation' by the government minister Tessa Jowell (2005). Jowell outlined the three principles of the government's 'better regulation': first, making a distinction between adults who are free to spend their time and money as they choose, and children who need special protection. This is illustrated in the increased protection for children in the 2003 Licensing Act and the 2005 Gambling Act.

Second, Jowell claims that the nature of 'better regulation' involves variation between cases, so that the government can justify apparent inconsistencies. The example she gives is that the criminalisation of smoking in enclosed public places (implemented in July 2007 in England) can be justified because even one cigarette is bad for both smokers and those around them, whereas the increased facilitation of drinking alcohol in the very same leisure venues (implemented in 2005) can be justified because one or even several drinks do not necessarily result in adverse consequences for drinkers or those around them. The extension of pub trading hours in the 2003 Licensing Act was justified by the government as extending freedom for the 'sensible majority' to drink later, while clamping down on the 'troublesome minority' and aiming to reduce closing-time congestion problems and drink-related disorder. Similarly, the expansion in British casinos has been justified by the government as increasing access to gambling for the sensible majority, while it claims that it will not increase overall rates of problematic gambling in the general population.

Third, Jowell has also suggested that this 'new politics of behaviour' requires a change of attitude by politicians and the public, to result in 'grown-up politics' in action, with a recognition that the government needs to engage in dialogue with the public regarding these issues.

A more critical perspective would be that the British government is torn between a prohibitionist stance towards deliberate and excessive intoxication by individuals (particularly, intoxicated youth and young adults in public places) and a libertarian stance towards those businesses that facilitate intoxication through alcohol (or gambling), for example through a policy of self-regulation both by individuals and by the drinks, gaming and leisure industries through corporate responsibility (see, for example, Prime Minister's Strategy Unit, 2004; HM Government, 2007). This is occurring within the wider context of the growing 'marketisation' of the control, regulation and policing of the night-time economy, dominated by alcohol-based leisure pursuits often undertaken in corporate-owned mainstream 'urban playscapes' (Chatterton and Hollands, 2002; Hollands, 2002; Hadfield, 2006). As Hobbs et al note, 'the marriage of leisure and commerce within after-dark post-industrial urban centres is a union consummated by deregulatory pragmatism and ordained by implicit governmental sanction and an expectation of righteous consumption' (Hobbs et al, 2003: 245). We argue here that illicit intoxication (with illegal drugs) and excessive intoxication (with alcohol) fall outside of righteous and respectable consumption in the eyes of the British government and are the focus of a proactively prohibitionist stance.

British drug and alcohol policy has tended to prioritise the relationship between alcohol, drugs and *crime*, resulting in both increased medicalisation (based on outdated notions of addiction and compulsion) and increased criminalisation (revolving around 'war on drugs' and crime-prevention discourses). Medicalisation through the potentially compassionate treatment of problem users is based on an exaggeration of the drugs–crime relationship that has been used to justify coercion into treatment since the establishment of quasi-compulsory treatment in the UK with the 1998 Crime and Disorder Act, and further prioritised in funding (for example with a £93 million increase in funds for drug treatment announced in June 2006). Coercion into treatment through the government's 'Tough Choices' Drug Interventions Programme requires drug users to attend initial and follow-up assessments after a positive testing for the presence of Class A substances, following arrest for a trigger offence. Coercion is extended by new provisions in section 20 of the 2005 Drugs Act, which allows intervention orders to be attached to Anti-Social Behaviour Orders (ASBOs), requiring individuals to attend drug counselling when their anti-social behaviour is deemed to be drug related. Non-attendance, and failure to remain for the duration of assessments, results in the individual being guilty of an offence under section 14 of the 2005 Drugs Act and liable to a fine and/or imprisonment (HMSO, 2005). Thus, non-compliance with coercive drug treatment becomes a criminal offence in itself and can result in criminal sanctions for a drug user who may not have been charged with any other offence. Such changes to the regulatory environment have occurred despite the recognised theoretical complexities of the drugs–crime relationship (Simpson, 2003; Seddon, 2006), despite empirical evidence to suggest that the group of problematic drug users for whom this relationship is significant is probably no more than 250,000 (Bramley-Harker, 2001; Hough et al, 2003) and despite research that suggests that the efficacy of quasi-compulsory treatment cannot easily be evaluated (McSweeney et al, 2006).

Meanwhile, millions of youth and young adults attend pubs and clubs in the UK and consume legal and illicit drugs for recreational purposes on at least an occasional basis, yet they fit neither the medical model of addiction nor the discourses of crime and compulsion. It is argued here that this policy vacuum is being filled by a new wave of criminalisation of contemporary cultures of intoxication through amendments to the 1971 Misuse of Drugs Act, alongside the 1998 Crime and Disorder Act, the 2003 Licensing Act and the 2005 Drugs Act. This has occurred in contrast to the diversion from criminal justice to treatment interventions for daily, dependent and chaotic drug and alcohol users, and the expansion of the criminal justice system's role in drug policy (with government spending on criminal justice-led drug treatment recently overtaking spending on community drug services: Chater, 2005: 26). With neither an individual desire for abstinence nor a policy of coercion into treatment, non-dependent intoxication falls between government aims and loses out on resources.

The new wave of criminalisation

In part, recent changes in the legislative and regulatory landscape of the night-time economy display historical continuities, that is, the enduring 'official' ambivalence to leisure and pharmacological pleasure (Measham, 2006a; Hayward and Hobbs, 2008). However, it is argued here that such official ambivalence is increasingly focused on particular segments of youth and young-adult culture, with very real consequences for those involved. In relation to illicit drug use, while there has been some evidence of a shift from the margins towards the mainstream in terms of the normalisation of recreational drug use by youth and young adults in the UK (Parker et al, 1998, 2002), the government has responded by increased criminalisation of illicit and excessive intoxication, with four developments particularly pertinent to youthful and young-adult leisure spaces.

First, the 1971 Misuse of Drugs Act has been repeatedly extended in recent years to include the classification and/or reclassification of a growing repertoire of drugs used for recreational purposes. This includes:

- the classification of GHB as a Class C controlled substance in an amendment to the 1971 Misuse of Drugs Act in 2002;
- the classification of fresh psychedelic mushrooms (containing psilocybin and psilocin in all forms) – previously legal if not prepared for consumption – as a Class A controlled substance in the 2005 Drugs Act;
- the classification of ketamine – previously controlled by the 1968 Medicines Act – as Class C in 2006;
- increased sanctions against methamphetamine with its reclassification from Class B to Class A in 2007;
- a press campaign in 2007 by the Medicines and Healthcare Products Regulatory Agency (MHRA) to reiterate that the sale of benzylpiperazines (BZPs or 'PEP' pills) and nitrous oxide (or 'laughing gas') is illegal under the 1968 Medicines Act and that retailers are liable to prosecution;[2] and
- restrictions on the recreational use of khat and Viagra also currently under consideration.

Thus, within the space of five years six drugs have either been criminalised or had their sanctions increased and/or re-emphasised by regulatory authorities.

These extensions to the 1971 Misuse of Drugs Act, to include an ever greater number of drugs used for recreational purposes, have occurred despite minimal evidence existing either of widespread use of these emergent drugs or of significant crime, health or social problems as a result of the use of these drugs, and despite little consultation with professional drugs agencies or other NGOs. This 'frenzied law making' (*Independent Online*, 2006) has occurred within the broader context of the British government's 'law and order' agenda and a wider 'culture of control' (Garland, 2001), where the meaning of certain transgressive pleasures develops from the interaction between individual identity, social group interactions, market forces, government policy and governance practices, whereby 'kids, criminals, and legal authorities [become] caught up in a process of symbolic meaning and official reaction' (Ferrell, 2005: 63). Such were the concerns about the lack of evidence-based harm pre-empting a new wave of criminalisation, while at the same time the classification of cannabis was reduced (from Class B to Class C in 2004) in spite of growing evidence on the relationship between long-term heavy use and psychiatric illness, that the House of Commons Science and Technology Committee (2006) asked whether the government had 'made a hash' of drug classification. Indeed, the government recognises that, rather than responding to a pre-existing drug problem, it has justified this body of legislation as a pre-emptive move to stop a problem from developing. Thus, this new criminalisation fits the long-standing British drug policy of proactive prohibition where, in contrast to the US for example, the main aim is deterrence rather than addressing an existing problem. This can be exemplified by MDMA (ecstasy) and its chemical cousins becoming Class A Schedule 1 controlled drugs in 1977 in an amendment to the 1971 Misuse of Drugs Act, despite no evidence of their availability, use or harm in the UK at that time.

A second, more embryonic development within this new wave of criminalisation involves the 2005 Drugs Act and issues surrounding 'social supply'. The Act amended section 5 of the 1971 Misuse of Drugs Act to provide for a presumption of intent to supply where the defendant is found in possession of a particular amount of controlled drugs. Initial threshold recommendations in 2005 were deemed by the government and the Advisory Council on the Misuse of Drugs to be excessive, although later recommendations (June 2006) were criticised for being set too low (Newcombe, 2006). The resulting recommended thresholds for ecstasy tablets, for example, stood at five, so that if an individual was caught in possession of more than five ecstasy tablets the onus would rest on defendants to establish that they were not drug suppliers. In effect, individuals would be presumed guilty of the more serious offence of intent to supply (as opposed to possession) – with a maximum sentence of life imprisonment for supplying Class A drugs in the UK – unless and until they proved themselves not guilty. Yet, according to the annual *Mixmag* dance magazine survey of its clubbing readership (see Sherlock and Conner, 1999), in 2005 the average number of ecstasy tablets bought at one time was 10, while the average number of tablets consumed in one session was 4.5 (*Mixmag*, 2005). In 2006 Home Secretary John Reid halted plans by his predecessor to set thresholds in relation to possession and supply, although he signalled a potential review of the thresholds policy in the future. This possibility, not unlike the erosion of 'due process' safeguards in other aspects of anti-social behaviour enforcement action, is perhaps the most worrying development in terms of human rights. As both Transform (2005a) and Release (2005) maintain, any reversal of the burden of proof in criminal proceedings, from the prosecution to the defence, must be considered within the framework of the right to a fair trial enshrined in Article 6 of the 1998 Human Rights Act. Article 6(2) requires that 'everyone charged with a criminal offence shall be presumed innocent until proved guilty according to law'.

The third development is the increased criminalisation of drunkenness and drink-related disorder through alcohol ASBOs, alcohol disorder zones and widespread use of on-the-spot £80 fines for minor offences such as urinating in public. It has been argued elsewhere (Measham and Brain, 2005) that increased access to alcohol, the promotion of new alcoholic beverages, venues and marketing, alongside the increased regulation of drink-related disorder, result in the combined seduction and repression of British drinkers within the night-time economy. What we can see here is the contrast between official facilitation of drinking through the 2003 Licensing Act and continued self-regulation by the drinks industry rather than state intervention, alongside the increased official condemnation of drunkenness, evident in the National Alcohol Strategy (HM Government, 2007). Thus, while moderate drinking (and therefore mild intoxication) is acceptable, excessive intoxication or drunkenness resulting from immoderate alcohol consumption (as defined by the government) is not. Although, as implied earlier, this may be less a question of intoxication as such, than of *who* is drunk and *where* they are drunk.

The fourth point relates to the repeated rejection of calls for a review of the basic regulatory framework in the UK governed by the 1971 Misuse of Drugs Act and the classification system embedded within it. Criticisms of the UK drug classification system have been raised in the Runciman Report (Police Foundation, 1999), the House of Commons Home Affairs Select Committee report (2002), the House of Commons Scientific and Technology Committee report (2006), and also by non-statutory drugs organisations such as Transform, Release and Drugscope and, most recently, the Royal Society of Arts (2007) and *The Lancet* (Nutt and Blakemore, 2007). Thus government policy towards intoxication remains replete with contradictions, highlighted even by those working within Whitehall. The House of Commons Science and Technology Committee review, for example, concluded that:

> with respect to the ABC classification system, we have identified significant anomalies in the classification of individual drugs and a regrettable lack of consistency in the rationale used to make classification decisions ... the current classification system is not fit for purpose and should be replaced with a more scientifically based scale of harm. (2006: 3)

The UK government has dismissed all recommendations for reform of drug laws, from the Runciman Report (Police Foundation, 1999) to, most recently, the Royal Society of Arts (2007) report. Instead, the government responded with the 2005 Drugs Act, which was considered by many within the field to be an ill-thought-out piece of legislation rushed through in the 'wash up' before the general election, with minimal consultation. Such discrepancies between Home Office policy and recommendations by a range of statutory and non-statutory bodies highlight the politically motivated nature of the classification system and underscore the government's reluctance to link classification of controlled drugs to scientific evidence of relative harm to the individual and/or society. This is despite the 1971 Misuse of Drugs Act, as noted by Shiner (2003), being based on a traditional medico-legal model of harm and addictive potential. Shaped by political and historical contingencies, 'anomalies in the classification system do matter, not least to the young person found in possession of ecstasy or magic mushrooms, which carry a prison sentence of up to 7 years' (Barnes, 2006: 9).

Home Office evidence of the efficacy of the deterrent value of the classification system, or indeed of prohibition itself, is virtually non-existent (HMSO, 2006), particularly in light of evidence of increased availability of illicit drugs and reductions in their real price in recent years, and despite this assumption of deterrence lying at the heart of UK drug policy. Indeed, the House of Commons Science and Technology Committee criticised the deterrence principle, saying:

> we have found no solid evidence to support the existence of a deterrent effect, despite the fact that it appears to underpin the Government's policy on classification. In view of the importance of drugs policy and the amount spent on enforcing the penalties associated with the classification system, it is highly unsatisfactory that there is so little knowledge about the system's effectiveness. (2006: 17–18)

The government rejected these criticisms, saying 'the Government fundamentally believes that illegality is an important factor when people are considering engaging in risk taking behaviour' (HMSO, 2006: 18). At least with respect to the recent criminalisation of ketamine, ongoing research by the authors challenges the government's position that prohibition has a deterrent value and reduces either drug prevalence or drug-related problems (Moore and Measham, 2006; Moore and Measham, 2008; see also Swaine, 2006). Furthermore, it highlights the inconsistency within government policy on various potentially addictive behaviours whereby we have seen the liberalisation of licensed leisure through increased access to gambling and drinking venues for the 'sensible majority', supported by claims that increased access will not result in a corresponding increase in problem gambling or problem drinking.

The dichotomy between coercive treatment for chaotic drug use and the criminalisation of recreational drug use also fits the broader government agenda that might ostensibly appear to be concerned with the individual welfare of, for example, drug users, yet suggests an underlying moral welfarism that prioritises treatment aimed at withdrawal and abstinence, while 'intense intoxication' (Hayward and Hobbs, 2008) and 'determined drunkenness' (Measham, 2006a) are perceived to be problematic in themselves. Analogies can be drawn here with British government policy on sex workers and trafficked women, where the focus of intervention is on policing criminal coercion into sex work and supporting exit strategies out of sex work, rather than harm-minimisation policies for those continuing in sex work, as noted by O'Neill and Campbell (forthcoming). A Home Office pilot study to be established in Ipswich will offer an 'exiting package' of counselling and lifestyle interventions for sex workers to exit prostitution, while increasing the criminal sanctions for those who continue to operate, through prosecution and ASBOs. This reflects the 'counselling or court' approach to drug treatment established ten years ago in the UK.

The legislative change outlined above will result in the increased criminalisation of young people who participate in the pursuit of altered states of intoxication, yet whose repertories fit neither the addiction–treatment nor the drugs–crime motivations for intervention. This new wave of criminalisation in the 21st century will fall disproportionately hard on specific cultural groups and distinctive local leisure 'scenes', such as clubbers in mature post-rave dance scenes whose participation is characterised by prolific polydrug repertoires. Those who choose not to exit these local leisure scenes face disproportionate criminal justice intervention. Yet arguably, young people do attempt to operate within the law; for example, fresh mushrooms were seen as an acceptable, legal psychedelic high increasingly available in British high street 'head' shops in the early 21st century, yet have recently been criminalised, in part because of increased use (Roe, 2005).

In the broader context, the pleasures of this 'controlled loss of control' (Measham, 2002) resulting from illicit and excessive intoxication fall outside of the government's concern with respectable behaviours and 'righteous consumption' (Hobbs et al, 2003: 245), demanding further governmental intervention within the context of young people's night-time leisure spaces and beyond. It is argued that powerful industry forces make a move towards the liberalisation, economic deregulation and normalisation of certain leisure practices (such as drinking, gambling, attendance at sex clubs) that are at odds with the increased regulation and criminalisation of those impermissible pleasures (including recreational polydrug use, outdoor sex between consenting adult strangers and increasingly drunkenness and other so-called 'anti-social' behaviours) that do not have powerful industry backing, corporate/consumer respectability or large-scale revenue-raising potential. In such terms, 'anti-social behaviour' becomes increasingly a question of social context.

Overall, the contradictory forces of deregulation and criminalisation are leading to an ill-planned experiment in the policing of pleasure in contemporary Britain and a new wave of criminalisation of the vibrant and distinct cultures of intoxication developing across the UK. Historically, this targeting continues the UK government's regulation of dance culture, evident in a series of pieces of legislation introduced or reintroduced in response to the 'decade of dance' 1988–98, resulting in the first criminalisation of a specific musical and cultural form and epitomised by the 1994 Crime and Public Disorder Act (Thornton, 1995; Linton, 1998; Measham et al, 1998, 2001; Hill, 2002). Local leisure scenes, with their distinctive cultures of intoxication, continue to experience discriminatory policing and differential targeting and enforcement alongside the deluge of recent legislation, evident in a recent conflict between the police and illegal ravers in Manchester.[3]

Discussion: the proactive prohibition of pharmacological pleasure

The 'otherness' of the night-time economy (Lovatt, 1996: 144), particularly in relation to dance/club culture and its continuing associations with a 'netherworld' (Presdee, 2000: 9) of illegal drug use and gang involvement (Hobbs et al, 2003), has provoked 'law and order' responses from both national and local governmental agencies, with official society 'criminalising as it goes, and making punishable the previously unpunishable' (Presdee, 2000: 9). Urban space becomes manicured, manipulated and mapped by these forces of criminalisation, as impermissible pleasures generated by transgressive leisure activities and identities become subject to regulation, surveillance and control, for example, with club fly-posting and flyering penalised and police stop and searches conducted on nightclub queues. Government policy and market forces combine to produce the lived realities of pleasure seekers participating in dance music, polydrug, pub and club scenes. In particular, the illicit and excessive intoxication of urban night-time revellers is viewed as requiring official moral-legalistic responses: through legislation, policing and enforcement by the criminal justice system and local city councils; through health discourses of drugs education, treatment and prevention supported by multi-agency research and harm-reduction initiatives (see Hughes and Bellis, 2003); and as reality television entertainment for the 'sensible majority' (Hayward and Hobbs, 2008).

Specific cultures of intoxication have attracted blanket official responses, such as the 2005 Drugs Act, that are likely to impact disproportionately upon clubbers, given their polydrug repertoires, resulting in the criminalisation of certain forms of intoxication by youth, young adults and 'ageing clubbers' (see Gibson, 2005). Other behaviours related to specific cultures of intoxication, such as public disorder and interpersonal violence linked to excessive alcohol consumption in urban night-time settings, are framed as being the consequence of a small minority of 'rough' youth and young adults, the actions of whom should not be allowed to spoil the liberties of the law-abiding majority of sensible drinkers, within the logical needs of the free-market, neoliberal consumer economy (Hall and Winlow, 2005). Legislative changes exemplified by the repeated extensions to the 1971 Misuse of Drugs Act have been essentially political decisions in response to developments in popular culture and perceived social threat rather than evidence-based responses to medical harm or police concerns about crime-related problems relating to these specific drugs, and together they form the crest of a new wave of criminalisation of contemporary cultures of intoxication and an increasingly repressive regime of governance.

In the absence of evidence of harm to the individual and/or society and with a drug policy drawing on the discourses of addiction, compulsion and the drugs–crime relationship, the policy vacuum is being filled by the proactive prohibition of emergent recreational polydrug use and determined drunkenness. Illicit and excessive intoxication is positioned as an 'impermissible pleasure' demanding greater governmental intervention that appears to be motivated by the desire to criminalise pharmacological pleasure in itself. Thus, current government policy effectively criminalises particular sociocultural forms and participants (such as clubbing and clubbers), providing little room for a pragmatic model of 'sensible' recreational drug use through harm-minimisation strategies and the rarely mentioned 'flip-side', namely pleasure maximisation. While we have yet to see whether the new criminal status of these emergent drugs will have the government's desired deterrent effect on potential and current users (Willis, 2006), prohibition remains part of the 'lived politics' (Ferrell, 2005: 63) of leisure and pleasure in the British night-time economy.

Notes

[1] This paper draws on a presentation by Fiona Measham (2006b) at the British Society of Criminology annual conference.

[2] In a recent 'off the record' telephone conversation with one of the authors, an MHRA spokesperson indicated that its recent concentration on BZPs and nitrous oxide 'is due to increased use in nightclubs' (28 April 2007).

[3] See 'Illegal rave attracts undesirables', (www.whathappenedlastnight. com/, accessed January 2007).

References

Barnes, M. (2006) 'DrugScope's critical view from the inside', *Drugs and Alcohol Today*, vol 6, no 3, p 9.

Blair, T. (2004) 'Alcohol the "new British disease"', (http://news.bbc. co.uk).

Bramley-Harker, E. (2001) *Sizing the UK market for illicit drugs*, Research Development and Statistics Directorate, Occasional paper no 74, London: Home Office.

Chater, D. (2005) 'Criminally minded: why we need to redress the crime bias', *Drugs and Alcohol Today*, vol 5 no 2, pp 26–8.

Chatterton, P. and Hollands, R. (2002) 'Theorising urban playscapes: producing, regulating and consuming youthful nightlife city spaces', *Urban Studies*, vol 39, no 1, pp 95–116.

Ferrell, J. (2005) 'Style matters', in J. Ferrell, K. Hayward, W. Morrison and M. Presdee (eds), *Cultural criminology unleashed*, London: Glasshouse Press, pp 61–6.

Garland, D. (2001) *The culture of control: Crime and social order in contemporary society*, Chicago: University of Chicago Press.

Gibson, L.H. (2005) 'Popular music, lifecourse, lifestyles, and identities: A case study of ageing club cultures', Master's thesis, University of Manchester.

Hadfield, P. (2006) *Bar wars: Contesting the night in contemporary British cities*, Oxford: Oxford University Press.

Hall, S. and Winlow, S. (2005) 'Night-time leisure and violence in the breakdown of the pseudo-pacification process', *Probation Journal*, vol 52, no 4, pp 376–89.

Hayward, K. and Hobbs, D. (2008: forthcoming), 'Beyond the binge in "Booze Britain": liminality and the spectacle of binge drinking', *British Journal of Sociology*.

Hill, A. (2002) 'Acid house and Thatcherism: noise, the mob and the English countryside', *British Journal of Sociology*, vol 53, no 1, pp 89–105.

HM Government (2007) *Safe, sensible, social: The next steps in the National Alcohol Strategy*, London: TSO.

HMSO (2006) *The Government Reply to the Fifth Report from the House of Commons Science and Technology Committee Session 2005–2006*, London: HMSO.

Hobbs, D., Hadfield, P., Lister, S., and Winlow, S. (2003) *Bouncers: Violence and governance in the night-time economy*, Oxford: Oxford University Press.

Hollands, R. (2002) 'Divisions in the dark: youth cultures, transitions and segmented consumption spaces in the night-time economy', *Journal of Youth Studies*, vol 5, no 2, pp 153–71.

Hough, M., Clancy, A., McSweeney, T. and Turnbull, P.J. (2003) *The impact of Drug Treatment and Testing Orders on offending: Two-year reconviction results*, Research Findings No. 184, London: Home Office.

House of Commons Home Affairs Select Committee (2002) *The government's drug policy: Is it working?*, Third Report of Session 2001–02, London: The Stationery Office.

House of Commons Science and Technology Committee (2006) *Drug classification: Making a hash of it?*, Fifth Report of Session 2005–06, HC 1031, London: The Stationery Office

Hughes, K. and Bellis, M.A. (2003) *Safer nightlife in the North West of England: A report by the North West Safer Nightlife Group*, Liverpool: Liverpool John Moores University.

Independent Online (2006) 'Blair's "frenzied law making": a new offence for every day spent in office', 16 August.

Jowell, T. (2005) Press release, London: Department for Culture, Media and Sport, 6 February, condensed version of Jowell, T. (2004) in *Fabian Review*, December, (available at: www.culture.gov.uk/global/press_notices/archive_2005/dcms016_05.htm).

Linton, M. (1998) 'The rave commission – the only culture police in the western world', *International Journal of Drug Policy*, vol 9, pp 305–10.

Lovatt, A. (1996) 'The ecstasy of urban regeneration: regulation of the nighttime economy in the transition to a post-Fordist city', in J. O'Connor and D. Wynne, *From the margins to the centre: Cultural production and consumption in the post-industrial city*, Aldershot: Arena, pp 141–68.

McSweeney, T., Stevens, A., Hunt, M. and Turnbull, P.J. (2007) 'Twisting arms or a helping hand? Accessing the impact of "coerced" and comparable "voluntary" drug treatment options', *British Journal of Criminology*, vol 47, pp 470–90.

Measham, F. (2002) '"Doing gender" – "doing drugs": Conceptualising the gendering of drugs cultures', *Contemporary Drug Problems*, vol 29, no 2, Summer, pp 335–73.

Measham, F. (2006a) 'The new policy mix: alcohol, harm minimisation and determined drunkenness in contemporary society', *International Journal of Drug Policy*, Special edition: Harm reduction and alcohol policy, vol 17, pp 258–68.

Measham, F. (2006b) 'Cultures of intoxication, local leisure "scenes" and the new wave of criminalisation', British Society of Criminology annual conference, Glasgow, July 2006, Unpublished conference paper.

Measham, F. and Brain, K. (2005) 'Binge drinking, British alcohol policy and the new culture of intoxication', *Crime, Media, Culture*, vol 1, no 3, pp 262–83.

Measham, F., Parker, H. and Aldridge, J. (1998) *Starting, switching, slowing and stopping: Report for the Drugs Prevention Initiative Integrated Programme*, Drugs Prevention Initiative Paper No. 21, London: Home Office.

Measham, F., Aldridge, J. and Parker, H. (2001) *Dancing on drugs: Risk, health and hedonism in the British club scene*, London: Free Association Books.

Mixmag (2005), February.

Moore, K. and Measham, F. (2006) 'Ketamine use: minimising problems and maximising pleasure', *Drugs and Alcohol Today*, vol 6, no 3, pp 29–32.

Moore, K. and Measham, F. (2008) '"It's the most fun you can have for twenty quid": meanings, motivations, and consequences of recreational ketamine use in Britain', *Addiction Research and Theory*, Special edition: Ketamine.

Newcombe, R. (2006) *Quantity thresholds for distinguishing drug possession from possession with intent to supply in Britain: A review of relevant evidence*, Manchester: Lifeline.

Nutt, D. and Blakemore, C. (2007) 'Development of a rational scale to assess the harm of drugs of potential misuse', *The Lancet*, 23 March.

O'Neill, M. and Campbell, R. (forthcoming) 'Regulating prostitution: social inclusion, responsibilisation and the politics of prostitution reform', *British Journal of Criminology*.

Parker, H., Aldridge, J. and Measham, F. (1998) *Illegal leisure: The normalization of adolescent recreational drug use*, London: Routledge.

Parker, H., Williams, L. and Aldridge, J. (2002) 'The normalisation of "sensible" recreational drug use: further evidence from the North West England longitudinal study', *Sociology*, vol 36, no 4, pp 941–64.

Police Foundation (1999) *Drugs and the law: Report of the independent inquiry into the Misuse of Drugs Act 1971* (The Runciman Report), London: The Police Foundation, (available at: www.druglibrary.org/schaffer/Library/studies/runciman/default.htm).

Presdee, M. (2000) *Cultural criminology and the carnival of crime*, London: Routledge.

Prime Minister's Strategy Unit (2004) *Alcohol Harm Reduction Strategy for England*, London: Strategy Unit.

Release (2005) 'Response to the Drugs Bill 2005', (available at: www.transform.org.uk, accessed January 2006).

Roe, S. (2005) *Drug misuse declared: Findings from the 2004/05 British Crime Survey, England and Wales*, Home Office Statistical Bulletin 16/05, London: Home Office.

Royal Society of Arts (2007) *Drugs – facing facts: The report of the RSA Commission on Illegal Drugs, Communities and Public Policy*, London: RSA.

Seddon, T. (2006) 'Drugs, crime and social exclusion: social context and social theory in British drugs-crime research', *British Journal of Criminology*, vol 46, no 4, pp 680–703.

Sherlock, K. and Conner, M. (1999) 'Patterns of ecstasy use amongst club-goers on the UK "dance scene"', *International Journal of Drug Policy*, vol 10, pp 117–29.

Shiner, M. (2003) 'Out of harm's way? Illicit drug use, medicalization and the law', *British Journal of Criminology*, vol 43, pp 772–96.

Simpson, M. (2003) 'The relationship between drug use and crime: a puzzle inside an enigma', *International Journal of Drug Policy*, vol 14, pp 307–19.

Swaine, K. (2006) 'BZPs – can classification protect public health?', *Drugs and Alcohol Today*, vol 6, no 3, p 14.

Thornton, S. (1995) *Club cultures: Music, media and subcultural capital*, Cambridge: Polity Press.

Transform (2005a) *Response to the Drugs Bill 2005 Second Reading Briefing*, (available at www.tdpf.org.uk, accessed January 2006).

Willis, P. (2006) 'Making yet another hash of it?', *Drugs and Alcohol Today*, vol 6, no 3, p 8.

SIXTEEN

ASBOs and working women: a new revolving door?

Jo Phoenix

Introduction

The casual observer would be forgiven for assuming that the regulation of prostitution in the UK has changed dramatically in the last decade or so. In 1999, the Department of Health and the Home Office issued new guidelines for how young people in prostitution were to be dealt with – guidelines that stressed diverting young people away from the criminal justice system and into statutory and voluntary welfare agencies, and punishing adults who commercially sexually exploit anyone under the age of 18 years. New statutes have been put in place to deal with facilitating or encouraging child prostitution and human trafficking for the purposes of sexual exploitation, with an accompanying range of much higher tariffs (including life imprisonment). The Home Office and the Local Government Association have made available funds and resources to provide women trafficked into prostitution with housing and accommodation, all with the aim of helping them leave (or 'exit') prostitution. The Home Office funded research in ten different locations to evaluate the sort of policies and practices that work best. Shortly afterwards, the then Home Secretary initiated a review of prostitution–related legislation and practice that resulted in the publication of a set of recommendations to police constabularies and local authorities on how to provide a coordinated strategy on prostitution. These recommendations, in common with those made regarding young people and victims of trafficking, are geared towards helping women exit prostitution. They highlight the difficulties that adult women encounter in terms of exploitation, violence, homelessness, lack of economic opportunities, debt and drug and alcohol addictions. In addition, these recommendations highlighted the problems caused to both sex workers and communities by the criminal organisation of prostitution and/or criminal men involved with or exploiting sex workers.

In view of all this, a casual observer could be forgiven for assuming that, unlike previous decades, the new millennium has signalled a shift in the official stance on prostitution – or more particularly prostitute women – which is less punitive. Unfortunately, the casual observer would be wrong for two main reasons. First, many of the reforms are reforms on paper only (perhaps with the exception of guidance dealing with young people). Many of the reforms are little more than a drawing together of established practice already in place. So, for instance, the consultation document *Paying the price* (Home Office, 2004) and the accompanying response *A coordinated prostitution strategy* (Home Office, 2006) make no new suggestions for working with the men, women and young people in prostitution in the UK. Second, the tolerance that would seem to mark the reforms is framed within an intolerant system of regulation and intervention that targets the most socially, economically and politically vulnerable and excluded women in prostitution (street workers) for punishment or coercive state-sponsored welfare. For, despite the rhetoric of welfare and support, the last decade has also seen the introduction and use of Anti-Social Behaviour Orders to police street workers and the suggestion that the sentencing orthodoxy of fining women convicted of soliciting or loitering for the purposes of prostitution be removed and that instead a graduated tariff of harsher punishments be considered.

The aim of this chapter is to place the use of ASBOs in policing prostitution into the broader context of the regulation of prostitution and, in doing so, to make two main arguments. The first argument is that ASBOs are not at odds with recent reforms to the regulation of prostitution – despite first impressions – and are not particularly innovative or new measures used by criminal justice agencies in the policing and regulation of prostitution. The second argument is that ASBOs represent a broader shift in the way prostitution is regulated towards harsher, deeper, targeted state-sponsored, coercive and punitive regulation of some of the most excluded, marginalised and impoverished individuals in prostitution – street sex workers. In order to make these arguments, the chapter is divided into two main sections. In the first section I place ASBOs in the context of the regulatory system as put in place by the Wolfenden Report (Home Office, 1957) and which has been in operation for the last 60 years. In the second section I explore the recommendations set out in the Coordinated Strategy in order to contextualise some of the observations made in the first section.

Formalising partial criminalisation – the Wolfenden Report and the problem of visible prostitution

The 1950s was a turbulent decade in regard to the formal legal regulation of sex. The 1956 Sexual Offences Act consolidated many of the pre-existing sexual offences and attempted to create a more coherent set of laws (and punishments). The Wolfenden Committee met to recommend changes to laws regarding prostitution and homosexuality and, as part of those changes, recommended the decriminalisation of male homosexuality and the partial criminalisation of prostitution. These changes did not, however, just emerge. They were part and parcel of a larger challenge to the established view that the law could and should specify limits to and levels of sexual morality (Weeks, 1985). Many commentators of the time noted that the law was no longer capable of responding to or reflecting the immense social changes in regard to openness and plurality that were taking place in British society. In this way, the approach to regulating prostitution recommended by the Wolfenden Report and institutionalised in the 1959 Street Offences Act represented a realignment of the law and sexual morality as much as it formalised a particular view of what was in need of regulation.

The Wolfenden Committee was very clear on what it viewed should be the relationship between sex, sexual morality and the law. The function and role of the law was:

> to preserve public order and decency, to protect the citizen from what is offensive or injurious and to provide sufficient safeguards against exploitation and corruption of others, particularly those who are specially vulnerable because they are young, weak in body or mind, inexperienced or, in a state of special physical, official or economic dependence. (Home Office, 1957: 9–10)

The committee then continued: 'It is not in our view the function of the law to intervene in the private lives of citizens, or to seek to enforce any particular pattern of behaviour, further than is necessary to carry out the purposes we have outlined' (Home Office, 1957: 10).

In drawing this line of distinction between criminal justice interventions and matters of private morality, the Wolfenden Committee defined prostitution in general as a matter of private morality. The only exceptions were activities and behaviours that caused an affront to public decency or a public nuisance. The Wolfenden Committee stated: 'ordinary citizens who live in these areas [that is, those in which street prostitution takes place] cannot, in going about their daily business, avoid the sight of a state of affairs which seems to them to be an affront to public order and decency' (Home Office, 1957: 82).

Prior to this moment, the laws pertaining to prostitution tended to be fragmented and seldom evenly enforced, but by the end of the 1950s the 1956 Sexual Offences Act and the 1959 Street Offences Act provided, at least in theory, a uniform, universal approach to regulating prostitution. The central principles of this system were a basic legal tolerance of the sale or purchase of sex, and the use of criminal justice to keep in check the negative consequences of prostitution – the primary negative consequence being identified as the nuisance and affront that visible prostitution was presumed to cause. In practical terms, this has meant a system of regulation that criminalises known prostitutes who loiter or solicit in a public place for the purposes of prostitution. Prostitution per se is not criminalised. Further, the centrepiece of the system of punishment that Wolfenden inaugurated was the use of 'prostitutes' cautions', in which women (and only women) suspected of loitering or soliciting for prostitution are given two cautions before being charged as common prostitutes. In common with Anti-Social Behaviour Orders, the evidence required to obtain a 'prostitute's caution' is less than the evidential requirements or burden of proof required in other criminal proceedings. To receive a prostitute's caution a woman must be suspected by a police officer of prostituting. Once she has been cautioned twice as being a suspected prostitute, then she can be arrested for soliciting or 'loitering by a common prostitute'. As many commentators have noted before, prostitutes' cautions are a form of regulation that reverses the legal maxim of innocent until proven guilty. Before any formal adjudication of guilt or innocence is made, women charged with soliciting or loitering are already deemed guilty (see also Edwards, 1997). The Wolfenden Report also recommended that the punishment of prostitution-related offences should start with a fine and become progressively more severe and culminate with imprisonment for up to three months.[1] In 1982, sentencing guidance was introduced that altered the punishment for soliciting or loitering to fines only.

So, the basic framework of regulation of prostitution that exists within the UK is one in which the sale and purchase of sex are tolerated, but any visible evidence that such exchanges take place is not. Aside from the wide discretion available to street-level enforcement (like the ASBO) and the ambiguities regarding 'due process' (such as the reversal of the burden of proof – again, like the ASBO), there are many ironies in regulating prostitution in such a way. With the exception of those who sell sex privately and individually from indoor locations, the way in which the Wolfenden Committee partially criminalised prostitution has meant that most sex workers will, at some point in the course of their prostituting activities, break the law and be subject to criminal justice punishments (unlike the men who purchase sex). And, the burden of criminal justice regulation falls disproportionately on the shoulders of those women least able to afford it – street-working women. Specifically, two centuries of research has established that many of the individuals who sell sex from the street are those whose lives have been shattered by the aggregate effects of poverty, social exclusion, violence and abuse in the home, drug and alcohol problems, homelessness and housing difficulties and a range of other social, personal and welfare problems (McLeod, 1982; May et al, 1999; Church et al, 2001; O'Neill, 2001; Phoenix, 2001; Sanders, 2005). Despite the fact that involvement in street-based prostitution rarely secures women any degree of financial or social stability, for these women selling sex may appear as a plausible and rational choice. However, fining these women for their prostituting activities creates a revolving door. In order to pay their fines, the women often return to prostitution, or in many cases merely let their fines accrue and then face prison sentences for fine defaulting (see Phoenix, 2001; Matthews, 2005).

One other ironic effect of tolerating the sale of sex and yet not tolerating where and how it is sold is the comparative under-enforcement of provisions designed to protect women sex workers (Edwards, 1997; Phoenix, 2001; Matthews, 2005; Sanders, 2005). Take, for example, the provision in the 1956 Sexual Offences Act against 'living off the earnings of prostitution', that is, pimping, and 'exercising control over a prostitute', that is, brothel keeping. The focus of criminal justice attention on the visible aspects of prostitution has enabled the less visible activities to go virtually unregulated (Matthews, 2005). In 2003, 30 convictions and 4 cautions were secured for living off the earnings of prostitution or exercising control over a prostitute. The same year saw 2,627 convictions and 902 cautions for soliciting or loitering in a public place for the purposes of prostitution (source: Office for Criminal Justice Reform, Home Office).

At the beginning of this chapter, I commented that ASBOs and their use in the policing of prostitution are not particularly new ways of regulating prostitution. ASBOs do provide local authorities and police constabularies with yet another mechanism of control and punishment in their periodic 'clampdowns' on prostitution. As many studies have confirmed, the active policing of prostitution has always been selective and periodic. Although the last 20 years have seen the police working much more closely with outreach organisations and other multi-agency organisations in order to encourage street-working women to work in ways that minimise the difficulties caused to local residents (Matthews, 2005), 'purges' and periods of 'zero tolerance' of street prostitution have also been well-used strategies. Typically, a 'purge' would involve local beat officers and any vice officers (in constabularies with vice squads) being deployed specifically for the purposes of arresting any and all women working in a particular area on a particular night. Phoenix (2001) notes that some 'purges' meant that women were being arrested twice and three times in one evening.

ASBOs have provided the police with a mechanism through which similar ends can be achieved – sudden and dramatic 'clampdowns' that target specific areas and individuals selectively and unevenly. In other words, rather than being a means by which police and local authorities can build on and develop the good relations that multi-agency work often permits, the use of ASBOs targets street-working (not indoors-working) prostitute women (not their clients) in a punitive and repressive fashion. But more than this, ASBOs are based on the notion that the 'real' problem of prostitution is not the poverty that often drives women and locks them into selling sex as a form of economic survival, nor the exploitation that is so endemic in the quasi-legal form of prostitution that is present in the UK. It is based on the notion that the 'real' problem is the distress that prostitution causes to wider communities. The Respect Task Force, which arguably has taken over the work of the Anti-Social Behaviour Unit, makes the following claim:

> Prostitution and kerb crawling cause nuisance and anti-social behaviour and can lead streets and residential areas into decline. Sexual activity from *street sex markets* can take place in empty car parks, play grounds and private gardens, and kerb crawling is often a problem in these areas. *Residential areas* can experience nuisance and disturbance when nearby dwellings are used for prostitution and drug dealing. During a one day count of anti-social behaviour carried out in September 2003 (covering kerb crawling, soliciting, prostitutes cards in telephone boxes, discarded condoms and inappropriate sexual acts), 1,099 reports related to prostitution were recorded, suggesting 274,750 reports per year. (Home Office, 2007; emphasis in original)

Leaving aside the issue that the count itself is open to question (see Matthews and Briggs, Chapter Four in this volume), the claim being made is clear. Prostitution is a particular type of nuisance – it is, by definition, anti-social. The Respect Task Force goes on to state that the anti-social behaviour of prostitution takes the form of noise or arguments (between prostitutes and their clients and between prostitutes and local residents), litter (such as condoms), slowing down of traffic (especially concerning kerb-crawling) and the soliciting of women not in prostitution or men who are not clients. These activities are anti-social because, claims the Respect Task Force, local people 'often have their sleep disturbed' and the general nuisance 'has a degenerative effect, making an area unpleasant and unsafe' and can 'impact on property values and insurance premiums' eventually leading to a spiral of decline. To deal with such problems, the Respect Task Force recommends that enforcement actions are taken against kerb-crawlers and prostitutes. The enforcement actions recommended against prostitutes are prostitutes' cautions, except where the activities of any individual woman are persistent and 'extreme', in which case Anti-Social Behaviour Orders and exclusion orders are deemed more appropriate.

As identified earlier in this chapter, such an approach is not new. The framework of regulation put in place with the 1959 Street Offences Act was framed by very similar understandings of the problem of prostitution and recommended similar interventions (that is, targeted repressive action against street-based sex workers). That said, the introduction of ASBOs has presented an unintended consequence: the reintroduction of imprisonment for prostitution-related offences, albeit through breaches of ASBO conditions rather than soliciting or loitering per se. One of the difficulties of making such an assertion is that neither the Home Office nor local authorities or police constabularies keep records of the types of behaviour for which ASBOs are served. Notwithstanding the lack of official statistics, many multi-agency outreach services, as well as other criminal justice agencies (such as the National Association of Probation Officers), have commented that ASBOs are being used to 'clean the streets' of those considered undesirable and that some of the conditions placed on sex workers are unrealistic. So, for example, Rowlands (2005) noted that one of the conditions attached to one sex worker's Anti-Social Behaviour Order in Manchester was that she was prevented from carrying any condoms in the same area where the drugs clinic that was working with her (and providing her with condoms) was based.

Growing intolerance – enforcement plus support?

During the final months of 2006 the bodies of five murdered women were found in the countryside around the relatively small market town of Ipswich. The one thing that all the dead women had in common was that they worked as street-based sex workers. These events focused the world's media attention on Ipswich and on questions about safety and vulnerability of sex workers as well as national and local strategies for dealing with the 'problems' of prostitution. Some four months after the discovery of the last of the dead women, Ipswich's Crime and Disorder Reduction Partnership published its prostitution strategy (Ipswich CDRP, 2007), in which it highlighted as the main objective removing street prostitution from Ipswich altogether. Its own strategy was developed in accordance with the dictates and recommendations laid out in *A coordinated prostitution strategy and responses to* Paying the price (Home Office, 2006). Therein it is recommended that the aims of any prostitution strategy are to disrupt sex markets – especially street-based prostitution – to develop routes out of prostitution for individuals involved, to reduce all forms of sexual exploitation and to ensure safety and justice for communities 'blighted' by the problems of street-based prostitution. On first reading, the Ipswich Street Prostitution Strategy, like *A coordinated prostitution strategy*, is difficult to critique. Ipswich's strategy has five main objectives:

1 to monitor street prostitution in Ipswich in order that all agencies are aware of the difficulties faced by street workers and communities so that appropriate resources can be developed and targeted;
2 to develop routes out of prostitution for individual women using a 'proactive' case management approach;
3 to disrupt the demand for street-based sex workers through an enforcement-based approach to kerb-crawlers;
4 to facilitate education and prevention work with young people to ensure that young people are adequately protected against sexual exploitation; and
5 to ensure that there is effective communication between the local authority and local residents regarding the prostitution strategy.

In regard to street-based sex workers, the cornerstone to this strategy, however, is not the development of services and resources for those in prostitution, but rather the integration of support services with enforcement. So, the 'proactive' case management approach to street-based sex workers is one in which the women are informed of and referred to various welfare and support agencies to help address their personal and social welfare problems *at the same time* that various criminal justice responses are made. Thus, for a woman who is identified as soliciting or loitering in Ipswich, she will be told about various support agencies in the locality at the same time that she is given her first prostitutes' caution. The second time that she is identified, she will be 'encouraged' to access the support services and given her second caution. The third time she is seen, she will still continue to be encouraged to access the support services, at the same time as being arrested and charged with soliciting or loitering. On the fourth time that she is identified as soliciting or loitering, she will be arrested and charged and an ASBO on conviction will be applied for. In this respect, one of the significant developments in prostitution policy in the UK within the last decade has been the official shift away from tolerating the exchange of sex for money, to an explicit abolitionist agenda (that is, abolishing prostitution).

One of the ironies of how ASBOs are being used to 'help' women out of prostitution has its roots in the shifting official constructions of the problem of prostitution and in particular the recognition of the violence and exploitation that many women in prostitution experience. Earlier in the chapter I traced one official construction: that of prostitution being a problem of public nuisance. In this section I put the use of ASBOs to police prostitution in a new context: that of constructing the problem of prostitution as being one of the victimisation of women. Conceptualising the problem of prostitution in such a manner creates an imperative for action, and the action that is recommended is a greater use of welfarist-based interventions – not as an alternative to criminal justice sanctions, but backed by the full range of criminal justice sanctions. This construction is made explicit in two of the most formative documents in prostitution policy of recent times: *Paying the price* (Home Office, 2004) and *A coordinated prostitution strategy* (Home Office, 2006). Together these documents shape current practice and provide, arguably, a new framework for thinking about prostitution, based not on tolerance, but on intolerance, of prostitution, of street work and ultimately of many sex workers themselves.

Paying the price and *A coordinated strategy* regularly repeat that the 'problems' that need tackling are:

1 the exploitation of women and children;
2 trafficking of individuals for commercial sexual exploitation;
3 the ways in which debt and drug addiction trap individuals into prostitution; and

4 the links between drug markets, serious and organised crime and prostitution.

Throughout both documents there are constant references to 'pimps', 'traffickers', 'dealers', 'sexual abusers', 'coercers' and a host of other hyper-masculine criminal men. These references are important because they form part of the 'explanation' for women's involvement in prostitution that underpins the reforms. This explanation is one in which the poverty, the constrained social and economic difficulties that women experience and the ways in which women make choices to be involved in prostitution are rendered invisible and irrelevant. This is despite the nearly two centuries of research on women's involvement in prostitution in the UK that highlights the ways in which women do often choose to sell sex but that their choices are constrained by the shattering and aggregate effects of poverty, abuse, homelessness and housing problems, drug and alcohol difficulties *and* the desire to be independent and secure some type of financial and economic stability. Instead, official understandings of prostitution define it as a public nuisance and, when it is not, almost entirely in relation to the misdeeds of criminal men. And it is these criminal men's presence that contributes to the understanding of prostitution as causing an even wider community problem – that is, the very destruction of local communities:

> Prostitution undermines public order and creates a climate
> in which more serious crime can flourish. Street prostitution
> is often associated with local drug markets, bringing Class
> A drugs and gun culture to local communities. (Home
> Office, 2004: 74)

Contemporary official policy draws on the stereotype of a prostitute-victim. In policy documents, doubt is cast about any expression of choice on the part of the women:

> Debt and drug addiction play a major part in driving
> people into prostitution as a survival activity. They are
> also significant factors, along with the threat of violence
> from pimps/partners, in making it difficult to leave. Those
> involved in prostitution can be particularly difficult to reach,
> claiming that prostitution is their choice and that they don't
> want to leave – through a combination of fear, the process of
> normalisation or in an effort to maintain their dignity. While

preventative work at an early age is important we must also
work to address the safety of the thousands already trapped
by debt and drug addiction. (Home Office, 2004: 55)

The casting of doubt on any expression of choice or voluntarism on
the part of the women is not new. It echoes Victorian concerns with
the 'White Slave Trade' and more importantly forms the basis of the
guidance on dealing with young people in prostitution as victims of
sexual abuse and exploitation, in the first instance (Department of
Health/Home Office, 2000). Perversely, though, framing 'the problem'
of prostitution in terms of the victimisation of women puts in place the
conditions for increased levels of regulation and, indeed, criminalisation
of some women in prostitution. This occurs for two reasons: first, the
stereotype of the prostitute-victim is treated as though it is an adequate
explanation; and, second, the enforcement-plus-support approach to
'victims' in prostitution reinforces the centrality of repressive, coercive
state responses to women who do not leave prostitution – voluntarily.
I will explain each of these in turn.

In *Paying the price* and *A coordinated strategy*, individuals in prostitution
are seen as victims because they do not voluntarily consent to sell
sex. They are victims because something or someone else has forced
or compelled them. Put another way, policy defines consent and
voluntarism as the capacity to make a different choice than to be
involved in prostitution – or to choose not to work in prostitution. The
key problem that policy now addresses is therefore to create the situation
in which women make their own choice to leave prostitution.

While such an understanding is certainly attractive, it contradicts
ethnographic research that argues that women do make choices, albeit
not in conditions of their own choosing (Phoenix, 2001; Sanders,
2005). The experiences of these women plainly do not fit the model
of explanation framing current moves towards intolerance of the sex
trade on the grounds of protection. So, while many street-working
women suffer some form of victimisation and exploitation, they are
not all victims waiting to be saved by the police or other agencies.
Many are just poor women struggling to survive.

As indicated in the example of Ipswich's own prostitution strategy,
the enforcement-plus-support approach buttresses the centrality of
criminal justice sanctions in the regulation of prostitution. This is a
result of the very demarcation between victims and offenders that
is at the heart of current policy. This is an approach in which, unless
there is the presence of a 'pimp' or other such controlling man, the
responsibility for involvement in prostitution is placed solely within

poor choices made by the individual, in which the question of necessity simply does not appear:

> The current offence of loitering or soliciting is a very low-level offence and, as such, the court will usually only consider imposing a fine. This is said to have very little deterrent effect and does not address the underlying causes of the offending behaviour. To rectify this situation, the Government intends to publish proposals for legislative reform to provide a penalty specifically tailored to the needs of men and women in prostitution. The intention will be for the courts to be able to order an appropriate package of interventions to address the causes of the offending behaviour where that behaviour is persistent. (Home Office, 2006: 37)

> Following from the review, it was concluded that the introduction of a co-ordinated strategy for prostitution would reduce the risks associated with prostitution and would also reduce many of the costs currently associated with prostitution. The implementation of a prostitution strategy will ensure that in every area where prostitution is an issue, a *coherent and holistic response* will be available to reduce the numbers creating the demand for a sex market, and to provide routes out to support those already involved in prostitution. Enforcement without support is not only ineffective in the longer term, but can place those in prostitution in even greater danger (Home Office, 2005: 7; emphasis added)

In practice, this has meant a variety of interventions, which include: voluntary self-referrals to outreach programmes; the use of civil Anti-Social Behaviour Orders and Intervention Orders by the police and local authorities compelling women into drug treatment or other treatment programmes (breach of either of which constitutes the possibility of a prison sentence of up to five years); pre-charge diversion in which individuals are referred to drug intervention programmes; conditional discharges; mandatory drug testing and compulsory attendance at drug intervention programmes following charge; as well as the full range of ordinary criminal justice sanctions following repeated conviction. The aim is clear:

Under this staged approach those women (and men) who respond to informal referrals and seek help from support services to leave prostitution, and those who engage with the CJIT (Criminal Justice Integrated Team) workers to receive treatment and other support, *may* avoid further criminalisation. However, for those individuals who, for whatever reason, continue to be involved in street prostitution, the criminal justice system will respond with rehabilitative intervention to reduced re-offending and to protect local communities. (Home Office, 2006: 39; emphasis added)

In the final analysis, then, coercive criminal justice responses are justified not only in terms of reducing the 'public nuisance' of prostitution (as before) but also to 'help', or force, women into making better choices. The best choice is, simply, to exit prostitution. In this context, ASBOs provide a potent mechanism through which local authorities and police constabularies can continue to clamp down on the activities of those most vulnerable in prostitution – street-based sex workers.

Such an increased level of coercive measures does not necessarily ensure that fewer women sell sex from the streets. Instead, as indicated in the Home Office's own evaluation of enforcement measures, 'crackdowns' on prostitution (in the name of protection or in the name of public nuisance) often result in geographical and temporal displacement. Women simply find other, perhaps less safe, places to work or wait for the purges and crackdowns to end before returning to the streets (Hester and Westmarland, 2004).

Conclusion

At the beginning of this chapter I indicated that, in regard to prostitution, the introduction and use of ASBOs is not particularly new or innovative and, more, that they signify a shift in official attitude from one that tolerated selling sex – so long as such activities did not cause or constitute a public nuisance – towards a growing intolerance of the sex trade, on the grounds of victimisation and, indirectly, of street-based sex workers. The irony contained at the heart of contemporary prostitution policy, however, is that, in order to better protect the vulnerable, harsher and more repressive measures taken against sex workers are warranted. What I have not provided is a detailed account of the levels of victimisation, or indeed the endemic poverty that marks the lives of most street-based sex workers. This is partly because such accounts are well documented elsewhere, but more because the objective of this chapter was to place the use of Anti-Social Behaviour Orders and the entire notion of what is considered 'anti-social' about prostitution in the wider context of prostitution policy. Further, I have not provided the reader with detailed figures about the numbers of sex workers given ASBOs or the statistics on the breaches of those orders. Because there are no requirements to record the grounds on which ASBOs are given, such statistics are of limited value anyway, as they are likely to be highly unreliable. Instead, I have tried to indicate that the introduction and use of ASBOs in the context of prostitution has a profound symbolic significance. Despite the rhetoric of help and support offered to street-based sex workers, and despite the fact that selling sex is not illegal, current prostitution policy is little more than institutionalised intolerance. Street-based sex workers *will be helped* to exit prostitution on pain of increased levels of control through Anti-Social Behaviour Orders and increased criminalisation.

Note
[1] The Wolfenden Report was implemented through the 1959 Street Offences Act. However, the 1956 Sexual Offences Act also consolidated some prostitution-related offences and made it illegal to control the activities of, live on the immoral earnings of or procure a prostitute. As will be seen later in the chapter, these provisions protecting women in prostitution are not policed at the same rate or level.

References

Church, S., Henderson, M., Barnard, M. and Hart, G. (2001) 'Violence by clients towards female prostitutes in different work settings: questionnaire survey', *British Medical Journal*, vol 332, pp 524–5.

Department of Health/Home Office (2000) *Safeguarding children in prostitution*, London: HMSO.

Edwards, S. (1997) *Sex, gender and the legal process*, London: Blackstone Press Limited.

Hester, M. and Westmarland, N. (2004) *Tackling street prostitution: An holistic approach*, Home Office Research Study 279, London: Home Office.

Home Office (Committee on Homosexual Offences and Prostitution) (1957) *Report of the Committee on Homosexual Offences and Prostitution*, (the Wolfenden Report), London: HMSO.

Home Office (2004) *Paying the price: A consultation document*, London: The Stationery Office.

Home Office (2005) 'Regulatory impact assessment: a coordinated strategy for prostitution', (available at www.homeoffice.gov.uk/documents/cons-paying-the-price/Paying-the-Price-RIA.pdf?view=Binary).

Home Office (2006) *A coordinated prostitution strategy and a summary of responses to* Paying the price, London: The Stationery Office.

Home Office (2007) 'Prostitution and kerb-crawling', (www.respect.gov.uk/members/article.aspx?id=7662, last updated 30 April 2007).

Ipswich CDRP (Crime and Disorder Reduction Partnership) (2007) *Ipswich Street Prostitution Strategy 2007–2012*, Ipswich: Ipswich CDRP.

Matthews, R. (2005) 'Policing prostitution: ten years on', *British Journal of Criminology*, vol 45, pp 877–95.

May, T., Edmunds, M. and Hough, M. (1999) *Street business: The links between sex and drug markets*, Police Research Series, Paper 118, London: Home Office.

McLeod, E. (1982) *Women working: Prostitution now*, London: Croom Helm.

O'Neill, M. (2001) *Prostitution and feminism*, Cambridge: Polity Press.

Phoenix, J. (2001) *Making sense of prostitution*, London: Palgrave.

Rowlands, M. (2005) 'The state of ASBO Britain – the rise of intolerance', European Civil Liberties Network Essays no 9, (available at www.ecln.org/essays/essay-9.pdf).

Sanders, T. (2005) *Sex work: A risky business*, Cullompton: Willan Publishing.

Weeks, J. (1985) *Sexuality and its discontents: Meanings, myths and modern sexualities*, London: Routledge and Kegan Paul.

Part Four
Anti-ASBO: criticising the ASBO industry

SEVENTEEN

'ASBOmania'[1]

Shami Chakrabarti and Jago Russell (Liberty)

> For eight years I have battered the criminal
> justice system to get it to change. And it was only
> when we started to introduce special anti-social
> behaviour laws, we made a real difference. And now I
> understand why. The system itself is the problem. We
> are trying to fight 21st century crime – anti-social
> behaviour, drug dealing, binge drinking, organised
> crime – with 19th century methods, as if we still
> lived in the time of Dickens. The whole of our system
> starts from the proposition that its duty is to protect
> the innocent from being wrongly convicted. Don't
> misunderstand me. That must be the duty of any
> criminal justice system. But surely our primary duty
> should be to allow law-abiding people to live in safety.
> It doesn't mean abandoning human rights. It means
> deciding whose come first. (Blair, 2005)

Tony Blair's meteoric career is well documented. His most significant brief before ascending to the leadership of his party, and then the country, was that of Home Secretary Michael Howard's shadow. It was then that the famous 'tough on crime, tough on the causes of crime' slogan was first coined. It was then that Mr Blair began developing one of the most significant elements of his phenomenal political success.

New Labour's belief in social justice (as greater equality in opportunities and outcomes is now so often described) would no longer be a bar to aggressive law and order policy. Quite the contrary, it would be the greatest justification for it. All sections of society might fear and loathe crime and nuisance but, the argument went, it was often the poorest and most vulnerable who were most exposed to it. Thus, even that notoriously authoritarian Conservative might be outflanked in a key, vote-winning comfort zone.

In the ten years of New Labour under Tony Blair, law and order policy has been characterised by radical extensions of summary powers to police and local authorities to 'take on the wrongdoers' and tackle 'anti-social behaviour'. Whitehall departments have published documents entitled *Delivering simple, speedy, summary justice* (DCA, 2006) and *Rebalancing the criminal justice system in favour of the law-abiding majority* (Home Office, 2006).

The Anti-Social Behaviour Order or ASBO has been the flagship measure of this aggressive law and order policy, and the UK has been in the grip of what Alvaro Gil-Robles (the Council of Europe's Commissioner for Human Rights) has described as 'Asbomania' (Gil-Robles, 2005: para 113). Over eight years since the ASBO was first created, it seems that they are being used now more than ever before (but now – more frequently added to other criminal penalties, see Burney, Chapter Seven in this volume) (Metropolitan Police Authority, 2007: para 35).

This approach to law and order has been founded on the view that traditional criminal justice values, born in this country, exported around the world – equality of arms, the presumption of innocence and the proportionate and dispassionate meting out of punishment by the state, those values that preceded the post-war universal human rights consensus and became so central to it – simply will not do. They are neither fundamental and inalienable nor even potentially expendable. Instead, their disposal is a matter of social duty and considerable urgency.

The presumption of innocence, the golden thread, the paradigm of natural justice, is considered too cumbersome. The system built upon it is too slow, expensive and uncertain in outcome. As Prime Minister Blair told us repeatedly, 'the concern of a 19th century criminal justice system was too many of the innocent being convicted' (Blair, 2006). But in the 21st century, the greater concern is that too many of the guilty go free.

The evidence base for such a bold contention has never been made clear. In particular, is it based on actual outcomes or on public perceptions? Nonetheless, once the conclusion is settled, that natural justice (or fair trial procedure) protects the individual wrongdoer instead of his past and future victims, the unworthy from the worthy poor, we are a short hop from placing natural and social justice at direct odds with each other as societal values. Criminal lawyers and judges are caricatured as vested interests who were fiddling while Rome or Swindon burned. A new, communitarian view of criminal justice is born.

Traditional fair trial principles were not always seen as running counter to social justice or community protection. Above the entrance to the Old Bailey (our central criminal court, erected on the site of the infamous Newgate prison in 1907) we can still see the famous inscription:'Defend the children of the poor and punish the wrongdoer.' But who are the 'children of the poor' encapsulated in this motto? Are they, as some may seek to argue, simply the victims of crime, seeking the protection and redress of the criminal court? That is certainly one possible interpretation of a phrase that so obviously juxtaposes this vulnerable class of humanity against the perpetrators of crime. Alternatively, do we take the call to 'defend' quite literally, so that the 'children of the poor' are simply defendants or those who lack the means to defend themselves?

There is, in fact, a far more satisfactory way of interpreting the inspirational slogan. For in 1907, as in 2007, the 'children of the poor' are especially prominent among victims and defendants – of both the innocent and the guilty varieties. Indeed, during a lifetime, or even only a lunchtime, a person can in fact be in all three categories.

This is one of the greatest difficulties with the Prime Minister's bold assertions about 'whose human rights come first'. How would he distinguish the decent majority from the criminal minority, even if the categories were hermetically sealed? Do the bad guys always wear hoodies? Generations of jurists struggled with this enterprise and, notwithstanding their noblest endeavours and aspirations, sometimes sent innocents to the gallows or prison. The Prime Minister's answer was far too simple and as old as the hills:'I can't physically come onto your street and stop the anti-social behaviour. But I can give the police the powers to do it. They know who the troublemakers are.'[2]

When one moves into the territory of collective liability or guilt by association, as political slogans about 'bad parenting' and 'problem families' appear to do, determinations of guilt become even more perilous. By contrast, the Old Bailey inscription, like the system it represents, promotes the best representation of justice for all, with the aim of punishing not the usual suspect or sometime offender, but the true perpetrator of a present and particular crime. This is the justice that both victim and defendant are entitled to. It is an exacting standard based not on reputation or likelihood but, as nearly as possible, on certainty of guilt (and usually guilt of mind as well as action).

There is no question that the standard is incredibly exacting and notably different from that applied when private persons bring their own disputes before the civil courts. Why so exacting? Why so different? It seems necessary to revisit the very role of criminal justice in civilised society.

The whole of our social existence is a series of relationships, at home, with our friends, neighbours, associates and others. Some are of our choosing and others not. They are long and short, simple and complex, simultaneous and sequential, evenly balanced or asymmetric in nature. To a greater or lesser extent, modern civilisations regulate these relationships with legal ties and obligations that, for the most part, seem almost invisible to the naked eye.

Of course, progressive societies tend to give particular regard to power imbalances and broader aspirations in the framing of such laws. Often these relationships generate conflict or breakdown, with or without fault on either side. Where parties are unwilling or unable to reach their own resolution and have the means to seek the state's adjudication, they will come to the civil courts for redress. Sometimes there is simple uncertainty about mutual obligation. More often, there may be a sense of having been wronged by another person or party.

But some wrongs are thought to be special, so grave for the individual 'victim' or so counter to wider societal interests, that to breach the obligation and wrong one's neighbour is to wrong the whole of society by departing from its non-negotiable core. This is the paradigm of crime, properly so called and framed. It is not best reflected or advanced by a whole host of minor and regulatory offences that have mushroomed in recent years. The advent of anti-social behaviour law may be the greatest blurring of the boundaries of civil and criminal procedure. But this may have seemed less of a sin after regulatory law (in a whole host of public policy areas) had so effectively blurred the conceptual boundaries between civil and criminal obligation.

If the gravity of a wrong or danger and societal solidarity with a victim were the only factors, we could have the police bringing defendants to civil courts where legal aid lawyers helped victims conduct their civil cases against the accused.

The ultimate reason for special criminal *procedure* with presumptive innocence at its heart lies in the grave consequences for the accused of criminal conviction. By graver opprobrium and punitive sanction (up to and including imprisonment) for the offender, criminal law is graver. Further, the massive inequality of arms caused both by the baying mob outside the court door and the resources that the state may deploy within it, the risk of abuse and tyranny, cry out for special protection for the criminal accused.

Of course, there were never completely bright lines in terms of opprobrium or consequence for civil and criminal wrongdoers. Few baying mobs assemble for parking offenders and some civil suits result in personal bankruptcy. Those who breach injunctions have long faced prison for contempt. Had the post-1997 philosophy been framed or applied differently, anti-social behaviour laws might be just another such minor blurring, a hybrid attuned to deal with serious nuisance or petty crime. Instead, whatever the original intentions, and notwithstanding the House of Lords' decision in the *McCann* case of 2003 (regarding the standards of proof to apply in ASBO cases),[3] the reality of ASBOmania in 2007 is reflected in the Prime Minister's statements and the history of its application: a new mutant strain of criminal law.

But the traditional process of criminal justice should not be left without reflecting upon the Prime Minister's exasperations with it. Whatever the efficiencies of modern technology and management, criminal due process is slow, or at least slower than the alternatives, and, in particular, slower than arbitrary or police justice. The high standard of protection for the accused inevitably requires time and expense.

Further, both our legal tradition and the human rights values it protects make for a necessarily adversarial system requiring an inevitable additional pressure or even anguish on the part of victims whose veracity is to be scrutinised and judged in the process. In the context of crime of all degrees of seriousness, an individual victim may perfectly rationally decide to stay away from court, thus allowing the wrongdoer's escape from justice and the wider community's loss of future protection.

The system will invariably lead to some acquittals, not least because of presumptive innocence and the evidential protections surrounding it. This makes for a potentially long and expensive process with an uncertain outcome (not an unfamiliar scenario in the context of public services more generally). Uncertainty of outcome is the ultimate strength or weakness of the system, depending upon your world-view. Is it protection from injustice, even tyranny, or a fault on the conveyor belt? Human rights proponents can only have one answer. However, the all-important reality check is the constant facts of an overwhelming majority of criminal defendants pleading guilty and survey after survey suggesting a massive discrepancy between perceived or even reported crime and that which ever reaches the courts.[4]

By contrast the statistics for Anti-Social Behaviour Order applications demonstrate breathtaking certainty of outcome. Of the 1,200 ASBOs applied for in London between April 1999 and December 2005, the courts refused only 40 (Metropolitan Police Authority, 2007).

Finally, from the prime ministerial perspective, the sanctions imposed by the criminal justice system both must be proportionate and inevitably require further state administration and cost. For the most part, and with limited exception, punishment looks to the past rather than the future, to proven deeds rather than future propensity, and may therefore seem particularly unsuited to affecting the future conduct of minor miscreants within the envelope of proportionality.

Of these various concerns, the need to protect immediate victims is most commonly shared by the human rights analysis of the criminal justice system. For too many years it seemed that the necessary procedural protections for an accused were accompanied by an almost gratuitous disregard for the dignity, worth and inevitable vulnerability of witnesses and victims. Procedural and substantive issues around the law of sexual offences were an obvious case in point.

To its credit, the early days of New Labour under Blair produced much complex and valuable work in this area and demonstrated how the recasting of substantive criminal law, and, more importantly, resources and support for victims within the criminal justice system, might improve the victim's experience and encourage participation without undermining the procedural protections of the accused. However, this kind of work is painstaking to conceive and often costly to implement. It lacks the quick fixes and robust rhetoric of summary police justice and community-imposed punishments.

In fairness, it is to be remembered that human rights values bring their own additional concerns with criminal justice as a mechanism of preference for dealing with social problems, particularly in the context of the young, for the severity of stigma, opprobrium and sanction that comes with criminal law is not always the best way to improve the life chances and future societal participation of the convicted offender. Criminal procedure may provide Rolls Royce protection for the innocent, but criminal sentencing has never provided the equivalent in rehabilitation for the guilty with which wider social policy must be concerned.

Further, the rush to criminal or even civil law can be an unnecessarily harsh, formal and dehumanising process for all concerned, particularly in the context of minor offending involving neighbours, the young and the otherwise vulnerable. Hence the proper continuation of informal resolution of minor disputes in even the most advanced societies and, in the context of our own society, the growth of mediation-type mechanisms.

So much for traditional criminal justice. What of its mutant cousin, the 'battered criminal justice system' of which the Prime Minister boasts?

The first observation to make about 'anti-social behaviour' is the sheer breadth of its definition. At its lowest, the statutory definition provided in section 1 of the 1998 Crime and Disorder Act encompasses behaviour 'likely to cause harassment, alarm and distress'. In our informal private dealings with each other, we have long been used to extremely broad and evolving concepts of what is socially welcome, acceptable, inept and anti-social. Tony Blair has described anti-social behaviour legislation as being 'manifestly on the side of the decencies of the majority', 'deliberately echoing some of the moral categories – shame, for example – that were once enforced informally' (Blair, 2006).

Does such breadth and informal evolution make just or good law? The guest who arrives late, hogs the conversation, lights a cigarette without permission in the close proximity of diners or children, proceeds to become drunk and obnoxious, makes an unwelcome pass at his hostess and a swing at his host has undoubtedly engaged in a range of bad behaviour according to cultural norms (depending on the context and times), and certainly within the statutory definition. But exactly how much of this behaviour should be regulated by the law, let alone mediated by police, local authority and court intervention?

Yet it is the sheer breadth and flexibility of the definition that, while worrying its critics, excites its supporters. When asked in a television interview to clarify the parameters of anti-social behaviour, as Minister of State in the Home Office, Hazel Blears replied: 'It means whatever the victim says it means.'

The breadth of the definition is the key to understanding this populist communitarian philosophy that places such absolute trust in both the police and other professionals and seems to have no trouble distinguishing between poor, worthy complainants and false accusers (who, incidentally, have been given ASBOs themselves). It seems completely untroubled by the variety of ways and ease with which people may be 'distressed' by those of another class, race or generation, by those who are irritating rather than threatening (in any objective sense), those who are themselves vulnerable or just plain different.

The thinking behind this definition has become the driver for a range of summary police powers. In 2001, for example, Penalty Notices for Disorder were introduced, enabling the police to impose fixed fines of up to £80 on those involved in low-level anti-social behaviour. They are described on the Home Office website as tools 'to tackle low-level anti-social behaviour and to reduce police bureaucracy'. In practice, they have sanctioned against foolish but harmless drunken jibes – an Oxford student who called a police horse 'gay' – as well as legitimate political protests – pro-hunting campaigners selling or just wearing 'Bollocks to Blair' T-shirts. They have also provided convenient tools to enable police forces to meet sanction and detection targets set by central government.

However, the new paradigm (in both breadth and ripeness for replication), the law to end all laws, appears to be the Anti-Social

Behaviour Order or ASBO. The ASBO model has been replicated in Parenting Orders (ASBOs for parents) and the more constructive-sounding Individual Support Order (ISO) – constructive sounding, that is, until one realises that failure to take up the 'support' offered is punishable by a fine of up to £1,000. More recently, it has also been replicated in measures designed to tackle serious crime, the Gangster ASBO.

The ASBO is, of course, a 'civil' order made on the application of the police, local authorities, registered public landlords and possibly any one of a range of other authorities designated by statutory instrument. For the most part it will be made in the magistrates' court sitting in its civil capacity, although it may also be made in other contexts, including that of criminal sentencing. The court must be satisfied to a high standard (in effect, the criminal one) that the individual has engaged in past anti-social behaviour, but then has a freer judgment about whether the prohibitions contained in the order are necessary for the purposes of protecting people in the locality (not specifically defined) from further anti-social acts.

The conditions imposed under the ASBO are often extremely vague, broad and significant in impact over an offender's life. Breach is a serious criminal offence carrying a sentence of up to five years in custody, although the breach proceedings (if not the proceedings that set the conditions themselves) take the form of a conventional criminal trial.

Before our highest courts and in official parliamentary pronouncements, the government speaks of ASBOs as preventative rather than punitive. As Professor Andrew Ashworth has so brilliantly described, the result is the subversion of the human rights standards that apply in the criminal context (Ashworth, 2004). As a result, the application for an ASBO involves the more flexible civil procedure, crucially allowing a great deal of hearsay (including police and local authority witness statements) to replace the classic need for the live evidence and cross-examination of possibly reluctant witnesses and victims. ASBOs can be obtained on the basis of gossip and rumours that the defendant cannot interrogate.

The language of prevention and reform does not, however, feature prominently in the government's public rhetoric about ASBOs and in fact runs directly counter to the Prime Minister's political pronouncements about being 'tough' on low-level crime and anti-social behaviour. This, the public face of ASBOs, is closer to the reality. Over time, the new anti-social behaviour justice system delivers swifter, easier and harsher accusation, proof and punishment.

Talk of prevention and reform is even less convincing when the ASBO model is applied in the context of serious crime. The Serious

Crime Bill, working its way through Parliament at the time of writing, would create Serious Crime Prevention Orders or 'Gangster ASBOs'. These have been described by Ministers as 'tough new powers to crack down on serious and organised crime ... to make life more difficult for serious criminals by disrupting their activities in both big and small ways, making it harder for them to cause damage or defraud innocent people' (Home Office, 2007). Notwithstanding this tough talk, the government expects the courts to be convinced that the Gangster ASBO, like its predecessor the ASBO, is preventative rather than punitive and can therefore be imposed without the full rigours of criminal due process. As the parliamentary Joint Committee on Human Rights has pointed out, such an argument is far from convincing when the behaviour in question is self-evidently of a criminal nature, when a Gangster ASBO can impose such severe restrictions on individual freedoms and when it can last for up to five years and be renewed indefinitely.[5]

In 1998 ASBOs, by contrast, may just have seemed like a possible mechanism for avoiding a criminal conviction for the first-time offender. They may also have seemed more suited to affecting the future conduct of minor miscreants than criminal punishment.

Today, however, it is clear that ASBOs have in fact operated as a short cut into criminal convictions rather than a way of avoiding them. Up to December 2003, 42% of all ASBOs were breached, with 55% of breaches resulting in custody.[6] This suggests that, like the traditional criminal justice system, ASBOs are very good at achieving what has never been this government's stated objective – namely, higher levels of incarceration. Even in relation to those ASBOed for recognisable low-level crime, the five-year breach penalty can lead to the inadvertent raising of custody tariffs for what was originally very low-level offending.

ASBOs are also often accompanied by wide-scale local publicity by way of local authority leafleting campaigns and press releases. Indeed, Home Office guidance, which is a greater guide to the dangers of ASBOmania than the legislation, positively encourages this. The justification for this 'naming and shaming' is of course that the policing of injunctions contained in an ASBO, quite often including wide-scale restrictions on the offender's movements, requires a great deal of community vigilance. It is difficult to identify as 'criminal' behaviour that, but for the terms of an ASBO, is entirely lawful. However, stories of reprisal attacks against ASBOed families (including innocent and vulnerable relatives of offenders) highlight the fine line between vigilance and vigilantism in this context. In 2006 a scheme was launched in East London whereby CCTV camera feeds will connect directly to the television screens of certain members of the local community to aid their do-it-yourself monitoring of those serving ASBOs.

ASBOs involve less central government involvement, not to mention expense, than the criminal process. The Prime Minister aspires to a day when the community rather than the state defines and polices unacceptable behaviour:

> One day when I am asked by someone whose neighbourhood is plagued with anti-social behaviour; or whose local school is failing; or whose hospital is poor, 'what are you going to do about it', I want to be able to reply: 'We have given you the resources. We have given you the powers. Now tell me what you are going to do about it.' (Blair, 2005)

The famous Home Office gaffe, the unfortunate slogan 'stop moaning and take action', is perhaps not too far from the truth.

One can certainly see obvious attractions of the ASBO model. Specific victims are under less pressure to come forward and can be replaced by confident police or local residents who have knocked on a variety of local doors before coming up with the desired case against the troublemaker. Home Office guidance is careful to advise that court files be kept short and to the point in order to minimise the risk of challenge by defence lawyers (a far cry from the onerous disclosure obligations of criminal due process). The whole system is capable of being cheaper, faster, more certain in outcome and flexible in content than conventional criminal law.

For the human rights proponent, in addition to the comfort of victims, ASBOs have the potential advantage of avoiding a criminal conviction for the first-time offender. However, whatever the good intentions, after eight years on the statute book, the natural and social justice and constitutional concerns about how ASBOs have been designed and applied are almost endless.

The breathtaking breadth of behaviour deemed anti-social, as well as the conditions imposed, has blurred the constitutional divide between legislation and enforcement to the point where different 'penal codes' may, in effect, apply in different communities or in respect of different individuals. Smoking may be profoundly unhealthy and fast becoming socially unacceptable, indeed unlawful in enclosed public spaces, but is it right that, without national parliamentary debate of any kind, local authorities and police should have the ability to use ASBOs to criminalise the practice of smoking on public streets?

This is not fanciful, in a context where ASBOs have been made so as to prohibit people from begging, swearing, speaking sarcastically, wearing certain types of clothing or not enough of it. Inevitably, these 'personalised penal codes' (as described by Gil-Robles [2005]) create a grave risk of arbitrary, discriminatory and unjust treatment. It is, to say the least, difficult to reconcile ASBOs with the most basic tenet of the rule of law – the idea that we are all, from the child growing up on a council estate in south London to the Prime Minister in Number 10, subject to the same law.

The lack of definition and procedural protection, combined with police and local authority involvement, also gives little regard to constitutional concerns about how such broad powers may be used and abused by accident or design by central or local government in years to come. One wonders whether Tony Blair can have stopped to think how a local authority controlled by a political party of the far right might choose to exercise such powers.

The breadth of ASBO conditions, combined with the ease with which they may be obtained, blurs the civil and criminal law not just in a way that causes legalistic, theoretical or aesthetic distaste but in a way that offends against the presumption of innocence and makes injustice more likely. This is not to say that an ASBO has never been properly or proportionately framed against an offender. But we must not forget the many ways in which the innocent and the vulnerable have been swept up with the guilty.

What of the kids with ADHD or Tourette syndrome who are banned from swearing and set up for inevitable failure? The suicidal woman banned from bridges? What of the mentally ill and the homeless banned from begging under pain of criminal sanction? The examples multiply by the day and can no longer be completely ignored. When did these people move from the category of those worthy to those unworthy of respect? In an analysis that respects human rights, such a distinction is both unnecessary and wrong.

Finally, one must ask the ultimate question of whether the move to summary, arbitrary and loosely defined community justice is really improving the flavour of our society. Does it make a greater or lesser contribution to a culture of respect than traditional criminal justice principles? It is our view that anti-social behaviour laws have to date been, at best, neutral and, at worst, positively damaging in this regard and that it may be time for a new prime minister to pause for reflection over the way in which criminal justice solutions to complex and perennial social problems have enjoyed such apparent political primacy over education, health and housing under a reforming government.

Notes

[1] This chapter is an expanded version of a paper presented at a British Institute of Human Rights lunchtime lecture by Shami Chakrabarti on 10 January 2006. The original version is available at www. liberty-human-rights.org.uk/publications/3-articles-and-speeched/ asbomania-bihr.PDF.

[2] *Sun*, 6 January 2006.

[3] *Clingham v Kensington and Chelsea LBC*; *R (McCann) v Crown Court of Manchester* [2003] 1 AC 787 (see www.parliament.the-stationery-office. com/pa/ld200102/ldjudgmt/jd021017/cling-1.htm).

[4] In 2005, for example, fewer than 4% of the 5.6 million recorded crimes ended up with a contested trial in the courts.

[5] 'Legislative Scrutiny: Fifth Progress Report', HL 91/HC 490, 2006–07, para 1.13.

[6] Up to December 2005, 47% of all ASBOs were breached (57% for juveniles).

References

Ashworth, A. (2004) 'Social control and "anti-social behaviour": the subversion of human rights?', *Law Quarterly Review*, vol 120, pp 263–91.

Blair, T. (2005) Speech to Labour Party Conference, September.

Blair, T. (2006) Speech on the Respect Action Plan in Bristol, 10 January.

DCA (Department for Constitutional Affairs) (2006) *Delivering simple, speedy, summary justice*, London: DCA.

Gil-Robles, A. (2005) *Report by Mr Alvaro Gil-Robles, Commissioner for Human Rights, on his visit to the United Kingdom, 4th–12th November 2004*, CommDH (2005)6, Strasbourg: Council of Europe.

Home Office (2006) *Rebalancing the criminal justice system in favour of the law-abiding majority: Cutting crime, reducing reoffending and protecting the public*, London: Home Office.

Home Office (2007) 'New powers to tackle serious crime: Home Office publishes Serious Crime Bill', Press release, 17 January.

Metropolitan Police Authority (2007) *The use of Anti-Social Behaviour Orders across London*, London: Metropolitan Police Authority.

EIGHTEEN

The responsibility of respecting justice: an open challenge to Tony Blair's successors

Dawn E. Stephen

> So these times challenge us to ask – what kind of
> society do we together want to become?
> (Brown, 2006)

Writing this chapter in the week Tony Blair finally announced his resignation as prime minister, it seems appropriate to reflect upon this vital question posed by his immediate successor, not least in respect of the concluding note of humility in Blair's resignation speech, in which he offered his apologies 'for the times I have fallen short' (Blair, 2007). It is to one of the key areas where his stewardship arguably 'fell short' that this chapter will turn, for Brown's question cannot be answered without looking at the society Britain has become. The imperative to make this assessment is spurred by the recent UNICEF report that revealed the profound malaise permeating the lived experiences of young people in contemporary Britain (UNICEF, 2007). This seems not to be a society in which young people share a sense of inclusion, of well-being, or of social justice. Despite the optimism that pervaded New Labour's election in 1997, and some unquestioned successes of his premiership, Blair's detrimental legacy is a society seemingly less tolerant, more condemnatory and less just than when he entered Downing Street. This chapter, therefore, will examine profound deficiencies in the bequest of 'respect' by responding to Blair's own challenge, announced in his speech to accompany the launch of the Respect Action Plan, for a 'genuine intellectual debate about the nature of liberty' (Blair, 2006) to which few have yet responded, despite the passage of time.

Notwithstanding, there were some grounds to believe that such political debate might come when the Leader of the Opposition, David Cameron, seemed to promote a greater culture of tolerance towards young people in his 'hug a hoodie' speech:

> We've got to be optimistic about young people, otherwise we'll forever be dealing with the short-term symptoms instead of the long-term causes. And I think there are three things that are vital if we're to make all our communities safe and give every young person the chance they deserve. The first thing is to recognise that we'll never get the answers right unless we understand what's gone wrong. (Cameron, 2006)

There was a sense of optimism here that the climate might change in approaches to young people, but sadly there was insufficient momentum, or commitment, to sustain a more humane approach to understanding young people's problems. 'Understanding what has gone wrong' does not involve greater scrutiny of young people but, instead, draws attention to exploring 'what has gone wrong' with society and, especially, how the Respect Agenda is actively undermining the foundations of respect in many important ways. Notwithstanding the sentiments expressed above, Cameron's subsequent calls to restore respect through his proposed 'revolution in responsibility' and by privileging 'civility' and 'responsibility' towards others as the means of reinvigorating our social bonds (eg Cameron, 2007) tend to suggest that the obsession with 'respect' is unlikely to diminish with Blair's departure. Indeed, no one can deny that this is the kind of society within which we all aspire to live, but we must move beyond such rhetoric to explore the ways in which, through misguided attempts at enforcing respect, 'tolerance, acceptance and common decency' are being eroded without consideration 'of the consequences' as expressed lucidly here:

> [I]t is unrealistic to suppose that legal restrictions and criminal punishments can increase the number of people who genuinely love their neighbours as themselves.... As the number of laws that cannot be realistically enforced increases, so does the risk that a growing number of people will lose their respect for, and fidelity to, the rule of law more generally. Extending law's scope to spheres of life in which it is likely to be practically pointless may be only another way to weaken public confidence in the legal system as a whole. But even when criminalising what is morally objectionable (or legally requiring what is morally mandatory) *would* make an appreciable positive difference in the way people actually do behave, the (moral) *costs*

incurred in carrying the legal enforcement scheme out are
in certain cases likely to be so great as to overshadow the
prospective benefits. (Kuflik, 2005: 186).

Later reminding us that 'in a free society people will *not completely agree*
on *what is morally* right or wrong in the first place' (Kuflik, 2005: 197;
emphasis in original), Kuflik's paper provides an important note of
caution to the effect that politicians' persistent attempts to legislate for
a climate of greater respect will more than likely serve to undermine
respect in the long run, an outcome diametrically opposed to the
government's stated intentions on its upbeat website:[1]

- It's about nurturing and, where needed, enforcing
  a modern culture of respect, which the majority of
  people want.
- It's about showing tolerance, acceptance and common
  decency towards the people around us – our family,
  friends and peers, people who are older or younger
  than us, people from different walks of life or who
  follow different cultures or religions.
- It's about being considerate of the consequences of
  our behaviour for others.

The Respect Agenda seeks to promote community order and
security in profoundly insecure times, not least for political authority.
Accordingly, full debate is indeed long overdue for, to date, politicians
have (rather tellingly) failed to present their case beyond, 'the crude
level' of 'populist' measures, as Blair's (2006) commentary demonstrated.
In offering symbolic assurances through populist appeals to 'respect', the
public's concerns are assuaged. Yet, in their misguided attempts to appeal
to the public, politicians have not faced up to the fact that populist
responses have 'in the past, produced unjust, brutal and discriminatory
policy' (Bessant, 2005: 106). Neither have politicians acknowledged
that 'ill-conceived and discriminatory legislation' always impacts
disproportionately on the most marginal groups in society (see Thomas,
2003: 1232) and reinforces their sense of exclusion. Trends within the
Respect discourse are certainly indicative of entrenching abandonment
(see Clarke, 2005), not just of some citizens' needs, but of long-held
principles of justice and rights of citizenship. Couched in the rhetoric
of Respect, then, anti-social behaviour measures have extended 'law's
scope' to potentially all 'spheres of life', criminalising, in large part, that
which is 'morally objectionable', or offensive, itself. As Kuflik stresses,

this is a highly subjective and problematic assumption upon which to base both policy and law-making. As a result, the 'moral cost' being paid in pursuit of the communitarian dream is an entrenchment of intolerance and progressive erosion of taken-for-granted liberties, not least those enshrined within the 1998 Human Rights Act.

The politics of Respect, therefore, are not promoting inclusion, security and justice, but instead creating long-term insecurities and injustices, of much greater threat to communities and individuals. Notwithstanding concerns raised by the European Human Rights Commissioner (Gil-Robles, 2005), or by various pronouncements from the civil rights groups Liberty, AsboConcern and asbowatch, findings from one of the earliest evaluations of anti-social behaviour enforcement (Stephen and Squires, 2003) argued that the young people and families subject to Acceptable Behaviour Contracts, rather than punishment and the threat of eviction, needed 'respect' for their human rights, not least respect for their right to 'private and family life' (Article 8), a 'right to education' (Protocol 1, Article 2) and 'right to a fair trial' (Article 6) (see Stephen and Squires, 2004). Moreover, Scraton's (2005) paper identifies further specific breaches of human rights for young people, including: 'separation from parents and the right to family life' (Article 9); 'freedom of expression' (Article 13), 'the protection of privacy' (Article 16); and of key aspects of Article 40 (Scraton, 2005: 12).

Central to the progressive erosion of liberty witnessed since New Labour came to power, especially since the 1998 Crime and Disorder Act and, particularly, following 9/11 and the London bombings of 7 July 2005, are three interrelated developments: the growth of 'comfort legislation directed towards producing or maintaining public confidence' (Thomas, 2003: 1198) in response to real or perceived threats; 'burgeoning modes of repressive governance' (Goldson, 2004: 27); and the further 'criminalisation of social policy' (for example, Squires, 2006; Tisdall, 2006) in which politicians are, as Tombs and Hillyard (2004: 54) contend, 'bereft of the means or inclination to devise social policy responses to social problems' and 'have turned increasingly towards the extension of the criminal justice system and the criminalisation of economically marginalised groups'. These interrelated shifts are not exclusive to Britain alone, but what is perhaps unique to New Labour's world view is the moralistic underpinning of policy responses within which falsely dichotomous portrayals of 'decent law-abiding citizens' and *others* are so heavily apparent (cf Jamieson, 2005). This focus on the real or imaginary other has become an increasingly central aspect of late-modern regulation and control.[2] Criminalising interventions have increasingly replaced traditional Labour concerns for social justice, while conditionality has replaced universality. Nonetheless, the Respect Action Plan aims to 'truly tackle disadvantage' (Home Office, 2006: 3) and offered some welcomed initiatives, such as family support schemes, but these are predicated upon an understanding of support as conditional, as a means of risk management, a point admirably captured by Garland:

> The welfare mode, as well as becoming more muted, has become more conditional, more offence-centred, more risk conscious....The offenders ... are now less likely to be represented in official discourse as socially deprived citizens in need of support. They are depicted instead as culpable, undeserving and somewhat dangerous individuals who must be carefully controlled for the protection of the public and the prevention of further offending. Rather than clients in need of support they are seen as risks who must be managed. (Garland, 2001: 175)

The Respect Agenda offers a common-sense, comforting focus to show the 'law-abiding' public that something is being done to tackle the social malaise eroding their neighbourhoods; culpable individuals and families are targeted, subjected to swift interventions and, thus, contained. Contained only, for there is little sign of how those undeserving *others* are to be reintegrated fully into their communities and society at large, and how sustainable respect will be engendered in the long run. Thus, in accepting short-term and superficial interventions, it is possible to appreciate the real 'respect' the government seeks to foster: a sense of respect for the rule of law in the face of the apparent hopelessness felt by 'law-abiding citizens' arising from a putative 'justice gap':

> Critics need to answer the following question: if the criminal justice system was failing people, as it clearly was, what ought we to have done? To do nothing is one option. But surely it is to do better by the British people to devise relevant powers, limited by the rights of appeal, to ensure that communities do not have to live with unacceptable levels of fear and intimidation. (Blair, 2006)

Driven by the worthy commitment 'to rebalance the criminal justice system in favour of the victim and the community' (Home Office, 2004: 14), no one can deny that there are very real problems to address.

However, attempting to fill the gap, not by tighter enforcement of extant criminal law, or much more idealistically reinvigorated welfare policies, but by fortifying summary powers though civil injunctions based upon spurious notions of 'respect' and 'swift measures' that erode long-standing principles of justice (see Thomas, 2003) are not the means to cement community solidarity, nor 'respect' for the rule of law. Such 'swift' and opaque civil measures that ignore due process are devoid of the safeguards built into the criminal law (see, for example, Zedner, 2005: 529–31) and, as such, bring about much greater disrespect for the law (Kuflik, 2005), serving only to increase social fragmentation. Shami Chakrabarti, Director of Liberty, summed up these fundamental concerns on the day of the launch of the Respect Action Plan (and see Chakrabarti and Russell, Chapter Seventeen in this volume):

> one must ask the ultimate question of whether the move to summary, arbitrary and loosely defined community justice is really improving the flavour of our society. Does it make a greater or lesser contribution to a culture of respect than traditional criminal justice principles? I would suggest that anti-social behaviour laws have to date been at best neutral and at worst positively damaging in this regard ... The constant arousal of fears and expectations concerning crime and nuisance, the endless recourse to new laws and extra coercive intervention ... the constant denigration of ancient and modern human rights' values, of the idea of the worth of the individual. This is not the way to inspire respect but merely a vain attempt at imposing it. (Chakrabarti, 2006: 12)

Richard Sennett was singled out for particular mention in Blair's launch speech (2006), and in seeking to develop Chakrabarti's final sentence above, it is worth reminding ourselves of Sennett's own conclusion: 'Treating people with respect cannot occur simply by commanding it should happen. Mutual recognition has to be negotiated' (Sennett, 2004: 260). To his credit, Blair acknowledged something of this point himself (Blair, 2006). However, he clearly missed the thrust of Sennett's thesis about the need for mutual recognition. He rehearsed yet again the 'rights and responsibilities' rhetoric (see Clarke, 2005, for a tidy overview) and the need to tackle ASB as 'the most visible sign of disrespect' (Home Office, 2006) which still remains key to attaining New Labour's communitarian idyll. Within this idyll, there appears to be little space for the negotiation of 'mutual recognition' as Sennett suggests, not least of the premise underpinning the 1998 Human Rights Act 'of the equality of esteem in which each and every one of us is held in view of our humanity' (Gearty, 2005: 18). Instead, the encouragement of subjective notions of acceptable conduct, the admission of hearsay evidence and the absence of due process within the safeguards of criminal law further encourage climates of suspicion and exclusion, especially in already strained neighbourhoods.

There is no doubting that anti-social behaviour does bring high social and economic costs to communities and is, therefore, 'a major social justice issue' (Home Office, 2006: 5), but, as Chakrabarti and Russell (Chapter Seventeen in this volume) have highlighted, anti-social behaviour enforcement measures are bringing about much wider costs to the British human rights tradition that will be of greater detriment to these very same communities. This erosion of liberties was most clearly championed in *Confident communities in a secure Britain* (Home Office, 2004), which outlined the government's 'commitments to law abiding citizens' and set out to enable this supposed majority to feel safe through the fostering of 'strong and cohesive communities'. In seeking to create a 'culture of intolerance' and proposing a greater use of 'swift' measures to deal with anti-social behaviour (Home Office, 2004: 49), these 'remedies', now reinforced by the Respect Agenda, have been justified by idealised appeals to 'community'. However, the symbolic use of this elusive concept in the contemporary governance of disorder guarantees that 'community' can never be wholly inclusive, respectful of all, as Flint explains:

> Technologies of governance in advanced liberal democracies involve the identification and classification of *autonomous citizens* capable of regulating their behaviour on the one hand, and on the other, identifying *targeted populations*, whose deviancy from norms of behaviour require government interventions. (Flint, 2002: 249; emphasis in original)

At issue here is not the impossibility of distinguishing the parameters of anti-social behaviour (see 1998 Crime and Disorder Act, section 1(1)(a); and a good critical discussion in MacDonald, 2006), although that in itself raises numerous causes of concern. Rather, our concern directly relates to the injustices entailed by the measures themselves. An appreciation of the cases of people subject to ASBOs[3] is especially revealing here.

Fortified by the intention to further strengthen summary powers and civil measures (Home Office, 2006), the remedies outlined in the

Respect Action Plan – dealing with 'challenging' families, improving behaviour and attendance in schools, and increased activities for children and young people (Home Office, 2006) – suggest that the problems within marginalised communities can be addressed by focusing on the symptoms of social malaise. These symptoms are identified as: poor parenting, weak familial relationships, truancy and exclusion, neighbourhood disorder and neglect, and early involvement in anti-social behaviour (see Home Office, 2006: 5). These remain, however, mere indicators of the deeper roots of late-modern marginalisation, but this does not seem to matter. The Respect Agenda, as a firm exemplar of late-modern governance needs, requires that the focus is squarely upon the 'conduct of conduct' (Gordon, 1991: 3) through the 'decentring of crime and crime control' and 'blurring of crime and disorder' (Matthews, 2002: 224) within the Respect Agenda. What Foucault referred to as a 'micro-physics of power' (Foucault, 1979), the disciplining of individuals, therefore, becomes a means of understanding the potency of appeals to 'respect', but it fails to offer individuals meaningful and sustainable means of altering their behaviour to become full and active citizens with a sense of reciprocal belonging. We are not reaffirming any sense of justice. As Cook argues:

> If a society cannot guarantee 'the equal worth of all citizens', mutual and self-respect and the meeting of basic needs, it cannot expect that all citizens will feel they have an equal stake in abiding by the law, and it cannot dispense justice fairly and enhance confidence in the law. In these respects, criminal and social justice are inseparable. (Cook, 2006: 21–2)

In late-modern Britain, through the various 'social harms' (see Hillyard and Tombs, 2004) to which those on the margins, especially young people (for example, Cieslik and Pollock, 2002; Mizen, 2004; MacDonald and Marsh, 2005; Furlong and Cartmel, 2006; Margo et al, 2006) are particularly exposed, there is unequal access to this 'reciprocal belonging', and especially to the 'mutual recognition' advocated by Sennett (2004). Inequalities are compounded by heightening social fragmentation and 'the death of community' (Hall and Winlow, 2005: 42) requiring governments to manipulate desires and responses (see Newburn and Jones, 2005) in the promotion of supposedly bottom-up community 'collective efficacy' (Sampson et al, 1999) through 'comfort legislation' (Thomas, 2003) that offers a transient, if not also illusionary, sense of ontological security. They do so in the face of a crisis of political legitimacy (see Flint, 2002). Yet, for New Labour, populist legitimacy has been won by remoralised appeals to law and order concerns (see Jordan, 2005; Squires, 2006), and it is here that Foucault's concept of 'governmentality' (Foucault, 1991) provides further insight. 'Community', as the paramount ideological 'means of governing crime and disorder' (Flint, 2002: 249), offers a means of deconstructing contemporary political imperatives and the ways through which 'power and freedom are intimately related' (Naughton, 2005: 48). Thus, while there has been a growing critique of anti-social behaviour measures, there has been too little engagement with the consequences of these developments in terms of power and freedom for the whole population, and there are certainly consequences:

> The conclusion that 'people like us' have nothing to fear from security measures may thus be born of a naïve failure of imagination. To posit our loved ones or ourselves as possible subjects of security measures is no abstract act of jurisprudential conjecture. (Zedner, 2005: 515)

Zedner is speaking specifically of terrorism here, but her thesis has ready applicability to the anti-social behaviour arena. She continues: 'Rather, it is the stark, self-interested recognition that where measures are defined so as to capture every instance ... we too might find ourselves subject to the very provisions whose introduction we approved' (Zedner, 2005: 515). Zedner's pointed reminder, therefore, highlights the pressing need to challenge the progressive erosion of liberties in the name of 'safety' at a rather more pedestrian level than terrorism. This latter point is exemplified clearly in the context of the increasing criminalisation of public leisure, such as the right of young people to hang around in public spaces (for example, Stephen, 2006) or play games in the street. In this manner young people are being excluded, as Flint explains, 'from the civil rights of access to public space and commercial centres, further compromising their social rights of citizenship' (Flint, 2002: 261). But it is not just young people who are affected; adults are experiencing similar restrictions, for example, on their freedom to take photographs in the public domain[4] (see correspondence in *Amateur Photographer*) in the interest of security. It is, therefore, not necessary to enter the grander arena of terrorism; rather, it is through such basic illustrations of *Foucauldian biopower in action*, now firmly couched in appeals to 'respect', that responsibilised (see Garland, 2001: 124–7; Clarke, 2005: 451–2) citizens are actively denouncing once-normal pursuits without appreciating the increased penetration of legal regulation into their own lives and the consequential erosion of their liberties. Indeed, contemporary utilitarian political expediency accepts that nothing comes without cost, and to begin to appreciate this it is necessary to reflect upon Bauman's prescient caveat:

> [T]here is a price to be paid for the privilege of 'being in a community' – and it is inoffensive or even invisible only as long as the community stays in the dream. The price is paid in the currency of freedom, variously called 'autonomy', 'right to self assertion', 'right to be yourself'. Whatever you choose, you gain some and lose some. Missing community means missing security; gaining community, if it happens, would soon mean missing freedom. Security and freedom are two equally precious and coveted values which could be better or worse balanced, but hardly ever fully reconciled or without friction. At any rate, no foolproof recipe for such reconciliation has yet been invented. (Bauman, 2001: 4)

In the context of the Respect Agenda, this assuredly applies to the human consequences of contemporary enforcement practices and processes of criminalisation, and what, as Bauman suggests, we are gaining and losing. Human costs that take little account of understanding, or indeed addressing, 'human needs and social processes' (Squires, 2006: 163), but instead offer 'a deepening, almost evangelical, commitment to discipline, regulation and punishment' (Scraton, 2005: 12). This is also a commitment too heavily reliant upon a rather narrow conception of the casualties of 'disrespect'.

The need to problematise narrow and politically driven understandings of 'victim' (see Walklate, 2006) arises when reflecting upon the example of the creeping criminalisation of public leisure above. What is immediately gained by deconstructing the Respect Agenda is an insight into the significance of surface appearances within the public sphere, and Tisdall (2006) highlights this in respect of the 'persons not of the same household' aspect of the definition of anti-social behaviour (see 1998 Crime and Disorder Act, section 1(1)(a). Our aforementioned research on Acceptable Behaviour Contracts revealed the increased risk to which families became exposed as they struggled to address the 'anti-social behaviour' (rooted in abject special educational needs and mental health problems) of their children in the public domain. In exploring their unmet psycho-social needs, it also underlined the futility of reliance on official notions of 'victim' within political rhetoric (Stephen and Squires, 2003). The public focus of the contemporary Respect

Agenda, therefore, disregards that which goes on in the private domain, and thus devalues these hidden crimes, for example, the relatively high incidences of 'hidden' child abuse, domestic violence and elder abuse perpetrated behind closed doors by many of the supposed 'decent law-abiding majority'. The focus on 'respect' and 'community', the especial scapegoating of young people's 'anti-social' agency, the superficial support on offer in the Respect Agenda, does nothing for those already excluded from respect for their basic human rights and from societal responsibility for their well-being; neither does it offer respect, in terms of 'equality of esteem' of their essential 'humanity' (Gearty, 2005: 18). Behind the constructs of otherness usually lie lives with profound unmet psycho-social needs (for example, Jamieson, 2005). Yet, in the vacuous rhetoric and assumptions upon which appeals to Respect are founded, there is no sense of those *others'* innate humanity:

> No liberal democracy can countenance the tyranny of a minority in any of its communities. We, as government, will discharge our duties. We will attempt to create the conditions in which respect can flourish. I believe in the innate decency of the British people and I believe that, together, we will eradicate the scourge of anti-social behaviour and restore Respect to the communities of Britain. (Blair, 2006)

Working with young people on the margins of British society, there develops a deep scepticism about any such sweeping claims to 'innate decency' of many in the adult population. Nor is there any tangible sense of 'respect' for young people in the policy-related injustices and inequalities affecting young people (Bessant, 2005) in contemporary Britain (Mizen, 2004; Margo et al, 2006; UNICEF, 2007). Sadly, in the *realpolitik* of late-modern Britain, such truths do not win votes, although obsequious appeals to innate vanity do. But Blair still made a valid point: there is an 'innate decency' in British traditions – an 'innate decency' we are at grave risk of losing.

Described colourfully as 'a jurisprudential Frankenstein, cobbled together in the satanic mills of the Home Office' (Smith, 2005), ASBOs and all the other anti-social behaviour measures reflect a marked epochal shift in the rightly lauded British approach to justice; the advent of 'precautionary injustice' (Squires and Stephen, 2005) characterised by the erosion of fundamental human rights whereupon civil measures are being employed in place of criminal law and legal safeguards (for example, Rowlands, 2005). Now, indeed, the Respect Agenda privileges the rights of 'law-abiding citizens', but this is not an unproblematic category built on objective certainty, as illustrated above. This 'movement away from the rule of law, democratic standards and the fundamental notion that we will not be punished if we abide by our society's penal code' (Rowlands, 2005: 3) focuses our minds on what we are ceding in the wholly insatiable desire for security implicit in the Respect Agenda. It is instructive to return to Kuflik's insightful paper once more:

> There is likely to be good moral reason not to enforce by law all of what there is nevertheless perfectly good reason to do. The attempt to legislate and enforce 'morality as such' itself involves a misunderstanding of morality's own requirements. (Kuflik, 2005: 186)

A 'good moral reason' is social justice, the need to tackle the social and economic roots of anti-social and offending behaviour, not the symptoms. The Respect Agenda, while scoring high on moralising, does little to redress the progressive disrespect for rights, or indeed humanity, in late-modern Britain, nor is it fostering the kinds of 'mutual recognition' for which Sennett (2004) calls. As he shows, it is inequality, and the consequential loss of autonomy, that hinders opportunity. In illuminating the risks associated with 'compassion fatigue' (Sennett, 2004: 146–50) Sennett shows that we need just social policies that respect individuals' capacities and foster opportunities for self- and social development because it is only such respect that enables 'exchange … the social principle which animates the character of someone who gives back to a community' (Sennett, 2004: 64). Accordingly, 'morality's own requirements' are such that social, not criminal, understandings of 'justice' must be returned to the centre of a more humane policy framework if a culture of respect is to be kindled. As such, our political leaders must assuredly enter the debate on liberty, not least the basic liberties crumbling under their stewardship. There is still time to redress matters, as Gearty reminds below, but, as he also shows, for the British public there can be no room for complacency:

> The basic building blocks of human rights – equality of esteem; a respect for law; a commitment to the democratic process – remain in place in Europe and the United Kingdom, but the price that needs to be paid every day to ensure the survival of these ideals in these difficult times takes the form of constant vigilance, endless community energy, and ongoing civil libertarian solidarity.... And if

those who care about human rights let their attention wander, even for a short while, then they might return from their daydreaming to find a radically different society. (Gearty, 2005: 33)

Whatever our role, we must work to ensure rights are safeguarded within a principled approach to justice (see Zedner, 2005). Although apparently too cumbersome in the current climate of summary powers, only this will ensure that measures are transparent, and due process and genuine respect is afforded to all citizens. We must begin to consider a viable dialogue of reciprocity and respect, but, as this chapter has contended, this task is too important to be left to the politicians alone. Initiatives within the Respect Action Plan (such as increased roles for social workers) and, especially, late-modern modes of governance require the involvement of us all, whether as members of multi-agency partnerships or simply as 'activated, empowered, or responsibilized citizens' (see Clarke, 2005: 447). In this manner, structures exist to begin to reinforce respect for the humanity of every citizen and to promote policies and practices that engender social, rather than criminalising, justice measures (for example Stephen and Squires, 2007). It is only when we begin to address the social injustices facing significant numbers of our fellow citizens that the possibility of respect will be actualised, responsibility will be enabled and liberty will be secured. Whoever will be the next *elected* prime minister, there may be some grounds for optimism in some of the more inclusive-sounding rhetoric from both David Cameron and Gordon Brown. In the short term, Blair's immediate successor faces a huge challenge both in answering his own question (refer to the epigraph of this chapter) as well as ensuring that the policies developed will deliver the kind of society he has envisaged while embracing the values he claims to share:

The values that matter: freedom, democracy and fairness. The shared values we were brought up with and must not lose: fair play, respect, a decent chance in life. And let us reaffirm the truth, that as individual citizens of Britain we must act upon the responsibilities we owe to each other as well as our rights. Here is the deal for the next decade we must offer: no matter your class, colour or creed, the equal opportunity to use your talents. (Brown, 2006)

Notes

[1] See www.respect.gov.uk/article.aspx?id=9054.

[2] See, for example, the special edition of *Social Justice*, 2005, vol 32, no 1.

[3] See www.statewatch.org/asbo/ASBOwatch.html.

[4] See correspondence in *Amateur Photographer*: 'Policeman "deleted my pictures" claims MP' (15 October 2005: 5); 'Backchat' (17 December 2005: 4); 'Police spin' (7 January 2006: 97); 'Inquisitive officers' (14 June 206: 88), 'Editorial welcome' and 'AP editor in talks over photo rights code' (25 February 2006: 3 and 5 respectively).

References

Bauman, Z. (2001) *Community: Seeking safety in an insecure world*, Cambridge: Polity Press.

Bessant, J. (2005) 'Principles for developing youth policy: Kant's categorical imperative and developmental ethics', *Policy Studies*, vol 26, no 1, pp 103–16.

Blair, T. (2006) 'PM's Respect Action Plan launch speech', 10 January, (www.number-10.gov.uk/output/Page8898.asp, accessed 13 January 2006).

Blair, T. (2007) 'Resignation statement', 10 May, (www.labour.org.uk/leadership/tony_blair_resigns, accessed 11 May 2007).

Brown, G. (2006) Speech to the Labour Party Conference, 25 September, (http://politics.guardian.co.uk/labourconference2006/story/0,,1880666,00.html, accessed 30 September 2006).

Cameron, D. (2006) Speech to the Centre for Social Justice, 9 July, (www.conservatives.com/tile.do?def=news.story.page&obj_id=130823&speeches=1, accessed 11 May 2007).

Cameron, D. (2007) 'Civility and civil progress', Speech to the Royal Society, 23 April, (www.conservatives.com/tile.do?def=news.story.page&obj_id=136420&speeches=1, accessed 11 May 2007).

Chakrabarti, S. (2006) 'Asbomania: from social and natural justice to mob rule?', BIHR lunchtime lecture, 10 January, (www.liberty-human-rights.org.uk/press/2006/asbomania.shtml, accessed 13 January 2006).

Cieslik, M. and Pollock, G. (eds) (2002) *Young people in risk society: The restructuring of youth identities and transitions in late modernity*, Aldershot: Ashgate.

Clarke, J. (2005) 'New Labour's citizens: activated, empowered, responsibilized, abandoned', *Critical Social Policy*, vol 25, no 4, pp 447–63.

Cook, D. (2006) *Criminal and social justice*, London: Sage.

Flint, J. (2002) 'Return of the governors: citizenship and the new governance of neighbourhood disorder in the UK', *Citizenship Studies*, vol 6, no 3, pp 245–64.

Foucault, M. ([1976] 1979) *The history of sexuality, Volume 1*, London: Allen Lane.

Foucault, M. ([1978] 1991) 'Governmentality', in G. Burchill, C. Gordon and P. Miller (eds), *The Foucault effect*, Chicago, IL: University of Chicago Press, pp 87–104.

Furlong, A. and Cartmel, F. (2006) *Young people and social change: New perspectives*, Maidenhead: Open University Press.

Garland, D. (2001) *The culture of control: Crime and social order in contemporary society*, Oxford: Oxford University Press.

Gearty, C. (2005) '11 September 2001, counter-terrorism, and the Human Rights Act', *Journal of Law and Society*, vol 32, no 1, pp 18–33.

Gil-Robles, A. (2005) *Report by Mr Alvaro Gil-Robles, Commissioner for Human Rights, on his visit to the United Kingdom, 4–12 November 2004*, CommDH (2005) 6, Strasbourg: Council of Europe.

Goldson, B. (2004) 'Authoritarian drift', *Safer Society*, vol 23, Winter, pp 27–8.

Gordon, C. (1991) 'Governmental rationality: an introduction', in G. Burchill, C. Gordon and P. Miller (eds), *The Foucault effect*, Chicago, IL: University of Chicago Press, pp 1–52.

Hall, S. and Winlow, S. (2005) 'Anti-nirvana: crime, culture and instrumentalism in the age of insecurity', *Crime, Media, Culture*, vol 1, no 1, pp 31–48.

Hillyard, P. and Tombs, S. (2004) 'Beyond criminology?', in P. Hillyard, C. Pantazis, S. Tombs and D. Gordon (eds), *Beyond criminology. Taking harm seriously*, London: Pluto Press, pp 10–29.

Home Office (2004) *Confident communities in a Secure Britain: The Home Office Strategic Plan 2004–08*, London: Home Office.

Home Office (2006) *Respect Action Plan*, London: Home Office.

Jamieson, J. (2005) 'New Labour, youth justice and the question of respect', *Youth Justice*, vol 5, no 3, pp 180–93.

Jordan, B. (2005) 'New Labour: choice and value', *Critical Social Policy*, vol 25, no 4, pp 427–46.

Kuflik, A. (2005) 'Liberalism, legal moralism and moral disagreement', *Journal of Applied Philosophy*, vol 22, no 2, pp 185–98.

MacDonald, R. and Marsh, J. (2005) *Disconnected youth: Growing up in Britain's poor neighbourhoods*, London: Palgrave Macmillan.

MacDonald, S. (2006) 'A suicidal woman, roaming pigs and a noisy trampolinist: refining the ASBO's definition of "anti-social behaviour"', *Modern Law Review*, vol 69, no 2, pp 183–213.

Margo, J., Dixon, M., Pearce, N. and Reed, H. (2006) *Freedom's orphans: Raising youth in a changing world*, London: IPPR.

Matthews, R. (2002) 'Crime and control in late modernity', *Theoretical Criminology*, vol 6, no 2, pp 217–26.

Mizen, P. (2004) *The changing state of youth*, Basingstoke: Palgrave Macmillan.

Naughton, M. (2005) '"Evidence-based policy" and the government of the criminal justice system – only if the evidence fits!', *Critical Social Policy*, vol 25, no 1, pp 47–69.

Newburn, T. and Jones, T. (2005) 'Symbolic politics and penal populism: the long shadow of Willie Horton', *Crime, Media, Culture*, vol 1, no 1, pp 78–87.

Rowlands, M. (2005) 'The state of ASBO Britain – the rise of intolerance', ECLN Essays no 9, (www.ecln.org, accessed 6 January 2006).

Sampson, R.J., Morenoff, J.D. and Earls, F. (1999) 'Beyond social capital: spatial dynamics of collective efficacy for children', *American Sociological Review*, vol 64, no 5, pp 633–60.

Scraton, P. (2005) 'The denial of children's rights and liberties in the UK and the North of Ireland', ECLN Essays no 14, (www.ecln.org, accessed 6 January 2006).

Sennett, R. (2004) *Respect: The formation of character in an age of inequality*, London: Penguin.

Smith, R. (2005) 'Shocking behaviour', *The Law Gazette*, 17 March, (www.lawgazette.co.uk/features/view=feature.law?FEATUREID=226678, accessed 11 April 2005).

Squires, P. (2006) 'New Labour and the politics of antisocial behaviour', *Critical Social Policy*, vol 26, no 1, pp 144–68.

Squires, P. and Stephen, D.E. (2005) *Rougher justice: Young people and anti-social behaviour*, Cullompton: Willan.

Stephen, D.E. (2006) 'Community safety and young people: twenty-first century *homo sacer* and the politics of injustice', in P. Squires (ed), *Community safety: Critical perspectives on policy and practice*, Bristol: The Policy Press, pp 219–36.

Stephen, D.E. and Squires, P. (2003) *Community safety, enforcement and Acceptable Behaviour Contracts*, Brighton: HSPRC, University of Brighton.

Stephen, D.E. and Squires, P. (2004) '"They're still children and entitled to be children": problematising the institutionalised mistrust of marginalised youth in Britain', *Journal of Youth Studies*, vol 7, no 3, pp 351–69.

Stephen, D.E. and Squires, P. (2007) 'Rough justice: supporting young people and their families in the community', in S. Balloch and M. Hill (eds), *Care, citizenship and communities: Research and practice in a changing policy context*, Bristol: The Policy Press, pp 105–31.

Thomas, P.A. (2003) '9/11: USA and UK', *Fordham International Law Journal*, vol 26, no 4, pp 1193–233.

Tisdall, K.M. (2006) 'Antisocial behaviour legislation meets children's services: challenging perspectives on children, parents and the state', *Critical Social Policy*, vol 26, no 1, pp 101–20.

Tombs, S. and Hillyard, P. (2004) 'Towards a political economy of harm: states, corporations and the production of inequality', in P. Hillyard, C. Pantazis, S. Tombs and D. Gordon (eds), *Beyond criminology. Taking harm seriously*, London: Pluto Press, pp 30–54.

UNICEF (2007) *Child poverty in perspective: An overview of child well-being in rich countries*, Report Card 7, Florence: UNICEF.

Walklate, S. (2006) 'Community safety and victims: who is the victim of community safety?', in P. Squires (ed), *Community safety: Critical perspectives on policy and practice*, Bristol: The Policy Press, pp 169–80.

Zedner, L. (2005) 'Securing liberty in the face of terror: reflections from criminal justice', *Journal of Law and Society*, vol 32, no 4, pp 507–33.

NINETEEN

Asocial not anti-social: the 'Respect Agenda' and the 'therapeutic me'

Stuart Waiton

The demand for law and order, which at first sight appears to attempt a restoration of moral standards, actually acknowledges and acquiesces in their collapse. Law and order comes to be seen as the only effective deterrent in a society that no longer knows the difference between right and wrong.
(Lasch, 1977: 187)

Introduction

The promotion of respect in society, like the concern about anti-social behaviour, engages with issues that on the one hand are relatively small or insignificant – dropping litter or not saying 'thank you', for example. And yet on the other hand these issues are often felt to be significant both in themselves and also through their association with major social problems such as the 'breakdown of communities'. The 'ASBO agenda' has been criticised for its authoritarian dynamic – especially by those on the left. However, even for critics there appears to be an uncertainty about the nature of behaviour today and a certain sense that there are some real problems to be addressed. Some, for example, believe that we are living in a 'culture of greed' – a belief that raises questions not only about capitalism and consumerism, but also about the very nature of relationships between people – indeed about the nature of people themselves.

This chapter argues that there are some new problems to address today, but that the problem we face is ultimately not one of an anti-social society but of an asocial society. Seen in this way, the myopic focus on anti-social behaviour can be seen not only as a diversion but as something that actually reinforces the asocial nature of society itself.

The problem

Until the 1990s the term 'anti-social behaviour' had scarcely any public or political existence (although see the discussion in Squires and Stephen, 2005: chapters 2 and 3). In the last 15 years the awareness and construction of this social problem has grown and grown, and it is now understood to be a, if not *the*, problem facing society. So seriously does the government take this problem that immediately following the 2005 general election victory, Prime Minister Tony Blair launched the 'Respect Agenda' – an agenda that extends the politics of behaviour further still into the realms of politeness and manners. To reinforce the seriousness of this issue, the Respect Action Plan, published in January 2006 by the Respect Task Force, came with a footnote from each member of the cabinet – from the Health Secretary to the Secretary of State for Work and Pensions, and of course from the then Minister of Respect, Hazel Blears – explaining what contribution their departments would make to the battle against anti-social behaviour, and for respect.

Conservative leader David Cameron has also recently painted a gloomy picture of a society that has become resigned to the fact that 'behaviour is bad and getting worse' (*Guardian*, 23 April 2007). But Cameron is no Mary Whitehouse and this concern is not a rerun of past moral campaigns by conservatives. The very fact that the Labour Party is at the forefront of the push for respect suggests that something other than the Christian moralising of yesteryear is behind this development. Indeed the old divide between conservatives and liberals around issues of liberty versus growing police powers no longer holds, and past cries of 'moral panic', while remaining in relation to questions to do with the family, are less frequently heard in relation to issues of crime and safety. A MORI poll from June 2005, for example, found that around two thirds of *Guardian* readers supported the use of ASBOs: questions of freedom and an opposition towards state regulation of society appear to have declined over recent years.

Despite today's high levels of cynicism towards politics and politicians, this has not resulted in a rejection of state interference in people's lives or the rise of libertarianism among the electorate. Indeed an existing decline of libertarianism observed in the early 1990s has accelerated over recent years with, for example, the 2007 Social Attitudes Survey finding that only 15% of Labour voters opposed identity cards as compared with 45% in 1990. As Britain becomes the CCTV capital of the world – with little opposition from the public – Professor Conor Gearty has noted that, 'It is as though society is in the process of forgetting why past generations thought those freedoms to be so very important' (*Guardian*, 24 January 2007).

In part, this decline of libertarianism and the greater acceptance of new legal provisions, such as ASBOs, within the UK has come with a growing concern about the behaviour of others. The concern about incivility and the development of laws to deal with it has also become significant in other countries, and in particular the US, where a number of the specific issues such as curfews and the targeting of 'aggressive beggars' first developed. One of the best known American politicians outside of the president himself is the ex-Mayor of New York Rudolph Giuliani. His fame largely stems from his notorious promotion of zero-tolerance policing and his campaign launched in 1998 to improve the manners of pedestrians, motorists, taxi drivers and even the city's civil service. But Giuliani is not acting alone, rather – as in the UK – the American public appear to be more than keen on these initiatives. As Mark Caldwell observes in his *Short history of rudeness*, 'in recent years civility and the perceived trashing thereof have become an American obsession, from cultural critics to politicians' (1999: 2). Here he also notes how, in 1996, a *U.S. News & World Report* survey found that 89% of respondents felt that America was 'basically uncivil' (Caldwell, 1999: 5; although refer also to Squires, in the introduction to this volume, regarding the US as a 'polite' society).

On both sides of the Atlantic, issues that may have captured the imagination of some conservatives in the past now appear to be both more mainstream and to be taken more seriously by the authorities. In the US the transformation of 1970s' New York from a 'hip' and edgy urban space into today's 'Safe City' is striking, and suggests that the expectations of the public – and perhaps the nature of New Yorkers – have changed: the hard-boiled Americans of old apparently did not need campaigns to protect them from impolite taxi drivers – but now it seems they do.

Panics past and present

For some of those who question the 'panic' about anti-social behaviour and the promotion of 'respect', the 'problem' of behaviour is nothing new and today's 'panic' is part of a cyclical pattern of anxieties that fluctuate over time. In the early 1980s Pearson's *Hooligan: A history of respectable fears* (1983) illustrated the way that panics about crime came and went, with conservatives often harking back to a golden age 20 years since – a time, as Pearson noted, that in reality had very similar concerns and panics about crime. Caldwell likewise argues that the concern about manners has a 'cyclical character' and is something that has emerged both at the end of the 19th and then again at the end of the 20th century as 'part of a general syndrome of millennial jitters' (Caldwell, 1999: 3).

The 'theory' of millennial jitters may have some validity but is much too general and lacks historical specificity. Today, however, Pearson's more detailed thesis that located elite anxieties within the realm of national and, most especially, class conflicts equally appears to be out of date. The preoccupation among the elite with crime remains high, despite the working class being less of a 'threat' than it has been perhaps at any other time in its history.

With the decline of the working class as a political force in society there has also developed a curious transformation in the meaning of left and right, and to some extent the calls for regulation, control and 'respect', once the preserve of conservative campaigners, have become framed within a new form of radical conservatism.

In the 1970s and 1980s the questions of crime, behaviour and, indeed, civility were politicised and there was a radical opposition to the restrictions and behaviour codes promoted by conservative moralists. However, at the same time a number of the political battles of the 1980s around issues of equality themselves developed into new codes of behaviour – and a new form of etiquette emerged in society. The question of 'behaviour' is no longer simply a right–wing concern, and indeed many of the codes of conduct developed within workplaces and indeed more widely in society since the 1990s have incorporated issues to do with gender and race awareness.

The legalisation, or at least the formalisation, of behaviour around these new behaviour codes raises questions about the moral dynamic behind the 'politics of behaviour'. And despite the positive intentions behind these developments there are some who have raised doubts about the benefits of them. Caldwell, for example, examining the criminalisation of 'sexual harassment', asks whether this development portends a 'dangerous shift in our understanding of civility [and] a tendency to inflate conflicts once resolved informally into wounding gladiatorial combat' (Caldwell, 1999: 5). Conservatives like Gertrude Himmelfarb similarly argue that:

> The movement against 'hate speech' is not intended, as is sometimes claimed, merely to revive the old rules of civility. It has invented new rules, defining as violations of civil rights, and therefore punishable, remarks that were formerly regarded as boorish or vulgar. (Himmelfarb, 1995: 265)

Himmelfarb bemoans the decline of the old moral framework while denouncing what she describes as the New Victorians with their modern form of 'moral correctness'. The questions of civility, respect and the use of language are no longer simply conservative concerns – and as the arguments and somewhat extravagant reactions to events and 'words' in the *Big Brother* house have recently illustrated, it is often radical concerns regarding issues such as race that have to some extent become incorporated into the British (indeed Western) understanding of what is and is not *acceptable behaviour*.

Today the concern about behaviour and the demand for the regulation of it is more than a mere rerun of past conservative moral panics. The political framework of left and right has been transformed and has arguably helped to influence this development. While the behaviour of the public may have changed to some degree, questions must also be raised about the changing nature of the public itself – and of the individual's capacity and preparedness to deal with the tensions of everyday life. Compared to the 'hard-boiled' attitudes that appear to have existed in the 1970s, today, from Mayor Giuliani's campaigns to the reaction to Jade Goody and the 'N-word' on *Big Brother*, to the widespread support for ASBOs, the public appear to be – or at least those in authority appear to believe that they are – more easily offended.

Perhaps it is that we are more 'soft-boiled' today that explains the problem of 'offensive behaviour', rather than any change in behaviour itself?

The problem of the elite

Before we explore the meaning of the 'therapeutic me' today, it is of some benefit to go back to the quote by Christopher Lasch at the start of the chapter to examine, first and foremost, the changing nature of the elite itself in the latter part of the 20th century, a time when, Lasch argues, 'law and order [came] to be seen as the only effective deterrent in a society that no longer [knew] the difference between right and wrong'.

The quote is taken from *Haven in a heartless world*, written in 1977, and Lasch's argument was, fundamentally, that in the United States the move towards a tough law and order approach by the political elite in the 1970s did not, as it was understood, indicate a shift to the right, with a subsequent restoration of 'moral standards' in society. Rather, it indicated the reverse. The move by the elite to enforce standards of behaviour through law – rather than through moral or political arguments, campaigns and movements – indicated that, in fact, the elite had given up. They had lost the capacity and even the will to lead; now the best they could do was regulate and control a society that felt increasingly out of their control.

Bauman (2000a) has similarly described an unstable, directionless society – a *Liquid modernity*. This is a society within which the lost sense of control reflects the elite itself, that, as Bauman argues, has abdicated the responsibility of being the pilot of society. This is an elite that 'rules without burdening itself with the chores of administration, management, welfare concerns, or, for that matter, with the mission of "bringing light", "reforming the ways", morally uplifting, "civilizing" and cultural crusades' (Bauman, 2000a: 13). Where past rules were set down by the 'captains' of society and 'displayed in bold letters in every passageway' – rules that could be followed or challenged – today, in comparison, 'the passengers of the "Light Capitalism" aircraft ... discover to their horror that the pilot's cabin is empty' (2000a: 59).

For Lasch, American society was losing its engagement with the past and, perhaps more importantly, with any sense of the future. This more directionless and anxious society was, he believed, moving into an age of 'diminished expectations' where safety, limits and regulation were replacing the drive to 'go West', to 'boldly go' or even to find a past golden age to inspire the next generation. The lost sense of history and progress meant that American society both was less grounded and lacked a narrative about where it was going. Consequently, a new form of conservatism emerged, a kind of survivalism that could aspire to little more than the conservation of society as it was (Lasch, 1979).

For Lasch, and later on for Bauman as well, the elite were understood to have lost their way and consequently gave up on directing society in any meaningful way: managing what C. Wright Mills described as private *troubles* rather than engaging with social *issues* has subsequently become the core business of government (Mills, 1968).

It appears to be no accident that in the UK a similar process to the one that developed in 1970s' America can be observed from the late 1980s, as the political contestation of the old left and old right came to an end and the micro-politics of the 1990s developed into a managerial form of governing through an ever-greater range of laws and controls.

In Britain over the last two decades, the move towards using laws, regulations and codes of behaviour to resolve society's problems has developed at a relentless pace. Often narrowly understood within public debate as the actions of authorities on genuine issues of concern about rising crime, or of violence and abuse, relatively little is said about the extent to which this way of running society has come to dominate ahead of all others. In the UK an acceleration of new laws took off under the Conservative leadership of John Major in the early 1990s and has subsequently accelerated further under the Labour governments since 1997.[1] It has recently been observed that, almost unbelievably, there have been over three thousand new laws introduced since Labour came to power – one for every day they have been in office.[2]

Laws, regulations and the attempt to control the behaviour of the public have in the last decade or so become a replacement for politics and purpose, and through the eyes of the new elite *social* problems have been recast as problems of personal behaviour.

The Respect Agenda is one example of this development – an agenda that was launched in full directly following the 2005 election, an election that appeared as a mere political irritation that, once out of the way, could allow the government to carry on with the micro-management of society assisted by the introduction of another 45 new laws as announced in the Queen's Speech.[3]

Respect what?

The idea of 'respect' promoted by the government can be confusing and appear to be a mere replay of past moralising. When speaking to a more traditional audience like the Women's Institute, for example, Tony Blair in June 2000 explained that respect and the 'essential decency of the British character' was about 'honour, self discipline, duty and obligation' (*Guardian*, 18 May 2005). Sentiments that could have been expressed by Baden Powell, Winston Churchill or Mary Whitehouse here situate Blair firmly with the blue rinse '*Daily Mail* reader'. However, as with the call by Blair, following the killing of James Bulger in 1993, to challenge the 'moral vacuum' in society, this new call for respect may appear familiar but has emerged at a curious political and historical point in time – and one where traditional moral and political ideas have largely lost their meaning.

Even the terms used here by Blair, that would once have been self-evident in their meaning, are today more confused. 'Duty' to whom or what, for example, and whom or what should we 'honour'? The often-empty plinth at Trafalgar Square, where a statue to a modern-day hero should be, suggests the British elite themselves cannot easily answer this question. And 'self-discipline'? Self-discipline to what end – or is this now an end in itself, and how does this idea sit with the more recent idea of self-esteem?

When we look for a wider meaning to the Respect Agenda, despite the big words occasionally muttered, we are often left feeling more than a little empty. More often the issue of respect is shown up to be more about not disrespecting others than about who and what we should respect. A Labour council leader struggling to give some weight to the issue of respect explained that, 'The Respect agenda is not just about tackling unacceptable or anti-social behaviour', before elaborating that it was about creating 'a modern culture of respect by working on the underlying causes of bad behaviour, whether in school, community or elsewhere' (*Guardian*, 23 January 2007). Respect is not just about anti-social behaviour, it appears – it is about the causes of anti-social behaviour as well!

Despite attempts to give it a wider social or moral meaning, time and again we find that the meaning of 'respect' is simply to be respectful, and that the basis of a good society is to not be bad. Rather than elaborating upon key issues of duty, honour or obligation, politicians appear to fall back upon the basis of the good society being one where people are not anti-social. The tautology of respect appears to start and finish with the issue of bad behaviour. But explaining what we should not be is not the same as elaborating upon what we should be, and why.

In 2003 at the Labour Party conference Tony Blair, elaborating on the meaning of a 'just society', explained that, 'We cannot live in a just society if we do not put an end to the anti-social behaviour, the disrespect, the conduct which we would not tolerate from our own children and should not have to tolerate from any one else's' (*Guardian*, 18 May 2005). The very meaning of a just society is itself, for Tony Blair, about *preventing* anti-social behaviour, but surely we need more than a call to 'be nice' to fill the 'moral vacuum' in society or indeed to create a 'just' society.

Talk to the hand

The number of books on behaviour and, indeed, on manners has flourished in the past decade, as has the number of papers and pamphlets being written by think-tanks and Labour politicians themselves. One of the most successful of these books is the more populist *Talk to the hand: The utter bloody rudeness of everyday life*, written by the best-selling author Lynne Truss. Despite this book's obsessive focus on 'rudeness' (in a book that Truss herself accepts is a bit of a rant), there are arguably more real insights in *Talk to the hand* than in any document the government has produced in the last ten years.

The key to Truss's insight is that in her description of our 'hamster ball' society, a world made up of individuals living in their own private bubbles, she gets very close to describing the real problem we face today. *This is not a problem of anti-social behaviour, but of an asocial society.* A society that lacks the capacity to connect people with one another through a system of meaning.

Looking at the problem as one of an asocial society is useful, as it shifts the debate away from the often unhelpful preoccupation with anti-social behaviour. However, it also helps to make clear some of the genuine and new problems with behaviour between people today.

For example, in our more fragmented world, where the purpose of society is unclear and our individual role within it even more so, there has emerged a form of introspection and a new trend for people to relate only to their own rules: 'Hey, my bubble, my rules', as Truss puts it. This is a world where we walk around in our own private bubbles, and the public becomes simply an obstacle in our way as we listen to our iPod and text our friends. Living in our bubble world, Truss argues, when standards – or manners – are enforced from outside ourselves, we are more inclined to stick two fingers up. 'Authority', Truss notes, 'is largely perceived as a kind of personal insult' (2005: 33).

This sense of distance and separation between the individual and society rings true, a world where personal concerns override public interests, where our business is nobody else's, where the separation between public and private has broken down. As Truss observes, 'It's as if we now believe, in some spooky virtual way, that wherever we are, it's home' (2005: 102).

Describing the way we have become disconnected from one another and become inwardly focused, she explains that, 'The once prevalent idea that, as individuals, we have a relationship with something bigger than ourselves, or bigger than our immediate circle, has become virtually obsolete' (2005: 35).

The 'therapeutic me'

Truss's explanation for this type of behaviour is that society has become more individualised, more selfish and more greedy. This is an explanation that sits comfortably with many commentators from a variety of political persuasions. Labour advisor Geoff Mulgan in the Demos pamphlet *Freedom's children*, for example, has attacked the culture of greed and the young working-class 'underwolves' that he believes are a product of Thatcher's Britain – a product that had the capacity to 'ruin pretty much everyone's quality of life' (Wilkinson and Mulgan, 1995: 108). In America, Caldwell notes that support for Guiliani's zero-tolerance approach to incivility has come from many who see the problem as one of a 'rude culture of self-indulgence' that has trampled good manners (Caldwell, 1999: 2). The Respect Action Plan itself talks about the problem of behaviour as a problem that has emerged within the 'selfish minority'.

This idea of the selfish individual – a kind of 'neo-liberal citizen' – is widespread and is seen as a problem by communitarians and radicals alike. Thatcher's child – the spawn of 'Essex man' and the 'underclass' – has come back to haunt us in the form of the anti-social 'yob' and the 'neighbours from hell'.

However, this representation of a somewhat greedy, hard-boiled character does not ring true, and despite Truss's own sense of there being a 'climate of unrestrained solipsistic and aggressive self-interest', she also, more usefully, hints at an alternative explanation for the changes in behaviour today – changes that the sociologist Frank Furedi has categorised as being part and parcel of a wider *Therapy culture*. This is a society less of 'selfish', assertive and expansive individualism, than one where the mantra 'talk to the hand' expresses an inward-looking and rather fragile sense of the self – a defensive retreat into the world of self-esteem. Rather than there being a libertarian impulse for unrestrained freedom, the opposite is the case, as support for regulations, surveillance and restraint have developed in part to overcome the problem of 'offence' that is more acutely felt today than previously. The modern man or woman is less a greedy, aggressive individual than an anxious and vulnerable one (Furedi, 2004).

The modern fragmented individual may well be inclined to see the world from their hamster ball – and to often see authority as a personal insult – but this self-same individual is also inclined to have an exaggerated sense of the problem of the anti-social behaviour of others. *In this respect the 'anti-social offender' and the 'easily offended' should be understood as two sides of the same asocial coin.*

Despite some genuine concerns about the changing nature of relationships between people, Truss also, if only at certain times within her book, recognises that most of the people most of the time are pretty decent to one another. 'And yet', she notes, 'if you ask people, they mostly report with vehemence that the world has become a ruder place. They are at breaking point. They feel like blokes in films who just. Can't. Take. Any. More.' (Truss, 2005: 39).

Unlike the myriad government ministers who relentlessly take the preoccupation with anti-social behaviour at face value, Truss has the presence of mind to recognise the contradictory situation, where everyone feels that everyone else is rude. 'So what on earth is going on?', she asks.

What is going on is that the 'bubble world' we are living in has a pretty thin skin; it encircles a rather anxious and vulnerable *therapeutic me*. There has been a shift in recent years from the idea of 'public man' – a strong-willed citizen who can make decisions and take actions by himself – to 'therapeutic man', where we are increasingly seen as fragile, potentially damaged and in need of help from apparently benign authorities to manage not just our day-to-day lives but also our innermost emotions and feelings.

Behind today's therapeutic mindset there lurks the idea that humans are frail and weak; that we need constant protection from others and from the challenges thrown up by life itself. In *Therapy culture* Furedi notes how terms such as 'self-esteem', 'trauma', 'stress' and 'syndrome' have exponentially increased within newspapers since around 1993 as the understanding of social problems shifted onto the perceived 'emotional deficit' in society: an 'invisible disease that undermines people's ability to control their lives', and one that was predicated upon an 'intense sense of emotional vulnerability' (Furedi, 2004: 5). As this understanding of people becomes normalised it influences how we understand ourselves, what we expect from ourselves and how we experience the behaviour of other people.

The therapeutic culture, coupled with the more fragmented society we live in, has resulted in the 'anti-social behaviour' of even young children being experienced as more serious than it would have been in previous times. Already feeling somewhat vulnerable, in our disconnected society, where one of the few positive connections we have with other people is through polite exchanges we experience as we drift past one another, politeness has become more significant, not less. We may not all practise it, but, almost without exception, we are concerned about it – and when politeness is not forthcoming, we react in a more extreme way to this perceived snub. We 'rage', or more often we are, simply, internally outraged. In this respect 'anti-social behaviour' acts as a catalyst to our sense of alienation within our asocial society.

In a humorous description of how she feels holding the door open for people who refuse to say 'thank you', Truss notes her own sense of wounded dignity – 'you feel obliterated', she writes, 'Are you invisible, then? Have you disappeared?' She continues:

> Instead of feeling safe, you are frightened. You succumb to accelerated moral reasoning. This person has no consideration for others, therefore has no imagination,

therefore is a sociopath representative of a world packed with sociopaths. When someone is rude to you, the following logic kicks in: 'I have no point of connection with this person.... A person who wouldn't say thank you is also a person who would cut your throat.... Oh my God, society is in meltdown and soon it won't be safe to come out'. Finally you hate the person who did not say thank you. (2005: 54)

Disconnected

In a world where people had a strong sense of connection with society, with institutions, organisations and beliefs, and consequently with one another, the irritations of everyday life would pale into insignificance.

Again, this is something that Truss herself recognises when she looks at the issue of smoking. 'Personally', she explains, 'I hate smoking [but] ... I do remember a time when it just didn't bother me', so what has changed? It's not just the health issue, she notes, but rather that:

I used to accept something I truly don't accept anymore: that being with other people involved a bit of compromise. When you were not alone, you suspended a portion of yourself. You became a member of a crowd. You didn't judge people by your own standards. I believe we have simply become a lot more sensitive to other people's behaviour in a climate of basic fearful alienation. (2005: 188)

What Truss is describing is what Mills (1968), Rose (1996) and a number of sociologists have described as the diminution of the 'public', a development that in recent years has also come with a growing intolerance of other people. The world of 'my bubble, my rules' may have resulted in the emergence of a 'me generation', but this is a therapeutic me. A more introspective individual who, on the one hand, is inclined to be less aware of any social mores beyond their own self but, on the other hand, perhaps more significantly, is prone to overreact to those around them and demand protection of their own private world.

The strength of *Talk to the hand* is not in the identification of *The utter bloody rudeness of everyday life*, which is, after all, in our world of ASBOs and Respect Action Plans, hardly a novel outlook, but rather in the implicit recognition of the problem of an asocial society. Unfortunately, in the end, like another useful book that addresses the issue of behaviour – the Conservative Alexander Deane's (2005) *The great abdication* – the start and end point of *Talk to the hand* is a preoccupation with rudeness, or anti-social behaviour.

With Truss, this is forgivable, as she both acknowledges that her book is a bit of a rant and, once again, is perceptive enough to recognise the limitations of what she is proposing. What Truss ultimately aspires to, she concludes, is 'to be a zero impact member of society'. 'But', she continues, 'does this qualify me as the opposite of an anti-social person? Quite honestly I don't think it does, because that would be *pro*-social, which would involve acting on society's behalf, and I don't do that' (2005: 181).

Ironically, the 'bubble world' that Truss identifies as the ultimate problem people face in their dealings with one another ends up being the place that Truss herself retreats into. Only Truss would like 'her bubble, her world' to be a little bit more polite than it is at present.

Asocial politics

However, if the more profound problem we face is one of an asocial society, we need to address how we 'burst the bubble' and create a 'pro-social' society. Unfortunately, the trend at present is not to challenge many aspects of the asocial nature of society and of individuals' behaviour, but to endorse it and attempt to relate to it.

The world of 'my bubble, my rules', when it takes the form of teenagers wearing hoodies and drinking on street corners, results in new laws and forms of policing to prevent this type of behaviour. But when it means that individuals sue their local councils for tripping over a paving stone, or take their local hospital to court for an accident during surgery, we find that society endorses this type of asocial or indeed anti-'social' behaviour. Rather than people feeling that they are part of society, that accidents sometimes happen and that it would be wrong for them to drain the resources of their local authorities, today the 'my bubble, my rules' outlook is institutionalised through law and we are encouraged to 'blame and claim'.

Until relatively recently the idea that you would sue your council or health service for accidents that occurred, thus starving local authorities of desperately needed funds, would have been unthinkable. But today, the use of law to compensate individuals for every misfortune relates to and encourages a cultural climate that separates the interests of people from society while undermining a sense of personal responsibility.

In Scotland, where new anti-social behaviour laws and initiatives are constantly being churned out by the Scottish Executive and concern is raised about the expense of having to deal with litter and graffiti, little is said about the more troubling example of the £5 million worth of compensation that has been paid out to Scottish policemen and women over the last five years. In the latest case of police officers suing their own force, ex-police officer Tracey Ormsby is suing a chief constable for £1.5 million following events on a demonstration where she was hit in the chest with a pineapple. Even for the people who are meant to be defending the 'law and order of society', the sense of individual grievance and 'where there's a blame there's a claim' outlook appears to be overriding any wider sense of duty and responsibility.

Worse still, in terms of the loss of any sense of loyalty among individuals to society, is the example of the soldiers who have made claims against the Ministry of Defence for not providing them with a safe working environment!

You do not need to be a fan of the police or the British army to realise that when the police start claiming for bites they receive from their own police dogs, and soldiers for being put at risk – 'society' really is in trouble.

Rather than challenging these asocial developments, the state and the law have institutionalised mechanisms to allow the growth of a compensation culture. Unable to project and promote a national or social sense of purpose and responsibility, today's elite have incorporated the outlook of 'my bubble, my world' into the framework of society. The problem of the asocial society is that the relationship between the individual and society has broken down. However, politicians who lack the capacity to unite people around a common set of beliefs and values have attempted to engage with individuals within 'their world'. In the process, our individual bubbles are being fortified against society – a process that has developed across social institutions and within the culture of society.

This engagement with the individual self can be seen in the way key jobs for society, that once embodied a commitment to a wider purpose, are advertised today. The ads for the Royal Navy on the Glasgow underground never fail to amuse and depress me, with their promotion of a life full of sun and fun where you make new friends. Placed next to a Club 18–30 poster, these two adverts could hardly be told apart.

Similarly, the ads for teachers that promote teaching as 'enjoyable and stimulating', where the kids are the most exciting people you will ever meet, engage not with the important and socially responsible job of transferring knowledge to the next generation, but with the 'fun' that *you* as a teacher can have in a classroom. When kids start misbehaving and undermining their teacher's sense of 'well-being' it is perhaps unsurprising that they too feel 'obliterated' and 'frightened'.

The development of a culture that encourages people to be increasingly introspective appears not only to be doing little to challenge the various social problems we face today, but also to be encouraging a more insecure and vulnerable understanding of the self. Perhaps it is no surprise that, having promoted the problem of children being bullied for the last decade or so, teachers and teachers' unions have now begun to campaign around the problem of children bullying teachers. Past collective activities of unions and, indeed, of professional teachers' associations are increasingly being replaced by the engagement with teachers today through their sense of themselves as vulnerable individuals.

Within education itself, the trend is towards engaging with and reinforcing the more introspective outlook (or 'in'-look) of children, with the growing significance of self-esteem as the 'measure of man', and with the institutionalisation of 'bullying awareness' schemes. Rather than educating youngsters to climb out of their caricatured adolescent self-absorption we appear to be encouraging the preoccupation with 'how I feel'.

Also, within the criminal justice system the engagement with the vulnerable individual has grown rapidly over recent years and now, rather than law being enforced by the state – on all our behalves, against the criminal – we have victim-centred justice. A form of 'justice' that literally endorses the idea of 'my bubble, my rules' – or, in this case, 'my feelings, my law'.

The development of a victim-centred justice system should be understood less as the rise of the moral right than as the collapse of both moral individualism and any sense of the social. It is part of an asocial process that relates directly to the vulnerable individual and, more particularly, to our feelings and fears.

ASBOs are a perfect expression of this development. As Atkins et al note in *Taking liberties*, 'The British "common law tradition" means that you can do whatever you want as long as it is not illegal' (2007: 143). Labour may have introduced thousands of new laws but at least 'you still have to be found guilty of one of these to go to prison'. However, with Anti-Social Behaviour Orders, 'If you are doing something that isn't against the law, but someone else doesn't like, they can go to a magistrates' court and get one of these orders that bans you acting in that way. If you break the ASBO you go to jail!' (2007: 145).

This is literally a case of 'my feelings, my law' – and unpleasant (offensive) behaviour has become criminalised.

In a society that no longer knows the difference between right and wrong, the authorities are increasingly engaging with and relying upon individual subjective experiences to create and enforce new offences. This is a therapeutic form of justice that is based not on a social system of justice but on the management of individual anxieties.

'Self'-respect

Many arguments today, which appear to be coming from opposite sides of the fence, actually endorse the perspective of the asocial citizen. The reaction to the 'hoody' issue, for example, was not to raise a *public* debate about the use of CCTV cameras, but to cry 'my hoody, my rules', as if *Guardian* readers' lifestyle choice of wearing 'hoodies' was under attack. Similarly, the reaction to CCTV and ID cards is often to simply question who is inspecting the inspectors – can we trust the people behind the cameras or should they be regulated as well? The distrustful asocial outlook can be seen in those who favour CCTV cameras and want to be protected from the public, and also among those who oppose the cameras on the basis of wanting to be protected from the protectors.

Ironically, even within the government's Respect Agenda, the asocial outlook is actually encouraged rather than challenged and a kind of nimbyism of the self is actually reinforced.

In reaction to the concern about the problem of behaviour and a sense of a loss of community, the government has developed the Respect Action Plan. This action plan sounds like an old-fashioned attempt to instil good moral values into society. It also appears to be all about creating a more social society, with catchy subtitles such as 'Everyone is part of everyone else', and 'The whole is greater than the sum of its parts'. Unfortunately, hidden within the very meaning of respect promoted here is the same asocial and equally amoral outlook that is coming to dominate politics and social policy.

Until recently the idea of respect related to experience and achievement. Adults, for example, deserved respect from children due to the socially accepted notion that they, as mature, active subjects – the people who made society – were worthy of respect from children. Particular individuals were also given respect for great things they had done, with our heroes, for example, being people we looked up to – because they had achieved.

Here, respect was a socially ascribed category, something that was earned – it was a judgement of certain actions and individuals based on what they had done. There may have been battles over who should be seen as deserving of respect, from conservatives and radicals, but within both camps it embodied the celebration of actions and attributes of certain individuals and institutions.

Today, by comparison, the idea of respect is devoid of content or of *character*. Everyone, we are told, should be respected – adults and children alike. Respect young people, the Children's Commissioner tells us, and they will respect you (*Guardian*, 19 January 2006). The sociologist Richard Sennett's book *Respect* begs the question, how do the professional classes *give* respect to the poor? Here respect has become something handed down from above, rather than a set of values that we aspire towards that can take us beyond our *selves*.

'Give respect get respect', is the opening chapter of the Respect Action Plan, with quotes from young people, such as, 'Being able to be the way I am without being bullied or skitted. And vice versa', or 'Not offending or damaging someone else's feelings or property', to help explain what respect is all about. But this is a highly individualised, fragile and negative version of respect. Rather than respect embodying values of achievement and character – something we could look up to beyond ourselves, something that makes us change ourselves, mature and gain self-respect – it has become something we demand for *who we are*.

Through a preoccupation with anti-social behaviour framed within the fragile asocial individual, the demand for respect has become little more than about being nice to one another. Give respect, get respect, fundamentally meaning, 'be nice and others will be nice to you'. Rather than respect being a form of social judgement, we are told to be non-judgemental, to respect people for who they are. Indeed, respect for the individual's self-esteem is to be protected from any hurtful social judgement. But this is little different from the sentiment of 'talk to the hand', or the outlook of the child who challenges your right to question his behaviour by arguing, 'I know my rights'.

In essence, the idea of respect today is, 'Respect my bubble, my rules, and I will respect yours'. Rather than the individual being drawn out of themself through values that relate to society, society is validating the inward-looking and insecure outlook of the 'therapeutic me'.

Based on the defence by the state of the vulnerable individual, 'respect' becomes little more than the protection of one individual from the 'abuse' of another. It is not saying 'respect me because I have done something to deserve it'. Nor is it saying 'respect adults because they know best – they have made this society and should be respected for it'. It is saying 'respect everybody because if you do not you are undermining them and their self-esteem'; it is a statement related to bad behaviour and the defence of the vulnerable, rather than a defence of the strong-willed character who has achieved a status that should be recognised. By saying everyone should be respected – young and old alike – it actually undermines the idea of respecting adults and infantilises the notion of respect itself.

At a time when respect for society's institutions is in decline – and, according to a MORI poll, politicians are the least trusted group of people in society – the government is attempting to engage with the bubble-world of the individual. In the process, respecting others becomes contentless and a protection of all against all. Any sense of the 'social' informed by moral or political norms has been diminished, and today's political elite promote a Respect Agenda in which there is no sense of society beyond the feeling of the 'therapeutic me'. Through this process, people are encouraged to have respect for the 'self' rather than achieving self-respect. And manners become little more than acquiescence to the vulnerable individual: 'respect' for the therapeutic self.

Encouraging impotence

Traditionally, respect was given to adults because of their capacity to *act*. Today respect is about not acting – about not harassing, upsetting, abusing, alarming or offending the vulnerable individual. There is no sense of individual capacity or of social responsibility – except in ensuring our actions do not harm others (and, even then, only in certain selected ways).

This preoccupation with harm to others has been latched onto by a government that lacks any social or political capacity of its own and can only develop social policy around the framework of social control. Protecting the diminished subject – the fragile individual – is the basis for myriad anti-social behaviour initiatives. Disastrously, this approach takes the asocial self as the starting point and consequently reinforces the problem of the asocial society.

Rarely, if ever, are people encouraged to take responsibility for the behaviour of others. Rather, a framework is being established that encourages us all to resolve the irritations of everyday life, of noisy neighbours, rude commuters, rowdy kids and 'aggressive' customers, by contacting the growing array of authorities to deal with these problems for us. This both discourages any possibility of social norms being established by the public itself and it also adds to the sense of individual impotence.

Until recently, anti-social behaviour was understood as a problem to be resolved by people themselves. When children swore and dropped litter or neighbours were noisy, people were expected to take a socially responsible approach and act themselves. Today, we are less inclined to act and indeed are discouraged from doing so, due to the various anti-social behaviour laws and programmes being introduced. Now there is a whole range of community wardens, police initiatives and helplines we can contact to deal with problems we have with other people's behaviour.

Unfortunately, when we fail to take responsibility for these problems that, in our hearts, we know we should be doing something about, when we retreat into our bubbles, we diminish our sense of ourselves. Various forms of anti-social behaviour, in this respect, are reacted to in an exaggerated way, not simply because of the problem behaviour itself, but also because we sense our own impotence. Our frustration is felt and our insecurity reinforced by our inability to act. *By not acting we sense and reinforce our own diminished subjectivity.*

Despite New Labour's proclivity to replace a sense of purpose with an ever-growing list of statutes, laws cannot resolve society's problems. Truss herself notes that when a policeman kindly asks you to get out of your car, regardless of how politely this is done, this is not a form of good manners, but of force. Manners, she notes, cannot be enforced. Today, through the process of relating to others only through third-party mediators, individuals are not only not creating a new society of 'respect' but are actually being desocialised. One consequence of this is that we increasingly feel comfortable engaging with others only within a regulated environment – like the exchange between a customer and shopkeeper – rather than through a free exchange with members of the *public.*

Ultimately, despite some real issues of behaviour in our hamster-ball world, the preoccupation with anti-social behaviour has emerged because of the loss of connection we feel with society and with those around us. This is something that is being reinforced by an asocial elite who lack a social sense and are equally disengaged from 'public' life. By engaging with the asocial individual through their fears, not only is the 'my bubble, my rules' outlook not overcome, but the fragmented nature of society is reinforced.

Rather than examining how we can stop people being anti-social, the real question is how we can create a 'pro-social' society – how we can burst the bubbles we are all increasingly living in. With this starting point there is the capacity to move beyond the myopic focus on anti-social behaviour, to raise the expectations of individuals to act for themselves, and also to identify how today's elite are actually reinforcing rather than transforming the asocial nature of society.

Notes

[1] Across the Western world there is a similar trend towards the increasing regulation of society coming with, for example, a dramatic increase in the number of police officers – where Australia holds the record, with an increase of 97% since 1970 (Braithwaite, 2000: 53) – and, as Bauman observes, there has been a fast-growing number of people in prison or awaiting prison sentences, in almost every country (2000b: 33).

[2] See Nick Clegg, Speech to Liberal Democrat Party Conference, 18 September 2001.

[3] As Lord Phillips said about the ever-increasing range of laws being developed to resolve society's problems: 'We are being drowned, and there's no two ways about that. Inundated. I sometimes talk about parliamentary effluent – all the ghastly stuff that goes through Westminster and then out on the poor unsuspecting public' (Atkins et al, 2007).

Bibliography

Atkins, C., Bee, S. and Button, F. (2007) *Taking liberties*, London: Revolver Books.

Bauman, Z. (2000a) *Liquid modernity*, Cambridge: Polity Press.

Bauman, Z. (2000b) 'Social uses of law and order', in D. Garland and R. Sparks (eds), *Criminology and social theory*, Oxford: Oxford University Press.

Braithwaite, J. (2000) 'The new regulatory state and the transformation of criminology', in D. Garland and R. Sparks (eds), *Criminology and social theory*, Oxford: Oxford University Press.

Caldwell, M. (1999) *A short history of rudeness: Manners, morals and misbehaviour in modern America*, New York: Picador.

Deane, A. (2005) *The great abdication: Why Britain's decline is the fault of the middle class*, Exeter: Imprint Academic.

Furedi, F. (2004) *Therapy culture: Cultivating vulnerability in an uncertain age*. London: Routledge.

Himmelfarb, G. (1995) *The demoralization of western society*, London: St Edmundsbury Press.

Lasch, C. (1977) *Haven in a heartless world*, New York: Basic Books.

Lasch, C. (1979) *Culture of narcissism*, New York: Norton.

Mills, C.W. (1968) *Power, politics and people*. New York: Ballantine.

Pearson, G. (1983) *Hooligan: A history of respectable fears*, London: Macmillan.

Rose, N. (1996) 'The death of the social? Re-figuring the territory of government', *Economy and Society*, vol 25, no 3, pp 327–56.

Squires, P. and Stephen, D. (2005) *Rougher justice: Anti-social behaviour and young people*, Cullompton: Willan.

Truss, L. (2005) *Talk to the hand: The utter bloody rudeness of everyday life*, London: Profile Books.

Wilkinson, H. and Mulgan, G. (1995) *Freedom's children: Work, relationships and politics for 18–34 year olds in Britain today*, London: Demos.

TWENTY

Conclusion: the future of anti-social behaviour?

Peter Squires

High-profile symbols of action will be essential as
agencies continue their drive to tackle ASB and take
on board the wider Respect agenda.
(Ipsos-MORI, 2006: 3)

Anti-social behaviour has a past, even, as we have argued, a 'secret
history' (Squires and Stephen, 2005), but does it have a future beyond
the smoke-and-mirrors symbolism alluded to above? Is our recent and
relatively sudden adoption of the language of anti-social behaviour
(ASB) a temporary aberration, or does it imply something about the
particular preoccupations of the British regarding the behaviour of (in
particular) lower-class youth? Has 'law and order' and ASB management,
above all, become our 'comfort blanket' in the face of the discomforting
social changes of late-modern globalisation? In other words, has anti-
social behaviour become the 'signal crime' or signal disorder of late
modernity (Innes, 2004)? And is ASB here to stay, by virtue of its
providing authorities with just too useful a definition of selective and
flexible delinquency and too many and infinitely variable levels of
precautionary and pre-emptive intervention and bespoke injunctive
criminalisation? The apparatus of ASB management and the ASBO
itself are, on this score, just too useful to be dismantled, notwithstanding
(indeed more likely *because of*) their fundamental transformation of the
operating philosophy of British criminal law and procedure.

As was suggested in the introduction to this book, the broad aim
behind the range of articles comprising this collection involved the
attempt to reflect the full spectrum of advocacy, opinion, commentary,
research evidence and findings, professional practice and development,
debate, and critique surrounding anti-social behaviour – in short,
everything it was possible to say about ASB management and 'the
ASBO', in particular. The book aimed to embrace the broad debate
about the contemporary significance of anti-social behaviour: what

could, or should, be done about it and, indeed, what *was* being done about it and, not least, how effective this was proving to be.

The point has been made in the introduction, and by a number of commentators in the book, about the fast-moving field of law and order politics in the UK. This has been especially noticeable with regard to ASB policy, an issue on which Tony Blair placed so much emphasis. Now, with the departure of Mr Blair from 10 Downing Street, it could be that the future of ASB management is 'up for grabs'. Much time, energy and resources have already been invested in the ASB and Respect initiatives, the issue has entered popular consciousness and discourse, it is frequently in the news and evidently raises widespread concern. More prosaically, the acronym 'ASBO' has entered the *Oxford English Dictionary* and a range of ASB-awareness merchandising, including T-shirts, posters, mugs and badges is available for purchase. Verging on science fiction, police in Merseyside were considering investment in unmanned flying surveillance drones to monitor 'ASB hot spots' in the city, as a report in the *Daily Telegraph* suggested:

> Police chiefs are considering using unmanned surveillance drones to hover over problem estates as part of plans for Britain's first 'yob squad' to tackle anti-social behaviour. Merseyside Police's new Anti-Social Behaviour Task Force, already known locally as 'the yob squad', will have an annual budget of £1 million, and a staff of 137 drawn from the fire service as well as the police. Its leader is promising to bring an 'Al Capone approach' to anti-social behaviour, using 'any lawful means necessary'. Task force leaders are in discussions with the Civil Aviation Authority about the feasibility of sending surveillance drones to hover over problem estates. (Lusher, 2006)

According to the police superintendent heading up the ASB task force, 'It's a cheap way of doing aerial surveillance ... intelligence and evidence gathering. Put over an anti-social behaviour hot-spot, it is quite a significant percentage cheaper than the force helicopter' (Lusher, 2006). This may tell us a great deal about the scale and priority of ASB management operations even though, for the police, it appears that it was the particular mix of cheap surveillance that recommended this new technology to the task force. It is hard to imagine, when the ASB issue first surfaced, that it would be the catalyst that launched unmanned aerial surveillance as a policing tool in the UK. More familiarly then, just as the newspaper reminds its readers that the 'task force' is better known as the 'yob squad', no doubt the unmanned aircraft are likely to become similarly known as 'yob drones'. And even as space-age technology is enlisted in the fight to improve the state of the nation's morals with a no-holds barred, by 'any lawful means necessary', approach to 'yob-busting', the essential continuity of the enforcement-based approach is all too evident. The 'new policing' (McLaughlin, 2007) has undoubtedly come a long way; and an ASB industry is clearly up and running.

Nor are the problems associated with ASB, or discussion of them, likely to go away, for even if we turn to the places where government policies are most regularly criticised – in the pronouncements of opposition political parties – then even here we find substantial agreement on fundamentals. Disagreement is, rather, confined to the details. In two substantial speeches, made during 2006 and 2007, David Cameron, the Conservative Party Leader, approached the ASB issue. In July 2006 his theme was restoring public confidence in the criminal justice system and he criticised the 'legislative hyperactivity' of the Blair governments on law and order. He spoke of the trap into which, Conservatives often argue, governments are frequently drawn, the need to appear to be responding on every issue, passing symbolic but often ill-conceived legislation. He closed by calling for a 'revolution in social responsibility' rather than more 'government-led' initiatives.

There were certainly differences of emphasis here, but no real disagreement on the underlying issues: anti-social behaviour was a serious problem, it caused grave concern to substantial sections of British society, its origins were attributable to a growing disrespect for authority and a growing irresponsibility, evident especially in the behaviour and attitudes of the young. Cameron warmed to his theme in a speech to the Royal Society of Arts in April 2007. First, he sought to put some distance between his own position and that of a former Conservative leader that Blair's New Labour had so successfully exploited, and argued that, after ten years of Labour government the problems of Britain could no longer be blamed on the 'no such thing as society' philosophy of Thatcherism – although this is surely a debatable point, for after ten years any children born 'under Thatcher' would all be well into their teens and later adolescence. This issue aside, the Conservative leader went on to spell out what he referred to as a different vision, where the government did have a role to play in helping to establish:

> a responsible society, based on building and strengthening
> the institutions that encourage personal and social

> responsibility – strengthening families, devolving
> responsibility to communities, localism, trust, sustainability,
> welfare reform [and] by creating a framework of incentives
> that encourages people and organisations to behave
> responsibly. (Cameron, 2007)

Such remarks reflect the 'softer language' of social capital, community 'resilience' and 'collective efficacy' that communitarian commentators advocate and even a movement away from a reliance on enforcement alone. The comments also embrace the more varied responses to ASB that we have seen developing in different parts of the country (not that this is without problems, as we shall suggest). To a large degree, Cameron's commentary reiterates the essential localism that has become so central a feature of all three major political parties' responses to crime and disorder management. Above all, the comments reaffirm the centrality of an interpretation of ASB based on conceptions of personal irresponsibility and immorality evidenced by 'bad' behaviour. These are all critical questions as we try to draw together a conclusion about the future of ASB.

Unfortunately, anti-social behaviour, with its left-realist and community safety ancestry (Bottoms, 2006; Squires, 2006), seems to envisage a community of victims lacking the capacity or resources to assert core values in the face of 'unwelcome' social change. Unfortunately, these 'social capital deficit' arguments overlook important questions concerning the selective inclusiveness of communities and, in particular, *who* derives *what* benefits from *which* social capital. Halpern et al (2004) have acknowledged the potentially contested character of social capital – not every commentator does.

The street socialising of young people, their congregation in groups in key public locations, often over-defined as 'gangs' by older community members, the police and the media (Hallsworth, 2005), is often precisely what so alarms older people, especially in so-called 'hard pressed' areas (Bottoms, 2006). After all, perceptions are so very critical to the ASB phenomenon and there is a broad continuity here. As Brown (1998) has remarked of the various neighbourhood watch schemes and community crime prevention panels introduced throughout the late 1980s and 1990s, such initiatives were comprised primarily of middle-aged, white owner-occupiers who spent their time recycling 'respectable fears' about young people perceived to be troublesome. Furthermore, research reported recently by Hulley (2007) drew attention to the predominantly interactive and perceptual characterisation of ASB: the respective ages of labeller, perpetrator and victim were critical in structuring definitions of ASB. Yet, while anti-social behaviour certainly manifests itself at the cultural and political levels, as Giddens (1998) has argued, the forces driving this social division and exclusion, which we have come to understand through the lens of criminology and victimology and discourses on ASB, irresponsibility, demoralisation and disrespect, are structural, global and economic. They need to be addressed at these levels, because from definitions we quickly move towards interventions: what manifests itself at one level as a broad 'cultural politics' of anti-social behaviour becomes a matter of direct public policy, posing dilemmas of distributional justice – or who gets what.

Social and public policy commentators will be familiar with these issues. They originate in utilitarian conceptions of welfare promotion and connect to the mainstream academic study of policy making through the work of Richard Titmuss. A key insight of Titmuss's work was encapsulated in the notion of the 'social division of welfare', the idea that, often, to promote the interests of some groups, the particular interests of others might have to be curtailed (1963). The aspiration was an overall enhancement of 'social justice'. But, of course, social justice was never just a matter of simple distribution – in this respect, Richard Sennett's insightful observation (2003) that policy makers often have a poor grasp of psychology has a direct bearing on ASB policy implementation. How, indeed, are we to cultivate respect for those whose legal rights we restrict, whose motivations we question, whose integrity we doubt, whose behaviour we condemn and whose mugshots we reproduce on 'name and shame' leaflets distributed throughout their communities? When we add to this the routine scapegoating by tabloid media and politicians alike, it becomes difficult to reconcile real 'respect' with the ASB and 'Respect' agendas.

With such ideas as a backdrop, the questions we need to ask of anti-social behaviour management concern whether the pre-emptive criminalisation of relatively marginal youth (notwithstanding the fact that criminalisation may be a means by which more supportive behaviour management interventions are levered into place), already the victims of social and economic processes beyond their control, offers a plausible contribution to social justice. Similarly, does the ASB model of localised community control (naming and shaming, scapegoating and all that this entails) achieve anything more than the further ostracism of criminology's 'usual suspects' (McAra and McVie, 2005) – but now by whole communities of enthusiastic and responsibilised citizens rather than just the police? And finally, does it work? Does it deliver the reassurances we demand? At a time when the pressures of global criminogenic change (criminality both organised and transnational) are increasingly acknowledged in our local and domestic contexts, what is the purpose behind this targeting of the easiest to target, 'rounding up our usual suspects' or, to coin another phrase, 'picking the lowest-hanging fruit'. To do so may achieve the 'quick wins' so sought after in police performance management terms but how far does this huge investment in low-level disorder management really address our major crime problems or the chief risks to our peace, security and community safety – and what are the opportunity costs?

From the welfare state to the ASBO nation?

When setting out to compile this book, our specific aim was to reflect the wide range of debate about ASB management and the injunctive 'ASBO approach' to crime and disorder. We have tried to capture the full range of debate and disagreement about ASB and its reduction while not avoiding some of the difficult questions. By way of closing, the following summary seeks to reiterate some of the main emerging themes and issues:

1. Contemporary concern about ASB arose in the context of regeneration and neighbourhood housing management problems. 'Incivilities' and visible signs of disorder compounded problems of deprivation and social exclusion. In the 'broken windows' account, these incivilities became instrumental to the process of further community decline and desubordination. In the 'signal crimes' analysis, ASB represented an outward sign of more fundamental social dysfunction.

2. Persistence was the key to ASB, alongside the systemic mismatch between existing criminal justice processes that dealt with *individual* perpetrators and a victimological perspective that acknowledged the collective and accumulating victimisation of particular groups of people trapped in 'communities of fate'. ASB offered a way of taking individually and apparently minor crimes and nuisances – that the police had never effectively prioritised but that accumulated to make people's lives a misery – more seriously.

3. Given the focus on community impact, ASB became strongly associated with the local context at a time when 'localism' (Neighbourhood Policing, New Deal for Communities) was actively being fostered by all major political parties. Notions of 'empowering' communities and 'accountability' became closely associated with ASB governance and even led to suggestions about the local determination of ASB priorities. In one sense, this

reflected the emerging evidence about the links between social contexts and perceptions of ASB, although one corollary of this involved suggestions about 'postcode injustices' in patterns of ASB enforcement.

4. ASB soon came to be seen as especially related to the activities of lower-class youth in public space. This was in part because of our more historic conceptions of 'juvenile delinquency' and partly because of an idea about ASB as 'pre-delinquent' or entry-level bad behaviour. Although the ASBO was not originally intended for use with young people, a core ambition of the new system of youth justice introduced in 1998 – 'nipping youth offending in the bud' – soon became a primary objective of ASB management.

5. Alongside a rapid process of development, as the above point suggests, the ASBO form of intervention rapidly evolved. Acceptable Behaviour Contracts were introduced to precede the ASBO and likewise 'interim ASBOs'. Dispersal Orders, Control Orders and Sex Offender Orders extended this enforcement methodology to further categories of offender, and what the media came to call 'super-ASBOs' were proposed for serious, gang-related or more organised offenders. ASBOs 'on conviction' were introduced and now account for the majority of orders issued. In many areas Crime and Disorder Reduction Partnerships (CDRPs) increasingly began to use injunction proceedings alongside other enforcement action. In short, the ASBO methodology has undergone substantial 'mission drift' in a short period of time as authorities have discovered its enforcement potential. This has led to criticisms of the ASBO's net-widening effect.

6. In a related sense, from the introduction of the ASBO in 1998 we have seen a fast-developing series of centrally orchestrated political initiatives to increase the profile of the government's ASB strategy, from the passage of the Anti-Social Behaviour Act in 2003, to the 'Together Campaign' and the broad-based Respect Agenda of 2006 incorporating (among other issues) the Parenting Academy, the Young People's 'Respect Awards' and, announced in early 2007, the establishment of 40 'Respect Zones' around the country.

7. We have already alluded to the 'postcode injustice' issue. To some extent this is compounded around the country as a result of area-by-area variations in the frequency of resort to ASBOs, and by debate and disagreement within the community safety profession itself regarding the most appropriate ways of managing ASB. Legislation affords considerable discretion to CDRPs and responsible agencies in handling ASB. On the other hand, Home Office performance

targets apply, and some areas have shown themselves far more proactive than others in seeking ASBOs. Others only employ them among a wide range of potential remedies or adopt them only as a last resort. Practice varies, and this variety can be seen as a problem or as a necessary aspect of processes of flexible, local and accountable priority setting. As some contributors to this volume have also shown, variety (not to mention inconsistency, imprecise measurement and ineffective evaluation) continues to be an issue.

8. Important definitional problems are involved with respect to ASB, in particular, the vague nature of the circumstances that may occasion the granting of an order: for instance 'behaviour likely to cause alarm and distress' in the eye of the beholder. There is substantial interpretative leeway here: does the behaviour have to cause *actual* distress to anyone? Should the tolerance or sensitivity of the victim influence how the behaviour is regarded? Evidence suggests that tolerance levels differ by area, age, gender and social class. In any event, when the Home Office undertook its anti-social behaviour day count in 2003 most of the incidents reported would already have constituted criminal offences, suggesting that the real question did not involve factors intrinsic to the behaviour complained of, but rather concerned the capacity of the authorities to respond effectively and their willingness to take it seriously.

9. Media reporting and some research have pointed out that behaviour regarded as alarming and distressing has been dealt with by ASBO procedures even though the behaviour arises as a result of mental illness, depression, addictive behaviours or personality disorders. Criminal justice pressure groups have continued to lobby about the failure of the system to divert people suffering such conditions from criminal justice processing, whereas ASBO procedures seem likely to compound these problems. In addition, the localised enforcement of ASB issues returns the threat of criminalisation and imprisonment to groups in the population that parliament has specifically sought to remove from the penal system – in particular, prostitutes, chronic substance misusers and the homeless.

10. ASBO procedures give rise to important questions regarding due process, criminal justice standards of proof, the question of hearsay evidence, and the exemption from non-disclosure of proceedings involving juveniles – of which not all issues have been satisfactorily resolved. As we have seen, something of the rationale behind the use of ASB proceedings for young people involved the idea of 'nipping crime in the bud', which gave rise to questions of

'net-widening', pre-emptive criminalisation or 'precautionary injustice'. The fact that most ASBOs are now awarded 'on conviction' in addition to other criminal penalties adds a toughened-up 'deterrent conditionality' to many community penalties, increasing the consequences (imprisonment) for breach of orders.

11. In development of the above point, many legal commentators criticise the introduction of what they refer to as 'two-step' legal prohibitions that are embodied in provisions such as ASBOs or Dispersal Orders. Such orders breach the principle of universality (the idea that the law should apply equally to all) and replace it with a bespoke form of individualised conditionality (the requirement to avoid certain behaviours, places, people, etc.), breach of which constitutes a criminal offence punishable by imprisonment. One criticism here has been that some conditions can be almost impossible to satisfy, especially in the case of young people (for example, if a young person is required not to associate with certain others, is he responsible if he encounters them inadvertently or if they seek him out?). The more general criticism of such provisions concerns the de facto creation of a two-tier system of rights. A group of specially targeted persons – 'usual suspects' – is subjected to more exacting individual conditions or 'ad hominem criminalisation', and they may not do what everyone else is entitled to do (Simester and von Hirsch, 2006: 181). The principle of equality under the law is thereby compromised.

12. Concern has arisen about the rate at which ASBOs are breached, and this connects with a number of other issues regarding the variations in professional practice regarding ASB management (see point 7 above). The ASB strategy has attracted criticism for its seeming reliance on 'enforcement-led' interventions and, more generally, for the criminalisation of social policy this potentially entails. Commentators from within the practitioner community and researchers have argued the need to balance enforcement action with supportive interventions and mediation initiatives: either (a) to resolve issues without the need to resort to an ASBO at all, or (b) to enable those subject to ABCs or ASBOs to complete them satisfactorily and without resort to breach proceedings. This whole issue – support and/or enforcement – recalls the long-standing tension within social work or probation theory and practice concerning questions of 'care and control'. Furthermore, even at the 'supportive' end of ASB management, although some features of ASB professional practice suggest elements of voluntarism,

partnership, consent and contractuality, questions have arisen about just how genuine these elements are, given the more punitive alternative measures that are also available.

13. We have drawn attention to the ways in which the particular questions of ASB policy sit inside a bigger cultural and political question in the UK. It was ever thus; it is reflected in the earliest pronouncements of the former Prime Minister and is captured just as clearly in the Respect Agenda. How far governments can, or should, go in reforming popular morality remains an open question, although 'liberals' (loosely defined) and social scientists in particular remain sceptical as to the capacity of the law alone to improve hearts and minds. Mark Twain observed that 'nothing so needs reforming as other people's behaviour' and, in the present context, it is the behaviour of some very particular groups (our 'usual suspects') that appears to preoccupy most people most of the time. This tends to point to the fact that at the heart of the ASB question stands an important cultural divide that itself is a symptom of more fundamental divisions between an 'us' and a 'them'. The latter are invariably poorer and younger, their presence signals a certain threat and certain social changes that neither group can do much about. Accordingly, there remain some very important questions about the counterproductive nature of public policies that appear to perpetuate, and even exacerbate, the social exclusion of some social groups.

14. While ASB policies have been criticised for further stigmatising and excluding the already marginal (as opposed to reintegrative shaming) there is also some evidence claimed of a 'street resistance' whereby young people are said to regard ASBOs as virtual badges of 'street credibility'. More pragmatically, young people's resentment of the restrictive conditions attached to an ASBO can make compliance with more reasonable conditions more difficult to secure; alternatively, too exacting conditions can set people up to fail.

15. Anti-social behaviour is emphatically about perceptions, relationships and interactions and contexts. It is important for what it signals. In turn, the government has done a great deal to raise the issue and to change the terms of the 'law and order' debate. There is an element of Pandora's box about much of this. The issue is now 'out there', fuelling public expectations, and, consequently, government will be judged by what it is perceived to achieve. Armed with a new range of flexible and utilitarian enforcement powers, ASB management could well represent the leading edge of

a new governmental rationality. In the end it will be the utility of the new powers, driving a bridgehead through the supposedly dated formalities (and rights and freedoms) of a common law heritage, that will recommend the ASBO model to policy makers. It is likely to become an increasingly familiar dimension of contemporary enforcement action.

A much older but parallel development of immense subsequent significance for British public policy suggests itself. The first generation of economic liberals undertook the reform of the old English Poor Laws in 1834: their actions were described by the historian E.P. Thompson as 'the most sustained attempt to impose an ideological dogma, in defiance of the evidence of human need in English history' (Thompson, 1963: 276). The reformed Poor Law established a framework for the governance of poverty, distinguishing deserving from non-deserving poor with a deterrent test of entitlement that, even in the era of the 'welfare state', still haunted British welfare provision. The new law created both a language for understanding poverty and the poor (the 'work-shy' and the scrounger) and political technologies for dealing with each. In like manner, contemporary ASB management creates and disseminates a new discourse of appropriate behaviour while establishing new governmental practices of surveillance, policing and treatment intended to give effect to the new behavioural imperatives. And it does so largely in the face of any situated or interpretative understanding of the behaviour, motivations and opportunities of those subjected to its novel interventions.

Even though there are welcome signs that the government may be softening its aggressive rhetoric on ASB and youth (although there seems to be no shortage of volunteers willing to take up the call), and although the Respect Task Force has been replaced by the Youth Task Force in the Department of Children, Schools and Families, this is hardly the end of the story. A government press release of 5 October 2007 announcing the new task force declared that:

> Commitments in the Respect Action Plan published in January 2006, including setting up a national network of Family Intervention Projects to give support and challenge in order to change the behaviour of the most anti-social families, alongside rolling out parenting advice across the country, have been met.

Such a claim is unlikely to prompt anyone's belief that Britain has now been thoroughly remoralised; in any event, as we have argued, the real issue is quite different. A softening of the line on ASBOs is hardly the point. On this the revisionist community safety practitioner, critical criminologist and civil libertarian can surely come to agreement: it is not about ASBOs. The real issue concerns the ways in which the discourse of ASB has fast-tracked, augmented and relativised the process of criminalisation: a process that the former Prime Minister tended to justify as the necessary 'modernisation' of the criminal justice system.

References

Bottoms, A.E. (2006) 'Incivilities, offence and social order in residential communities', in A. von Hirsch and A.P. Simester (eds), *Incivilities: Regulating offensive behaviour*, Oxford: Hart Publishing.

Brown, S. (1998) *Understanding youth and crime*, Buckingham: Open University Press.

Cameron, D. (2006) 'Restoring public confidence in our criminal justice system', The John Harris Memorial Lecture to the Police Foundation, London, 10 July.

Cameron, D. (2007) 'Civility and social progress', Speech to the Royal Society of Arts, 23 April.

Giddens, A. (1998) *Beyond Left and Right: The future of radical politics*, Cambridge: Polity Press.

Hallsworth, S. (2005) *Street crime*, Cullompton: Willan Publishing.

Halpern, D., Bates, C., Beales, G. and Heathfield, A. (2004) *Personal responsibility and changing behaviour: The state of knowledge and its implications for public policy*, London: Cabinet Office.

Hulley, S. (2007) 'Disrespecting youth: the meaning of anti-social behaviour', Unpublished paper to British Society for Criminology Annual Conference, London School of Economics, September.

Innes, M. (2004) 'Signal crimes and signal disorders: notes on deviance as communicative action', *British Journal of Sociology*, vol 55, no 3, pp 335–55.

Ipsos-MORI (2006) *Understanding Crime and Justice*, London: Ipsos-MORI Research Department.

Lusher, A. (2006) 'Police want spy planes to patrol troubled estates', *Daily Telegraph*, 15 October.

McAra, L. and McVie, S. (2005) 'The usual suspects: street-life, young people and the police', *Criminal Justice*, vol 5, no 1, pp 5–36.

McLaughlin, E. (2007) *The new policing*, London: Sage.

Sennett, R. (2003) *Respect: The formation of character in an age of inequality*, London: Penguin/Allen Lane.

Simester, A.P. and von Hirsch, A. (2006) 'Regulating offensive conduct through two stage prohibitions', in A. von Hirsch and A.P. Simester (eds), *Incivilities: Regulating offensive behaviour*, Oxford: Hart Publishing.

Squires, P. (2006) 'New Labour and the politics of anti-social behaviour', *Critical Social Policy*, vol 26, no 1, pp 144–68.

Squires, P. and Stephen, D.E. (2005) *Rougher justice: Anti-social behaviour and young people*, Cullompton: Willan Publishing.

Thompson, E.P. (1963) *The making of the English working class*, Harmondsworth: Penguin Books

Titmuss, R. (1963) 'The social division of welfare', in R. Titmuss *Essays on the welfare state*, London: Allen and Unwin.

Index

Note: The abbreviation ASB is used for anti-social behaviour.